# Eastern Christians in Anthropological Perspective

THE ANTHROPOLOGY OF CHRISTIANITY

Edited by Joel Robbins

# Eastern Christians in Anthropological Perspective

*Edited by*

## Chris Hann and Hermann Goltz

UNIVERSITY OF CALIFORNIA PRESS

*Berkeley   Los Angeles   London*

University of California Press, one of the most distinguished university presses in the United States, enriches lives around the world by advancing scholarship in the humanities, social sciences, and natural sciences. Its activities are supported by the UC Press Foundation and by philanthropic contributions from individuals and institutions. For more information, visit www.ucpress.edu.

University of California Press
Berkeley and Los Angeles, California

University of California Press, Ltd.
London, England

© 2010 by The Regents of the University of California

Library of Congress Cataloging-in-Publication Data

Eastern Christians in anthropological perspective / Chris Hann and Hermann Goltz, editors.
    p.   cm.
Chiefly rev. papers from a conference held in Sept. 2005 at the Max Planck Institute for Social Anthropology.
    Includes bibliographical references and index.
    ISBN 978-0-520-26055-9 (cloth : alk. paper)—ISBN 978-0-520-26056-6 (pbk., alk. paper)
    1. Orthodox Eastern Church.   2. Europe, Eastern—Religious life and customs.   I. Hann, C. M., 1953–   II. Goltz, Hermann.

BX215.E28   2010
306.6'815—dc22                                              2009035398

Manufactured in the United States of America

18   17   16   15   14   13   12   11   10   09
10   9   8   7   6   5   4   3   2   1

This book is printed on Cascades Enviro 100, a 100% post consumer waste, recycled, de-inked fiber. FSC recycled certified and processed chlorine free. It is acid free, Ecologo certified, and manufactured by BioGas energy.

# CONTENTS

# ILLUSTRATIONS

## FIGURES

vii

## TABLES

## MAP

## MUSICAL EXAMPLES

PREFACE AND ACKNOWLEDGMENTS

I can date my awareness of the "otherness" of Eastern Christianity very precisely: at Easter 1981 I attended the rituals of the local Greek Catholics in a village church in the Polish Carpathians. Although the Easter liturgy had to be performed in a Roman Catholic church (since the Greek Catholics were not legally recognized by the socialist state, and their own church had been appropriated), its duration, sensorial range, and bodily practices differed radically from the Roman Catholic services I had been used to since childhood. My Catholic background helped me to familiarize myself with Eastern Christianity in this corner of Central Europe without having to endure awkward interrogation concerning motivations and conversion. It was an easy way to enter a field that has continued to fascinate me ever since, though I am well aware that my perspective on numerous matters has been skewed by this initiation: these Greek Catholics may have a foot in both East and West, but they remain marginal to both.

In 2003 my department at the Max Planck Institute for Social Anthropology launched a series of projects to investigate changes in the scope and nature of religion in postsocialist countries. Eastern Christianity has figured prominently in these projects. It quickly became apparent that the literature available in Anglophone anthropology to those working on Orthodoxy and Greek Catholicism in East-Central Europe was poor compared with the comparative literature on Islam available to those colleagues investigating religious changes in Central Asia; it was also poor in comparison with the literature on the other major streams of Christianity.

I was fortunate to find in Hermann Goltz a colleague in Halle who was an expert on the history and theology of the Eastern Christian churches and who had long been pursuing innovative anthropological agendas of his own in this field. His advice as we developed our projects on the Greek Catholics of Central Europe was invaluable. As a further step in our dialogue we convened a conference at the Max Planck Institute in September 2005 with a title closely resembling the title of this volume. The chapters of this book are for the most part revisions of the papers presented at this meeting.

In addition to Hermann Goltz, I am indebted to Juraj Buzalka and Vlad Naumescu, two of my doctoral students who helped in convening the conference, and to numerous other participants who made valuable contributions, among them Stephen Headley, Roger Just, Marcin Lubaś, Paul Robert Magocsi, Jacek Nowak, and Lucjan Turcescu. Anke Meyer's assistance in preparing several versions of the manuscript was indispensable. Finally, I express my warm thanks to Joel Robbins for his continuous support and many valuable suggestions, to Michael Herzfeld and Douglas Rogers for much constructive criticism of the manuscript, and to the latter for contributing a summary epilogue.

*Chris Hann*

# Introduction

## The Other Christianity?

Chris Hann and Hermann Goltz

### OTHER FOR WHOM?

The title of the introduction to this volume mimics the habit, common in the recent past in some parts of the West, of referring to the socialist bloc as "the other Europe." Otherness is a matter of perspective, and symbolic geographies are always contingent. Political boundaries between East and West have seldom coincided with religious boundaries. During the cold war, socialist countries such as Poland and Hungary belonged to the West in terms of their dominant religious orientation, while Greece, confusingly, was Eastern in its religious tradition but Western in terms of politics (it was admitted to the EU in 1981). Despite these inconsistencies the basic power relations are quite similar in the two domains. Mention Christianity, and most contemporary Western readers will think in the first instance of Roman Catholicism and Protestantism. They are unlikely to think of the belt of Oriental Christians stretching from Ethiopia through the Middle East into the Caucasus, with a significant offshoot in the South Indian state of Kerala. Western readers are more likely to recognize the terms Eastern Orthodoxy and Byzantium, associating them with stagnant empires and authoritarian rule ("caesaropapism"), which allegedly precluded the emergence of political liberalism and stifled the individual initiative that is essential for economic development. The tradition exemplified by Max Weber is still strong: it tends to be taken for granted that capitalist modernity is a phenomenon of the West (*das Abendland*), closely linked to Western Christianity, and above all to certain forms of Protestantism (Weber [1904–5] 2001).

Such stereotypes, and the skewing of the literature in virtually every discipline to laud the dynamism of the Western traditions, are prime examples of what Jack Goody has termed "the theft of history" (2007). As a result of Western global supremacy in the last two centuries, scholars such as Weber have misrepresented the preceding millennia of Eurasian history. They have produced teleological accounts that underestimate or deny the contributions of other civilizations. Whereas Goody is primarily concerned with comparisons across the entirety of Eurasia, the particular interest of the religious traditions addressed in this volume lies in the fact that Christianity, nowadays commonly perceived as the Western faith par excellence, is itself an Oriental religion by origin. The Eastern traditions of Christianity nowadays have large congregations (numbering well over 200 million), but they have attracted little scholarly attention to date from Anglophone anthropologists.

Analysis is complicated by the fact that, over the centuries the otherness of the Eastern Christian streams has often been acknowledged as such, sometimes to be applauded and sometimes denigrated, on the inside. As we know, "Orientalism" can be internalized. In their self-representations, rooted in their theology, Eastern Orthodox have emphasized the continuity of their traditions since the early fathers. The name Byzantium is a Western appellation. In their own name for themselves (as in the designation applied by their Ottoman Turkish conquerors) the Greeks of Byzantium expressed their direct connection to the Roman empire. Etic, external perspectives have often taken the emic stress on continuity much further. According to Protestant theologian Adolf von Harnack, key elements in "Greek Catholicism" were taken over unmodified from Hellenic cults. In his view the Eastern Church did not change fundamentally after the sixth century, and it was "at rest" from the iconoclastic controversies of the eighth and ninth centuries onward (1904: 222). More recently, anthropologist Charles Stewart has justified his "long synchronic approach" to Greek Orthodoxy by arguing that Orthodox doctrines really were "remarkably insulated from change" and held basic values "constant." According to Stewart, Orthodoxy is "the most conservative branch" of Christianity because its strong notion of tradition rules out rupture: "Orthodoxy is conceived to be a living tradition (*parádosis*), a continuous herme- neutic interaction in which individuals are guided by the Holy Spirit toward consistent interpretation of both Scripture and the existing body of tradition" (1991: 139–40; cf. Agadjanian and Roudometof 2005: 9). Even in matters of ecclesiastical organization, Stewart emphasizes long-term continuities.[1] Many in the Eastern churches have made the explicit commitment to continuity the basis for claims to a greater "authenticity," sometimes in order to assert a moral superiority that contrasts with and compensates for their economic inferiority and political subordination to the West. Such patterns have a long history. They have been particularly evident in postsocialist countries, where blanket allegations are put forward that a communitarian Orthodoxy is hindering recognition of individual human rights, contributing to the failure of "shock therapy" to implant market capitalism, and repressing competition in the religious marketplace.

Yet it is by no means obvious that the variation that now exists within Christian traditions can be adequately approached on the basis of a binary distinction between East and West. Certainly there has always been much diversity and plurality within, as well as between, the many Eastern churches. In contrast to the Western traditions, virtually no social science paradigms have been developed to analyze the patterns of the East. East-West differences can be traced back to the first centuries of the Christian church (Gahbauer 1991). But can shades of difference in theology and divergent forms of ecclesiastical organization be held responsible for long-run patterns of political and economic development? We suggest that, to the extent that such "genetic" factors have played a role, they can only be understood when set in the context of wider institutional changes, power relationships, and their consequences for self-understandings. This means questioning hallowed Western assumptions about the breakthrough to modernity. For example, rather than emphasize the absence in the East of a Protestant ethic based in interiorized asceticism, we may recognize in the Greek and Armenian Christian communities of the Ottoman empire proof that Orthodox Christian ethics, too, were conducive to dynamic commercial activity (Antoniadis-Bibicou 2007; Krikorian 1978; Zekiyan 1997).

Of course it is hardly surprising that Western traditions should dominate the literature on Christianity in the Western social sciences. The greater dynamism of Roman Catholics and Protestants in recent centuries can hardly be denied, and it appears to many contemporary sociologists that the Eastern Christian traditions remain significantly less global (Agadjanian and Roudometof 2005). However, we should recall that long after its earlier northward expansion among the Slavs the Byzantine tradition continued to spread across Asia under the Tsarist empire, generating many conflicts between Orthodox missionaries and the Russian political authorities (Tarasar 1975; Goltz 1996; Znamenski 1999; Oleksa 2002). Moreover, the Orthodox churches can stake a strong claim to be *more* global in the original Christian sense of church unity: they form a *global* structure of *local* churches, as distinct from the "globalization" of a local church, be it the West Roman, the Wittenbergian, or the Genevan.

The paradigm of East/West alterity developed slowly over many centuries, both before and after the Great Schism of 1054. We sketch this history briefly below, in the section "Church Histories, Wider Histories." To point to the constructed and contingent character of this particular East/West boundary is no mere antiquarianism, given the renewed force that it has acquired among scholars and in widely disseminated stereotypes on both sides. That is why it is so important to recall that the origins of Christianity lie far to the east of the dominant centers of intellectual production in subjects such as sociocultural anthropology. Influential writers such as Samuel Huntington (1996; see Bowman, this volume) may homogenize both Western and Eastern streams in order to oppose them to each other as distinct civilizations, but a common origin in the Middle East is indisputable. From the perspective of Eastern Christians in Iran, Byzantium (today's Istanbul) was a stronghold of the West. Christianity shares its roots and its homelands with Judaism and Islam, yet in modern Western consciousness these religions are firmly associated with the Middle East. Islam was perceived to have superseded Oriental Christianity in a kind of inverse Crusade (Lepsius 1922; Goltz 2004), and the lived reality of Christian life in the East was long lost to view. For this reason the West must bear a share of the responsibility for the destruction of so many of these communities, and, above all, the annihilation of Armenians in the last decades of the Ottoman empire (Lepsius 1897). Such perceptions and ideal-types of Christianity based on Western Christianity alone reveal a profound ethnocentrism; unfortunately, some contributions in sociocultural anthropology cannot be exempted from this stricture.

## THE EMERGING "ANTHROPOLOGY OF CHRISTIANITY"

This volume is the first to examine a range of Eastern Christian communities on the basis of ethnographic case studies.[2] The coverage is neither comprehensive nor systematic, and much more research is needed if this stream is to be adequately integrated into comparative agendas. The dominant perspective of the volume is that of contemporary sociocultural anthropology; even those contributors who are not formally affiliated with this discipline have made use of its main method—namely, fieldwork (ethnography)—in preparing their chapters.

The word *anthropology* has acquired different meanings in different scholarly traditions. On the one hand, it denotes a science that investigates the human being as a biological organism. Particularly in the German-speaking world, *Anthropologie* has also denoted philosophical inquiry into the unique human nature of our species. This usage was popularized by scholars such as Immanuel Kant and Johann Gottfried Herder, and followed by Karl Marx, among many others. In a sense these great figures of the European Enlightenment were merely using a new term for what philosophers and theologians had always been doing. Eastern Christianities also have an anthropology in this sense—that is, a distinctive view of what it means to be human. Unlike Marx's materialist account of man's "species being" (*Gattungswesen*), the anthropological understanding of Eastern Christianity emphasizes man's affinity to God. We return to this theme below, in the section "Theology and Anthropology."

But the most common reference point of anthropology among English speakers nowadays is the field of cultural or social anthropology (which we take today to form a single intellectual community). These anthropologists have generally sought to make sense of religion with reference to sociocultural contexts and often see in it the prime collective representations of society itself (Durkheim [1912] 2001). The sociocentric approaches of the Durkheimian school have become more problematic as, with accelerating globalization, it has become harder to define the boundaries of a society or a community. However, the decentralized organization of the Eastern churches and the high degree of congruence with secular, national identities leave considerable scope for investigating correspondences between cosmic and social orders. In the case of Greece numerous Anglophone ethnographers have tapped this potential by documenting the profound ways in which Orthodoxy structures the community at all levels—its use of space, its rituals, and the everyday social interaction of its members (Campbell 1964; Danforth 1982; Dubisch 1995; Hirschon 1989, this volume; Stewart 1991).[3] Much of this literature has emphasized a dichotomy between text and practice: popular ritual performances (orthopraxy) tend to deviate from scriptural doctrine (orthodoxy) and often draw on customs that can be traced to pre-Christian times.

Alongside inquiries into the distinctive features of religion in particular local or national contexts, some contemporary anthropologists have drawn on psychological research to pursue the cognitive universals that shape all religions everywhere (Atran 2002; Boyer 1994; Whitehouse 2000, 2004). Much of this literature, too, is pervaded by dichotomous models. The so-called world religions are contrasted to the others, and within the former category, scriptural religion is equated with orthodoxy and contrasted to popular or heterodox religion. The influential theory of Harvey Whitehouse is based upon a contrast between the doctrinal mode of religiosity and the imagistic mode, and he takes the latter to be exemplified by the veneration of icons. However, this is to overlook a large body of Orthodox theology concerning icons. As Sonja Luehrmann notes in her contribution to this volume, the antimaterialist Protestant stance that privileges texts and direct communication with God cannot be taken as the general Christian norm. Along with other contributors to this volume (see especially the chapters by Hanganu, Forbess, and Naumescu), Luehrmann shows that Eastern strands of Christianity pose problems for the standard dualisms of the anthropological theory of religion.

In between the particularist focus of the ethnographer and the universalist ambitions of the cognitive anthropologists there is the potential to develop middle range inquiries in the anthropology of religion. The "anthropology of Christianity" has been vigorously promoted as one such possibility. Joel Robbins (2003) has argued that this field remains poorly developed (e.g., when compared with anthropological investigations of Islam). While some of the early pioneers of sociocultural anthropology drew on Christian materials (Robertson Smith 1889), Christianity was by and large not strongly represented in twentieth-century ethnographies. Robbins finds that even when Christianity figures in anthropological accounts, it tends to be downgraded: the people concerned are usually converts, or the descendants of recent converts, and the Christianity of their culture is viewed by the analyst as somehow superficial (2007).[4] Robbins has suggested a dual "cultural" explanation for the relative neglect of Christianity:

> Christians are too similar by virtue of drawing on the same broad cultural tradition as anthropologists, and too meaningfully different by virtue of drawing on a part of that tradition that in many respects has arisen in critical dialogue with the modernist ideas on which anthropology is founded. Both the similarities and the pointed nature of the differences make Christianity more difficult than other religions for anthropologists to study. (2003: 192)

Joel Robbins and Fenella Cannell (2005, 2006) are the most active advocates of the emerging anthropology of Christianity. Both draw on earlier work by Talal Asad, in which he argued that the anthropological study of religion was suffused with Christian bias (1993). Specifically, according to Asad, the emphasis upon meaning, popularized above all through the work of Clifford Geertz, was a reflection of the modern Western self, an interiorized product of Christianity. This point was well taken, and it has continued to shape interesting work on meaning (and its absence) in contemporary Christianity (Engelke and Tomlinson 2006). However, as Renée Hirschon and Alexander Agadjanian and Kathy Rousselet argue in this volume, the notion of the self found in Eastern Christianities is not identical with that of the Latin tradition. Asad's critique needs to be qualified and reformulated accordingly.

Fenella Cannell, who has carried out fieldwork among Catholics in Bicol (Philippines) and among Mormons in the United States, argues that anthropological understandings of Christianity have been distorted by an exaggerated emphasis on ideas concerning asceticism and transcendence, which she traces from Hegel via Durkheim to Edmund Leach (2005, 2006b). She acknowledges that this dominant model has not hindered the writing of useful ethnographic studies that draw attention to the diversity of practices found in popular or heterodox religion, such as the work of João de Pina-Cabral in rural Portugal (1986). However, Cannell argues that popular Catholicism in Bicol presents a more radical challenge, since in this setting both ideas and practices (e.g., concerning the "dead Christ") diverge more radically from theological orthodoxy. Cannell provides strong support for Asad's critique of the bias of much previous work in the general anthropology of religion. However, like him she fails to consider the possibility that "orthodoxy" in the Christian tradition that actually bears this name might carry rather different meanings from the Western (primarily Protestant) model that she equates with Christianity as a whole. Indeed, some elements of her Bicolano ethnography—the downplaying of notions of transcendence and salvation and an emphasis instead on correct management of relations with ancestors—resemble the popular Orthodox world of the Romanian villagers documented by Gail Kligman (1988; see also Hanganu and Forbess, this volume).

Joel Robbins, who has carried out fieldwork among Pentecostalists in New Guinea, has developed somewhat different arguments to support the promotion of the study of Christianity in anthropology. Whereas Cannell argues that the discipline has been excessively Christian and hindered by its ascetic model of Christianity from adequate acknowledgment of heterodox beliefs and practices, Robbins attaches more significance to a deep incompatibility between Christianity and anthropology as a discipline (2007). He admits to simplifying the former through his reliance on Protestantism as an ideal-type but argues that it is exactly this Protestant strand that anthropologists have most difficulty recognizing. This is due to what he calls the "continuity thinking" that is embedded in the discipline, inhibiting practitioners from taking seriously the claims of those who emphasize their conversion experience as a massive rupture. According to Robbins, Christianity is unique in the emphasis it places at multiple levels on discontinuity: in the lives of individual converts but also in the history of communities and of the religion itself, with the life of Christ marking a disjuncture between the Old and New Testaments. He might have added the Reformation and the Great Schism to this list, as further prominent instances of rupture in the history of Christianity. But this argument loses its general validity once we recognize that, as noted above and in contrast to the model applied by Robbins, Eastern Christians tend to emphasize continuity in their self-representations. Their basic notions of time seem (at any rate among certain intellectuals in certain periods) to be quite different from Western temporalities.[5] Following Robbins's logic, since the emic views of the believers correspond to the continuity thinking of the anthropologists, one might expect to find a rich and satisfying literature on Eastern Christians. In fact, there is very little; far greater effort continues to be invested in understanding Latin Christianity's continuing expansion in the territories that used to be the colonies of Christian (Western) Europe (Hann 2007).

The arguments put forward by Cannell, Robbins, and others, emphasizing factors such as excessive familiarity, revulsion, and anomaly, do not suffice to explain the neglect of the Eastern stream within the emerging anthropology of Christianity. Orthodoxy certainly differs from the broad cultural tradition shared by most Anglophone anthropologists, but at the same time it hardly resembles the "repugnant other" (Harding 1991) represented by American Christian fundamentalists. Yet the latter have attracted far more attention from anthropologists (cf. Coleman 2000, 2008).

The main reasons for this neglect are perhaps rather prosaic. Eastern Christians live mostly in Eurasia, a landmass that has never been adequately addressed by the modern discipline of sociocultural anthropology (Hann 2006). Emigration has created a large diaspora, but by and large in recent centuries the Eastern Christian churches have not expanded through missionizing, so that the themes that have animated countless studies of Catholic and Protestant interactions with the religions of nonliterate peoples could not be pursued in the same depth for the Eastern stream.[6] Moreover, when sociocultural anthropology entered its heyday in the second half of the twentieth century, the homelands of many Eastern Christians were inaccessible for political reasons. It is surely no accident that we have a relatively abundant literature for popular religion in modern Greece, but little or nothing for most neighboring Orthodox countries. Those anthropologists who did manage to gain access to socialist countries were seldom able to place religion at the center of their inquiries. Even where "scientific atheism" was less rigorously imposed, the ideology of Marxism-Leninism proclaimed that religion was superstition, and that it was bound to disappear in the course of building communist society. Such dogmas also impeded scientific research by local scholars, whatever their disciplinary affiliation.

The situation was transformed by the collapse of socialist regimes in 1989–1991, but although political barriers were removed, other barriers have remained in place. Few researchers from the West have the historical knowledge and linguistic abilities to embark upon fieldwork projects in the former Soviet Union and the ex-socialist countries of Eastern Europe. Scholars in those countries have no strong tradition of research into contemporary religious practices on which to build as they set about exploring religious commitments in postsocialist conditions. Contemporary inquiries cannot proceed without careful reassessment of the transmission of religious beliefs and practices in the socialist era, despite strong secularization trends.[7] At present we still lack clear paradigms and are only just beginning to exploit the potential of the postsocialist conjuncture for the insights it can give into the enduring features of Eastern Christianity and the study of religion in general (see Rogers 2005; Hann et al. 2006).[8]

## CHURCH HISTORIES, WIDER HISTORIES

Western images of Eastern Christianity, at least since Gibbon's *Decline and Fall of the Roman Empire,* have emphasized the stagnation, sterility, and autocratic government of Byzantine emperors, which in the most extreme accounts is alleged to have provided the prototype for modern forms of totalitarianism.[9] The great figures of European historical sociology, from Max Weber to Norbert Elias and Michael Mann, hardly engage seriously with the civilization closest to their own (it is surely remarkable that Weber wrote much more about China and India). In any case the Western focus on Byzantium has always been too narrow. Although the division of the Roman empire in 395 did not call basic religious unity into question, the schism that followed in 451 between the Oriental Orthodox churches and East Roman ("Byzantine") churches had consequences that can still be recognized today. The former churches include the Syriac, Coptic, Ethiopian, Armenian, and Indian Oriental Orthodox churches. The latter are the Patriarchates of Constantinople, Alexandria, Antioch, and Jerusalem (and originally Rome).[10] For six hundred years after this first great rupture, until the Great Schism of 1054, the "Byzantine" branch remained in communion with the Church of Rome (although the tensions between them began as early as the fourth century, they remained genetically *one* imperial church uniting the eastern and western parts of the Roman empire). It follows that the large Orthodox churches that we commonly take to epitomize "the East," such as those of Greece, Russia, and Romania, which feature most prominently in this volume, might more appropriately be classified as intermediate, between the Western and Oriental Orthodox churches.

When the eastern boundary of the Christian Roman empire was threatened by Sassanid Persia, Constantine the Great shifted his capital to the Nea Romi, "New Rome." On the flags of the "Christ-loving" armies of Emperor Heraclius, the Persian enemies were shocked to see the Mandylion icon of Christ's face, which in its iconographical type resembles Medusa on the shield of the defender goddess Athena. The Virgin Mary became the defender (*Hypermachos*) of the city of Constantinople, and people pray to her as such even today by singing the popular Orthodox Akathistos hymn, which dates from the fifth century (Goltz 1988, 2005; Peltomaa 2001).[11] Constantinople was attacked by the Crusaders in 1204 and later threatened by the Ottoman Turks. Many Orthodox inhabitants preferred, as Grand Duke Lukas Notaras put it, to live under "the Sultan's turban than the Latin mitre" (Runciman 1985: 111; Ducas 1958: 329). Eastern Christians had to choose between maintaining their independent identity, thereby risking martyrdom under Muslim domination, and sacrificing that identity by becoming an integrated "rite" in the West Roman juridical hierarchy. The last emperor of Constantinople, Constantine XI Palaeologus, blackmailed by the West, agreed to a church union between East and West in order to obtain Western military support against the Turks. His people did not accept the deal, and it was never implemented. Despite the efforts of a small Genoese detachment from neighboring Pera, the Turks took the city of Constantine in 1453. Yet the Orthodox and Oriental Christian populations held on. It was another five hundred years before, under the pressure of a nominally "laicist" republican Turkish government, the numbers of Istanbul's Christians declined steeply (see Couroucli, this volume).

Historically the Christian churches consolidated a decentralized, conciliar structure in which nationality in the modern sense was unimportant. As in other religious traditions, for most people, most of the time, religion was simply the ultimate explanation of their place in the world. In the cases we consider in this volume that place has come to be fused with the "imagined community" of a modern nation: Greece, Russia, Romania, and others. This is a relatively recent development, and in some places it is still unfolding in complex ways, as Anna Poujeau shows below in her exploration of the recent history of the links between Greek Orthodoxy and pan-Arab ideology in Syria.[12]

Socialist rule, which was ostensibly devoted to the elimination of religion, eventually accentuated the tendency to fuse religious identity with a secular, national identity. Unlike the Polish Roman Catholic Church, Orthodox churches were seldom prominent in the mobilization of opposition to socialism. (However, it would be a mistake to exaggerate a contrast to the Western churches, some of which—for example, the Roman Catholic Church in Hungary—also forged close links to socialist power-holders.) In the postsocialist years several Orthodox churches have claimed a privileged position in the life of their respective nations and resisted external pressure to open up the religious marketplace (again using strategies that resemble those of dominant churches in certain Western countries). Opposition to foreign missionaries has been strong. In some places, notably Serbia, the nationalist component seems to have predominated over the religious (spiritual), and Orthodoxy has been mobilized for reactionary political goals and violence. Arguably, the dominance of Orthodoxy in Romania and Bulgaria delayed their admission to the European Union and continues to delay the expansion of the EU in the western Balkans and Ukraine. The Moscow Patriarchate is frequently perceived as nationalist and anti-European (see the chapters in this volume by Agadjanian and Rousselet and Caldwell). On the other hand, this Patriarchate maintains a delegation at Brussels and declares itself open to a "greater Europe"; it is opposed only to formulations of European identity in which Western Christianity is guaranteed pride of place.

Greece has witnessed a long-running debate about the links between religious and national identity, and conservativism or "rigorism" has emerged as a force to be reckoned within the Greek Orthodox Church (Yannaras 2007; Makrides 2004). In the view of significant sections of Greek society, only the orthodox symbolic, "negative" theology of the Eastern fathers can provide the basis for a stable Christian identity, while the West has been driven toward secularism and atheism as a result of its unbalanced positivist theology (Yannaras 2004). The official Church is now perceived as excessively "Protestant" by some Greek traditionalists, who prefer to see their religion not as a matter of interiorized faith but as the suffusing of all human life with the sacred. Their rejection of Western technology and consumerism is associated with a more general "cultural fundamentalism," which means first and foremost Greek nationalism but also solidarity with other Orthodox churches, notably the Serbian Church during the years of conflict in Bosnia (Herzfeld 2002a).

Of course similar affinities between religious rigorism (fundamentalism) and reactionary politics can also be found in other religious traditions. Disparaging and hostile attitudes toward this constellation in the Orthodox world continue a long Western tradition, for even well-intentioned commentators have tended to view Eastern Christians as basically inferior. Long before Adolf Hitler's tirades against *Untermenschen,* medieval Western Christian missionaries scorned the Slavs. The Slavic subpeople do stink, as we read in the *Vita* of Sturmi, Saint Boniface's disciple and missionary to the East (Sames 1993). Western attitudes to Eastern Christians have ranged from condescending to contemptuous, and East Slavs have attracted the most negative stereotypes. Roman Catholic clergy are confident of their central place in the very definition of Europe, and some still like to classify their Orthodox neighbors as members of another civilization.[13]

## THEOLOGY AND ANTHROPOLOGY

In order to counter pervasive stereotypes we have taken some trouble in the discussion above to point out that many patterns found among Eastern Christians are also to be found in the West, and vice versa. However, we do not wish to gainsay differences altogether. In this section we outline the key areas in which the ideas and doctrines of Eastern Christianities diverge from those of the West. Here too we need to distinguish carefully between myths and realities, while recognizing that crude simplifications can themselves have tangible consequences when thoroughly internalized by the actors.

The basic distortion is caused by approaching the East in narrow Western terms. The premise is that Eastern Christianities failed to develop the combination of political, legal, and economic conditions that allowed for a breakthrough to an increasingly secular and bureaucratized modernity in the West. The question posed by generations of Western writers is, then, to what underlying ideas can this failure be attributed? Vasilios Makrides (2005) has reviewed the evidence for alleged irrational, mystical elements in Orthodoxy, its lack of interest in "this-worldly" transformation and in the absence (at any rate until very recently) of a "systematic social ethic" as found in both Protestantism and modern Catholicism. He finds some truth in these diagnoses but calls for a much more subtle and discriminating analysis. Closer inspection reveals plenty of precedents in the East for modern concepts of rationality. Under the hagionym of Dionysios Areopagites (cf. Acts 17) an Orthodox theologian elaborated a highly rationalized concept of society, entirely consistent with Weber's notion of "rational-legal authority" (Goltz 1974). Perhaps the key difference is that between the capitalist experiment of a single globalized rationality and an Orthodox experiment that always remained grounded in local, "bounded" rationalities.

If, instead of asking Western questions, we turn to address Orthodox theological issues in Orthodox terms, we must begin by recalling that Orthodoxy emphasizes man's affinity to God. This is the anthropological root for the principle of icon veneration. It is the human being, the *anthropos* as icon and likeness of God, that makes the icon so central.[14] Genesis (1:27) tells us that the male and female *anthropos* were created in the image of God ("kat' ikóna Theou"; see *Septuaginta* 1965: 2; Hanganu, this volume). In Orthodox theological anthropology the first and highest image is that of the invisible God, the Creator, which became the visible icon of God in the second person of the Trinity, Christ, the creating Word (*Logos*), thereby rendering redundant the Old Testament's iconoclastic command. Men and women are the first and highest created likenesses of God.[15] Hence the Orthodox veneration of icons is not the veneration of the material pictures, as so many critics have assumed. Veneration is directed only to the archetype of the painted icon, the uncreated, invisible Trinity of God the Creator.[16]

Orthodox icons figure not only in individual veneration but also in liturgical interaction. One of the most famous is the image known as the *Philoxenia,* the *Hospitality of Abraham and Sarah,* also sometimes called the Holy Trinity of the Old Testament (cf. Gen. 18; see Vzdornov 1989). This image never ceases to astonish those who conceive of Orthodox iconography as limited to rigid copying. The reason for the variation found here is that Abraham and Sarah are serving the Trinity, while the Trinity at the Holy table is serving mankind through the Eucharistic offering of Christ. The Orthodox Divine Liturgy is the realization of this theological hospitality. The men and women of the parish traditionally stand to the left and right respectively, representing Abraham and Sarah. The icon is thereby integrated into the liturgical action, or one might say that God, sensuously present in his icon, integrates the parish in his action. The ethical and liturgical interaction of men and women with God in the medium of the icon is a vast unexplored field for socioanthropological research. In addition to the semiotic (Uspensky 1976, 1994), the sociological (Onasch 1993) and the material (Hanganu, this volume) dimensions, it is essential to appreciate the full liturgical framework.

Mention of the parish and congregation brings us to another core topic of philosophical anthropology and theology. The dichotomy between individual and collective has a long history in the West, but Eastern Christian understandings are based a notion of the person that negotiates the Charybdis of (supposedly Western) individualism and the Scylla of (supposedly Eastern) collectivism. Michael Herzfeld has recently deconstructed discourses of liberal individualism for the case of Greece and drawn attention to the variation to be found in constructions of the person elsewhere in Europe. His basic conclusion is that "the idea of a typically European individualism confuses the discourse with its subject matter" (2002b: 170). Orthodox theology in this context draws on Trinitarianism as a paradigm of Christian *koinonia* or *communion,* where the *individuum* is not lost but saved in personal relations of love (Williams 1972; Staniloae 1994: 245–80; Yannaras 2006). Several contributors to this volume highlight individualizing tendencies, including Renée Hirschon for the case of Greece since the 1970s and Jeanne Kormina for postsocialist Russia. Agadjanian and Rousselet shed further light on the complexity of the Russian case: while some citizens (such as the "religious tourists" discussed by Kormina) pursue a postmodern bricolage that is highly individualistic and antithetical to the parish community, others (such as the pilgrims discussed in the chapter by Naletova) are deeply embedded in a "thick" religious tradition. For the latter, it is above all deep inner reflection that binds them into a community, rather than the collective effervescence stressed by Émile Durkheim and Victor Turner. Inna Naletova defines this as a *kenotic* community, grounded as much in theological teaching as in sociology, "centred around a holy place and guided by a belief in God's suffering for humanity and His sacrificial death on the cross."

The distinctive mystical and charismatic (pneumatological) character of Eastern Christianities has long been recognized by scholars (Meyendorff 1974).[17] The origins are to be found in early Christian monasticism, which has exercised an influence over Orthodox parish life that persists to the present day, in close association with pilgrimages (e.g., to the hermits of Mount Athos; see Mendieta 1972; Mylonas 2000). Orthodox laity are almost everywhere closely related to their monasteries; the *bios angelikos,* the "angelic life" (Frank 1964) of monks and nuns is a strong magnet. The hermits who cut all ties with the "world" only succeed in strengthening those bonds, because they are hermits for the world's sake. Their prayers in the wilderness sustain the world, and the other inhabitants of the world are well aware of their debt to this minority. These seeming "unsocials" or even "anti-socials" aspiring to live in the transcendent heavenly world are in fact the foundations of the social world. Nuns and monks play a central role in transmitting religious knowledge (Forbess, this volume), in complementing parish-based institutional structures (e.g., through performing special rituals; see Naumescu, Poujeau, this volume), and in establishing claims to authentic belonging through their very presence in the landscape (Poujeau, this volume).

It is often claimed that Eastern Christians tend to place less emphasis on a transcendent God and more on the dispersal of the sacred in the natural world.[18] A theologian specialized in the Orthodox churches would reject the implicit "zero sum" assumption. According to the doctrines there is a *paradoxon* that has its insoluble basis in the *mysterion* of the Incarnation. Christ is at one and the same time the eternally ruling *pantocrator* over the entire *kosmos* and a crucified man. The *titulus* of the cross in certain icons of the Crucifixion gives a clue. In place of the New Testament's "Jesus of Nazareth, King of the Jews" one sometimes finds

"King of Glory" (Greek: Vasilevs Tis Doxis; Russian: Tsar Slavy) (Kaffka 1995: 100, 109, 199; Belting 1981: 160).

This brings us back to the more general argument of this introduction. In recent decades some Western theologians have applauded the Orthodox churches for their very "otherness." They see their Western Church as the Church of the Word and the Eastern Church as the Church of the Icon. These theologians (and the anthropologists tempted to follow them) have a more benign approach to West-East differences than their Western forerunners, but they do not know Orthodox Christianity. Eastern Christianities are deeply rooted in the Word; after all, many of the most celebrated icons depict Jesus or a saint with a book in his hands. Saint John Chrysostom, the most famous preacher of the universal church, the "Golden Mouth," was a preacher of the Christian East. The Orthodox developed the icon out of the Word (and more specifically from the Hymnos). The Eastern side does not yearn for the West, for the Word, in the way that so many Westerners have been attracted to icons. Arguably, the reason for this is that Eastern Christianities succeeded in evolving a multimedial expression of faith: the Word became Icon and the Icon became Word, just as the divine and creative Logos became a human being and the human son of God became the creative Word. Eastern Christians thus possess a sublime understanding of *theología,* but this is falsely interpreted by Western theologians as a low stage of development. *Theología* in the Eastern understanding is not a scholarly discourse *on* God; it is rather a liturgical discourse *of* and *between* God and human beings. What the West rediscovered with the help of the German Jews Martin Buber and Franz Rosenzweig—namely, the dialogical nature of human existence—the Orthodox had never forgotten (Goltz 2006b). The highest form of theology is the oral celebration of that dialogue, before and beyond all written or printed words (Goltz 2006a). The centrality of *paradoxon* in Orthodox theology causes Western critics to allege that it has yet to emerge from the Middle Ages and come to terms with the rationality propagated above all by the Enlightenment. But from the point of view of the East it is precisely the balance of positive and negative theology, of the mystical and emotional factors that necessarily accompany understanding of the Word (i.e., dogmas), that establishes their superior claim to continuity with the early Christians (see Markschies 1999).

Finally, let us again caution against attaching excessive causal weight to the intellectual divergences we have touched upon in this section. Vasilios Makrides argues that these differences have often been exaggerated and concludes that contrasting adaptations to globalization and modernity should not be attributed to "inner theological grounds" (2005: 185). Rather, we need to recognize a complex interplay between ideas and material, institutional factors. Instead of postulating an "Orthodox mentality" as a barrier to modernity, it is time to recognize the emergence of distinctive Orthodox patterns of modernity.

## ORTHODOXY AND ORTHOPRAXIS

Like most anthropologists who have written about world religions, Fenella Cannell, though critical of what she considers to be excessively ascetic approaches to Christianity, ends up working with a binary model—in her case, "orthodox versus heterodox." "Scriptural versus popular" is a closely related and widely used dichotomy, as is the opposition between "doctrine" and "practice," or "theology" and "practical religion" (Leach 1968). Somewhat less common nowadays is the contrast between "great and little tradition." With the rise of fieldwork as their prime method, sociocultural anthropologists have generally seen themselves as specialists in the latter. However, an emphasis on fieldwork and social context carries with it the danger of naïveté. The anthropologist who lacks all familiarity with the texts of a great tradition may get excited about a "discovery" that has long been a commonplace to historians and theologians. On the other hand, the anthropologist who remains fixated on scriptures and theological debates may classify all the noncanonical beliefs and practices documented during fieldwork as deviant, even though they are fundamental to the religion as it is lived. In Eastern Christianities, perhaps to a greater extent than in the West, there has always been a continuum between written canonical tradition and what believers have actually done. A broad definition of "church," one more in keeping with the traditional Eastern Christian understanding of the community of believers, must include those who venerate icons in heterodox ways and whose participation in pilgrimages appears to have more in common with the consumerism of a tourist than the devotion of a true pilgrim. Orthodox Christianity is perhaps best seen as a highly reflected pre- and postscriptural oral culture, where oral is understood to mean not a primitive but a superior, because *living,* mode of communication.[19]

The dichotomy between orthodox and heterodox is more than a little piquant when we come to consider Orthodox Christianity, and not merely because of the name. As we noted above, this tradition offers solid theological backing for attaching prime importance to practice. If orthodox refers in the first instance to consistency and continuity in belief, orthopraxy refers to correct behavior, to religion in action, in particular to ritual performance. James Watson has shown with regard to death rituals in early modern China that a uniform ritual structure was much more important in creating a sense of being Chinese than shared beliefs (1988). Belief is a problematic category because it implies a concern with internal states that, according to Watson, simply was not relevant in this case. Rather, in the absence of a church, it was the imperial officials who disseminated the uniform ritual structure of funerary rituals, which, then, in its actual implementation, showed remarkable regional and local variation.

The comparison with China is suggestive, especially given the decentralized organization of the Orthodox churches. Orthopraxy can, however, be explored in other ways, and it is not necessary to maintain, as Watson does, that perfor-mance always takes precedence over belief. Eastern Christianities offer instructive insights into the literature on how communication with the divinity is mediated through different forms of language and materiality (see Coleman 1996; Engelke 2005; Keane 1997, 2007; cf. Goltz 1979). Gabriel Hanganu (this volume) detects an affinity between Orthodox approaches to religious objects and academic theo-rizing about material culture, and argues that no social anthropology of religious practices can be complete without close attention to both matter and spirit—that is, human relations to material objects, on the one hand, and to spiritual beings, on the other. In this way, closer attention to both *doxa* and *praxis* in Eastern Christianity generates a better basis for the study of lived religious activity than the polarizing models that still dominate much of the literature. It is unhelpful to ground the comparative enterprise on ideal-types that prioritize the scriptural, the ascetic, and the transcendental. If Eastern Christianity rather than Protestantism were the basis of the ideal-type, then the similarities as well as the differences from other religions might appear with greater clarity. For example, we might then see that Oriental Orthodox churches such as those of the Copts, the Syriacs (Arameans), and the Armenians were very close indeed to particular strands of Islam. Instead of opposing beliefs to practices and theo-logical to practical religion case by case, analysts might instead begin to recognize more complex combinations of beliefs and practices, varying between different social groups, but also between individuals, and contextually variable even for the individual.

## IMPLICATIONS AND PROSPECTS
## FOR FUTURE RESEARCH

The risk in pursuing the differentiation strategy indicated above is that at some point the category "Eastern Christian" would dissolve. Actually this risk is basi-cally the same whether we are dealing with Christianity as a whole, or with the common amalgam "the Abrahamic faiths." Limited intermediate generalizations may still be possible. Thus Forbess and Naumescu (this volume; see also Naumescu 2007) argue that Orthodoxy represents a peculiar combination of the two modes of religiosity identified by Harvey Whitehouse, since the "imagistic mode" has never been displaced by the development of doctrinal rules but retained its cen-trality. Alternatively, it might be argued that Eastern Christians confound Whitehouse's dichotomy, which is left with at most a limited heuristic value. What is clear is that neither he nor any of the other protagonists in the current cognitive debates have looked at Eastern Christianities in any depth. The application of their theoretical framework to a range Eastern churches could lead to a breakthrough in historicizing their research programs.

The case studies of this volume focus on religion per se, but several chapters offer insights into the politics of church-state relations as well as wider contexts of anti-Westernism. There is undoubtedly scope for anthropologists to play a bigger role in interdisciplinary investigations of the gradual integration of Eastern Christianities into global networks (Roudometof, Agadjanian, and Pankhurst 2005). Rather than the bipolar models discussed above, it would seem important to identify at least four groupings: those "ordinary believers" who belong formally to a congregation; those who profess some form of belief and commitment but who remain "outside the walls" of the church; the official hierarchy of the church; and finally the rigorists or fundamentalists, often as critical of the official church as they are of deviant popular practices. In some cases it might be necessary to differentiate further; "monastery people" (see Kormina, this volume), for example, might form a separate group from parish clergy. Of course similar classifications can be applied to other religions; given that the major religious traditions face similar challenges and are in close competitive contact with each other, it is hardly surprising that virtually all have developed a "rigorist" current and are drawn into similar kinds of conflict.

Contemporary social transformation and conflict is just one context in which Eastern Christianity needs to be brought into wider comparative frameworks. Agadjanian and Rousselet argue that to understand the current situation in Russia it is important to draw together three distinct time frames: postsocialist processes of hybridization and eclectic individuality, the legacy of Soviet repression, and the "genetic" explanatory logic that traces some of the major differences between Eastern and Western branches of Christianity to the first millennium. When we turn our attention to the more distant past, many other research avenues open up. One of the most important concerns relationships to non-Christian religions. The Tsarist empire, larger in its day than any of the far-flung empires of the Western European powers, was very active in missionizing. However, despite the great interest of the theorists of postcolonialism in mission histories, few have begun to investigate Russian history from this perspective.[20] The influence of the Russian Orthodox Church spread beyond the Russian empire into North America; where this happened it is interesting to ask whether this was due to a closer fit with indigenous religious practices or to the warm response of native North Americans to a version of Christianity that allowed them to remain different from the religion of their colonizers.[21]

More historical work would give further insight into the themes of continuity and authenticity that pervade this volume. We have noted that it is much too simple to maintain that the Eastern stream represents an uninterrupted flow from the primordial early church. There have been countless moments of rupture within the churches now designated "Eastern." It is also important to recognize that all these churches have been in continuous contact with each other all along.

The Orthodox churches of Eastern Europe were profoundly influenced by both the Reformation and the Counter-Reformation in the West. Given all this interaction, the pursuit of "otherness" is ultimately suspect and futile. We would do better to recognize a pluralism of Eastern Christianities and to develop a multilevel comparative approach. This pluralism (of course the same applies to the Christianities of the West) should lead us to question the value of continuing to oppose East and West—after all the Nicene Creed, with its formulation of the "One, Holy, Catholic and Apostolic Church," is common to both. If for certain purposes this basic dichotomy may still be useful, it should not prevent us from investigating many kinds of internal differences: How does Greek Orthodox Christianity in Greece today compare with, say, Greek Orthodox Christianity in Syria? Does the condition of the Romanian Orthodox Church closely resemble that of the Russian Orthodox Church as a result of a common postsocialist conjuncture? What distinctive insights can be obtained from examining Eastern Catholics—Christians who are commonly perceived to constitute a bridge between West and East? Is the Vatican's recognition that the Greek Catholics of Central Europe possess a separate rite in fact to be understood as a (historically unwarranted) refusal to grant them the status of a juridically independent church? If so, this would be a clear example of the unequal power relations that have undermined conciliar structures ever since the first centuries of the Christian church (Meyendorff 1983).

Finally, more attention to Eastern Christians promises further dividends for the anthropologist, beyond the field of religion. We have in mind the zone where the two kinds of anthropology, the sociocultural and the philosophical, come together. Many sociocultural anthropologists have questioned whether "our" assumptions about what Hirschon (this volume) calls "the human subject" are shared all over the world. If "individualism" can be operationalized at all for social science analysis (i.e., if we can link it to specific features of social reality, beyond its rhetorical invocations), we must identify the concrete historical variables that promote or discourage it. In any case it is clear that many peoples draw no comparable dichotomy between individual and society. This has led distinguished anthropologists to contrast India with "the West," or Melanesian with "Euro-American" constructions of the human subject. But Eastern Christianity is deeply rooted in Europe, and Europe in Eastern Christianity! Greater familiarity with this stream therefore invites us to undertake some basic rethinking. One response might be simply to redraw the line and adjust the labels. If it is not necessary to go to India or Melanesia to find complex relational notions of the person, because very similar notions underpin the Orthodox worldview in Greece, then perhaps one might simply substitute "North Atlantic" for "Euro-American" and continue business as usual. Another way forward is to argue, as Hanganu does below, that Eastern Christianity represents an intermediate position between the individualism of the West and the "distributed personhood" found in many other parts of the world. Rather than recognize a non-Western "other" in the heart of Europe or view the Eastern Christian cases as somehow fuzzy or liminal, their closer investigation might lead us to a more radical questioning of this dichotomy, and thus to a more careful appreciation of the historical circumstances that shape models and practices of personhood everywhere.

## AN OVERVIEW OF THE VOLUME

The chapters grouped in part 1 examine some of the most distinctive features of the Eastern tradition. The icon cannot itself be the object of worship, but it is a legitimate artifact of mediation in facilitating communication with the divine. A number of concepts of Orthodox anthropology developed by early Christian writers, and in particular the conceptual pair "image-likeness," provide a frame within which contemporary Romanian icon-based religious practices can be discussed in relation to more general anthropological concepts, such as "distributed personhood" and "biography of objects." Gabriel Hanganu shows in chapter 1 that to understand the efficacy of an icon in a local context it is necessary to examine interaction between and within local social groups, as well as communication with the spiritual world, and also with the world of material objects, which, according to Orthodox theology, is itself divine in its potential. Sensorial experiences and bodily practices are central. In comparison with the privatization that has taken place in Western societies, they have remained public, located in the community. Knowledge is no less central, and some icons are known to have richer "social biographies" than others; their efficacy is related to this "charging." Hence, although in theory divine intercession can be secured through any icon, there is a strong preference for famous miracle-working images. On a more general level, the specific ways in which Eastern Christians conceive of the invisible world and the material realm, and the objectification of this understanding in contemporary religious practices, suggest a new perspective for their anthropological study, one that acknowledges and reflects Orthodox Christian anthropology itself.

In chapter 2 Sonja Luehrmann explores the use of icons in the Russian republic of Marii El, where many inhabitants have preserved traces of pre-Christian religious practices, notably in the veneration of distinctive natural objects in sites held to be sacred. For the Protestant missionaries active in the republic today, the use made of icons by Russian Orthodox Christians has to be condemned as an extension of such pagan superstitions. Many people nonetheless use icons publicly and maintain "icon corners" in their homes. In chapter 3 Stéphanie Mahieu demonstrates that, in the border zone of Central Europe, Greek Catholic churches are a hybrid form—an integral part of the universal Catholic Church for centuries, yet practicing the rite of the Byzantine East. The Vatican has encouraged these churches to reject Latinization and return to the purity of Eastern liturgical forms, but Mahieu shows that while younger priests and the Greek Catholic elite in general tend to favor "re-Orientalizing," many of the faithful and some of the hierarchy are reluctant to disrupt the status quo. Some prefer to maintain a plurality of options, arguing that icons and statues offer alternative, noncontradictory representations of the sacred (for further studies of the Greek Catholics of Central Europe, see Mahieu and Naumescu 2008). In chapter 4 Jeffers Engelhardt examines a different border zone, and we move from the visual to the aural. Orthodoxy is central to the social identity of the Seto in Estonia, and their distinctive singing is the purest expression of their faith and celebration of their tradition.

The chapters in part 2 explore the concepts of image and tradition further in three monastic contexts. In chapter 5 Alice Forbess shows that religious knowledge is transmitted to novices in a Romanian convent with little reference to text-based doctrine. Rather, adapting Harvey Whitehouse's cognitive model, she shows that Orthodox Christianity exemplifies the predominance of the "imagistic mode of religiosity," in which intuitive, sensuous forms of communication with the divine are preeminent. In his study in chapter 6 of how a splinter group of monks came to specialize in exorcism rituals in postsocialist Ukraine, where the demand for the emotional intensity of the imagistic mode rose in the uncertain conditions of postsocialism, Vlad Naumescu, too, draws on Whitehouse's dichotomy. In chapter 7 Anna Poujeau outlines the crucial role played by monasteries in the consolidation of the Greek Orthodox Church as a minority community in Syria. With the help of a full ritual calendar (in which some rituals are recent innovations), the new monasteries constructed at old shrines demonstrate the rooted authenticity of Christian tradition in an Arab-dominated land.

Questions of authenticity and syncretism, already raised by Luehrmann, Mahieu, and Poujeau, are the principal theme of the analyses of shrines and pilgrimage practices grouped in part 3. In chapter 8 Glenn Bowman examines three locations in Macedonia where "mixing" between Christians and Muslims has taken different forms. Countering an influential argument of Robert Hayden, he argues that the sharing of shrines does not necessarily mean antagonism: rather, intercommunal relations will always be sensitive to the wider social and political context. In chapter 9 Maria Couroucli describes contemporary Greek Orthodox celebrations on an island in the Bosporus that are attended by many Muslims from Istanbul, few of whom have any knowledge of the Christian faith. She proceeds to draw on archival evidence to investigate the nature of syncretic activities in the late Ottoman years and finds that there was neither a crude antagonism nor the full positive embrace of "the other" that some nostalgic romanticists imagine.

Chapters 10 and 11 provide complementary insights into pilgrimage and other aspects of "religion outside the church" in postsocialist Russia. Inna Naletova's account of pilgrims as forming kenotic communities that contribute positively to the reestablishment of generalized trust in Russian society is apparently contradicted by Jeanne Kormina, who turns the spotlight on urban dwellers whose bus trips seem better classified as "religious tourism" than as pilgrimage. Authenticity, closely tied to a "simple," "pure" natural environment, is crucial to these tourists' search for new individual and collective identities. The *avtobusniki* with whom Kormina traveled (like the Muslims encountered by Couroucli in the Bosporus) had very little knowledge of Christianity. Describing how the hosts at holy sites put on performances for ignorant guests, and borrowing the terminology of British sociologist Grace Davie, Kormina asks whether postsocialist Russia might resemble contemporary Britain in the widespread prevalence of "believing without belonging." She goes further and suggests that even belief may not be very important. The bus tourists are not interested in acquiring religious knowledge or joining a parish, but only in the experiential authenticity they can glean through visiting holy places as anonymous individuals.

In contrast, Naletova emphasizes the long-term subjective "echo" of the experience of holy places for the individual. She also notes the collective aspects of the ways in which pilgrims "achieve" their religiosity and suggests that the privileging of "we" rather than "I" is a distinguishing feature of Eastern Christianity generally. The "we" identified by Naletova also has a secular dimension, for many Russian pilgrims are deeply concerned with national literature, history, and their country's contemporary predicament.

The papers in part 4 pursue further the tight, multiple-level links between the individual and the collective, and also between religious and secular identities. In chapter 12 Renée Hirschon examines the Greek case, where the intimate link between the Orthodox Church and the nation has been increasingly threatened since the 1970s. She shows that, according to the Orthodox worldview, the church is identical with society, the sacrament of baptism marking the person's entry into both. However, modernization processes and Europeanization are threatening the relational human subject of Orthodoxy, in which the individual was encompassed, but not dominant. The change is evident in the "cosmological shift" represented by the celebration of birthdays instead of name days. In chapter 13 Alexander Agadjanian and Kathy Rousselet pursue the same themes in the context of post-Soviet Russia. They give the example of new rituals venerating the Romanov dynasty to show that religion plays a very important role in the remolding of identities at collective as well as individual levels, and indeed at other levels in between. In chapter 14 Melissa Caldwell explores widespread popular criticism of the Russian Orthodox Church's charity work. One reason for discontent is that many ordinary Russians are uncomfortable with the church's efforts to promote an ethic of personal responsibility, and to discriminate between different categories of "deserving" when distributing aid. Drawing on Marcel Mauss's theory of the gift, Caldwell argues that Russians increasingly perceive the Orthodox Church as an institutional actor that has abandoned its traditional principles for a new political and commercial agenda. The church appears to be left in a no-win situation. In postsocialist Russia the market principle is invading all domains, and consumers of religion are offered a variety of products by competing suppliers. Yet when the Russian Orthodox Church joins the neoliberal fray and expands its commercial activities, it is promptly condemned for its greed and corruption. It seems that the only strategy left to the church is to reaffirm its historic monopoly claims and adopt a nationalist stance that excludes non-Russians as recipients of Orthodox generosity.

Finally, in a concise epilogue, Douglas Rogers synthesizes the main themes of this collection and extracts a more general message. He draws attention again to the significance of long-term continuities (real as well as imagined) for Eastern Christians. Ritual practice as a living tradition is fundamental to their identities, both as persons and as communities. Rogers concludes that the study of Eastern Christianity presents a "coming of age" challenge for comparative anthropological science. Indeed, our broader aim with the research agenda initiated in this volume is simultaneously to free the category "East" from the political distortions of the Cold War era and to transcend the legacy of centuries of scholarly "Orientalism."

## NOTES

1. Some historians have drawn attention to shifts in doctrine and ecclesiastical organization, and others to ruptures in the corresponding political formations For example, Jaroslav Pelikan writes of the "subtle relations between continuity and change" in Eastern Christianity (1974: vii).

2. For institutional and liturgical comparative studies, see Baumstark 1958; Taft 1996.

3. The literature for other Eastern Christians is meager by comparison. However, there exists for most Orthodox countries (including Greece) a large literature devoted to popular religion and folklore that is all too often ignored by Anglophone researchers. Kligman 1988 is a noteworthy attempt to bridge research traditions for the case of Romania. See Barna 2004 for a sample of research histories in various European countries, both Eastern and Western.

4. This is analogous to the Western reclassification and misrecognition of Oriental Christians in the "inverse Crusade" noted above.

5. Stamatios Gerogiorgakis (2006) has argued that Eastern and Western understandings of time began to diverge sharply in the Middle Ages. While the former remained close to Aristotelian notions, the latter increasingly adopted linear notions of time, with far-reaching implications for notions of sin and individual responsibility.

6. The major exception is of course the expansion of Russian Orthodoxy throughout northern Asia. Eastern Christianities are also active in other regions; for example, the Orthodox Patriarchate of Alexandria organizes mission work in contemporary Africa.

7. Another subject of enormous interest that is hardly touched on in this volume concerns the way in which the church itself is dealing with the history of the socialist era. For discussion of one particularly famous martyr, see Goltz 1990. See also Kravec 2000–.

8. It is hard to avoid the conclusion that much of the anthropological literature on religion in the first decades of postsocialism steers away from systematic engagement with dominant Orthodox churches. Charismatic visionaries, shamanic revivals, "new age" movements, and the spread of Pentecostalism have all received more attention (Lindquist 2006; Valtchinova 2004; Wanner 2004).

9. For discussion and rebuttal of the most influential Western myths about Byzantium, see Arnason 2000. For fuller accounts, see Angold 2006 and Binns 2002.

10. See Gahbauer 1991.

11. The history of this hymn exemplifies the continuity of Eastern Christianities, which ranges through the Alaskan Akathistos to the miracle working of Our Lady of Sitka (Alaskan Akathist 2005) and is particularly strong in the Greek case (Alexiou 2002; Goltz 2007; see also Luehrmann and Engelhardt, this volume). The Akathistos hymn is sung every Friday at 8:00 a.m. in contemporary Odessa (to mention just one of countless local examples) as a token of gratitude to the Virgin, who helped save the city from the combined fleets of the English, the French, and the Turks during the Crimean War. An Akathistos hymn written in Stalin's Gulag by one of the thousands of imprisoned Orthodox priests was transformed into a Western oratorio by the English composer John Tavener (premiere in Westminster Abbey, 1988).

12. Such "nationalization of religion" is not unique to Eastern traditions. In some countries, perhaps most clearly in Poland, the Roman Catholic is strongly identified with the nation in a similar way.

13. Thus a Croatian bishop was once heard (by Hermann Goltz) to describe his Serbian neighbors as "Asian."

14. See the Greek Old Testament (*Septuaginta* 1965) Gen. 1:26 and 27: "God said: 'Let us create the *anthropos* according to Our [sc. God's] form/gestalt [icon] and likeness [*omoíosis*] [*kat' ikóna imetéran kai kath' omoíosin*].'"

15. Herein lie the roots of Orthodox ethics. Sin destroys and darkens our image of God. What Western Christian ethics derive from Thomas à Kempis's *Imitatio Christi*, the Orthodox Christian East had already derived from the notion that the *anthropos* was the image of God.

16. The Orthodox cathedral of Kerkyra (Corfu) contains an icon of the Byzantine empress of Armenian descent, Saint Theodora, who in 843 A.D. reinstalled the veneration of icons, as defined by the Seventh Ecumenical Council of Nicaea (787 A.D.). In her hands the canonized empress holds not only an icon of the Theotokos and Christ, but also a *rotulus* bearing the words "If you venerate the icons like God, you are three times condemned." For further analysis of the theology of icons, see Lossky and Ouspensky 1999.

17. The charismatic basis of Orthodoxy has been elaborated by the Czech scholar Thomas Spidlik (1978/1986). It has always been rich in Russia, and greater familiarity with pre-Soviet sources (e.g., Smirnov [1913]) would undoubtedly benefit anthropologists researching the charismatic dimension of contemporary, postsocialist Orthodoxy in Russia.

18. Cf. Eliade's concept of "cosmic Christianity" (1972: 251). See also Harnack's discussion of the implications of "the God-Man nature of the Saviour" (1904: 233–40).

19. In this respect Orthodox theology is neither pre-academic nor nonacademic, but rather a postacademic science. This highly reflected Orthodox theology of living experience surpasses the legalism of Roman Catholicism and Protestant scientism. It is perfectly expressed in the immortal religious-philosophical letters of the Armenian-Russian physicist and theologian Pavel Florensky (Florensky 1997).

20. See Geraci and Khodarkovsky 2001. Numerous publications of the Theological Faculty of the University of Kazan in the last decades of the Tsarist empire would be among the basic sources for such a fuller historical anthropological study. See also Glazik 1954, 1959; Goltz 1996.

21. See Znamenski 1999, 2003; see also Ivanov 1997 and Kan 1999 for the Tlingit case. We thank Sonja Luehrmann for drawing these issues to our attention.

## REFERENCES

Agadjanian, A., and V. Roudometof. 2005. Introduction: Eastern Orthodoxy in a global age—Preliminary considerations. In *Eastern Orthodoxy in a global age: Tradition faces the twenty-first century*, ed. V. Roudometof, A. Agadjanian, and J. Pankhurst, 1–28. Walnut Creek, Calif.: AltaMira Press.

Alaskan Akathist. 2005. Akathist service to the icon of Our Lady of Sitka. CD produced in accompaniment to the pilgrimage of the Sitka icon. Anchorage: RODA. http://www .asna.ca/alaska.

Alexiou, M. B. 2002. *The ritual lament in Greek tradition.* 2nd ed. Rev. D. Yatromanolakis and P. Roilos. Lanham, Md.: Rowman and Littlefield.

Angold, M., ed. 2006. *Eastern Christianity.* Cambridge History of Christianity 5. Cambridge: Cambridge University Press.

Antoniadis-Bibicou, H. 2007. *Byzantina et moderna: Mélanges en l'honneur d'Hélène Antoniadis-Bibicou*, ed. G. Grivaud et S. Petmezas. Athens: Alexandria Publishers.

Arnason, J. 2000. Approaching Byzantium: Identity, predicament, and afterlife. *Thesis Eleven* 62: 39–69.

Asad, T. 1993. *Genealogies of religion: Discipline and reasons of power in Christianity and Islam.* Baltimore: Johns Hopkins University Press.

Atran, S. 2002. *In gods we trust: The evolutionary landscape of religion.* Oxford: Oxford University Press.

Barna, G., ed. 2004. *Ethnology of religion: Chapters from the history of a discipline,* Budapest: Akadémiai Kiadó.

Baumstark, A. 1958. *Comparative liturgy.* London: A. R. Mowbray & Co.

Belting, H. 1981. *Das Bild und sein Publikum im Mittelalter.* Berlin: Mann.

Binns, J. 2002. *An introduction to the Christian Orthodox churches.* Cambridge: Cambridge University Press.

Boyer, P. 1994. *The naturalness of religious ideas.* Berkeley: University of California Press.

Campbell, J. K. 1964. *Honour, family, and patronage: A study of institutions and moral values in a Greek mountain community.* Oxford: Oxford University Press.

Cannell, F. 1999. *Power and intimacy in the Christian Philippines.* Cambridge: Cambridge University Press.

———. 2005. The Christianity of anthropology. *Journal of the Royal Anthropological Institute* 11, no. 2: 335–56.

———, ed. 2006a. *The anthropology of Christianity.* Durham, N.C.: Duke University Press.

———. 2006b. Introduction to *The anthropology of Christianity,* ed. F. Cannell, 1–50. Durham, N.C.: Duke University Press.

Coleman, S. 1996. Words as things: Language, aesthetics, and the objectification of Protestant evangelicalism. *Journal of Material Culture* 1, no. 1: 107–28.

———. 2000. *The globalization of charismatic Christianity: Spreading the gospel of prosperity.* Cambridge: Cambridge University Press.

———. 2008. The abominations of anthropology: Christianity, ethnographic taboos, and the meanings of "science." In *On the margins of religion,* ed. Frances Pine and João de Pina-Cabral, 39–58. Oxford: Berghahn.

Danforth, L. 1982. *The death rituals of modern Greece*. Princeton: Princeton University Press.

de Mendieta, Amand E. 1972. *Mount Athos: The garden of the Panhagia*. Amsterdam: Desclée de Brouwer.

Dubisch, J. 1995. *In a different place: Pilgrimage, gender, and politics at a Greek island shrine*. Princeton: Princeton University Press.

Ducas, M. 1958. *Istoria turco-byzantina (1341–1462)*, ed. V. Grecu. Bucharest: Romanian Academy of Sciences.

Durkheim, E. [1912] 2001. *The elementary forms of religious life*. Oxford: Oxford University Press.

Eliade, M. 1972. *Zalmoxis, the vanishing God*. Chicago: University of Chicago Press.

Engelke, M. 2005. Sticky subjects and sticky objects: The substance of African Christian healing. In *Materiality*, ed. D. Miller, 118–39. Durham, N.C.: Duke University Press.

Engelke, M., and M. Tomlinson, eds. 2006. *The limits of meaning: Case studies in the anthropology of Christianity*. Oxford: Berghahn.

Florensky, P. 1997. *The pillar and ground of the truth: An essay in Orthodox theodicy in twelve letters*. Trans. B. Jakim. Princeton: Princeton University Press.

Frank, K.-S. 1964. *Angelikos bios*. Münster: Aschendorff.

Gahbauer, F. R. 1991. *Die Theorie der Pentarchie*. Frankfurt am Main: Knecht.

Geraci, R. P., and M. Khodarkovsky, eds. 2001. *Of Religion and empire: Missions, conversion, and tolerance in Tsarist Russia*. Ithaca, N.Y.: Cornell University Press.

Gerogiorgakis, S. 2006. Zeitphilosopie im Mittelalter: Byzantinische und lateinische Vorstellungen. *Erfurter Vorträge zur Kulturgeschichte des orthodoxen Christentums* 5. University of Erfurt: Chair of Religious Studies.

Glazik, J. 1954. *Die russisch-orthodoxe Heidenmission seit Peter dem Großen*. Münster/Westfalen: Aschendorff.

———. 1959. *Die Islammission der Russisch-Orthodoxen Kirche*. Münster/Westfalen: Aschendorff.

Goltz, H. 1974. *HIERA MESITEIA: Zur Theorie der hierarchischen Sozietät im Corpus areopagiticum*. Oikonomia: Quellen und Studien zur orthodoxen Theologie 4. Erlangen: Lehrstuhl für Geschichte und Theologie des christlichen Ostens.

———. 1979. Antihäretische Konsequenzen: "Monismus" und "Materialismus" in der orthodoxen Tradition. In *Studien zum Menschenbild in Gnosis und Manichaeismus*, ed. P. Nagel, 253–74. Halle: Martin-Luther-Universität.

———. 1988. *Akathistos—Hymnen der Ostkirche*. Leipzig: Benno.

———. 1990. He backed the Logos to defeat the Chaos: The death of Pavel Florensky (1882–1937). *Religion in Communist Lands* 18, no. 4: 343–55.

———. 1996. Streiflichter aus der Geschichte der christlichen Mission in Russland bis zum 18. Jahrhundert; Bemerkungen zur christlichen Mission auf Kamtschatka im 18. Jahrhundert. In *Die große nordische Expedition*, ed. W. Hintzsche and T. Nickol, 100–102, 250–51. Gotha: Justus Perthes.

———, ed. 2004. *Armenien, Deutschland und die Türkei 1895—1925: Thematisches Lexikon*. Munich: K. G. Saur.

———. 2005. Freue dich, du Schatz des Lebens unerschöpflich: Zum Akathistos als Wort-Hymnos und Ikonen-Hymnos. In *Orthodoxe Theologie im Dialog*, ed. J. Weber, 71–95. Münster/Westfalen: LIT.

———. 2006a. Die biblische Gestalt des "Volkes Israel": Ein orientalisch-christlicher Typos in Händels Oratorium "Israel in Egypt." In *Händel-Jahrbuch* 52, ed. Georg Friedrich-Haendel-Gesellschaft, 13–24. Kassel: Bärenreiter.

———. 2006b. Narek and the Occident: Anxiety of the classic ages and contemporary materialism (an imaginary dialogue). In *Saint Grégoire de Narek, Théologien et Mystique*, ed. J.-P. Mahé and B.L. Zekiyan, 325–35. Orientalia Christiana Analecta 275. Rome: Pontificio Istituto Orientale.

———. 2007. Zur Ikonographie des Klosters der Panhagia von Sumela. *Anadolu ve Çevresinde Ortaçağ* 1: 113–38.

Goody, J. 2007. *The theft of history*. Cambridge: Cambridge University Press.

Hann, C. 2006. *"Not the horse we wanted!" Postsocialism, neoliberalism, and Eurasia*. Münster: LIT Verlag.

———. 2007. The anthropology of Christianity per se. *Archives Européennes de Sociologie* 47, no. 3: 383–410.

Hann, C., et al. 2006. *The postsocialist religious question: Faith and power in Central Asia and East-Central Europe*. Berlin: LIT Verlag.

Harding, S. 1991. Representing fundamentalism: The problem of the repugnant cultural other. *Social Research* 58: 373–93.

Harnack, A. 1904. *What is Christianity?* 3rd rev. ed. London: Williams and Norgate.

Hayden, R. 2002. Antagonistic tolerance: Competitive sharing of religious sites in South Asia and the Balkans. *Current Anthropology* 43, no. 2: 205–31.

Herzfeld, M. 2002a. Cultural fundamentalism and the regimentation of identity: The embodiment of Orthodox values in a modernist setting. In *The postnational self: Belonging and identity*, ed. Ulf Hedtoft and Mette Hjort, 198–214. Minneapolis: University of Minnesota Press.

———. 2002b. The European self: Rethinking an attitude. In *The Idea of Europe*, ed. A. Pagden, 139–70. Cambridge: Cambridge University Press.

Hirschon, R. 1989. *Heirs of the Greek catastrophe: The social life of Asia Minor refugees in Piraeus*. Oxford: Oxford University Press.

Huntington, S.P. 1996. *The clash of civilizations and the new world order*. New York: Simon and Schuster.

Ivanov, V. 1997. The Russian Orthodox Church of Alaska and the Aleutian Islands and its relation to Native American traditions: An attempt at a multicultural society, 1794–1912. Washington, D.C.: Library of Congress.

Kaffka, H. 1995. *"Die Schädelstätte wurde zum Paradies": Das Kreuz Christi im Gottesdienst der byzantinischen und slavischen Tradition*. Theol. D.-Thesis, Halle-Wittenberg. Oikonomia 35. Erlangen: Lehrstuhl für Geschichte und Theologie des christlichen Ostens.

Kan, S. 1999. *Memory eternal: Tlingit culture and Russian Orthodox Christianity through two centuries*. Seattle: University of Washington Press.

Keane, W. 1997. Religious language. *Annual Review of Anthropology* 26: 47–71.

————. 2007. *Christian moderns: Freedom and fetish in the mission encounter.* Berkeley: University of California Press.

Kligman, G. 1988. *The wedding of the dead: Ritual, poetics, and popular culture in Transylvania.* Berkeley: University of California Press.

Kravec, S. L., ed. 2000–. *Pravoslavnaya enciklopediya* [Orthodox encyclopedia]. Moscow: Cerkovono-nauchny centr "Pravoslavnaya enciklopediya."

Krikorian, M. K. 1978. *Armenians in the service of the Ottoman empire.* London: Henley and Boston.

Leach, E., ed. 1968. Dialectic in practical religion. Cambridge: Cambridge University Press.

Lepsius, J. 1897. *Armenia and Europe: An indictment.* London: Hodder & Stoughton.

————. 1922. Der umgekehrte Kreuzzug. In *Der Orient,* ed. J. Lepsius, 98–101. Potsdam: Tempel.

Lindquist, G. 2006. *Conjuring hope: Magic and healing in contemporary Russia.* Oxford: Berghahn.

Lossky, V., and L. Ouspensky. 1999. *The meaning of icons.* Crestwood, N.Y.: SVS.

Mahieu, S., and V. Naumescu, eds. 2008. *Churches in-between: Greek Catholic churches in postsocialist Europe.* Berlin: LIT Verlag.

Makrides, V. 2004. L' "autre" orthodoxie: Courants du rigorisme orthodoxe grec. *Social Compass* 51 (4): 511–21.

————. 2005. Orthodox Christianity, rationalization, modernization: A reassessment. In *Eastern Orthodoxy in a global age: Tradition faces the twenty-first century,* ed. V. Roudometof, A. Agadjanian, and J. Pankhurst, 179–209. Walnut Creek, Calif.: AltaMira Press.

Markschies, C. 1999. *Between two worlds: Structures of earliest Christianity.* London: SCM Press.

Meyendorff, J. 1974. *Byzantine hesychasm: Historical, theological, and social problems.* Collected Studies. London: Variorum Reprints.

————. 1983. *Catholicity and the church.* Crestwood, N.Y.: SVS.

Mylonas, P. M. 2000. *Bild-Lexikon des Heiligen Berges Athos.* 3 vols. Wasmuth: Verlag Tübingen.

Naumescu, V. 2007. *Modes of religiosity in Eastern Christianity: Religious processes and social change in Western Ukraine.* Münster: LIT.

Oleksa, M. 2002. *Orthodox Alaska: A theology of mission.* Crestwood, N.Y.: SVS.

Onasch, K. 1993. *Liturgie und Kunst der Ostkirche.* Berlin and Munich: Union.

Pelikan, J. 1974. *The spirit of Eastern Christendom.* Vol. 2 of *The Christian tradition: A history of the development of doctrine.* Chicago: University of Chicago Press.

Peltomaa, L. M. 2001. *The image of the Virgin Mary in the Akathistos hymn.* Leiden: Brill.

Pina-Cabral, J. de. 1986. *Sons of Adam, daughters of Eve: The peasant worldview of the Alto Minho.* Oxford: Clarendon.

Robbins, J. 2003. What is a Christian? Notes toward an anthropology of Christianity. In "The anthropology of Christianity," special issue, *Religion* 33, no. 3: 191–99.

————. 2007. Continuity thinking and the problem of Christian culture: Belief, time, and the anthropology of Christianity. *Current Anthropology* 48, no. 1: 5–38.

Robertson Smith, W. 1889. *Lectures on the religion of the Semites.* Edinburgh: A. and C. Black.

Rogers, D. 2005. Introductory essay: The anthropology of religion after socialism. *Religion, State and Society* 33, no. 1: 5–18.

Roudometof, V., A. Agadjanian, and J. Pankhurst, eds. 2005. *Eastern Orthodoxy in a global age: Tradition faces the twenty-first century.* Walnut Creek, Calif.: AltaMira Press.

Runciman, S. 1985. *The Great Church in captivity: A study of the Patriarchate of Constantinople from the eve of the Turkish conquest to the Greek War of Independence.* Cambridge: Cambridge University Press.

Sames, A. 1993. Zur Entstehung eines negativen Slavenbildes in der deutschen Historiographie. In *1000 Jahre Taufe Russlands—Russland in Europa,* ed. H. Goltz, 557–59. Leipzig: Evangelische Verlagsanstalt.

*Septuaginta.* 1965. *Septuaginta Id est Vetus Testamentum graece iuxta LXX interpretes,* ed. A. Rahlfs. 8th ed. Stuttgart: Württembergische Bibelanstalt.

Smirnov, S. [1913] 1990. *Drevnerusskij duchovnik.* Moscow: Sinodal'naya Tipografiya.

Spidlik, T. 1978/1986. *La spiritualité de l'Orient chrétien.* 2 vols. Orientalia Christiana Analecta 206/230. Rome: Pontificio Istituto Orientale.

Staniloae, D. 1994. *The experience of God.* Brookline, Mass.: Holy Cross Orthodox Press.

Stewart, C. 1991. *Demons and the devil: Moral imagination in modern Greek culture.* Princeton: Princeton University Press.

Taft, R. F., ed. 1996. *The Christian East: Its institutions and its thought.* Orientalia Christiana Analecta 251. Rome: Pontificio Istituto Orientale.

Tarasar, C. J. 1975. *Orthodox America, 1794–1976: Development of the Orthodox Church in America.* Syosset, New York: Orthodox Church in America Press.

Uspensky, B. A. 1976. *The semiotics of the Russian icon.* Lisse, Netherlands: The Peter de Ridder.

———. 1994. *Selected studies.* Vol. 1, *Semiotics of history, semiotics of culture;* vol. 2, *Language and culture* [in Russian]. Moscow: Gnosis.

Valtchinova, G. 2004. Constructing the Bulgarian Pythia: Intersections of religion, memory, and history in the seer Vanga. In *Memory, politics, and religion: The past meets the present in Europe,* ed. F. Pine, D. Kaneff, and H. Haukanes, 179–98. Münster: LIT.

Vzdornov, G. I. 1989. *Troica Andreja Rubleva.* Moscow: Iskusstvo.

Wanner, C. 2004. Missionaries of faith and culture: Evangelical encounters in Ukraine. *Slavic Review* 63, no. 4: 732–55.

Watson. J. 1988. The structure of Chinese funerary rites: Elementary forms, ritual sequence, and the primacy of performance. In *Death ritual in late imperial and modern China,* ed. J. Watson and E. Rawski, 3–19. Berkeley: University of California Press.

Weber, M. [1904–5] 2001. *The Protestant ethic and the spirit of capitalism.* Routledge Classics. London: Routledge.

Whitehouse, H. 2000. *Arguments and icons: Divergent modes of religiosity.* Oxford: Oxford University Press.

———. 2004. *Modes of religiosity: A cognitive theory of religious transmission.* Walnut Creek, Calif.: AltaMira Press.

Williams, R. 1972. The theology of personhood: A study of the thought of Christos Yannaras. *Sobornost* 6: 415–30.

Yannaras, C. 2004. *On the absence and unknowability of God: Heidegger and the Areopagite.* London: Continuum International Publishing.

———. 2006. *Person and eros.* Brookline, Mass.: Holy Cross Orthodox Press.

———. 2007. *Orthodoxy and the West: Self-identity in the modern age.* Brookline, Mass.: Holy Cross Orthodox Press.

Zekiyan, B. L. 1997. *The Armenian way to modernity: Armenian identity between tradition and innovation, specificity, and universality; an inquiry into the impact of the modern world on Armenian society from the Renaissance through Enlightenment up to the genocidal catasrophe of 1915.* Venice: Supernova.

Znamenski, A. A. 1999. *Shamanism and Christianity: Native encounters with Russian Orthodox missions in Siberia and Alaska, 1820–1917.* Westport, Conn.: Greenwood Press.

———, trans. 2003. *Through Orthodox eyes: Russian missionary narratives of travels to the Dena'ina and Ahtna, 1850s-1930s.* Chicago: University of Chicago Press.

# PART ONE

# Image and Voice

*The Sensuous Expression of the Sublime*

# 1

# Eastern Christians
# and Religious Objects

## *Personal and Material Biographies Entangled*

Gabriel Hanganu

One day in August 2000, during fieldwork in northwestern Moldavia, Romania, I happened to be driving back to the town of Piatra Neamț from a neighboring village when I encountered a lorry carrying several nuns. The nuns were holding a large, silver-coated icon of Saint Anna (Romanian: Ana), the Mother of Mary, on the open platform of the truck. I pulled over, turned around, and followed the lorry to its destination. It turned out that the icon, which was the property of the Orthodox Christian nunnery of Văratec, about sixty kilometers away, had been requested by the villagers, who planned to perform a special religious service to bring rain to the dry fields. When the lorry arrived in front of the village church the nuns unloaded the icon and brushed off the dust that had accumulated on them on the way. The local priest and parishioners were gathered in the church-yard to welcome the icon. People knelt in a long row along the alley leading to the church. The nuns lifted the heavy icon and carried it slowly down the alley, holding it upright above the people's heads. All joined the nuns in singing a hymn in honor of the Mother of God. The icon was then taken into the church, and people venerated it individually. A religious service followed, including special rain-seeking prayers.

## THE ICON IN PROCESSION

The next day the icon remained in the church and, according to one of the church readers, was venerated mainly by people who could not come to church the previous day. On the third day a special liturgy with two priests was performed early in the morning. Toward the end of the service the parish priests announced that

FIGURE 1.1. Icon procession to the fields, northwestern Moldavia, Romania, 2000. The Văratec icon (behind the two priests) is preceded by the painted cross, flags, and other icons of the local church. Photograph by Gabriel Hanganu.

a short rain-seeking service involving the carrying of the icon outside the church would be organized after the liturgy. The parishioners began to comment and express disagreement with the priests' decision. In their view, a successful ritual required the carrying of the icon through the streets and the performance of the rain-seeking ritual at the far end of the village. The priests, however, insisted that the service could be performed anywhere, and emphasized that the most important thing was that their prayers were heard by God. During further discussions in front of the church the nuns who had accompanied the icon mentioned that both faith and a moral life were essential if one's prayers were to be fulfilled. According to them, the icon would not perform miracles in communities with an inappropriate religious life. After about an hour of further negotiations the priests finally gave in. A "proper" icon procession began, with a crowd of about a hundred people accompanying the icon in the midday heat over dusty village roads to the village border (fig. 1.1). There, adjacent to the closest arable fields, the priests blessed the waters, read another set of rain-seeking prayers, and then sprinkled holy water on people's heads and on the nearby fields (fig. 1.2).

As soon as the ritual was completed, the icon and accompanying nuns followed a group of parishioners from another settlement who had come to the fields to

FIGURE 1.2. Religious service in the fields, northwestern Moldavia, Romania, 2000. Some people kneel while priests bless the waters and read intercession prayers. Photograph by Gabriel Hanganu.

welcome the icon. As previously arranged, the icon was to stay with them for a similar three-day period of night vigil, day veneration, and procession to the fields. According to the nuns, in periods of severe drought the icon might travel from one village to another for as long as several weeks. Its efficacy in securing rain was usually rewarded with substantial amounts of money and gifts in kind, which the nuns collected on behalf of the nunnery of Văratec.

Many of the participants had expected to have rainfall as soon as the procession began. Others hoped that it would begin when the priests sprinkled the holy water onto the fields. However, when the service ended there was still no sign of clouds in the sky. In fact it only rained a couple of days later. In the meantime the villagers kept discussing the event and produced various explanations for the apparent inefficiency of the ritual. Six main opinions were expressed, which are summarized below in the people's own terms.

1. The priests: "See, we were right! Carrying icons to the fields is useless. The real problem is our poor praying power. We have to learn to pray properly when we are in church. One should focus on the service rather than leave one's mind to carelessly wander about."

2. The nuns: "As we've said before, in certain villages the icon won't work any miracle. You need to find and do something about those brothers and sisters of yours whose poor moral life prevents you from getting the blessing of rain."

Four main attitudes were common among the villagers:

3. Some echoed the priests' opinion: "Carrying icons [in procession] is useless as long as we don't attend services properly."
4. Others were closer to the nuns' view: "It's not the icon's fault. How could it be? It's definitely something to do with us. We've got people among us who live shamefully, and it's about time we did something about it.
5. Others were very disappointed and questioned the efficacy of the Văratec icon: "This [icon of] Saint Ana is not a wonder-working one. We should never borrow it again."
6. Finally, some were skeptical about the practice of carrying icons in procession: "All this rain-seeking business doesn't make any sense. It will rain when it will rain. There's nothing one can do about it."

When it eventually rained a couple of days later most people interpreted the event along the lines of their previous opinions. The majority tended to perceive the rain as the direct result of the ritual, just a bit delayed for various reasons, while a small minority dismissed any possibility that the icon had influenced the rainfall. Nevertheless, the issue was less hotly debated than during the immediate aftermath of the procession, as if the joy of having their major agricultural hope fulfilled made them less keen to argue with each other anymore.

The villagers who insisted on carrying the Văratec icon to the fields, hoping that it would be able to save their crops, behaved as if they feared that, by not performing the full-blown ritual, rain might fall within the village, but the surrounding lands would remain dry. Michael Herzfeld's view, quoted by Sonja Luehrmann in relation to a village icon that has received the grace to cure cancer, is equally relevant in this situation: the icon, in its located materiality, refracts a power whose source lies elsewhere (Herzfeld 1990: 111; Luehrmann, this volume). The villagers' insistence on carrying the icon in procession showed that both the intercession of the depicted spiritual beings and the physical location of the icon mattered to them for the successful fulfillment of the ritual. For the priests, however, the ritual's main power came from the special prayers read during the rain-seeking service. To them any icon would have been equally useful as a means for prompting the depicted saint to intercede on behalf of the community. They tolerated the villagers' excitement about hosting an allegedly wonder-working icon but saw their enthusiasm as a sign of superstitious behavior stemming from poor religious education. As for the nuns, they carefully warned the villagers from the beginning about the potential failure of the ritual. The icon was very powerful, they said, but it wouldn't work miracles in communities hosting people who didn't follow righteous moral conduct.

One can identify in these accounts the potential hidden agendas of the groups involved in the negotiation generated by the icon's presence in the village. For instance, by trying to perform the rain-seeking service just outside the church—thus minimizing the importance of the procession, and implicitly of the icon—the priests might have been concerned to preserve their local religious authority. Similarly, the nuns might have simply wanted to make sure that the icon's reputation—and that of their nunnery—would not be compromised in case of ritual failure. The villagers might not have been fully convinced of the positions they advocated, but perhaps took sides according to kin-related or interest-driven preferences. While I acknowledge all these possibilities, I would like to argue that unless one takes account of two supplementary levels, the anthropological study of Eastern Christian communities risks remaining superficial, if not altogether misleading. One of these levels refers to the theological and spiritual backgrounds associated with the religious practices under scrutiny. The other concerns the visual and material frameworks in which these practices unfold and have an impact on personhood and social agency.

## RELIGIOUS KNOWLEDGE
## AND SPIRITUAL BIOGRAPHY

A closer inquiry into the villagers' cultural backgrounds revealed that their explanations of the apparent failure of the ritual were consistent with their religious knowledge and spiritual experience. Some explanations were affected, for instance, by the fact that people did not know who the saints depicted on the Văratec icon were; others by the fact that people had had the chance to pray in front of the more famous wonder-working icon of Saint Ana at Bistriţa. An in-depth study of the contexts of the Văratec icon's visit revealed that a small proportion of villagers were ambivalent about the practice of carrying icons to the fields, although they displayed and prayed with icons at home. To them, an allegedly wonder-working icon, spiritually more powerful than the others, did not make any sense. They joined the procession mainly because they did not want publicly to express their doubts about the efficiency of the ritual. However, when the priests explained that praying should be more important than the procession itself, these persons agreed, and they were the first to point this out when it did not rain at the end of the ritual.

The vast majority of the villagers, nevertheless, were convinced that carrying the icon to the fields was extremely important. Their opinion was in most cases based on a combination of accounts of the lives of the saints, previous personal

FIGURE 1.3. Religious service in the church, northwestern Moldavia, Romania, 2000. In front of the adorned Văratec icon the villagers have placed candles and food offerings to be blessed and shared among the community on behalf of the deceased. Photograph by Gabriel Hanganu.

experiences, and stories heard from older kin and other acquaintances. Many were aware that the Văratec icon depicted Saint Ana. Indeed, despite the misleading posture, which is very similar to that of the Mother of God holding Christ (the Hodighitria type), the Văratec icon displayed Saint Ana holding her daughter, the future Mother of God. This knowledge of the saint's name apparently triggered mental associations that affected people's sense of identity and relationship. Many villagers felt that, by virtue of their nominal connection with the saint, those whose name was Ana in the community (both living and deceased), and to some extent their close kin, were involved in the ritual in a particular way. Therefore, the opportunity created by the icon's visit was used to commission religious services in memory of the deceased named Ana and their kin. Special lists of names (*pomelnice*) were written and handed to the priests to be read during the services, and ritual offerings of food were blessed and distributed among the villagers (fig. 1.3). Since many families had persons named Ana among their close living or departed kin, these services reinforced the sense of physical and spiritual kinship among the nominally connected visible and invisible communities, similarly to the horizontal and vertical solidarity mentioned by Renée Hirschon (this volume) with respect to the Orthodox name-day celebrations in Greece.

Those who were fully aware of the identity of the icon's prototype were more inclined to associate the efficacy of the ritual with Saint Ana's intercession. To them the icon was precisely an icon of Saint Ana, and Saint Ana was renowned for her rain-interceding specialty. Therefore they largely adhered to the nuns' interpretation of the failure of the ritual as a sign that something was morally amiss in their village. Saint Ana's intercession was all-powerful by virtue of her historical and spiritual biography; and her icon, as a visible expression of that intercession, shared in her power. Therefore to them the only element that could explain the apparent failure of the ritual was their own incapacity to "activate" the icon's power through appropriate moral behavior and ritual engagement.

Most of the villagers who knew that the icon's prototype was Saint Ana were familiar with her biography. In the tales of the saints' lives—which traditionally reached Orthodox believers as church readings, and more recently as published literature—Saint Ana is described as a pious wife who miraculously becomes fertile despite her very old age. This element of her hagiography was paralleled in popular beliefs with the dry farmlands turning fertile through her intercession and divine agency, thus contributing to the idea that one of Saint Ana's "specialties" was interceding for rain. The countless accounts of people who reported rain-making miracles as a result of carrying Saint Ana's icons in procession confirmed the saint's renown and supplemented her historical biography with narrative layers of invisible spiritual activity. The villagers who knew that the icon was of a rain-seeking "professional" tended to attach greater importance to the procession, which they saw as an extraordinary event performed by a specialist saint on a particular occasion. By contrast, those who believed that the same result would have been achieved if they had employed the icon of any other saint were more inclined to associate ritual failure with other factors, such as the devotional or moral features of the community, or the efficiency of the icon itself.

The priests' and nuns' responses must also be placed in the context of their religious education and spiritual experience. For a number of reasons, during the socialist decades—and to a certain extent after 1990—the training of priests paid little attention to the role of religious representation in Orthodox cosmology and teleology. The two village priests were able to discuss the basics of the theological meaning of icons, but when asked about the minute articulation of icon-based religious practices they provided explanations rooted in the moral rather than the mystical areas of Orthodox theology. In such circumstances it was not surprising that during the negotiations with the villagers they played down the ability of icons to bear Spirit and dismissed the need to carry them to the fields, emphasizing instead the importance of engaging in prayerful communion with the whole Church (of which the interceding saint was but a part). Similarly, the ascetic religious experience and moral education the nuns received as novices played an important part in the conception of their explanations. Trained to live less for themselves and more for the community, they thought it was their duty to warn the villagers that they might live next door to someone whose moral conduct was inappropriate. Further conversations with the nuns revealed that their warning had less to do with a fear of being "contaminated" by the neighbors' dubious morals than with their concern that people might behave carelessly with their fellows. Seen in this light, the nuns' warning that the icon might not work miracles in certain communities appeared in a new perspective. There might have been some interest in protecting the spiritual credentials of their icon and nunnery in the case of failure; it might equally have been their religious education and experience that influenced their utterances.

## MATERIAL PRESENCE AND SENSORY EXPERIENCE

Unlike other older and more famous Romanian wonder-working icons, the Văratec icon has been carried in procession for only a few years. In 1997 a group of nuns received permission from their superior to take it from the church and accompany it to the places most affected by drought, having been approached by the villagers, who went to the nunnery to ask for intercession. The model of the borrowing was provided by a famous icon preserved at the monastery of Bistriţa, near the town of Piatra Neamţ—a much older and richly adorned medieval icon, renowned throughout Moldavia for its wonder-working activity.[1] According to a range of local popular accounts, in the past five centuries the icon of Bistriţa has never failed to provide rain in drought seasons when ritually carried in procession to the fields.

Despite being much younger (early nineteenth century) and having far less impressive spiritual credentials, the Văratec icon was believed to be equally powerful, to the accompanying nuns and the group of devout villagers who had negotiated its borrowing. Initially the parish council could not decide which icon to solicit, but in the end a group of villagers who often traveled to Văratec for spiritual guidance persuaded the others that the icon hosted there would be the most appropriate. Apparently, over the past few years it had often succeeded in bringing rain to the fields of devout villagers in the neighborhood. However, its rain-seeking "fame" was still being formed, and remoter villages less connected spiritually with Văratec were not yet fully aware of it.

Most participants knew of the existence of the older and more famous icon of Saint Ana at Bistriţa. Some mentioned that they had traveled to the monastery on various occasions and had had a chance to see and venerate it in the church.[2] Those who had shared its physical presence recalled their experience in terms of awe, deep reverence, and compunction of heart. Yet absorbing the spiritual power of the icon did not inhibit their ability to record a number of visual and material features related to the icon. On the contrary, their sensorial perception seemed to have been enhanced during those moments, since after many years they could remember certain physical details, the accuracy of which I was able to check later myself. Unsurprisingly those who had physically experienced Saint Ana's icon at Bistriţa were equally sensitive to the visual and material qualities of the Văratec icon. For instance, the silver coating of both icons and their display of precious stones in silver mountings seems to have helped associate the two in terms of spiritual efficiency. However, where some saw similarities, others saw differences. The badly damaged painting of the Bistriţa icon—allegedly the result of the count-less rainfalls endured—was seen by some as an evident sign of spiritual efficiency, which radically distinguished it from the relatively newer icon of Văratec, with its better preserved painting. Those who noticed such visual and material differences between the two icons, and suggested parallels with similar differences of spiritual power, tended to interpret the ritual failure as the result of having used an insuf-ficiently "experienced" icon. They pleaded for borrowing the Bistriţa icon in the future, as the only one capable of infallible religious efficacy.

The nuns' relationship with the Văratec icon was of a different nature than that of the villagers'. According to my participant observation in Văratec and other Orthodox monastic locations, nuns spent about half of their time in church, during which they experienced significant multisensorial intake. This included reading and singing sacred texts and music, wearing symbolic vestments, ritually handling symbol-rich religious paraphernalia, inhaling incense, listening to ritual bell tolling, and prostrating in front of icons and relics, all under the physical eyes of the monastic community and the invisible eyes of the spiritual beings depicted on church walls. In addition to training in spiritual awareness and devotional activity, monastic life comprised the appropriation of a daily sensory continuum, which informed the nuns' subsequent perception and interpretation of spiritual matters. A body trained in a spiritually permeated sensory environment was thought capable of both providing enhanced commun-ion with God and activating God's presence in the world through human activity. In this sense, these Romanian nuns' liturgical practice was similar to that of the members of the Estonian church choir described by Jeffers Engelhardt (this volume), for whom church singing was not just music, but aural rendition of the divine prototypes.

One of the nuns mentioned that her praying place in the church had always been in front of the icon of Saint Ana. As she spent most of her praying time there, she gradually developed a particular relationship with the saint. This eventually materialized in her requesting the superior to be allowed to accompany the icon to the villages that asked for spiritual intercession. When I questioned whether she thought of the icon just as a means of facilitating prayer, or as an item spiritu-ally powerful in itself, she thought for a moment and then replied:

Both. I have some icons of Saint Ana in my cell as well, and in my daily prayers I often ask the saint to protect and intercede to Christ for me. But with the big Saint Ana in the church it's different. I feel protected when I'm next to it—and even without praying. Just being there, that's enough for me.

Sharing sacredness sensorily was clearly an important issue for this nun. The big icon was an expression of her particular relationship with the saint, materialized in a sort of "respectful familiarity" that allowed her daily to ask for intercession. But at the same time it was perceived as a physical object charged with spiritual power, which she approached with the sense of being protected and filled with sanctity simply by sharing its physical proximity.

To sum up, in addition to deconstructing individual and group agendas, the "bread and butter" of anthropological research, supplementary elements need to be taken into account in order to build a full picture of the religious practices under study. The way in which people conceive of spiritual beings, and the experience of their relationship with them, can dramatically influence their participation in religious practices. Addressing Saint Ana daily in prayer, or spending considerable amounts of time in front of her icon, may lead to different effects than those achieved by only being vaguely familiar with her hagiography. Certain aspects of religion don't happen only because human groups interact socially, but because they engage differently with the other realms of the universe, including the spiritual and the material. Despite their apparently irrational character, these less obvious relationships are important because they are thought of and acted upon as real by those involved. Most villagers I interviewed were familiar with Saint Ana's icons displayed both in church and at home, and believed any of them would be able to convey their prayers to the saint, and through her intercession farther on to Christ. However, faced with the prospect of severe drought, they had decided to request a special icon of Saint Ana for their rain-seeking ritual, an icon they believed was more efficient than the others. How was it possible for them to think and act in different ways at the same time, without any apparent conflict? In order to provide an appropriate context for discussing this issue I first need to highlight a few points about the particular Orthodox understanding of the terms "image" and "likeness," and to reveal the impact of this view upon religious practices that emphasize the material and biographical qualities of icons.

## ORTHODOX PERSON AND MATTER

The particular understanding of the human person in Orthodox anthropology is based on both biblical references and patristic accounts passed orally from master to disciple and later materialized in written form.[3] Thus, according to Genesis, the first humans were made in the image and likeness of God: "Let Us make man according to Our image and likeness."[4] Two points in this brief formulation require special attention, as they have been interpreted differently by Eastern and Western Christians, resulting in distinctly placed accents that can still be identified in the contemporary religious practice of each group. One concerns the terms "image" and "likeness"; the other, the plural person (Us, Our) in which God speaks about human creation.

Unlike Western theologians, the early Christian fathers held that the first humans were perfect, but only in a potential sense. They had been endowed with God's image from the beginning and were supposed to grow to full divine likeness through their own efforts and the assistance of God's grace. "Image" in this context refers to an innate feature of the human race, while "likeness" denotes a potentiality that each individual is called to attain. For Saint John of Damascus wearing the "image" of God refers to humans' free will, moral responsibility, and rationality—everything that singles them out from the natural world and makes them human "persons."[5] Made in God's "image," humans have the innate capacity to know God and have communion with him. But they are also endowed with free will, and therefore they can take or reject the opportunity to enter into communion with God. If they choose to channel their lifetime energy toward communion with God they can fulfill their inherited "image" with the gradually acquired divine "likeness," and thus become "humans deified," or "gods by grace."[6] This view was interpreted differently by Augustine and resulted in a new understanding of "image" and "likeness" in Western Christianity. According to Augustine, humans were made perfect by God in all aspects: their perfection was fully accomplished from the very beginning. As a result the consequences of the Fall appeared more dramatic to Western Christians, who tended to emphasize the fundamentally expiatory role of Christ in relation to the human condition. Eastern Christians preferred to maintain a balance between the ontological meaning of Christ's sacrifice and the ongoing activity of the Holy Spirit. They emphasized God's call to synergetic partnership with him, by which both humans and the surrounding natural world can be transfigured.

This pneumatological aspect of Orthodox theology, also mentioned by the volume editors in the introduction, brings us to the second point of interest in the Genesis quote. As Hirschon (this volume) points out, for Christians, God is a relational being. Father, Son, and Holy Spirit are a Trinity of persons in relationship, undivided, distinct and not confused, each of whom dwells in the other two by virtue of a perpetual movement of love. Across Eastern and Western Christians one particular point of this doctrine continues to remain difficult. While Orthodox theologians emphasize the "monarchy" of the Father, who is seen as the unique originator and source within the Godhead, Western Christians ascribe this feature to the Son as well. By regarding both the Father and the Son as the source of the Holy Spirit, the Father ceases to be the unity principle of the Trinity and is replaced with the divine essence the three persons share. Therefore, Orthodox hold, by emphasizing the divine essence at the expense of the divine person, Latin Scholastic theology risks assimilating God with an abstract idea that needs metaphysical arguments to prove its validity. The Orthodox, arguably, downplay the need for theorizing about God and urge experiencing him in direct, personal encounter.

Apparently a specialist theological issue, the practical consequences of building one's religious life around this conception of God are far from trivial. If one believes the human person is made in the image of God, and God is a Trinity of persons, then one is likely to see one's personal and social destiny in the light of the Trinitarian doctrine. Humans are free to make choices during their lives and express their own individualities, thus mirroring the distinct individuality of each person of the Trinity. But at the same time they are invited to reflect in their own lives the other complementary aspect of the Trinity: the loving relationship between persons. In other words, while preserving one's unique individuality, one's full destiny as a human person can be accomplished only by sharing one's life with others in a bond of unconditional, sacrificial love.

This complex Orthodox view of the human person is paralleled by a particular understanding of matter, similarly rooted in early Christian cosmology and teleology. Orthodox hold that on the Last Day, like the human body, the entire natural world will be turned by God into a qualitatively superior realm.[7] This belief in the universal redemption of the cosmos is also rooted in the book of the Genesis, according to which the world was made good by God. This theme of the original "sacredness of the world" was expanded in the seventh century by Saint Maxim the Confessor, who, following Dionysios Areopagites, maintains that the Creator endowed each created thing with a *logos,* or inner principle, that makes each thing uniquely and distinctively that which it is, and at the same time connects it with God in an essential yet invisible manner. It is through these subtle cosmic links, nourished by divine energies, that the world is preserved and developed. Building on Saint Maxim's cosmology, Dumitru Stăniloae, an important modern Orthodox theologian, also emphasizes the "holiness of matter," by associating it with man's potential holiness, and by affirming a powerful solidarity between the human race and the realm of nature (Stăniloae 1994). Within this context, the whole world becomes an unfinished work of the Creator, and man, as a synergetic partner with God, is called to set his own imprint on it, as through his own labor and creative imagination he can bring to fulfillment potentialities yet unrealized within Creation. As we can see, the "potentiality-fulfillment" type of metaphor suggested by the "image-likeness" conceptual pair can also be used for describing the created material world. Matter is potentially holy by virtue of the original creation and the connections maintained with God through the divine energies. At the same time it has the possibility to fulfill this potentiality by being involved in human activity performed "in synergy" with God.

## ICON IN THEORY AND PRACTICE

Seen from the perspective described above, objects created by people are part of their work of transforming nature. People are asked to add their contribution to the *logoi* God originally implanted in the constitutive materials of the objects and to the flow of divine energies keeping the whole world in existence. By virtue of their free will they can make and use objects either toward or against the fulfill- ment of nature's sacred potentiality—hence their responsibility for both the natural world and their own creation. Religious objects comprise a particular category of objects that are meant to be employed for prompting and facilitating people's relationship with God. Their "proper" use can open up invisible channels by means of which spiritual energies are directed to the various realms to the benefit of animated and unanimated elements of the cosmos. As religious objects, icons are an even more specific category of goods created by people. In addition to being material objects produced and employed in the visible world, they are also images providing representations of the invisible spiritual realm. The Orthodox Christian understanding of icons is founded on the premise that the transcendent God can be represented visually in the immanent form of the icon, since his incarnation as human has demonstrated the possibility of combining in one and the same being both divine boundlessness and human delimitation. Many Byzantines of the seventh and eighth centuries believed that images were not merely external signs, arbitrarily or causally linked to the realities they repre- sented, but rather that an ontological relationship existed between the spiritual beings and their painted images. In the formulation of the Second Ecumenical Council of Nicaea (787 A.D.), "the honour paid to the images passes on to that which the image represents, and he who does worship to the image does worship to the person represented in it" (Mathews 1997: 20). David Freedberg (1989) calls this particular type of aesthetics, in which the devotional image is employed as a straight, unmediated connector between the beholder and the deity, an "aesthetics of presence." Within an "aesthetics of presence" the direct visual relationship prompted by the divine image is associated with specific bodily and material devotional practices, or in Christopher Pinney's terms a "corpothetics" (2001: 157, 161), inasmuch as the image points to a personalized, rather than abstract, presence.

In contrast to this type of aesthetics, transmitted through Byzantine art to Russia and the Orthodox Christian countries of the Balkans, Freedberg holds, Latin Christianity maintained a circumspect view on the ontological transparency of the connection realized by means of religious images. For Aquinas, Christian images could be used for the instruction of the unlettered, who might learn from them as from books. They could also be successfully used as reminders of the important historical events of Christianity: "The mystery of the Incarnation and the examples of the saints might remain more firmly in our memory by being daily represented to our eyes" (Aquinas, quoted in Freedberg 1989: 162). For Bonaventura, the need for images came from our human shortcomings: the ignorance of our mind, the sluggishness of our emotions, and the unpredictability of our memory. Religious images "stood for" the "heavenly kingdom," but no ontological link was required between them and their referent (166). Both Aquinas and Bonaventura located religious images within a "semiotic aesthetics." Unlike Orthodox Christianity, which integrated icon veneration within the liturgy, Latin Scholastic theology removed images from the spiritual core of the Church and assigned them a mere instrumental and representational role.

Icons in Eastern Christian churches are displayed according to a centuries-old spatial and temporal program. During religious services they are venerated by both clergy and laity with a mixture of verbal, mental, and bodily devotion, such as kneeling, crossing, prostrating, and kissing, which involve a crucial embodied relationship with the depicted prototypes. Pilgrims often visit famous icons hosted in monasteries and spend long hours praying in front of them, passing under them, and touching them. Many rub against their glass covers clothes belonging to sick relatives or friends, in the belief that the icons' spiritual power can be transferred through physical contact with another material, thus being able to cure "by delegation." Icons are also carried in processions outside the church—for instance, on battlefields or to farming lands—in the belief that the spiritual beings represented on them can intercede on behalf of the community and ensure success. On special annual occasions, such as before Christmas or Epiphany, the icons of the approaching feast are carried by the priests to every household so that they can be venerated by the faithful and the houses ritually sprinkled with holy water. People commonly display icons at home and employ them in daily devotion by crossing themselves, kissing them, and kneeling and lighting candles and oil lamps in front of them. Together, these icon-centered religious practices create a particular sensory background, which adds to the conceptual and psychological layers of religiosity, and influences the devotees' relationship with the divine and, equally important, with their fellow humans and the surrounding material world.

In many Orthodox Christian Churches a strong correlation between theological formulations and religious practices has been preserved to the present day. This is partly because the process of confining religion to the private sphere that has affected Western Christianity since the Renaissance was less well developed in the East. In spite of the decades of atheist totalitarian regimes in southeastern Europe, religious practices survived and emerged strongly in the public domain after 1990. As a result. even groups and individuals with little religious education continued to be exposed to visual and material expressions of popular religiosity by being involved in collective practices performed regularly in both urban and rural locations. Baptisms, weddings, funerals, and other socially salient rituals have preserved a key religious practice component, which in most cases is still acknowledged and (at least formally) accepted even by those who do not consider themselves religious or do not regularly go to church. Thus in the Romanian case study presented above, even the villagers who were not believers or regular churchgoers were familiar with these diffusely distributed forms of devotional activity. Previous social events in which they had taken part had familiarized them with the idea that spiritual power can be ritually associated with human bodies and material objects.[8]

This kind of community-induced logic of the spiritual potential of matter can help us understand the apparently conflicting views of the villagers, according to whom all the icons of Saint Ana were equally capable of conveying prayers, while at the same time the particular icon of Saint Ana of Văratec could intercede on the villagers' behalf more efficiently than the other icons. Why were all the icons of Saint Ana equally powerful? Because they all pointed to the same spiritual being, and as potentialities each could accomplish the intended aim of facilitating spiritual exchange. Why could some icons be more efficacious than others? Either because the prototype had endowed them with more spiritual power at a particular moment, or because their material bodies have gradually "charged" over time as a result of being repeatedly involved in spiritual mediation. In other words, all the icons of Saint Ana were visual and material interfaces, which when devotionally prompted allowed for the manifestation of the prototype's spiritual agency. In addition to this form of external agency, wonder-working icons like Saint Ana of Bistrița—and possibly Văratec—possessed some sort of spiritual agency of their own, acquired as a result of their particular biographies, and uniquely attached to their physical bodies. This paradoxical form of spiritual agency, neither fully external nor fully self-contained, or (if we prefer) both reflective and accumulative, is consistent, as we have seen, with the "image-likeness" model of the human person, which anchors its realization both externally, in God's image, and internally, in the gradual accomplishment of the divine likeness through synergetic collaboration with God.[9] This paradoxical understanding and use of both "ordinary" and wonder-working icons by Eastern Christians suggest that we need to take account of a distinctive Orthodox view of personhood, materiality, and relationship, according to which the agency of religious objects must be seen in relation to both their potential for mediating spiritual exchange with the prototypes they depict and the fulfillment of this potential by participating in social and material fellowship. Similarly, human personhood needs to be ascertained in relation to both the unique physical and biographical identity of each individual and the relational energy distributed within the material, social, and spiritual realms. In both cases the "potentiality-fulfillment" model suggested by the "image-likeness" theological pair provides a recognizable pattern. Interestingly, as I will show in the next section, these ideas resonate with theoretical concerns in anthropological scholarship, to which Eastern Christian views of personhood and materiality may provide some theoretical alternatives for future development.

## PERSONS AND THINGS IN
## A TEMPORAL PERSPECTIVE

Various scholars have emphasized the importance of studying material aspects of religion in the context of practices associated with their production and consumption, thus complementing—and sometimes challenging—previous theological and art historical approaches. An important contribution to this body of research was made by visual anthropologists and material culture scholars who emphasized that materiality affects social relationship. In addition to words, visual symbols, and social convenience rules, people construct their identities and relate with each other through material culture elements. Visual anthropologists such as Marcus Banks and Howard Morphy have argued that a common theoretical and methodological framework should be used for studying both material culture elements and the "visual systems" of the communities that produce and employ them (1997: 14). Referring more specifically to the materiality of photographic representation, Elizabeth Edwards has pointed out that "while the analytical focus has been on the semiotic and iconographical in the representation of race and culture, material forms of images are integral to this discourse" (Edwards 2002: 67). Communication scholars and anthropologists informed by media studies have also addressed the topic of object-mediated relationship and called for a more serious examination of the materiality of communication across cultures. As Faye Ginsburg, Lila Abu-Lughod, and Brian Larkin have observed, in addition to expanding the study of media production and audience contexts, more research needs to be done on the physical and sensory properties of the media technologies themselves (2002: 19). Visual historians such as David Morgan (2001, 2005) have emphasized that word-based communication models should be employed cautiously where material religious practice is concerned, suggesting that, more than a mere illustration or accessory to word-based interpretation, material culture is "co-constitutive of religion" (2001: 16).[10] In studies informed by material culture and anthropology of art the shifting of the objects' meaning as they move through circuits of exchange has been a recurrent topic. Researchers such as Arjun Appadurai (1986), Nicholas Thomas (1991), George Marcus and Fred Myers (1995), and Daniel Miller (1995) have pursued the implications of cross-cultural exchange (of objects, narratives, and technologies) for culture making and personhood by showing that the clear distinction between persons and objects, usually taken for granted in Western Europe and North America, is made in other societies along different lines, with objects and people connected through networks of relations. This research has challenged previous work based on the long-established animate-inanimate distinction developed in antiquity and revived during the Renaissance. If objects in some societies are seen as capable of developing some form of social agency, researchers have to describe how they come to be socially bound to their producers and audiences with invisible threads of past and present relationship. In order to have access to their full "social lives" one has to study all the contexts relevant to the manifestation of this particular form of agency, as Pinney did in his study of the cultural politics informing the shifting rapports between religious image and studio photography in India (1997).

Other authors have focused their research on the "biographical" dimension of the objects' "social lives." Janet Hoskins (1998), for instance, has described "biographical objects" as material culture elements used to create and sustain the meaning of people's lives. According to Kopytoff (1986), things cannot be fully understood by looking at only one point of their existence, and their processes of production, exchange, and consumption need to be documented and analyzed as a whole. Objects change throughout their existence and have the capability of accumulating histories; therefore their present meanings are partly determined by the persons with which they interacted and the events they were part of. A significant number of studies have followed this theoretical path and analyzed the ways in which objects accumulated "cultural biographies" as a result of their circulation within and across communities.[11] Building on the extensive literature developed around the gift-commodity distinction, Marilyn Strathern (1988) has developed a theory of Melanesian sociability in which people and objects are seen as moving moments within networks of relations. In this model, objects are seen as detached parts of people moving among social groups, while people are conceived of as distributed items composed of all the objects they have made and exchanged throughout their lives. A person's agency may have effect at a distance from the individual's body and may continue to have effect after the person's death. Following similar ideas, Alfred Gell (1998) has developed a theory of art and agency, according to which material culture items are seen as social actors of some sort, in the sense that they affect social relationship in ways that would not occur if they did not exist. Art objects are secondary agents that act as extensions (indexes) of their makers' or users' agency, and have effect by virtue of being enmeshed in social relationship. These theories have major implications for the idea of biography. Objects are not merely external supports or measures of an internal life, but rather people and things have mutual biographies, which unfold in culturally specific ways (Gosden and Marshall 1999: 173).

In the light of the scholarship emphasizing the invisibly connected biographies of objects, how should material culture be documented and represented by anthropologists who have traditionally relied on "realist" modes? Are some methodological tools more appropriate than others for investigating and representing the world of "entangled objects"? Such questions are especially important in devotional contexts, because of the enhanced entangling potential of religious objects, with both the visible and the invisible, the material and the immaterial, realms of existence. Biographies of religious objects are interlaced with the biographies of their producers and users, and at the same time with those of the spiritual beings they represent. Additionally, and crucially for this discussion, by virtue of their material "bodies" religious objects are able to connect these biographies with the natural realm to which their material constituents belong.

The temporal quality of icons can be usefully described in terms of "internal and external narratives" (Banks 2001). This terminology has been employed by Banks in the context of photographs and postcards, but it can be used for other types of images as well. For Banks the internal narratives of an image refer to its visual content—the visual text, or "the story that the image communicates." The external narratives, by contrast, describe "the social context that produced the image, and the social relations within which the image is embedded at any moment of viewing" (2001: 11). This distinction indicates that the narratives associated with people and objects located both inside and outside the image frame gradually accumulate in time, and that by studying them one is likely to come across fragments of the biographies of those who produced and employed them.[12]

Like the photographs discussed by Banks, the internal and external narratives of religious images consist of layers of relationship established in time with their producers and audiences; however, additionally they are entangled with the invisible beings addressed by devotees during religious practices. In certain cultural traditions, where religion essentially involves physical, as well as aural and mental, devotional participation, supplementary levels of entanglement occur, including involvement with the materials of which religious objects are made.

In the particular case of Orthodox Christian icons, the theological assumption that the constitutive materials maintain an invisible connection with God is combined with the belief that the honor paid to the image passes on to whomever the image represents.[13] This double determination of the icon, which reflects the double determination of the human person in Orthodoxy, suggests an alternative method that can be employed in the anthropological study of Eastern Christians—a method that is informed by Orthodox anthropology and focuses on the religious objects produced, circulated, and employed within the community. This alternative method should be seen as complementing previous approaches, such as those that analyze the politics of representation within religious communities. In the case of Eastern Christians, with their specific understanding of personhood and materiality, this method significantly enhances overall research results by taking into account the social, spiritual, and material aspects of relationship suggested here.

## CROSS-REALM BIOGRAPHIES OF RELIGIOUS OBJECTS

The new model I propose for the study of Eastern Christian communities would supplement the "direct" documenting of religious phenomena with "indirect" accounts of exchange between the visible and the invisible, as described and effected by the members of the religious communities themselves. The researcher's direct observation of religion-based social interaction can be complemented with a biographical study of the material culture elements involved in these processes, which are seen primarily as relational nodes connecting the material, social, and spiritual worlds. On the basis of such premises, anthropological developments, such as those informed by the "cultural biographies of objects," would share some common ground with the Orthodox conceptualization of personhood and materiality, according to which spiritual beings, humans, and religious objects undergo entangled transformations and accumulate layers of relational biographies.[14]

The new model proposed here attempts to build on such similarities between anthropological theory and Orthodox theology, and to bring to center stage two features of religious objects: their cross-realm relational potential and their multilayered biographical dimension. From this perspective the full biography of an icon can be seen as the product of a collaboration of various categories of agents (animate and inanimate, human and nonhuman, visible and invisible). It consists of the interlaced biographies of four distinct elements: (1) producers, (2) audiences, (3) prototypes (spiritual beings depicted on icons and invoked in religious devotion), and (4) materials included in the icon's "body." All these "agents" affect the icon's existence variably at various moments of its biography, and at the same time they mutually influence each other and have an impact on the larger realms of existence to which they belong. The successive layers of relationship created in this way imprint themselves visibly or invisibly upon the icon and continue to influence its subsequent existence, just as biographical events affect people's lives.

Most of the anthropological scholarship on icons (e.g., Kenna 1985; Herzfeld 1990; Dubisch 1995) has focused on the study of their cultural biographies acquired through circulation and use, which in the context of a cross-realm biography covers mainly area 2, "Audiences" (see fig. 1.4). Research into these different areas would benefit from a coordinated theoretical and methodological agenda, with the aim of documenting and analyzing the icons' "full-blown" cross-realm biographies. Future studies will need to include issues only tangentially discussed or alluded to in this paper, such as the effect of material culture contexts on icon production (especially as southeastern Europe shifted from socialist to postsocialist regimes), producers' status as icon-entangled agents despite the apparently severed links with the icons they completed, and the nature of the relationship that icons maintain with the natural world by virtue of the raw materials of their physical bodies. Last but not least, more attention may need to be paid to the

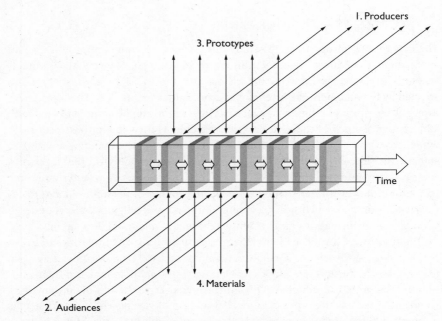

1. Producers

3. Prototypes

Time

4. Materials

2. Audiences

FIGURE 1.4. Cross-realm biography of an icon. Original diagram by Gabriel Hanganu.

spiritual dimension of the icons' biographies, by including both the official and local, historical and spiritual, biographies of the prototypes involved in devotion. In addition to providing a more complete picture of the social and religious interplay in Eastern Christian communities, this model would be useful for rethinking the role of agency and materiality in religious mediation more generally.

## CONCLUSION

In this case study from Romania I showed that by paying attention to the biographical and material qualities of icons one can venture beyond the models traditionally employed in anthropology, art history, and communication studies. A broader perspective is likely to enhance our understanding of icons as spiritually, socially, and materially connected objects with constantly evolving biographies. The temporary presence of the Vǎratec icon of Saint Ana in the host village confronted the local population with issues they were not prepared to deal with, such as the role of the clergy vis-à-vis that of devotional objects in common and exceptional religious practices, the management of religious activity in individual and collective rituals, and the social and spiritual negotiation of apparent ritual failure. It questioned existing individual and group identities and generated heated social and religious debate within the community. The visiting icon's biography and materiality were central to the processes of religious mediation that took place in the village.

On a more general level, the specific ways in which Eastern Christians conceive of the invisible world and the material realm, and the objectification of this understanding in contemporary religious practices, suggest a new perspective for their anthropological study, one that acknowledges and reflects Orthodox Christian anthropology itself. As I have shown, the "image-likeness" theological dyad informs the understanding of the human person and material culture in Orthodox theology and explains the use of icons by the faithful as both reflective and accumulative agents of spiritual power. Time and relationship are essential in this conceptual framework, where people and icons can move during their lives from an innate potentiality to its relationally dependent fulfillment. A similar temporal and relational model lies at the heart of the "biography of objects" approach in anthropology, according to which objects change throughout their existence and accumulate in time layers of relationship. These similarities suggest alternative avenues into the anthropological study of agency and personhood. The apparently clear-cut distinction between the understanding of the individual as a self-contained unit, informed by Western Christianity, and the various non-Christian forms of distributed personhood is challenged by a paradoxical Eastern Christian intermediary position.

## NOTES

1. The Byzantine emperor Manuel II Palaeologus (1391–1425) gifted the icon to the Moldavian prince Alexandru cel Bun and his wife, Ana. The prince then endowed it to Bistriṭa Monastery, which he had founded.

2. An old man mentioned that in the late 1940s he happened to accompany the icon in a horse-driven cart to another village that had requested it. According to him, clouds began to gather as soon as they got out of the monastery, and by the time they reached the border of the village, rain began to pour so heavily that he and his companions had to cover the icon with their clothes. The priests and villagers welcomed the icon in their church, venerated it, and performed a thanksgiving service, while rain poured outside for a couple of hours; then they sent the icon back to Bistriṭa with money and gifts they had collected in advance.

3. The Orthodox Christian theological material in this section draws in part on Ware [1963] 1997.

4. Gen. 1:26.

5. John of Damascus *Patrologia graeca* 94: 920B.

6. "I said, you are gods, and all of you sons of the Most High." Ps. 81:6; cf. John 10:34–35.

7. "Then I saw a new heaven and a new earth; for the first heaven and the first earth have passed away." Rev. 21:1.

8. For instance, one Romanian villager confessed that although he was a nonbeliever, when he traveled for the first time to Western Europe he felt very strange entering churches without crossing himself, as he would normally do at home when entering churches for wedding or baptism ceremonies.

9. This is also consistent with the Eastern Christian view of deification, according to which the devotee is capable of complete fusion with God while preserving his own individual features. For a popular account, see the famous encounter of the Russian saint Seraphim of Sarov and his disciple Motovilov in Fedotov 1950.

10. Religious objects should not be seen simply as substitutes for religious words, but as the "nonverbal articulation of space, property, kinship, status, value, power, affection, order, ethnicity, race, gender." (Morgan 2001:16).

11. For a useful account of the "biography of objects" scholarship, see Gosden and Marshall 1999.

12. In another paper (Hanganu 2004) I have discussed these issues in the context of the multiple performances of a photographic collage of a miraculously founded Romanian Orthodox Christian nunnery. The multiple "dormant" copies of the image produced in the 1950s went into public oblivion following the sentencing of the authors by the communists, but a surviving copy of the original negative instantly "woke up" when I began documenting its production context.

13. The social expression of this concern for materials may be reflected in opposite ways. For instance, some icon makers emphasize the need for "pure" or "blessed" materials for icon painting, while others are totally indifferent to these aspects, as they believe that irrespective of production contexts icons can become sacred in time as a result of their being used in religious devotion.

14. Needless to say, this apparently overlapping conceptual zone should be explored with extreme care, as the processes described by terms such as "relationship" and "biography" are different in the two contexts. While social scientists generally conceive of these processes in an abstract and symbolic sense, for Orthodox Christian patristic writers and contemporary faithful the realities described are of a concrete and personal, albeit invisible, nature.

## REFERENCES

Appadurai, A., ed. 1986. *The social life of things.* Cambridge: Cambridge University Press.

Banks, M. 2001. *Visual methods in social research.* London: Sage.

Banks, M., and H. Morphy, eds. 1997. *Rethinking visual anthropology.* New Haven: Yale University Press.

Dubisch, J. 1995. *In a different place: Pilgrimage, gender, and politics of a Greek island shrine.* Princeton: Princeton University Press.

Edwards, E. 2002. Material beings: Objecthood and ethnographic photographs. *Visual Studies* 17, no. 1: 67.

Edwards, E., and J. Hart, eds. 2004. *Photographs, objects, histories: On the materiality of images.* London: Routledge.

Fedotov, G. P. 1950. *A treasury of Russian spirituality.* London: Sheed and Ward.

Freedberg, D. 1989. *The power of images: Studies in the history and theory of response.* New York: Columbia University Press.

Gell, A. 1998. *Art and agency: An anthropological theory.* Oxford: Clarendon Press.

Ginsburg, F. D., L. Abu-Lughod, and B. Larkin, eds. 2002. *Media worlds: Anthropology on new terrain.* Berkeley: University of California Press.

Gosden, C., and Y. Marshall. 1999. The cultural biography of objects. *World Archaeology* 31, no. 2: 169–78.

Hanganu, G. 2004. Photo-cross: The political and devotional lives of a Romanian Orthodox photograph. In *Photographs, objects, histories: On the materiality of images,* ed. E. Edwards and J. Hart, 148–65. London: Routledge.

Herzfeld, M. 1990. Icons and identity: Religious orthodoxy and social practice in rural Crete. *Anthropological Quarterly* 63, no. 3: 109–21.

Hoskins, J. 1998. *Biographical objects: How things tell the stories of peoples' lives.* London: Routledge.

Kenna, M. A. 1985. Icons in theory and practice: An Orthodox Christian example. *History of Religions* 24, no. 4: 345–68.

Kopytoff, I. 1986. The cultural biography of things: Commodization as process. In *The social life of things: Commodities in cultural perspective*, ed. A. Appadurai, 64–91. Cambridge: Cambridge University Press.

Marcus, G., and F. Myers, eds. 1995. *The traffic in culture: Refiguring art and anthropology.* Berkeley: University of California Press.

Mathews, T. F. 1997. Religious organization and church architecture. In *The Glory of Byzantium: Art and culture of the Middle Byzantine era, AD 843–1261*, ed. H. C. Evans and W. D. Wixom, 20–35. New York: Metropolitan Museum of Art.

Miller, D., ed. 1995. *Worlds apart: Modernity through the prism of the local.* London: Routledge.

Morgan, D. 2001. Introduction to *The visual culture of American religions*, ed. D. Morgan and S. M. Promey. Berkeley: University of California Press.

———. 2005. *The sacred gaze: Religious visual culture in theory and practice.* Berkeley: University of California Press.

Pinney, C. 1997. *Camera Indica: The social life of Indian photographs.* London: Reaktion.

———. 2001. Piercing the skin of the idol. In *Beyond aesthetics: Art and the technologies of enchantment*, ed. C. Pinney and N. Thomas, 157–79. Oxford: Berg.

Stăniloae, D. 1994. *The experience of God.* Trans. and ed. I. Ionita and R. Barringer. Brookline, Mass.: Holy Cross Orthodox Press.

Strathern, M. 1988. *The gender of the gift.* Berkeley: University of California Press.

Thomas, N. 1991. *Entangled objects: Exchange, material culture, and colonialism in the Pacific.* Cambridge, Mass.: Harvard University Press.

Ware, T. [1963] 1997. *The Orthodox Church.* London: Penguin.

# 2

# A Dual Quarrel of Images
# on the Middle Volga

## Icon Veneration in the Face
## of Protestant and Pagan Critique

Sonja Luehrmann

"Russians and baptized people pray onto an icon (*moliatsia na ikonu*), *chimari* pray onto a tree, onto a candle." This is how a Mari villager, speaking in Russian, described the differences between two of the religions that are practiced in the Republic of Marii El in the Volga region of the Russian Federation.[1] Whereas "pray" is the verb commonly used locally to refer to lay religious activity within any denomination, this woman used a slightly unidiomatic turn of phrase to locate the difference not in who the prayers are *addressed to,* but what they are *directed onto,* what object focuses and mediates them.[2] Her expression aptly captures how, for many people in Marii El, Orthodox Christians' use of icons in prayer is one of the significant marks distinguishing them from unbaptized *chimari* ("pure Mari," often referred to as *iazychniki,* "pagans," in Russian), as well as from Muslims and from the adherents of the Protestant churches whose membership has been growing in the region since the early 1990s. As intentionally visible attributes of Orthodox churches and households featured in most rituals of the Orthodox Church, icons can readily become a focus of critique, an issue around which outsiders formulate what seems wrong or strange to them about Orthodoxy. For some observers, icons, trees, and candles are too much alike in their idol-like materiality; for others, icons lack important qualities that make trees and beeswax candles more suitable vehicles for contact with nonhuman beings. Both lines of critique have taken on new inflections during the recent history of Soviet atheism. But their general thrust is already anticipated in the Orthodox theology of the icon, which, having been elaborated through centuries of fierce controversy, has given liturgical practices of icon veneration an aspect of demonstrative defiance performed before an imaginary audience of critics.

Given that the defense of the veneration of images in the Second Nicaean Council of 787 depended on the distinction between the material image, not worthy of veneration on its own, and the prototype, who was the true recipient of the honors shown to the image, it is important to the contemporary Orthodox clergy to impress on believers the correct understanding of this semiotic relationship, an understanding that they often find lacking among their parishioners. In reference to these long-standing debates about the proper role of the material and the sensual in worship, often filtered through standards of credibility inculcated through decades of Soviet education, the precise differences and similarities between icons, trees, and candles become highly meaningful for some religious practitioners. The woman I quote above, however, an unbaptized middle-aged mother who has had her children baptized in the Orthodox Church, treats the three classes of objects as equivalent to each other, merely associated with the practices of different people. As I trace debates about icon veneration in this chapter, it is important to remember that current polemics draw on layers of argument from many centuries, some of which have been constitutive of current practices but are not necessarily present or relevant to all current practitioners. It is precisely the variety of stances toward the use of material and sensual media in worship contained within theories and practices of icon veneration that deserves the attention of anthropologists studying Christianity.

## ICONS AND ICONOCLASM

In the Orthodox theology of the image, as elaborated in the course of the iconoclastic controversy, the distinction between prototype and image, the being represented and the representation, is crucial. The visual representation of spiritual reality is justified by God's own diverse image-making activities. According to the eighth-century apology regarding icon veneration written by Saint John of Damascus, God first formed images in his mind of the things and beings he was going to create (conceptual images), then created humankind in his own likeness (image as imitation). Most importantly, God authorized the depiction of uncreated divinity through its incarnation in the person of Jesus Christ, "the first natural and undeviating image of the invisible God" (John of Damascus 2003: 96–98; quote from 96 [3.18]).

The prohibition against making images in the second commandment, the main argument of the iconoclasts, was interpreted by the defenders of icons to prohibit the worship of images as divine beings (*idolatreia;* Russian: *idolopoklonstvo*), as distinct from showing them honor and veneration as representations of a divine or saintly prototype (*eikonodulia, proskynesis;* Russian: *ikonopochitanie*). The Nicaean Council, which established icons as worthy of veneration, condemned those who refused to venerate images of Jesus Christ, the Mother of God, and the saints, and also those who worshipped them as divine beings (Besançon 1994: 231). In a list of heresies, John of Damascus calls iconoclasts "Accusers of Christians" (*Christianocategori*), because they accuse iconodules "of worshipping as gods, after the manner of the Greeks, the venerable images of our Lord Jesus Christ, of our immaculate lady, the holy Mother of God, of the holy angels, and of His saints" (John 1958: 160).[3] He thus agrees with the iconoclasts that Christians should not do as the Greeks, who, he claims, make no distinction between gods and their images. This agreement makes the accusation of idolatry a charge both sides take very seriously, something that is still evident in interreligious debates in today's Russia.

The difference between proper Christian *veneration* and "Greek" or pagan *deification* of images thus depends on the idea that icon portraits render visible a world of invisible "prototypes"—that is, divine or saintly persons who lived in the past, have a lasting personal, though invisible, existence in the kingdom of heaven, and remain distinct from their representation in paint. The Orthodox insistence on the distinction between material image and spiritual prototype may seem to fit comfortably into narratives about Christianity as they have been proposed in recent anthropological work on materiality and semiotics, whose authors have pointed to the role of theological debates within Western Christendom for fueling anxiety about proper distinctions between signs and their meaning, material objects and immaterial referents. Concerns elaborated in Reformation-era debates about the Eucharist and the veneration of relics and statues, some scholars argue, were later echoed in such divergent contexts as colonial missionary denunciations of "fetishism" (Keane 2007; Kohl 2003) and the Saussurean model of the arbitrary relationship between signifier and signified (Keane 2003). Christianity thus appears as a force promoting an increasing separation between the realm of things, on the one hand, and realms of meaning and human agency, on the other, in European history as well as in the colonial and postcolonial worlds (see also Engelke 2005).

A problem with this extremely fruitful line of inquiry is that in their focus on the links between Christianity and modernity these studies tend to take the anti-materialism of pietistic Protestantism as their paradigmatic case, sometimes almost treating it as the most logical consequence of early Christian teachings. That seems problematic as a starting point for comparative research on other branches of Christianity, not least because it is very close to the narrative Protestants like to tell about themselves. A careful consideration of what is at stake in the Orthodox distinction between icon veneration and idolatry can help bring to the fore some aspects of Christian engagement with the material world that may also be present within Western denominations under different guises and that deserve more attention in an emergent anthropology of Christianity.

The work of art historian Hans Belting (2000, 2001) resonates to a certain extent with that of Webb Keane and Karl-Heinz Kohl. Belting pursues the emergence of the Western concept of art, in which the main function of an image is to visually represent a reality external to itself, and the "image" (what is represented) is considered to be independent of the "picture" (the material manifestation of this representation, including the cloth and frame in the case of a painting, or the stone or metal in the case of a statue). In his account, however, it seems less clear whether developments within Christianity propelled the development of Western art or stood at odds with it. The Byzantine icon in particular occupies a transitional place in his analysis. According to Belting, Christian art took shape at a time when a historically more common understanding of images as sites of presence was encountering a new understanding emerging in the Greek ecumene, of images as visual representations of a reality in which they did not themselves participate. In the understanding of image-as-presence, the image of the emperor literally stood for him, in the sense of making him present at places where he was not, and hence was accorded the honors due to his person. Visible resemblance of the image to the person represented ("iconicity" in the language of semiotic anthropology) was often of little importance compared to what Peircean semiotics would consider its indexical capacity to be endowed with the power or aura of that person (Peirce 1955; cf. Gell 1998). With the emergence of realism in Greek funerary art, Belting argues, came a new focus on the capacity of images to depict a reality that existed (or had perished) independently of them. This also opened up the possibility of a critique of the image as unable truly to do justice to the original, all the more so if, as in Platonic philosophy, the person or object represented was itself considered to be only a transitory manifestation of spiritual reality (Belting 2001: 171–73).

In Belting's analysis, the Byzantine theology of the icon preserves a hybrid notion of image. The icon is necessary to the worshipper because it is an index of the presence of God's grace, but the worshipper is also enjoined to remember constantly that the source of this grace is God, not the image itself. This relationship of mediation is made more complicated when the icon depicts not Jesus as one of the persons of the Trinity, but the Mother of God or a saint. Standing before the icon, the believer is in the presence of the saint, who is him- or herself a recipient and mediator of the grace of God. Prayers addressed to the saint are supposed to ask him or her to pray to God for the supplicant or to use healing powers that have been bestowed on the saint by God (Belting 2000: 11–19). In the Orthodox East, this complex relationship was carried into liturgical texts from different periods, as in this stanza from the *akathistos* (a hymn in praise of Mary, a saint, or a feast day) to the Kazan icon of the Mother of God, approved for liturgical use in 1867 (Shevzov 2007: 69):

> Desiring to bestow grace upon those who venerate You lovingly, oh Birthgiver of
> God, you deposited the gracious power that is Your own in Your sacred icons, for
> the divine grace which rests upon them always works signs and miracles and gives
> all those who approach with faith healing of all spiritual and bodily ills through Your,
> oh Mother of God, incessant prayers to God for those who sing to Him: Halleluiah.
> (*Akafist* 2004: 23–24 [Kontakion 12])

Divine grace is the true source of the signs and miracles accomplished through
the icon, and God is the one who heals the supplicant, motivated by the prayers
of Mary, but the icon is necessary as a "deposit" of grace. During my fieldwork I
found educated Orthodox clergy and laypeople very careful to stress both aspects
when they spoke about icons. For example, on our way to visit a recently painted
copy of a Greek miracle-working icon in a rural church, a woman explained to
me that "the Lord has been blessing this icon in recent times; there have been
many healings." A leaflet distributed in the church explains that this icon type,
representing the Mother of God enthroned as Vsetsaritsa (Queen of All), "*has
received the grace* to heal the most terrible illness of contemporary humanity,"[4]
namely, cancer. The particular icon copy is an irreplaceable instrument of healing
that people take pains to visit, because, in Michael Herzfeld's analysis, in its
localized materiality it manages to "refract" a power whose source lies elsewhere,
with the intercessions of the Mother of God and ultimately God himself
(Herzfeld 1990: 111).[5]

## POLEMICAL LITURGIES

Liturgical performances of the theology of the icon often explicate the distinction
between the image and the various beings whose powers are mediated through it
in a context in which "unbelievers" criticize Orthodox practices. For example,
another stanza from the *akathistos* to the Kazan icon reads:

> Strange and doubtful it sounds to the unbelievers how from Your icon flow streams
> of grace and living odors exude: but we, believing the word You said, oh Ruler, to
> the first-painted icon, "With you is My grace and strength," are full of hope, for with
> this icon also Your grace is always: that is why standing before it reverently we kiss
> it, bow to it, as to You Yourself, for the honor shown to the icon ascends to the
> prototype, and Your grace through this icon works signs and miracles for all
> who come to You with faith and sing to God: Halleluiah. (*Akafist* 2004: 16–17
> [Kontakion 8])

This stanza shows the polemical and demonstrative side of the theology of the
icon, where self-consciously adopting the proper attitude toward an icon—veneration, but neither worship nor rejection—is necessary because of the actual or
imagined presence of critics of the church. Veneration is justified by the assur-

FIGURE 2.1. The feast of the Triumph of Orthodoxy in the Ascension Cathedral, Ioshkar-Ola. In the foreground, with his back to the camera, stands Archbishop Ioann, confirming each anathema with a knock of his staff. In the background, with his back to the iconostasis, the deacon is reading out the list of anathemas. He stands in front of a large Mandylion icon, a smaller version of which, barely visible between the heads of the worshippers, is laid out in the center of the church for veneration. Photograph by Sonja Luehrmann.

ances of the Virgin herself and the church fathers: the phrase "for the honor shown to the icon ascends to the prototype" is an unmarked quote from the fourth-century theologian Saint Basil the Great (Belting 2000: 173–74).

On the feast day of the Triumph of Orthodoxy (Torzhestvo Pravoslaviia), held every year on the first Sunday of Lent in memory of the end of iconoclasm in 843, anathemas are pronounced over all the ancient heresies and in contemporary Russia also over Baptists, Jehovah's Witnesses, neo-pagans, and a host of other nationally and locally active religious groups (fig. 2.1). During the service in honor of the feast in the cathedral of Ioshkar-Ola (the capital of Marii El) in 2005, the icons brought out for veneration were the Savior Not Made by Human Hands (known in the West as the Mandylion—a depiction of the cloth on which Jesus made an imprint of his face for the king of Edessa, today's Urfa, who requested to see him) and the Mother of God of the Sign (showing Mary presenting an image of the infant Jesus before her on a shield), both pointing to the incarnation of the divine Word as the origin and justification of Christian images (Ouspensky 1992).

The gospel and epistle readings spoke of the need for a unified church: Jesus giving his disciples the "power of the keys" ("Truly I say to you, whatever you bind on earth shall be bound in heaven, and whatever you loose on earth shall be loosed in heaven," Matt. 18:18), and the apostle warning Christians to preserve unity by twice admonishing, then shunning people who teach heresy (Titus 3:10).[6] The iconoclastic controversy is thus placed in a larger narrative of perpetual danger to the church from various false teachings, and icon veneration comes to stand metonymically for faithful adherence to Orthodoxy, while the miracles worked through icons over the centuries serve as evidence of the ongoing presence of the grace of God in the church.

The liturgy of this feast day ties the correct understanding of images to the survival of the church itself and the integrity of its Christological and ecclesiologi-cal teachings. This implies concerns about worshippers' reflexive capacity to dis-tinguish between proper agents of grace and objects without autonomous agency, concerns reminiscent of those of the Dutch Calvinist missionaries in Indonesia described by Keane (2007: 184). These missionaries worried about proper distinc-tions between interior Christian prayer and what they saw as unconverted Indonesians' tendencies to ascribe material effects to the words of a prayer or to address prayers to a sacrificed chicken. But the liturgy of the Triumph of Orthodoxy dramatizes concern not only about people who mistake the object that prayers are directed onto for the addressee of the prayer, but also about those who reject mediating objects altogether. And the test of right observance it offers is ultimately the collective one of participation in the rites of the Orthodox Church, rather than a probing of individual awareness. These two factors, as we will see, allow Orthodox clergy considerable latitude in deciding which forms of engagement with material objects are acceptable in Christian worship, while at the same time leading them to reject the solutions espoused by Calvinist-inspired churches.

## CONTEMPORARY CRITIQUES

In the liturgical texts, the presence of external critics is assumed, but Orthodox Christians never actually need to encounter them. In fact, the biblical texts often quoted on this question, Titus 3:10 and Matthew 18:15–17, advise the faithful to avoid contact with heretics and persistent sinners, and Archbishop Ioann of Marii El, when asked during a Bible study how to convince "sectarians" of the errors of their ways, counseled against entering into arguments with them.

But in Marii El, the Orthodox do indeed face both other Christians who do not venerate icons and people who are commonly known as "pagans" (iazychniki), the term that is used for the Hellenic "gentiles" in Russian translations of the Bible. Protestants often adopt the position of the "unbelievers" in the hymn quoted above, finding Orthodox practices of icon veneration "strange and doubtful" or simply condemnable. One woman, talking about the time before her conversion to a Charismatic-Pentecostal branch of Protestantism, remembered her confusion when encountering the icons in an Orthodox church: "Back then we went to an Orthodox church and asked, Who is the main god here? Here is God's mother, also a god; here is Nicholas the Miracle Worker, he works miracles, that means also a god. Who is the strongest of them?" A standard phrase I heard among Baptists, Charismatics, and Lutherans was that Orthodox Christians "worship something created"—that is, the piece of wood on which the icon is painted, or the physical image itself—while Protestants worship "the living God" and "have no mediator except Christ." These Protestants effectively repeat iconoclast arguments by accusing the Orthodox of deifying images and thus practicing polytheism. In the words of a Lutheran deacon, "Orthodoxy is just another kind of paganism." Like Reformation-era Protestants rejecting the Catholic cult of relics (Kohl 2003: 66–68), these Russian Protestants are scandalized by the idea that material things can be repositories or media of divine grace.

Protestants thus accuse the Orthodox of confusing the material medium with the divine source of power, and assume that such confusion is inevitable when material things are used during worship. To pagans Orthodox images are suspect because they uphold the distinction between medium and source too strictly, and thus offer no indexical proof that the source actually exists. "Jesus Christ is an image painted by someone," the *chimari* high priest of Marii El, Aleksandr Tanygin, said in an interview with me. He was referring to the low reliability of biblical reports about Jesus's teachings, and at the same time pointing out that the gods the Mari worship are so real that they need not be depicted but can be immediately experienced in groves where sacred trees grow as a result of their creative energy. From this point of view, the icon becomes at best an unnecessary addition to places that are already inherently sacred, at worst a weapon of hostile takeover by the church. A woman formerly active in a Mari political movement and now supporting herself as a cultural entrepreneur by selling embroidery and organizing tours of healing springs told me how she resented finding icons displayed near more and more springs. In one village the people proudly told her: "Batiushka [an affectionately respectful term for an Orthodox priest] came and consecrated our spring." She bristled at the recollection: "Batiushka, batiushka! I told them nature herself consecrated your spring, because the water contains silver. Maris are like that: they think they are nothing by themselves; only when a batiushka has come, then it must be something." This woman also held that only real beeswax candles should be used in prayer, not the paraffin ones sold in church, because beeswax had the same cell structure as the universe and everything in it.

While both pagans and Protestants criticize the Orthodox for worshipping man-made things instead of going directly to sources of divine power, they each do so from a different side of the fine line between idolatry and iconoclasm prescribed by Orthodox doctrine. Protestants—especially those whose teachings have roots in radical evangelical traditions, such as Baptists and Pentecostals—consider any attempt to approach divine power through the mediation of material ("created") things as misguided and blasphemous. In *chimari* worship, by contrast, sacred places, sacrificial foods, and other materials used in worship are not taken to be signs pointing to an outside spiritual reality but are said to be endowed with efficacy by virtue of inherent qualities—the sacred groves in which sacrificial ceremonies are held are thought to have been discovered to be sacred by ancestors who first established a given village, not to have been made so through consecration. Both sides thus deny what Herzfeld (1990: 116) identifies as the social (one might also say ecclesiological) consequences of the essential nonequivalence of icon and prototype: as multiple, conventionalized tokens of a unitary spiritual reality, icons can simultaneously represent the segmentary interests of families and communities and make them mutually equivalent parts of a transcendent whole. Neither the moments of spontaneous prayer favored by evangelicals nor spatially bound sacred trees and candles that must consist of a specific material are enduring, transposable, and easily reproducible in quite the same way.

## ECHOES OF SOVIET SCIENCE

Before the Soviet period, inhabitants of the Mari region would probably not have argued that devotional objects must share in the cell structure of the universe in order to be effective. Protestant and *chimari* critiques of icon veneration gain persuasiveness through standards of credibility and habits of thought inculcated by Soviet educational institutions, whose influence is also evident in Orthodox responses. Soviet atheist propaganda often focused on denouncing visible and public practices of folk Orthodoxy, such as the veneration of bleeding, weeping, or oil-exuding icons. Antireligious lecturers and traveling agitational groups presented stories of such miraculous occurrences as deliberate attempts by the clergy to take advantage of the ignorance of the population. They performed chemical experiments to demonstrate how "blood," "tears," and "oil" could be deliberately made to appear by human agents (Nekhoroshkov 1964). The assumption was that knowledge of natural laws would liberate people from believing in the supernatural explanations propagated by self-interested clergy.

The fruitfulness of this strategy of public enlightenment was disputed even among Soviet antireligious activists. But the fact that virtually everyone alive in Marii El today went through an educational system that stressed that nothing in the world happens without a scientific explanation means that today there is a large number of people for whom the way in which icons accomplish the effects ascribed to them is problematic and in need of such explanation. For critics, the answer can be that apparent effects are the result of deception or self-deception, which keeps people from seeking out true sources of power, be they in an out-of-the-world God or in natural phenomena themselves. Apologists can stress that icon veneration protects against the deceptive influences of other forms of visual media.

Acknowledging that deliberate deception was not sufficient to explain the effect of icons, Soviet critics took recourse to theories of the role played by visual perception in shaping people's convictions. The following analysis of the perfidious influence of icons repeatedly mentions the eyes and processes of sight as the channels of interaction between humans and icons, in order to construct an argument that the icon is a way for "church people" to influence people's thoughts and behavior in the most intimate spheres of life:

> The veneration of icons was inculcated in children from the earliest age. As a rule, icons were *colorful*, with a *shiny* wreath around the image, which unwittingly *attracted the interest and attention* of the children. In all the most important events in a person's life the icon inevitably participated. . . . All family members several times daily went down on their knees and prayed, *looking at the icon*, asking god to send down a better life and health. . . . Everyone who came into the house *turned his eyes* first of all toward the god-shelf [*bozhnitsa*], to the icons, and finding them, crossed himself, bowed, and only after this greeted the inhabitants of the house. (Nekhoroshkov 1967: 15; emphasis added)

The idea that visual impressions are important in forming convictions was well developed in postwar Soviet educational psychology, and lecturers and propagandists were trained in producing "visual aids" (*nagliadnye posobiia*) in order to enhance their effect on audiences.[7] The author of the above quote, instructor of natural sciences at the teacher's college and one of the most prominent antireligious activists of the Mari Republic in the 1950s and 1960s, evidently understands icon veneration in this framework and treats icons as competition to the Communist Party's attempts at visual persuasion.

Twentieth-century Orthodox theology also contains many reflections on icons as, first and foremost, objects to be seen (Ouspensky 1992), and contemporary apologists seem to find it easiest to defend icons by analogy to other visual media. "A mother who kisses a photo of her son does not cause you disgust. Why then is an Orthodox Christian who kisses the image of the Savior an idol worshipper?" is the Orthodox response to critics suggested in a handbook for debates with "sectarians" (Rubskii 2003: 94). Icons, in this interpretation, function a bit like the tools of persuasion atheist theorists suspected they were, or rather as aids in protecting a devotee's senses from other visual influences. During a rare occasion of actual polemical engagement between representatives of different denominations in Marii El, Orthodox clergy argued that Christians who refuse to use icons exposed themselves to uncontrolled outside influences on their visual imagination of sacred beings. Participating in a dispute between representatives of Protestant churches and Orthodox priests conducted in the Charismatic Ioshkar-Ola Christian Center in the capital of the republic, Father Oleg Steniaev from Moscow answered critical questions about icon veneration by relating a conversation he had had with a Baptist woman:

> She says: "I don't need icons; Christ is in my heart." I asked her: "And what does he look like?" You know, this woman got confused a little bit, and says: "He is not very tall, red-headed." And somehow got even more disturbed. I say: "What is bothering you?" She says: "He looks like one man. When I was young I knew this one man. He was some kind of accountant, very religious." . . . When we speak about Christ, whether we want to have icons or not, in the consciousness of each of us some kind of image arises. One young Orthodox boy, he was thirteen, went to see the film by Zeffirelli, *Jesus of Nazareth.* And then for a whole month he could not free himself from that hallucination. He says: I get on my knees to pray and I have, he says, that actor before my eyes, and there's nothing I can do about it. The icon exists to filter out this sensual image, sensual apprehension. It shows another world, in a way. And sensuality goes to the sidelines a little bit. And what are Pastor Timofei and Pastor Sergii [Timofei and Sergei are the names of his Protestant opponents] if not icon painters when they tell about Christ in their sermon? He is crucified, the hands, legs pierced by nails, a crown of thorns on his head?[8]

According to Father Oleg, it is uncontrolled visual imagination that leads to idolatry, whereas icons with their canonically sanctioned conventions restrain idolatrous impulses. Paradoxically, Protestants in Ioshkar-Ola seemed to worry far less than this Orthodox priest about the potential idolatrous effects of images, as long as they were used didactically, and enthusiastically used film to propagate their faith. In 2005, a Baptist church showed Mel Gibson's *The Passion of the Christ* on Maundy Thursday, and a montage of mute scenes from the same film formed the visual backdrop to a song about the sufferings of Christ during an Easter evangelizing concert organized by a Pentecostal church. Immediately following this view of Christ being flagellated, carrying his cross through the streets of Jerusalem and dying painfully on the cross, the pastor's exhortation developed imagery from the scenes, encouraging listeners to go even further in their visual imagination:

> You know, it was no coincidence that Jesus died in just the way which you saw today in the scene from the movie. He was flogged, he was simply torn to pieces, the skin is taken off, there was not a living piece of flesh on him, the blood was flowing and pouring in streams, maybe he would even have died just from the loss of blood. So much blood all around! Why such a death? Why blood? No forgiveness without bloodshed. You remember how we said in the beginning? Passover—that is the lamb that had to be offered as a sacrifice for sin, sacrifice for salvation.[9]

The use of a film for emotional-didactic effect easily falls into Steniaev's category of the kind of "sensuality" (*chuvstvennost'*) that icons help to avoid. A Protestant image that is in some ways more similar to icons is a city map used in the Charismatic Christian Center (fig. 2.2). This congregation presents an extreme case of Protestant mistrust of material media: it meets in a former cinema and emphatically denies the need for any special architectural space or any requisites other than the seats, microphones, and loudspeakers necessary to make sure everyone can sit and hear the words of the preacher and the music of the band. However, one "visual aid" they used at the time of my fieldwork, and even carried with them when they had to move their worship space from the auditorium to the foyer during renovations, was a commercially produced map of the city onto which someone had glued the heading "God Loves the City of Ioshkar-Ola" in hand-drawn letters. This map hung from one of the loudspeakers on stage, and during prayers for the evangelization of the city all church members stretched out their arms toward it. Like an icon, a map is considered to be a faithful representation whose accuracy is partly assured through resemblance to the physical shape of the prototype, and partly through adherence to symbolic conventions familiar to viewers. In the Peircean classification of signs, both the icon and the map thus combine aspects of "icon" and "symbol" (Peirce 1955: 102–3). Perhaps because of this combination of realism and obvious stylization, the map, much like the icon, lends itself to use as a medium of contact not with the physical reality of the city, but with the unseen spiritual world that surrounds and permeates it, and in which angels and demons battle over its fate, a battle in which the prayers are intended to intervene.

The use of the map by this strictly iconoclastic group confirms Steniaev's argument that it is hard to sustain religious practice without resort to visual imagination. But for members of this church it is also significant that this map was "simply bought in a store" (as they explained to me when I photographed it). Unlike Orthodox icons, it makes no claim to significance by virtue of either its beauty or its "biography" (Hanganu, this volume) and hence does not relieve worshippers of the obligation to find an indexical point of contact with God's majesty in their hearts, not in the fittings of the church. If the simple white robes used by the Zimbabwean Pentecostals described by Matthew Engelke are an "anti-fashion," and the pebbles they use as prayer tokens, by analogy, anti-objects (Engelke 2005: 127, 131), then the map in the Christian Center is an anti-icon. It is also an anti-icon from an Orthodox point of view, since instead of being a conduit of divine grace toward the supplicant, the image functions as a reverse index, where the flow of causality is from the image to the reality it depicts, and that can be influenced through it.

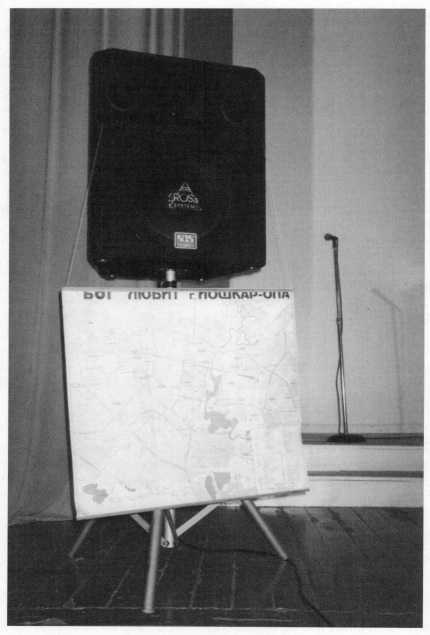

FIGURE 2.2. City map used during prayers for evangelization, Ioshkar-Ola Christian Center. The text on top reads: "God loves the city of Ioshkar-Ola." Photograph by Sonja Luehrmann.

## BEYOND VISUAL INTERACTIONS:
## THINGS AND PERSONS

As mentioned earlier, it was relatively rare, and not always recommended by spiritual superiors, for Orthodox Christians in Marii El to engage directly in interreligious polemics. More commonly, the concern of clergy and educated laypeople about correct practice expressed itself in criticisms of folk and village Orthodoxy, framed as a struggle of the "teaching of the Holy Fathers [of the church]" against the "teaching of the grandmothers."[10] In settings where the assumed audience consisted exclusively of clergy and those laypeople familiar with and loyal to church practices (*votserkovlennye,* or "churched" people), criticism of the practices of less "churched" Christians sounded very similar to Protestant criticism of Orthodoxy in general. During a conference dedicated to the feast day of Saints Cyrill and Methodius, the paper entitled "Faith and Superstition" presented by a priest from a small rural town resonated strongly among other members of the clergy. In his paper, Father Viacheslav Mikhailov cited cases of "paganism in the church": for instance, the widespread opinion that candles that were passed through the church to be placed before an icon must be passed only over the right shoulder or only after crossing oneself a certain number of times, or when people understood candles to be a direct payment that obliged God or the saint to answer their prayers. All this, the speaker claimed, confused the spiritual, symbolic significance of lighting a candle as a sign of prayer with the concrete acts involved. The priest's immediate superior, the superintendent of the northeastern part of the diocese, confirmed that the fact that "almost everyone believes only superstitiously" (*veriat tol'ko sueverno*) was one of the greatest theological problems facing the Russian Orthodox Church.[11]

Part of "believing superstitiously" is mistaking material media for immediate sources of grace, but another part is caring more about the immediate personal benefits of acts of veneration than about becoming a part of the church as a translocal and transgenerational Christian community. This is where the ecclesiological aspect of correct veneration lies. During a procession with a copy of the Smolensk icon of the Mother of God, which traveled through the republic in June 2005, the priests stressed the blessings that Mary had decided to bestow on individual villages as well as the republic as a whole and tied them to the need to atone for the atheism of the Soviet period. They repeatedly reprimanded people who shoved others aside to receive a larger dousing of holy water or who kept running ahead of the icon in order to pass under it again and again. In Father Viacheslav's terms, these people could be said to display "a consumerist attitude" toward the blessings of the church, coming to "consume [*potrebliat'*] grace while leaving nothing in return."[12]

When Orthodox clergy sometimes accuse their parishioners of paganism in ways that are close to Protestant critiques, what seems to worry them is not necessarily the parishioners' understanding of the fine distinctions between worship and veneration, but rather their lack of consideration for the church as a community and an institution. As Charles Stewart describes for twentieth-century Greece, and Vera Shevzov for prerevolutionary Russia, priests and laypeople can share the understanding that the distinguishing factor between acceptable Christian practice and condemnable magic or superstition is whether or not a rite is performed by an ordained priest or at least with his blessing (Shevzov 2004: 123–25; Stewart 1991: 41–42). What matters from this point of view is the spirit of reverence or willfulness in which people encounter such grace-filled objects as icons, rather than where they locate the source of the grace. This criterion allows for a variety of stances toward the materiality of an icon, a variety perhaps best accommodated by thinking of icons as persons.[13] During the procession described above, villagers greeted the icon as an honored guest, spreading hay and flowers on the village road and preparing tables of food and drink as refreshments for her train of pilgrims. The custom of crouching down in front of the icon to have it pass over one's head—encouraged by the priests unless people did it so often that it slowed down the procession—deliberately used the material qualities of the icon as a fairly large rectangular "picture" to allow people to enact this respectful greeting of a revered visitor (fig. 2.3; cf. Hanganu, this volume).

While, as we have seen, contemporary defenders of icon veneration tend to speak of icons as a form of visual media, the treatment of icons as persons blurs distinctions between visual and nonvisual qualities of images, as well as between forms of engagement sanctioned and frowned upon by the church. Crouching under an icon during a procession is an example of a nonvisual, but officially sanctioned mode of engagement, although there are few references to it in contemporary apologetics. When an icon, with its fixed convention of depicting a given saint, provides an opportunity to recognize this saint in living people, this is an unintentional effect of sanctioned practices of visual contemplation. One devout Orthodox woman told me that as she was filling out her applications for a state pension, she saw a small old woman in a head scarf pass by, murmuring "trouble, trouble." She thought that the woman looked familiar, and when she really ran into trouble with her application, she remembered that the woman looked like Saint Matrona of Moscow (1885–1952), a twentieth-century "fool for Christ" whose cult became popular in the 1990s. All three Orthodox churches in Ioshkar-Ola displayed icons of Matrona at the time of my fieldwork, and a laminated reproduction of one hung on this woman's kitchen wall. Having recognized Saint Matrona in the old woman, she immediately went to confession and ordered a prayer service for the saint, after which her pension came through.

FIGURE 2.3. Procession with the Smolensk icon of the Mother of God passing through a village in Zvenigovo district, Republic of Marii El, June 2005. Photograph by Sonja Luehrmann.

Although such apparitions challenge Steniaev's argument that icons protect against the "hallucinations" caused by exposure to cinematic representations of Jesus Christ, the idea that a simple old woman may resemble a saint also resonates with church teachings about iconic resemblances across different layers of the Christian community. At the most general level, every human being, even in the present fallen state, is assumed to be an image of God. More specifically, clergy and especially bishops are treated as images of Christ, who, in turn, is the only unadulterated image of God and of humanity before the Fall. To show reverence for his status as image of Christ a priest is greeted with a kiss of his hand, and the visit of a bishop to a parish is an occasion for a reenactment of Christ's entry into Jerusalem, with a carpet of flowers replacing the biblical palm bows. The title bestowed on a monastic saint, *prepodobnyi*, literally means "most similar," referring to the way in which monastic life is thought to bring a person closer to man's original state of likeness to God. Building a relationship with saints through emulation and prayerful contemplation in turn enables lay devotees to move toward such likeness (Ouspensky 1992). Iconic resemblances among people and between people and divinity thus unite living and dead, clergy and lay members of the church. The conclusions drawn by the pension applicant—to go to confession

FIGURE 2.4. Icon corner in a Mari household, Baisa village, Kirov region, June 2005. Photograph by Sonja Luehrmann.

and order a prayer service—would most likely save her vision from being censured as "superstitious" in Father Viacheslav's terms, because they demonstrate that she is a "churched" Christian, who combines respect for sacraments and willingness to support them financially with recognition of personal responsibility through repentance.

The affinity between icons and churched persons also helps us to understand how the tolerance of the church can extend to cases where the character of the icon as visual representation is almost eliminated. As Belting notes, the capacity of images to index an absent prototype does not necessarily depend on their visual qualities. Indeed, it may not depend on images being seen at all—they may be hidden in a temple, be displayed only on certain feast days, or be accessible only to a certain class of people (Gell 1998: 136). In rural households in Marii El, for example, icons remain hidden from view most of the time, contrary to what Soviet critics of icon veneration lead us to expect. In Mari villages, most houses I visited had icon corners. In most cases, the shelf supporting one or more icons was fitted into a corner and shielded by an embroidered curtain, creating a niche in which the icons were barely discernible (fig. 2.4).

The curtain is lifted on occasions that require candles to be lit in front of the icons (family celebrations, memorials, and Christian feasts observed in the village), but for most of the year the embroidery is far more visible than the images behind the curtain. This practice is not unique to the Mari but is also found in Russian villages of the republic and in some regions of central Russia. It is often explained as a way to keep the saints from seeing everything that goes on in the household (Tsekhanskaia 2004: 130–31), but a folklorist in Marii El recorded a different explanation in a village of Russian Old Believers in 2004: "They [the icons] can see us anyway, but passersby can't see them" (Marina Kopylova, personal communication, January 2007). Both explanations point to a desire to keep visual interactions with the image under the control of members of the household. At the same time, the lavish embroidery and the emphasis on the festive moments of opening the curtain can be seen as expressions of love and reverence for the prototype, which may explain why I have not heard priests condemn the practice or interpret it as selfish willfulness.

Unlike the Greek and ethnic Russian communities studied by other scholars of Orthodoxy, not all inhabitants of Marii El consider themselves to be Christian. But even unbaptized Mari often have icons in their houses, indicating that the understanding of icons as devices to materialize a presence can not only be reconciled with church doctrine, but can also make them equivalent to other objects that people of various religious affiliations "pray onto." In a village that had been the center of an Orthodox parish before the revolution but that was also famous for its continuous observance of Mari sacrificial ceremonies, even the house of one of the pagan priests had an icon corner. One of the newer houses, however, contained no icons, although the corner opposite the stove in each of the two rooms was still partitioned off with an embroidered curtain, behind which a candle was fixed to a small board fitted across the angle. When I asked why there were no icons, the sister of the owner of the house, herself visiting, answered: "Oh, they simply didn't buy one." Her sister-in-law, the lady of the house, added: "We have to order one. Or no, they sell them in the church; you can buy them there."

As I later learned, it had been seventeen years since the couple had built the house, so they had obviously felt no great need for icons, and their professed intention to buy one may have been for my benefit as a stranger with unknown religious sympathies. But the point is that the corner without an image worked in much the same way as an icon corner. Family videos showed that the curtain was lifted and the candle lit in it for birthdays and other important events in the lives of its members, as would be done in front of the icon in other households. In terms of providing the presence of a powerful being, icons, candles, and even trees dedicated to particular gods may do much the same work, especially when they are placed in locations that are themselves charged with force, such as the "forward corner" of the house or, in the case of trees, the family vegetable plot or a grove on a hilltop at the village boundary.

Thinking back to Belting's analysis of icons as hybrids between image-as-presence and image-as-representation, one could say that rural Mari icon corners put the emphasis on the first understanding, to such a degree that for some people it becomes irrelevant if they contain an actual icon. Comparable ideas about the location of power in the corner itself rather than the icon have been reported from regions with a purely Russian Orthodox population (Paxson 2005: 219). In Russian folklore studies, these ideas have sometimes been interpreted as instances of *dvo-everie* (dual faith), a kind of syncretism in which "pagan beliefs and practices are preserved under a veneer of Christianity" (Levin 1993: 31). Eve Levin has rightly criticized this approach for assuming that all folk practices are of pre-Christian origin, and for underestimating the formative influence of church rituals on the popular imagination (cf. Stewart 1991 for a critique of similar assumptions about Greece). In the Volga region, where indigenous religions exist as living traditions alongside Orthodox Christianity and Islam, the concept of syncretism may be more appropriate, as the use of icons by people who do not consider themselves Christians exemplifies. But cases where people establish equivalences between practices that they recognize as appropriate for different people, such as praying onto icons versus praying onto trees or empty corners, are perhaps better described as religious parallelism rather than syncretic mixing. Whereas Protestant churches actively seek to avoid practices that can be construed as parallel to *chimari* ones, the position of the Orthodox Church is more complex. As suggested by the indifference with which the owner of the iconless house acknowledged that she should go buy an icon in the church, one of the relevant distinctions between Christian and non-Christian devotional practices lies in whether a family cares enough about its connection to the church to visit the nearest functioning one and either purchase a consecrated icon or pay for the rite of blessing a reproduction or self-painted image. From the point of view of Orthodox doctrine, the blessing enables the icon to link individual devotees to the Christian community in the way discussed by Herzfeld, because it ensures that the power refracted by the presence behind the curtain is the grace of God on the church, not one of the forces evoked in the parallel practices of other religions.

## CONCLUSION: ANTIHERETICAL CONSEQUENCES

Hermann Goltz (1979) has argued that the insistence of the early church on the moral neutrality of the material world and its participation in God's plan of salvation, elaborated in polemics against Gnostic and Manichaean dualisms, had a lasting effect on Eastern Orthodox thought, up to the iconoclastic controversy and beyond. In the light of these long-standing controversies, a variety of practices in contemporary Marii El, some of them arguably inspired by phenomena as recent as the atheist campaigns of the 1960s, appear as the latest manifestations of the two deviations of iconoclasm and idolatry, or, in even older terms, of the rejection or deification of matter. For anthropological reflections on the role of Christian theology in the emergence of modern forms of dualism between matter and spirit, signs and meanings, it may be important to note that the Orthodox diocese of Marii El seems to allow itself far more latitude in tolerating practices that lean toward the side of idolatry, by giving credit to the love and reverence involved in ambiguous practices and relying on a theology of incarnation and divine image-making. Only the complete denial of a need for church blessings on sacred sites and objects or the conscious address of prayers and offerings to beings outside the heavenly hierarchy seems to place a person among the "pagans and neo-pagans" anathemized during the Triumph of Orthodoxy. On the side of "icono-clasm," the line is drawn far more quickly, and a large number of groups considering themselves Christian, from "Baptists and Anabaptists" to "the followers of the Ioshkar-Ola Christian Center," end up in the roll call of anathemas.

While it is easy to interpret these anathemas as an appeal to history in order to legitimize current claims to power, a more complex question would concern the demands that their double-sided theological distinctions place on practitio-ners and researchers, within Orthodoxy and in other Christian denominations. Other branches of Christianity may not place the same emphasis on avoiding the two extremes of rejecting or deifying matter and may have different ways of linking the acts of committed believers to the collective context of the church, but all preach the physical incarnation of God and the idea of the church as the body of Christ. Taking a cue from the feast of the Triumph of Orthodoxy, greater atten-tion to the intersections between liturgics, ecclesiology, and ideas about material-ity may prove fruitful in studies of these other traditions as well.

## NOTES

My fieldwork in Marii El in 2003 and 2005–6 was funded by the German Academic Exchange Service, the Wenner-Gren Foundation, and the University of Michigan's International Institute and Center for Russian and East European Studies. I am also grateful to Angie Heo, Webb Keane, Valerie Kivelson, Douglas Rogers, Ilya Vinkovetsky, and two anonymous readers for comments on a draft of this chapter.

1. Marii El, a republic of about 750,000 inhabitants, is located five hundred miles east of Moscow, on the western border of Tatarstan. The Mari, who make up about 44 percent of the population, have been missionized by the Orthodox Church since they became subjects of Muscovy in the sixteenth century, but worship of Mari gods in sacred groves continued in many villages through the Tsarist and Soviet periods. Approximately 6 percent of the population is Tatar, many of them Muslims. Russians and other Eastern Slavs, most of them from traditionally Orthodox families, make up almost half the population. Baptists and Pentecostals have been present in the republic since the 1940s, but current Protestant churches were either started or significantly enlarged in the early 1990s with support from the United States and Finland, a country with which the Mari intelligentsia is forging ties by reference to the Finno-Ugric origin of the Mari language. On the prerevolutionary religious history of the region, see Werth 2002; on religious life in the post-Soviet era, see Luehrmann 2005.

2. In Russian, the usual way to say "pray to someone" involves use of the dative case, *molit'sia komu-to*. Instead, this woman used the directional preposition *na* and the accusative case, *molit'sia na chto-to*. It is unusual to speak about icons in either way, more common phrases being "to pray before the icon" (*molit'sia pered ikonoi*) or "to lay oneself onto the icon" (*prilozhit'sia k ikone*), referring to the act of venerating an icon by touching one's forehead to it and then kissing its lower edge. Although I have not heard anyone else use the same expression as this woman, an important commonality it shares with the latter two phrases is that all describe the devotee's bodily orientation in relation to a material object during the act of praying, rather than making a statement about the addressee of the prayer.

3. "Greek" refers here to the ancient Hellenic, pre-Christian (i.e., "pagan") civilization.

4. Emphasis added.

5. A similar effect of refraction can be achieved by Catholic images. See Mahieu, this volume, for a discussion of the differences and conditions of interchangeability of Eastern-style icons and Western-style statues.

6. Author's field notes, 20 March 2005.

7. Two examples of the abundant literature on the topic, one theoretical and one a practical advice book, are Zankov 1958 and Gorfunkel' 1976.

8. Transcript of audiorecording of the discussion (without exact date, ca. 2003) provided by the Missionary Department, Orthodox Diocese of Marii El.

9. Author's tape of interdenominational Protestant Easter concert in the Puppet Theater, Ioshkar-Ola, 8 May 2005.

10. I heard this expression from several Orthodox Christians in Marii El, who all ascribed it to Archbishop Ioann. The phrase "teaching of the grandmothers" refers to the successive generations of old women who served as authorities on Orthodox practices through the Soviet period. The current church hierarchy publicly praises them for their role in transmitting the Christian faith during the period of socialism but also attributes many cases of nonconformity between church doctrine and folk practices to these women's tendency to appropriate undue authority to themselves.

11. Author's notes on Father Viacheslav Mikhailov, "O vere i sueverii" (paper presented at the VIII annual conference "Christian enlightenment and Russian culture," Ioshkar-Ola, 26 May 2005).

12. Ibid.

13. A comparative analysis of ethnographic examples of images being treated as persons is given in Gell 1998.

## REFERENCES

*Akafist.* 2004. *Akafist Presviatoi Bogoroditse v chest' ikony Ee Kazanskoi.* Moscow: Sretenskii Monastyr'.

Belting, H. 2000. *Bild und Kult: Eine Geschichte des Bildes vor dem Zeitalter der Kunst.* 5th ed. Munich: C. H. Beck.

———. 2001. Bild und Tod: Verkörperung in frühen Kulturen. In *Bild-Anthropologie: Entwürfe für eine Bildwissenschaft*, 143–88. Munich: Wilhelm Fink.

Besançon, A. 1994. *L'image interdite: Une histoire intellectuelle de l'iconoclasme.* Paris: Gallimard.

Engelke, M. 2005. Sticky subjects and sticky objects: The substance of African Christian healing. In *Materiality*, ed. D. Miller, 118–39. Durham, N.C.: Duke University Press.

Gell, A. 1998. *Art and agency: An anthropological theory.* Oxford: Clarendon Press.

Goltz, H. 1979. Antihäretische Konsequenzen: "Monismus" und "Materialismus" in der orthodoxen Tradition. In *Studien zum Menschenbild in Gnosis und Manichäismus,* ed. P. Nagel, 253–74. Halle: Martin-Luther-Universität.

Gorfunkel', P. L. 1976. *Psikhologicheskie osnovy nagliadnosti v lektsionnoi propagande: V pomoshch' lektoru.* Izhevsk: Udmurtiia.

Herzfeld, M. 1990. Icons and identity: Religious orthodoxy and social practice in rural Crete. *Anthropological Quarterly* 63, no. 3: 109–21.

John of Damascus. 1958. On heresies. In *Writings,* trans. F. H. Chase, Jr., 111–63. New York: Fathers of the Church.

———. 2003. *Three treatises on the divine images.* Trans. A. Louth. Crestwood, N.Y.: SVS.

Keane, W. 2003. Semiotics and the social analysis of material things. *Language & Communication* 23, nos. 3–4: 409–25.

———. 2007. *Christian moderns: Freedom and fetish in the mission encounter.* Berkeley: University of California Press.

Kohl, K.-H. 2003. *Die Macht der Dinge: Geschichte und Theorie sakraler Objekte.* Munich: C. H. Beck.

Levin, E. 1993. *Dvoeverie* and popular religion. In *Seeking God: The recovery of religious identity in Orthodox Russia, Ukraine, and Georgia,* ed. S. K. Batalden, 31–52. DeKalb: Northern Illinois University Press.

Luehrmann, S. 2005. Recycling cultural construction: Desecularisation in post-Soviet Mari El. *Religion, State and Society* 33, no. 1: 35–56.

Nekhoroshkov, M. F. 1964. *Vliiat' na soznanie i chuvstva: Iz opyta raboty kluba ateistov Mariiskogo gosudarstvennogo pedagogicheskogo instituta im. N. K. Krupskoi.* Ioshkar-Ola: Mariiskoe knizhnoe izdatel'stvo.

———. 1967. *Sem'ia i religiia.* Ioshkar-Ola: Mariiskoe knizhnoe izdatel'stvo.

Ouspensky, L. 1992. The meaning and content of the icon. In *Theology of the icon,* trans. A. Gythiel and E. Meyendorff, 1: 151–94. Crestwood, N.Y.: SVS.

Paxson, M. 2005. *Solvyovo: The story of memory in a Russian village.* Bloomington: Indiana University Press.

Peirce, C. S. 1955. Logic as semiotic. In *Philosophical writings of Peirce,* ed. J. Bucher, 98–115. New York: Dover.

Rubskii, V. 2003. *Posobie po razgovoru s sektantami.* Kiev: Pochaev.

Shevzov, V. 2004. *Russian Orthodoxy on the eve of revolution.* Oxford: Oxford University Press.

———. 2007. Scripting the gaze: Liturgy, homilies, and the Kazan icon of the Mother of God in late imperial Russia. In *Sacred stories: Religion and spirituality in modern Russia,* ed. M. Steinberg and H. Coleman, 61–92. Bloomington: Indiana University Press.

Stewart, C. 1991. *Demons and the devil: Moral imagination in modern Greek culture.* Princeton: Princeton University Press.

Tsekhanskaia, K. V. 2004. *Ikonopochitanie v russkoi traditsionnoi kul'ture.* Moscow: Institut etnologii i antropologii RAN.

Werth, P. 2002. *At the margins of Orthodoxy: Mission, governance, and confessional politics in Russia's Volga-Kama region, 1827–1905.* Ithaca, N.Y.: Cornell University Press.

Zankov, L. V., ed. 1958. *Sochetanie slova uchitelia i sredstv nagliadnosti v obuchenii: Didakticheskoe issledovanie.* Moscow: Izdatel'stvo Akademii pedagogicheskikh nauk RSFSR.

# 3

# Icons and/or Statues?

## The Greek Catholic Divine Liturgy in Hungary and Romania, between Renewal and Purification

Stéphanie Mahieu

Byzantine icons and Latin statues belong to two different, if not opposite, religious worlds: Orthodoxy and Roman Catholicism. Yet they can be found together in many Greek Catholic churches in contemporary Hungary and Romania.[1] This chapter, based on ethnographical fieldwork conducted in northern Transylvania (1998–2001) and northeastern Hungary (2004–2005), focuses on liturgical, aesthetic, and architectural transformations within the Greek Catholic churches in Romania and Hungary. These churches, like the other Greek Catholic churches of Central Europe, are located on the border between Eastern and Western Christianity and present an original synthesis of Catholic canon and Byzantine ritual, a mixture of Latin and Eastern traditions, and of "official" and "popular" religious elements. While officially always following the Byzantine rite, these churches have been subjected to Latinization through the centuries. A space of negotiation has always existed between the hierarchy and the flock: over the centuries these churches, originally established "from above" by political elites, have constantly been reshaped by the faithful, creating a "syncretism from below" (Hann 2005) that integrates popular Latin devotions such as the cult of the Sacred Heart and the rosary into the Byzantine liturgy.

However, since 1990, with the promulgation of the *Code of Canons of the Eastern Churches* by the Vatican, a liturgical "purification" aimed at eliminating Latin elements has been actively promoted "from above," both by the Vatican through the Congregation for the Oriental Churches and by local Greek Catholic authorities.[2] Its main goal is to "introduce recovery of the Eastern liturgical authenticity, according to the Tradition which each Eastern Church has inherited from the Apostles through the Fathers" (Silvestrini 1997: 7). This "purification" affects all dimensions of religious life: not only the Divine Liturgy of Saint John Chrysostom itself, but also church architecture, interior decoration, and hymns, since unlike Roman Catholicism, Eastern Christianity integrates icon veneration and Orthodox singing within the liturgy (see Engelhardt and Hanganu, this volume). I will focus on debates concerning icons, architecture, and church interiors, which are the most visible aspects of transformation and probably the fields in which both priests and believers have the most autonomy vis-à-vis the church hierarchy. Since icons are a central part of the liturgy, any change in this field has consequences for the Greek Catholic religious experience in its totality.

Ana,[3] a young Greek Catholic who lived in Cluj and studied English literature at the university, summed up the problem as follows:

> My brother is a student at the Greek Catholic seminary in Rome, and every time he comes back home and sees that people have put statues in our churches, and that they are losing the [Byzantine] rite, he's very upset, and he says: "I can't believe that you're losing the rite like that; it is so beautiful!" But how does one explain to younger people that it is a beautiful rite, when what they like are statues, short liturgies, with nice hymns and the organ?

The views expressed here are becoming stronger not only in Romania but also in Hungary, where a move to return to an "authentic" Byzantine tradition started in the 1970s. This attempt at Orientalization is the latest stage of a four-century-long debate that began with the inception of the Greek Catholic churches in Central Europe in the sixteenth century. A pendulum between Latinization or Occidentalization and Byzantinization or Orientalization has long been evident.[4] On the one hand, Occidentalization was a way for many Greek Catholics, often considered "second class Catholics" (Hann 2005: 217), to escape their social backwardness and to fight Eastern Christian popular practices, which were often considered superstitions (Hitchins 1999: 90). The boundary between official and popular religion was more porous in the Eastern Christian world than in the West (Badone 1990; Stewart 1991). Certainly many Greek Catholics have seemed to pay more attention to the "religion as practiced" than to the "religion as prescribed" (Christian 1981: 178). On the other hand, the Orientalizing trend stressed the need to keep the specificity of Eastern Christianity and restore the "purity" of the Byzantine rite, which was considered deeper and more intense that the Latin rite.

C. Stewart and R. Shaw (1994; and Stewart 1999) have set out a relational and dynamic framework within which to examine syncretism and antisyncretism. They emphasize that religious mixture is an ongoing process, negotiated at the local level, where it can be studied ethnographically (Stewart and Shaw 1994: 7). Syncretism has close ties to concepts such as hybridity, bricolage, and creolization (Benhabib 2002; Stewart 2007; Werbner 2001; Zehner 2005). The Greek Catholic churches represent an interpenetration of Latin and Byzantine Christianity, but the rise of nationalism in the secular domain has fostered the "politics of anti-syncretism"—that is, the assertion and protection of religious boundaries (Stewart and Shaw 1994). Antisyncretism is very often associated with the notions of "authenticity" and "purity." Yet Stewart and Shaw insist that the former does not necessarily depend on the latter: "Both putatively pure and putatively syncretic traditions can be 'authentic' if people claim that these traditions are unique, and uniquely their (historical) possession" (1994: 7). Claims to authenticity depend therefore on uniqueness rather than purity, and syncretic blends can plausibly be seen as unique, because "historically unrepeatable" (Stewart and Shaw 1994: 7). Hence the debate on liturgical changes focuses on the Greek Catholic rite as it has actually developed in both Romania and Hungary, rather than on purity.

The quest for authenticity is very often supported with spurious traditions designed to fake continuity where it does not exist (Hobsbawn and Ranger 1983). The Greek Catholic Church in Romania presents an interesting case in this respect. As a result of forty years of prohibition (1948–1989), the "chain of belief'"(Hervieu-Léger 2000) was institutionally interrupted. After 1989 everything had to be renegotiated. But the Greek Catholics, and indeed Eastern Christianity in general, pose a deeper challenge to anthropological theory. Joel Robbins (2007) has argued that social anthropology has developed with a strong bias toward the study of continuity. This explains why, in his view, the anthropology of Christianity has been slow to develop. The discipline has not been able to incorporate the ruptures and radical changes that characterize Christianity. However, while it is easy to see how this applies to the Protestants studied by Robbins, other Christian traditions have placed a greater emphasis on continuity. The very term Orthodoxy indicates that the true teachings of the divine revelation have been faithfully transmitted: the Orthodox Church "remains the Church of continuity and tradition" (Meyendorff 1996: ix). Reform or innovation can be contemplated only on the margins of religious life (Pott 2000). Icons, considered the heart of Byzantine theology (Belting 1994; Kokosalakis 1995), deny any idea of invention. A Byzantine icon is always based on an earlier icon, thereby establishing an uninterrupted chain with the prototype (see Luehrmann, this volume). For B. Uspensky (1976), icons are like the translation of an original text. They establish a direct relation between the worshipper and the supernatural entity (be it Jesus, the Holy Virgin, or a saint). They are "both containers and refraction of the divine essence" (Herzfeld 1990: 111). Because they establish a chain of continuity, individual creativity on the part of the icon painter is precluded (Kenna 1985: 348). How, then, can icons and a Latin representation of the Sacred Heart be combined in the same church, sometimes on the same iconostasis? Icons are a metonymy of the saint they represent, and constitute a totally different way of worshipping than that fostered by Western art.

Anthropological literature on icons has focused on their production, and the uses made of religious images by worshippers (Hanganu 1997 and this volume; Herzfeld 1990; Kenna 1985; Kokosalakis 1995; Luehrmann, this volume; Manolescu 1999). These studies all refer to strong Orthodox traditions in Greece, Romania, and Russia, where the Byzantine icon, with its regional variations, is at the center of both church and domestic religious life. But the Greek Catholics are a very different case: for many of my informants, Western images, too, can create a deep encounter with God. As members of an Eastern church, the Greek Catholics illustrate the continuity of Christianity and present themselves as bearers of an uninterrupted tradition dating to early Christianity (Pelikan 1989; Pott 2000). Yet because their faith was banned for more than four decades under communism, they show how transmission of the Christian message can be interrupted, at least formally. V. Pospishil (1989), in a discussion of the debate over liturgical reform within the Greek Catholic churches, shows what is at stake. The rite represents a system of symbols and pictures that become mediators and embody the presence of the holy in specific forms. When those forms are said to be reformed, as in the Byzantinization process, the risk is that the symbols (i.e., the existing "syncretic" Greek Catholic rite) will lose their meanings. The flock will then be unable to make contact with the symbols, since "the Eastern rites . . . require more explanatory information" (Pospishil 1989: 203). Many of my informants commented on the problematic nature of the quest for a purified Eastern liturgy: "If one went to the Byzantine liturgy without proper training, one might not receive the message, because it is too demanding." The opposite risk was Latinization and the disappearance of Greek Catholicism itself. The younger generations were not satisfied with syncretic forms associated with popular religion, which nowadays have less to do with "little Christian" practices labeled "superstitions" in the eighteenth century than with practices hugely popular among elderly women, such as the rosary or the cult of the Sacred Heart. (Pospishil 1989: 203).

In this chapter I shall argue that the Greek Catholic Church needs to offer an "authentic" Eastern, intense, mystical option to believers who will otherwise opt to join the Roman Catholic Church or not go to any church at all. But there is a tension here, expressed in the quotation above. For Ana's brother, current practices have to change because the rosary and statues are seen as tepid, bastardized forms of religiosity, good only for elderly people. But for Ana herself, as I discovered in further conversations, what mattered was that people liked the rite the way it was; in her view too radical an attempt to change it would drive people out of the church. Bruno Latour (1990, 2001) has theorized this tension by suggesting that all Christian churches have been confronted since early times with a double and contradictory obligation: on the one hand, fidelity to the Christian message and, on the other, renewal in the transmission of this message. Latour shows that, in the Christian world, the "messengers" cannot be distinguished from the message they re-present. Two traps endanger religious transmission: tedious repetition (in the case of excessive fidelity), and heresy (in the case of excessive renewal). For Latour, what is peculiar about the Christian message is that "it cannot appear as a new idea," precisely because one cannot distinguish between the message and the messenger; yet "it is mendacious if one does not have the impression one is hearing it for the first time" (Latour 2001: 229). I will present ethnographical illustrations of this tension, drawing on the discussions I witnessed about religious art and architecture within Greek Catholic communities in Hungary and Romania. Basic modalities of the encounter with God are at stake. When discussing the need to eradicate Latin elements or, on the contrary, to keep them, the faithful I met are not discussing mere aesthetic details but how best to encounter God. Should the encounter be more accessible but less intense (the Latin version), or deeper but more demanding (the Eastern version)? If changes are too radical, some people might turn away from the church and migrate to Roman Catholicism, while if no changes are made some might turn to the Orthodox Church, which offers a "real," intense religious experience. These dilemmas assume a different shape in the two countries, partly because of the contrasting paths of the two Greek Catholic churches during the socialist period. Thus I turn first to an outline of this context.

## THE GREEK CATHOLICS IN ROMANIA AND HUNGARY

The Romanian Greek Catholic Church (hereafter RGCC), established in 1697 in Transylvania (Union of Alba Iulia) in the context of the Counter-Reformation, after the Hapsburg conquest, numbered 1,559,857 believers (10 percent of Romania's population) in 1948.[5] On 21 October 1948, a forced ecclesiastical "reunification" synod of the Greek Catholic Church with the Orthodox Church took place. The majority of the Greek Catholic priests and all the bishops refused to comply with this "union," and many were sentenced to prison. In December 1948, Decree no. 358 disbanded the Greek Catholic Church and transferred its properties to the Romanian state. The Council of the National Rescue Front abrogated this decree in December 1989. At this point the RGCC was in a very precarious situation: it had been banned for more than forty years, had almost no surviving hierarchy, and its churches and other goods had been nationalized by the socialist regime and were generally in the hands of the Orthodox Church (Iordachi 1999; Mahieu 2004). The number of believers was less than 15 percent of the 1948 level: 223,327 according to the 1992 census. By 2002 the number was even smaller: 195,481, less than 1 percent of the total population. The RGCC has the status of a metropolitan church and has five dioceses.

In Hungary the situation is very different. The Hungarian Greek Catholic Church (hereafter HGCC) was the only Greek Catholic Church of the region to

escape political repression during the socialist period. It is a product of the tumul-
tuous history of the Carpathian basin and, more specifically, of the Magyarization
of populations of Rusyn and Romanian origin (Mayer 1997; Molnár 1997). The
establishment of a Rusyn Greek Catholic Church in Subcarpathia dates to the
Union of Uzhhorod (1646). In 1912, Pope Pius X created the Eparchy of
Hajdúdorog for 162 Hungarian-speaking Greek Catholic parishes. In 1924 an
Apostolic Exarchate was established at Miskolc for 21 Rusyn parishes that remained
in Hungarian territory after the creation of Czechoslovakia. At the time these
parishes used Slavonic in the liturgy, but by the 1940s they had all switched to
Hungarian. The Apostolic Exarchate of Miskolc is administered today by the
bishop of Hajdúdorog, whose jurisdiction was extended in 1980 to all Greek
Catholics in Hungary. The church was not abolished in the socialist era. Like other
Greek Catholic churches, the HGCC is a *sui iuris* (self-governing) church.
However, unlike its sister churches in Romania, Ukraine, and Poland, it does
not have the status of a metropolitan church, and it lacks a body of canon law.
In consequence, the HGCC remains officially under the authority of the
Roman Catholic Archbishop of Esztergom. According to the 2001 census,
there are 287,000 Greek Catholic believers in Hungary (2.8 percent of the
total population).

Unlike Romania, where the number of believers has declined since 1989 and
where property conflicts with the Orthodox Church have remained endemic,
the HGCC seemed to me to exude wealth, dynamism, and self-confidence.
It boasted a brand new seminary, three theological journals, many vocations,
and full churches. The miraculous weeping icon in Máriapócs has cemented its
position as the main pilgrimage center for Greek Catholics of the entire
Carpathian region. However, I found that debates over the nature and forms of
the liturgy were more lively in Romania than in Hungary. Priests who had shared
clandestine religious life with their parishioners under socialism continued in
the new conditions to conduct an open dialogue with them, whereas in Hungary
the clergy tended to adopt a more normative position and to refrain from
such dialogue.

Both churches are affiliated with the Congregation for the Oriental Churches
in the Vatican. Unlike Orthodox churches, with whom they share a rite, they are
obliged to conform to the centralized norms of the Vatican, especially in liturgical
matters. The Vatican renewed its attempt to return to the "authentic" tradition as
the Greek Catholic churches were all finally freed from socialist repression.
Many priests and students went to Rome in the 1990s, and the re-Orientalization
of the liturgy was high on the agenda at meetings between members of the
Congregation for the Oriental Churches and the Greek Catholic hierarchies.
However, some Greek Catholic priests complain about the idea of standardizing
the Eastern tradition:

For me, it is a complete mistake to think in a Western way about Eastern things. For them [in the Vatican] being Oriental means having a certain tradition, and then they say: "You should come back to the true Eastern tradition," but it is constrained! It is a Latin way of thinking that aims to make things uniform according to a certain canon, which I don't know anything about! And the Second Vatican Council says two contradictory things: "You should renew ancient traditions, and innovate if the community needs it." It is hard to combine the two! (Father József, interview by author)

Father József summarizes the ambiguity of the antisyncretic trend encouraged by the Vatican: as Stewart and Shaw (1994) and Zehner (2005) suggest, the move conceals invented and hybrid features of its aim. Let us examine the antisyncretic and syncretic trends in more detail, to understand how they interact.

## TO (RE-)ORIENTALIZE OR TO COMBINE

In 1964, the Second Vatican Council decree entitled *Orientalium Ecclesiarum* explicitly encouraged the Greek Catholic churches to preserve and/or rediscover their "ancestral traditions."[6] The HGCC was the only church in a position to implement this advice, since the other Greek Catholic churches of Central Europe had been repressed. But the HGCC was also very Latinized, especially in its architecture and iconography. The baroque style has had an especially great influence in the Carpathian basin (Puskás 1991). In Romania, the liturgy has been less influenced by Latin elements, although many of today's Greek Catholics attended the Roman Catholic Church during the socialist period. After the fall of socialism the promulgation in 1993 of the *Code of Canons of the Eastern Churches* again invited the Greek Catholic churches to "rediscover authentic traditions" by "eliminating that which has altered them" (Silvestrini 1997: 12). In the field of sacred art, the external form of sacred buildings, and the arrangement of the interior space they were to implement an "organic recuperation of the proper usages" in order to "avoid hybridisms" (Silvestrini 1997: 57). The HGCC did not implement these instructions immediately, but many young priests, like Ana's brother, who favor a "purified" Byzantine liturgy, have now returned from Rome, and this trend is gaining momentum.

There is a tension in both countries between the advocates of a return to the "true" traditions of the East and those who want to defend the status quo (i.e., a combination of Eastern and Latin elements). Recent political and religious transformations in postsocialist Hungary and Romania have intensified this tension, which illustrates the double and contradictory obligation of all Christian churches in the sense argued by Latour (1990, 2001): on the one hand, fidelity to the Christian message and, on the other, renewal in the transmission of this message. My informants agreed that both sides should find a compromise, since otherwise believers would join a "quieter church." It was pointed out that in both countries religious mobility had increased. Those who advocated re-Orientalization were mainly well-educated, and they included many members of the Greek Catholic elite. Many (paradoxically enough) acquired their strong Eastern sensibility during studies in Rome. However, the tension between the two sides cannot be reduced to a mechanical opposition between the elite and the people, between modernity and tradition, between official and popular religion. A fraction of the elite defends the status quo, either because they want to differentiate their church from a dominant Orthodox Church (the Romanian case), or to avoid unnecessary tensions and to maintain a certain autonomy from the Vatican (the Hungarian case). Moreover, if we consider the classical opposition between tradition and modernity, it is striking that the advocates of a return to—sometimes invented— tradition are, sociologically speaking, the most "modern"—that is, city dwellers, who typically travel abroad frequently. They argue that the only way to stem the massive drop in church attendance, especially among young people, is to follow the current trends in European religion, notably the promotion of sporadic but highly emotional religious experiences (based in this case on Eastern spirituality) rather than regular weekly services (based on the syncretic current Greek Catholic rite) (see Hervieu-Léger 2000; Davie 2000). Rather than oppose bounded and immutable entities (Western Christianity versus Eastern Christianity), there is a need to focus on the "dialectical character of their interrelationship" (Badone 1990: 6), and to recognize that the distribution of ideas among social groups is complex and dynamic. The example of Ana and her brother is striking in this respect: they come from the same educated family but hold very different views about the best way to sustain the dynamism of the RGCC. For Ana it is vital to take into consideration the tastes of the mass of the faithful, while for her brother it is a pity if the "beauty" of the rite is allowed to atrophy, because this can lead only to a tepid religious life.

The major arguments put forward to promote a return to the "true" rite are that the Divine Liturgy of Saint John Chrysostom is a sacred part of Greek Catholic tradition, that it is deeper and more intense than the Latin tradition, and that such a return would maintain the continuity of Eastern spirituality. In Romania, the liturgical model is clear, since it is provided by the dominant Romanian Orthodox Church. In Hungary, however, there is no "national" Orthodox Church.[7] In the quest for a "purified" liturgy, the model is neither that of Subcarpathian Rus nor that of Romania, but that of Greece. This is evident in iconography, in the design of new churches, and also in historical narratives asserting the presence of a significant Byzantine church in Hungary in the Middle Ages (Cselényi 1994). This reference to Greece is not new: when Pope Pius X created the Eparchy of Hajdúdorog in 1912, the use of Hungarian was to be limited to nonliturgical functions. According to papal decree, the liturgy was to be celebrated in Greek, and the clergy were given three years to learn it. World War I intervened, and the requirement to use Greek was never enforced. Eventually, in 1965, Hungarian was formally recognized as a liturgical language (Ivancsó 1995). The attempt to locate an authentic tradition in Greece is paradoxically a way to make it more Hungarian. The small size of the local Orthodox Church seems to make "going East" easier in Hungary than in neighboring countries. The preference for Eastern traditions was indeed marked among those I spoke to in Hungary compared with Romania. The trend represented by the Hungarian "Orientalizers" resembles the Greek neo-Orthodox movements in its antisyncretic quest (Herzfeld 2002; Kokosalakis 1995; Makrides and Uffelmann 2003). However, unlike their counterparts in Greece and Russia, the Hungarians are profoundly pro-European and do not profess nationalist claims.

The arguments put forward by the defenders of the status quo are very different in the two countries. In Hungary, where the Greek Catholic Church was not prohibited under socialism, religious transmission was not interrupted. When I asked believers what they thought about liturgical changes, they usually answered that they saw no reason to do anything differently from what their ancestors had done. Among the youngest cohorts, except for the most devout, my informants were not really aware of the existence of an Eastern trend. In Romania, however, where everything, including the definition of the rite, had to be reconstructed following forty years of prohibition, the arguments given were much more explicit. This was probably because the majority of the Greek Catholic believers I met had been attending either a Roman Catholic church or an Orthodox church during the socialist period, and therefore had some knowledge of what constituted a "pure" Latin or Orthodox rite. They made frequent comparisons between rites and sometimes argued with their priests about the appropriate form of the Greek Catholic liturgy. Some wanted their favorite Roman Catholic prayers to be included.

Simona, for example, was a Greek Catholic in Cluj who had visited the Catholic shrine of Medjugorje in Bosnia-Herzegovina, where she attended the Adoration of the Divine Mother. She had later tried to convince her parish priest to incorporate it into the liturgy and commented on his refusal: "Maybe the hierarchy up there thinks it is too Latin." She added that the sobriety of the Bosnian church had pleased her:

> I remember Medjugorje: the church was very simple; there were only three statues, Saint Peter and Saint Anthony facing Mary the Mother of God; there were no icons. The Byzantine rite is over-ornate [*prea încărcat*], heavier; when you are used to it, you like it, but once you have been in Medjugorje, you feel that it is too heavy, too many things.

Alina is another Greek Catholic in Cluj, who, like Simona, is an university graduate. She attended both Roman Catholic and Orthodox churches before 1989, which gave her several ways of "meeting" God. She found the Orthodox liturgy, with the higher emotions generated by icons and hymns, more intense but less accessible. For her, Latin churches, with their statues and their shorter masses, were less beautiful but more appropriate for normal celebrations like a Sunday mass. Urban parishioners in Cluj were continuously debating these matters. Many preferred, like Simona, to have a plurality of options, and in addition to the Greek Catholic church they have continued to frequent a Roman Catholic and/or an Orthodox church (Mahieu 2006).

## CHURCH ARCHITECTURE AND INTERIORS

Architectural preferences reveal a lot about the options favored by a religious community. Can Eastern icons and Latin representations of the Sacred Heart be combined in the same church? According to Eastern theology, the answer is no. Indeed, the positions taken by Eastern and Western Christianity toward religious images are so different that "the way the Byzantine Church imagined the production of religious images is one of the principal reasons for the schism between Latin Christianity and the Christian East" (Barbu 1998: 50; see also Zeitler 1994). For Michel Evidokimov, "Art in the West, above all with the Gothic, is representation, when in the East it is presence" (2000: 102). The differences between East and West became even more apparent after the thirteenth century with the adoption of a linear perspective in the Latin tradition, whereas in the East inverse perspective continued to be used. Western artists were increasingly able to invent, to innovate, to *represent* (to be faithful to the original) instead of *re-presenting* (to make present again) (Latour 1990, 2001). The icon painter, however, was always more constrained by a chain of continuity. As a result the relationship between the worshipper and the icon is more personal and intense than in the Western tradition.

Attitudes toward statues also differ. In the East, statues were suspected of being idols, and icons were favored; in the West, sculptures were seen as a counter to the ancient idols of the barbarian civilizations (Belting 1994). However, statues of Catholic saints like Saint Anthony or Saint Therese, and representations of the Sacred Heart, were allowed into Greek Catholic churches over the centuries, and they are still popular.

My Greek Catholic informants often challenged the familiar dichotomy between Western and Eastern religious representations. For some of them, including some priests, the Latin image of the Sacred Heart did not contradict their rite. For others, on the contrary, all Latin elements should be removed from churches. The same dilemma arises in old churches as in the numerous new churches that have been constructed since 1990 (fig. 3.1).

FIGURE 3.1. Altar, Greek Catholic church, Bixad, Romania, 2007. Photograph by Stéphanie Mahieu.

FIGURE 3.2. Narthex, Şes Greek Catholic church, Ieud, Romania, 2000.
Photograph by Stéphanie Mahieu.

Ieud is a large, wealthy village in the Iza Valley of the Maramureş region, in northwestern Romania. The Greek Catholic Church was dominant here before 1948. Ieud's wooden Şes church was built in typical Maramureş style in 1700,[8] though the local Orthodox priest claims that it was actually built in 1697, before the union of the Greek Catholic Church with Rome. After 1948 it became Orthodox, and it was the main church of the village until a new one was built in 1984. Having tried in vain to regain possession peacefully, a group of Greek Catholics broke a padlock on the Şes church in December 1990 and occupied the building. When I first visited the church in 2000 I was overwhelmed by the interior: the narthex walls were covered with Latin reproductions of the Sacred Heart, Jesus Christ, and the Holy Virgin; and a statue of the Holy Virgin occupied one corner (fig. 3.2). In the *naos,* or inner part of the church, Latin images of Jesus Christ and the Virgin Mary had been placed above the old wooden iconostasis. The unmistakable impression was that the believers who had taken back their church (themselves Orthodox believers between 1948 and 1989) now wanted to emphasize its Catholic character. Ieud is an interesting example because the Şes church was one of the first to be taken back by Greek Catholics after the RGCC became free to operate again (Mahieu 2004).[9] The redecoration of the interior was organized without any intervention of the hierarchy. A priest was only appointed a few years later. He made it clear to me that in several domains (notably funerals) his parishioners would not let him take any initiative. The church's use by the

FIGURE 3.3. Statues for sale at a fair during the Assumption pilgrimage, Máriapócs, Hungary, 2005. Photograph by Stéphanie Mahieu.

Orthodox until 1984 probably intensified the parishioners' will to "Latinize" the interior.

All together, only 80 (out of 1,800 claimed) churches were given back to the RGCC. In the majority of those I visited, reproductions of the Sacred Heart and other Latin images were not to be found. However, people did buy them at fairs organized around the big pilgrimages, particularly at the feast of the Assumption (15 August), and displayed them in their homes (fig 3.3).

The most important Greek Catholic pilgrimage site in Romania is Bixad, in the Oaş region. When I was there for the feast of the Assumption (Praznic Adormirii Maicii Domnului [Sfînta Maria Mare]) in 1998 and 2007, two pilgrimages, one Orthodox and one Greek Catholic, were organized at the same time. Vendors were selling all kinds of religious souvenirs on the main street, including reproductions of Byzantine icons, Orthodox religious literature, and also statues and reproductions of the Sacred Heart.

In Hungary, the equivalent shrine is that of Máriapócs, with its weeping icon (the Könnyező Szűzanya). The feast of the Assumption (Nagybúcsú) draws crowds from all over Hungary, and also from Slovakia, Romania, and Ukraine. The weeping icon was painted in 1675 in a popular Carpathian baroque style (Puskás 1991). It is said to have wept for the first time in 1696. It was then transferred by the emperor's troops to St. Stephen's Basilica in Vienna, where it never wept again. A second icon was painted, which shed tears twice, in 1715 and 1905. What remains of it has been put in a golden frame and is displayed inside the Máriapócs Basilica, which also has an enormous baroque iconostasis. In 2004 and 2005 I found a wide range of Latin images, mostly representing the Sacred Heart, the Last Supper, and the Holy Virgin, on sale for the pilgrims, together with reproductions of the weeping icon and Greek Orthodox color-print icons. Inside the walls of the basilica only Eastern icons were on sale, but in the fair organized outside the walls the quest for a "purified" iconography was abandoned in the interests of popular religiosity.

In Cluj, the intellectual capital of Transylvania, the parish of Sfânta Fecioara Maria was created in 1994 in the Grigorescu district. A new church was built and consecrated in 2001. The architectural style, both external and internal, is very different from that of the church at Ieud. The white walls of the Cluj church display a representation of the Via Crucis (Calea Crucii). There is no iconostasis but an altar with a crucifix, and two statues. Outside the church, there is a replica of the Lourdes Grotto. The two priests in charge of the parish are father and son. The father was educated clandestinely during the 1980s. His son was educated after 1989 and studied in Germany. Even though the son seems to be more keen on a "return to the East" than his father, he emphasizes that icons and statues have the same function:

> In Eastern churches, you tend to find icons, and in Latin churches statues. But we want to combine both: statues and icons, because they have the same goal: they both represent the saints.

It is hard to say how prevalent statues were in Romanian Greek Catholic churches before 1948, but many informants told me that after 1989 they received "secondhand" statues from Roman Catholic parishes in Western countries. One woman complained about this:

> Our brothers from the West, they believe they help us by sending us old statues they don't use anymore, but we are starting an action to get rid of them, because this is not our rite. Still, we have to be flexible, because is not the object in itself that people worship, but God, and therefore, it is the same thing, an icon or a statue.

This quotation illustrates how difficult it is for the RGCC to define its liturgical norm. In the early 1990s the lack of buildings and interior artifacts was so acute that the small communities who wanted to relaunch Greek Catholicism had no alternative but to improvise: masses were said in private houses or in the open air, and any help, such as gifts of religious books and statues, was welcome.

By contrast, in Hungary, where the Roman Catholic Church is dominant, the popularity of Latin images is probably much older, but the advocates of a return to Eastern tradition are determined to get rid of them all, and to replace them with Byzantine icons. Nyírszőlős is a dormitory town of Nyíregyháza, situated twenty kilometers from the city center. When the priest, a young lecturer who taught at Nyíregyháza theological seminary, was appointed to this Greek Catholic parish, he thought that the small, rustic church needed some rearrangement. He had previously participated in the painting of a neo-Byzantine fresco in a new church, and he had two icon painters and an art historian in his immediate family. He decided to install a small wooden iconostasis in front of the altar, and to remove several old paintings and statues, explaining to me that many iconostases had been removed from Greek Catholic churches when Hapsburg Hungary was dismembered in 1920. At that time, Greek Catholicism was considered backward; Greek Catholics, who were mostly peasants of Rusyn and Romanian origin, wanted to show their fidelity to the Catholic Church and to the Magyar state (Pusztai 2005). This situation has changed. Greek Catholics are no longer challenged in their Hungarianness, and the region around Nyíregyháza has experienced significant economic growth. In this context, changing the church interior also expressed a change of social status. This small-scale restoration illustrated an erasure of the religious past comparable to that which occurred in Ieud, but in this case the traces eliminated (statues, thrones, etc.) were Roman Catholic.

A region that has not been prosperous offers another example. Ózd is a town of 45,000 situated in a crisis zone of northeastern Hungary, close to the Slovakian border. It has a Greek Catholic parish, which erected a neo-Byzantine church in 1996. The exterior resembles a traditional Byzantine church, with a six-sided cupola, but the decoration is modern. Even though the need for new churches is not as urgent as in Romania, several new churches have been built in Hungary since the 1980s. The neo-Byzantine style was initiated by architect Ferenc Török, and others have followed him. Their designs make explicit reference to Greece, even though, as Father József explained, it was vain to attempt to imitate the Greek style literally:

It is a synthesis between the old and the new, with elements of tradition, like the cupola, the center that reflects the Byzantine liturgy. And then, without copying baroque churches, it is something modern, something new, but at the same time Byzantine. And the bishop, through his friendship with Török, is following this direction, doing something with a Byzantine flavor, but without making a servile copy of the past.

A similar spirit prevails in icon painting. Hungary has many valuable baroque iconostases, mostly from the eighteenth century, but in new churches, like that in Ózd, a neo-Byzantine style was favored. The walls were covered with a fresco. The artist who painted it was Orthodox and came from Romania. Romanian icon painters were popular not only because their fees were lower, but also because the tradition of icon painting was said to be stronger in Romania than in Hungary. Among Hungarian Greek Catholic icon painters, László Puskás and Zsolt Makláry, his son-in-law, are the most famous. For the latter, what defined an icon was not so much whether or not it looked like an icon, but what it expressed:

> For instance, if we consider the icons on the iconostasis in the Greek Catholic church of Rozsáktere in Budapest, despite the fact that the general style of the image has become Latin, certain elements were kept. For instance, Jesus Christ is facing us, as in the East, and he blesses with his right hand, as on the icons; his left hand is holding a book, there are Greek letters, those elements have remained, and these are more important that the color of the clothes. Anyway, these images painted during the twentieth century are still icons. For me, the fact that these images can be venerated like icons shows that one can paint icons in different ways. What I always do when I start painting an icon is to look at the elements that confirm the inner logic of the icon. Today, as an icon painter, I have to make decisions, and it is not easy to make such decisions. I have to take into account many aspects, like the proportions of the bodies, and to ask whether I want to stress spirituality or not. What do I want to stress with the colors? But the most important is to follow our own tradition, with our personal inspiration. Anyway, in Hungary, the situation is much freer than in Greece.

This icon painter addressed the question that was central for all my informants, be they priests or peasants. Most agreed that the defining features of an icon were the intention of the painter, and the uses to which the icon was put by the worshipper. This might be considered a heresy in countries like Greece, where the Byzantine tradition is more standardized than in the Carpathian basin. In Hungary, a crossroads for different artistic and religious influences, it makes sense. Zsolt Makláry represents a neo-Byzantine style (see fig. 3.4, a fresco painted by him in Rakaca), and he is a self-conscious Orientalizer, closer to the antisyncretic trend encouraged by the Vatican. At the same time he illustrates the tensions to which I have drawn attention throughout this chapter. Even though the purification process that aims at eliminating Latin elements from the Greek Catholic liturgies is receiving increasing official support in both countries, the "authentic" tradition that has to be "restored" can in practice only be based on the synthesis of two religious trends, Eastern and Western. As Stewart and Shaw (1994) showed, authenticity does not necessarily equate with purity. However, there remains a significant difference between the two countries as a result of the strength of the Orthodox Church in Romania. Even though at first sight the Orientalizers are much more radical in Hungary than they are in Romania, they are at the same time more open to a syncretic (Latinized) Greek Catholic rite, in the name of Hungarianness.

FIGURE 3.4. Fresco by Zsolt Makláry, Greek Catholic Center Paraklisz, Rakaca, Hungary, 2004. Photograph by Stéphanie Mahieu.

## CONCLUSION

Liturgical changes in the Romanian and Hungarian Greek Catholic churches are still proceeding, shaped both by local factors and by more global developments, such as Catholic-Orthodox dialogue. In the postsocialist years it has been possible to witness vivid discussions among Christians about issues as fundamental as the mystery of the icon, the connection between the form of the prayer and its content, and the conditions and intensity of encounters with God. These debates are framed by the peculiar situation of the Greek Catholic churches, which link the Latin and the Byzantine religious worlds.

After forty years of repression, everything in Romania had to be reorganized, including the definition of the rite. Many of my Greek Catholic informants in Romania had attended two or even three churches during their lives: Roman Catholic, Greek Catholic, and Orthodox. They were in a position to compare the different rites. The Orthodox rite was usually presented as more intense and more mystical, but overloaded and more demanding. By contrast, the Latin rite was presented as more accessible and well suited to standard occasions, but more sober. Many expressed a wish to combine the best of both rites (intensity and accessibility) in the Greek Catholic Church. While older priests trained during the socialist period were generally closer to their faithful, with whom they had practiced the Greek Catholic rite clandestinely, a new generation of young priests trained in Rome is returning home and tends to favor a return to the Byzantine tradition. However, this is not an easy task in Romania, as the Ieud example shows. Many faithful and priests still want to differentiate themselves from the Orthodox Church to which they belonged before 1989 by decorating their church with Latin images and statues, or even, as in Cluj, by building an entirely new church in the Latin style.

In Hungary, religious transmission was never interrupted, and the general situation of the Greek Catholic Church has remained much more favorable. In the absence of a strong Hungarian Orthodox Church, those wishing to implement the Vatican's instructions to "rediscover authentic traditions" have looked instead to Greece as their point of reference: hence the choice of a neo-Byzantine style in church architecture, as in Ózd, or in icon and fresco painting, as in Rakaca. These examples can be considered "invented traditions." The lack of a local Orthodox tradition, however, is also a source of strength, since it enables the HGCC to offer worshippers an intense and mystical religious experience, without having to differentiate itself from a dominant Orthodox Church. Latin influence is nonetheless still very tangible, especially during popular events such as the pilgrimage at Máriapócs. Both Hungary and Romania show the importance of recent historical developments in the study of Eastern churches. As Robbins (2007) argues, social anthropology has developed with a strong bias toward the study of continuity. Even though the Eastern tradition has put a greater emphasis on continuity than the Protestants studied by Robbins, the case of the Greek Catholics shows the necessity to focus on discontinuities as well.

In both countries there is tension between the advocates of a return to Byzantine traditions (though no one wishes to impose this by force) and those who think that such "purification" is not needed, because an icon, a Latin image, and a statue offer more chances to encounter God than an icon alone. This tension is not a mechanical opposition between the politics of syncretism and antisyncretism, between the elite and the people, or between modernity and tradition. The classical opposition between tradition and invention is blurred, and the advocates of a purified liturgy are not necessarily moral conservatives. This tension illustrates the double and contradictory obligation of all Christian churches theorized by Latour (1990, 2001): on the one hand, fidelity to the Christian message and, on the other, renewal in the transmission of this message. Religious transmission is threatened by both tedious repetition (in the case of excessive fidelity) and heresy (in the case of excessive renewal). The Greek Catholic churches, too, are confronted with such a tension. It seems, however, that the Eastern trend has become stronger in both countries. Discussion has been more vivid in Romania than in Hungary, but the general debate is one that affects Eastern Catholic churches all over the world as they seek to maintain their vitality and distinctiveness within the universal Catholic Church.

## NOTES

I am grateful to Boris Najman for his help throughout this work. I would like to thank the Free University Brussels and the Van Buuren Foundation, Brussels, for their financial support of my doctoral dissertation, defended at the EHESS Paris in 2003. My main field sites were the villages of Bixad and Ieud and the city of Cluj. I am grateful to Alban Bensa, my PhD supervisor at the EHESS; to Elisabeth Claverie, Rose-Marie Lagrave, Paul Robert Magosci, and Albert Piette, members of my PhD jury; and to Vintilă Mihailescu. I would like to thank Gabriela Coman, Iulia Haşdeu, Adina Ionescu-Muscel, and Adriana Oprescu for their help during my field trips, and all the Greek Catholic priests and believers who helped me in the course of this project. Work in Hungary was funded by the Max Planck Institute for Social Anthropology. My main field site was located around the city of Nyíregyháza. I would like to thank Kristóf Buza, Péter Csigó, Anita Halász, Zsolt Horváth, Bertalan Pusztai, and Irén Szabó. I am also grateful to two anonymous readers for comments on a draft of this chapter.

1. Greek Catholic churches are also called Eastern Rite Catholic churches or Uniate churches, although many Greek Catholics consider the latter a derogatory term. The official name of the Romanian church is Biserica Română Unită cu Roma, Greco-Catolică; that of the Hungarian church is Magyar Görög Katolikus Egyház.

2. This policy was initiated a century earlier, when the Latinization process was still very strong; nevertheless, attempts were made to bring it to a halt and to promote the specificity of "Eastern roots." In 1894, Pope Leo XIII's encyclical, *Orientalium Dignitas,* threatened any missionary who persuaded Eastern rite followers to transfer to the Latin rite deposition. See Pospishil 1989.

3. Except for public personalities, the names of my informants have been changed.

4. The terms Latinization and Byzantinization refer to changes in ritual, while Occidentalization and Orientalization refer more generally to the exposure to Western or Eastern influence (see Hann 2005: 217).

5. Rance 1994: 22.

6. Decree *Orientalium Ecclesiarum* 1964: §6.

7. According to the 2001 census, there are approximately 15,000 Orthodox believers in Hungary, split up into Rumanian Orthodox (5,598), Russian Orthodox (3,502), Greek Orthodox (2,473), Serbian Orthodox (1,914), Bulgarian Orthodox (508), and other Orthodox (1,303). See http://www .nepszamlalas.hu/eng/volumes/26/tables/load1_1.html.

Both the Greek Orthodox Church and the Russian Orthodox Church claimed ownership of the Dormition Cathedral in Budapest. In the legal case that developed, the plaintiff was the Hungarian exarchate of the Patriarchate of Constantinople, and the defendant was the Hungarian diocese of the Moscow Patriarchate. The latter's right to the cathedral was recognized by the Hungarian supreme court in 2005.

It seems that there have been several cases of conversion from Greek Catholicism to one of the Orthodox churches, mostly in Budapest, by young, educated, urban people, but the figures remain insignificant.

8. Şes is the regional form of the Romanian word *jos,* which means "down."

9. In the other places in which I conducted fieldwork the return to the Greek Catholic Church was much slower; the numbers, too, were generally smaller than in Ieud, where in 2001 a third of the village was Greek Catholic.

## REFERENCES

Badone, E. 1990. *Religious orthodoxy and popular faith in European society.* Princeton: Princeton University Press.

Barbu, D. 1998. *Byzance, Rome et les roumains : Essai sur la production politique de la foi au Moyen-Âge.* Bucharest: Babel.

Belting, H. 1994. *Likeness and presence: A history of the image before the era of art.* Chicago: University of Chicago Press.

Benhabib, S. 2002. *The claims of culture.* Princeton: Princeton University Press.

Christian, W. 1981. *Local religion in sixteenth-century Spain.* Princeton: Princeton University Press.

Cselényi, I. 1994. Bizánci nyomok a magyarországi görög katolikus rítusban [Byzantine traces in the Hungarian Greek Catholic liturgy]. *Poszbizánci Közlemények: Studia Postbizantina Hungarica* 1: 103–10.

Davie, G. 2000. *Religion in modern Europe: A memory mutates.* Oxford: Oxford University Press.

Decree on the Catholic Churches of the Eastern Rite, Second Vatican Council *Orientalium Ecclesiarium.* 1964. http://www.ewtn.com/library/COUNCILS/V2EAST.HTM.

Evdokimov, M. 2000. *Les chrétiens Orthodoxes.* Paris: Flammarion.

Hanganu, G. 1997. If Roublev had been given a video camera: On inverse perspective, transcendental style, and ethnographic film. *The Museum of the Romanian Peasant Anthropology Review* 2: 94–102.

Hann, C. 2003. Creeds, cultures and the "witchery of music." *The Journal of the Royal Anthropological Institute* 9, no. 2: 223–39.

———. 2005. The limits of Galician syncretism, pluralism, multiculturalism, and the two Catholicisms. In *Galicia: A multicultured land,* ed. C. Hann and P. R. Magocsi, 210–39. Toronto: University of Toronto Press.

Hervieu-Léger, D. 2000. *Religion as a chain of memory.* Cambridge: Polity Press.

Herzfeld, M. 1990. Icons and identity: Religious orthodoxy and social practice in rural Crete. *Anthropological Quarterly* 63, no. 3: 109–21.

———. 2002. Cultural fundamentalism and the regimentation of identity: The embodiment of Orthodox values in a modernist setting. In *The postnational self: Belonging and identity,* ed. U. Hedetoft and M. Hjort, 198–217. Minneapolis: University of Minnesota Press.

Hitchins, K. 1999. *A nation discovered: Romanian intellectuals in Transylvania and the idea of nation, 1700–1848.* Bucharest: Encyclopedy/The Romanian Cultural Foundation.

Hobsbawm, E., and T. Ranger, eds. 1983. *The invention of tradition.* Cambridge: Cambridge University Press.

Iordachi, C. 1999. Politics and inter-confessional strife in post-1989 Romania: From competition for resources to the redefinition of national ideology. *Balkanologie* 3, no. 1: 147–69.

Ivancsó, I. 1995. Harminc eves bizánci liturgia [Thirty years of Byzantine liturgy]. *Poszbizánci Közlemények: Studia Postbizantina Hungarica* 2: 89–100.

Kenna, M. 1985. Icons in theory and practice: An Orthodox Christian example. *History of Religions* 24, no. 4: 345–68.

Kokosalakis, N. 1995. Icons and non-verbal religion in the Orthodox tradition. *Social Compass* 42, no. 4: 433–49.

Latour, B. 1990. Quand les anges deviennent de bien mauvais messagers. Special issue, *Terrain* 14: 76–91.

———. 2001. "Thou shalt not take the Lord's name in vain"—Being a sort of sermon on the hesitations of religious speech. *Res* 39: 215–34.

Mahieu, S. 2004. Legal recognition and recovery of property: Contested restitution of the Romanian Greek Catholic Church patrimony. In *MPI Working Papers* 69. Halle (Saale): Max Planck Institute for Social Anthropology.

———. 2006. (Non-)retours à l'Église gréco-catholique roumaine, entre adhésion et transmission religieuse. *Social Compass* 53, no. 3: 513–31.

Makrides, V. 2004. "L'autre orthodoxie": Courants du rigorisme orthodoxe grec. *Social Compass* 51, no. 4: 511–21.

Makrides, V., and D. Uffelmann. 2003. Studying Eastern Orthodox anti-Westernism: The need for a comparative research agenda. In *Orthodox Christianity and contemporary Europe,* ed. J. Sutton and W. van der Bercken, 87–121. Leuven: Peeters.

Manolescu, A. 1999. Icônes sans visage: Une mise en image de la transcendence. *Martor: Revista de Antropologia a Muzeului Taranului Român* 4, http://martor.memoria .ro/?location=view_article&id=93 (accessed 30 July 2009).

Mayer, M. 1997. *The Rusyns of Hungary: Political and Social Developments, 1860–1910.* New York: Columbia University Press.

Meyendorff, J. 1996. *The Orthodox Church: Its past and its role in the world today.* Crestwood, N.Y.: SVS.

Molnár, I. 1997. Mióta magyarok a magyarországi görög katolikusok? [Since when have Hungarian Greek Catholics been living in Hungary?]. *Posztbizánci Közlemények: Studia Postbizantina Hungarica* 3: 46–52.

Pelikan, J. 1989. The church between East and West: The context of Sheptyts'kyi's thought. In *Morality and reality: The life and times of Andrei Sheptyts'kyi,* ed. P. R. Magocsi, 1–12. Edmonton: Canadian Institute of Ukrainian Studies, University of Alberta.

Pospishil, V. 1989. Sheptyts'kyi and liturgical reform. In *Morality and reality: The life and times of Andrei Sheptyts'kyi,* ed. P. R. Magocsi, 201–27. Edmonton: Canadian Institute of Ukrainian Studies.

Pott, T. 2000. *La réforme liturgique byzantine: Étude du phénomène de l'évolution non-spontanée de la liturgie byzantine.* Rome: C.I.V. Edizioni Liturgiche.

Puskás, B. 1991. "L'influence du baroque sur la peinture d'icônes dans la région des Carpathes. In *Le baroque de l'Europe occidentale et le monde byzantin,* Académie serbe des sciences et des arts 59; Classe des sciences historiques 18: 29–36.

Pusztai, B. 2005. Discursive tactics and political identity: Shaping Hungarian Greek Catholic identity at the turn of the nineteenth and twentieth centuries. *National Identities* 7, no. 2: 117–31.

Rance, D. 1994. *Roumanie: Courage et fidélité; L'église gréco-catholique unie.* Mareil-Marly: AED.

Robbins, J. 2007. Continuity thinking and the problem of Christian culture: Belief, time, and the anthropology of Christianity. *Current Anthropology* 48, no. 1: 5–36.

Silvestrini, A. 1997. *Instruction for applying the liturgical prescriptions of the Code of Canons of the Eastern Churches.* http://www.christusrex.org/www2/greek-catholic/library/book001_left.html.

Stewart, C. 1991. *Demons and the devil: Moral imagination in modern Greek culture.* Princeton: Princeton University Press.

———. 1999. Syncretism and its synonyms: Reflections on cultural mixture. *Diacritics* 29, no. 3: 40–62.

———. 2007. *Creolization: History, ethnography, theory.* Oxford: Berg.

Stewart, C., and R. Shaw, eds. 1994. *Syncretism/anti-syncretism: The politics of religious synthesis.* London: Routledge.

Uspensky, B. 1976. *The semiotics of the Russian icon.* Lisse: Peter De Ridder Press.

Werbner, P. 2001. The limits of cultural hybridity: On ritual monsters, poetic licence, and contested postcolonial purifications. *The Journal of the Royal Anthropological Institute* 7, no. 1: 133–52.

Zehner, E. 2005. Orthodox hybridities: Anti-syncretism and localization in the evangelical Christianity of Thailand. *Anthropological Quarterly* 78, no. 3: 585–617.

Zeitler, B. 1994. Cross-cultural interpretations of imagery in the Middle Ages. *The Art Bulletin* 76, no. 4: 680–94.

# 4

# The Acoustics and Geopolitics of Orthodox Practices in the Estonian-Russian Border Region

Jeffers Engelhardt

Early on the morning of the feast of Holy Pascha in 2003, I rode with Father Andreas Põld from the town of Värska to the village of Saatse (Satserinna), both of which lie in the Estonian-Russian border region of Setomaa or Petserimaa (map 4.1).[1] It was cold, and we had slept only a few hours since the All-Night Vigil and Divine Liturgy of Holy Pascha ended at the Church of St. George in Värska at about 2:30 that morning. These overcrowded services brought to brilliant culmination the fast of Great Lent and Holy Week with nearly ceaseless communal singing of the Paschal *troparion* in both Estonian and Slavonic: "Christ is risen from the dead, trampling down death with death, and upon those in the tombs bestowing life!"[2]

That morning, worshippers in Saatse joyously sang these words to the same melody heard in Värska. This traditional Russian Orthodox melody is common to a global community of Eastern Christians whose musical and liturgical practices have been shaped by Russian Orthodoxy through imperial and missionary encounter (see Geraci and Khodarkovsky 2001; Kivelson and Greene 2003; Werth 2002; Znamenski 1999). At the same time, this community continues to transform the musical (Morosan 1994; von Gardner 1980, 2000), iconographic, material, and ritual nature of "Russian" Orthodoxy through myriad local innovations and ideological reforms (see Shevzov 2004). These Eastern Christians are part of a soundscape and religious imaginary extending from Western Europe through Eurasia and East Asia and into North America (see Kan 1999; Stark 2002; Stokoe 1995). The global dimensions of these Russian-influenced Orthodoxies reflect the deterritorialized nature of many Eastern Christianities and their place among other global Christianities. The "Easternness" of Eastern Christians, then, might

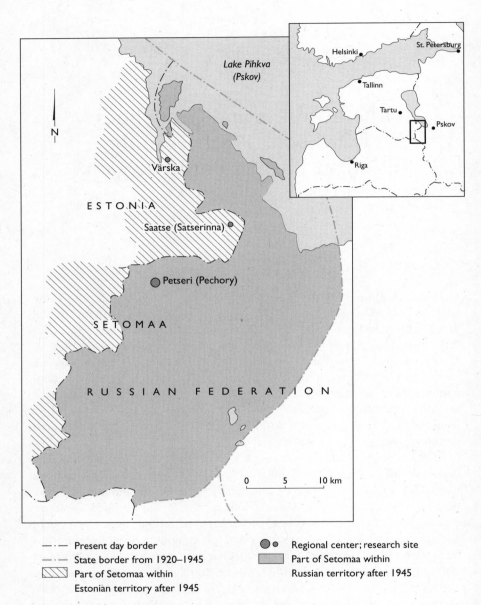

Lake Pihkva
(Pskov)

N

Värska

E S T O N I A

Saatse (Satserinna)

Petseri (Pechory)

S E T O M A A

R U S S I A N    F E D E R A T I O N

0      5      10 km

Helsinki
St. Petersburg
Tallinn
Tartu
Pskov
Riga

-··- Present day border
-····- State border from 1920–1945
Part of Setomaa within
Estonian territory after 1945

Regional center; research site
Part of Setomaa within
Russian territory after 1945

MAP 4.1. Field site in Setomaa.

be less about hemispheres and civilizations and more about particular ethical and social norms, beliefs about sound and ways of singing, attitudes toward liturgy, doctrine, and tradition, and beliefs about personhood, human ecology, and soteriology.

While part of a global community of Eastern Christians, Orthodox believers in Saatse and elsewhere in Setomaa maintain distinctive musical practices and oral traditions, commemorate local saints, visit local holy places and village chapels (*tsässonad*), celebrate together at village parties (*kirmaskid*) and calendric festivals (*praasnikud*), and integrate Orthodoxy into cultural activism and plans for regional development. Orthodoxy in Setomaa creates intimacy and addresses social and spiritual problems; it is where clerical and lay interests and institutional authorities interact; it accommodates non-Orthodox beliefs and practices; it responds to secularism and compensates for religious knowledge lost in the Soviet era; it both transcends and intensifies dominant ethnolinguistic and geopolitical ideologies in post-Soviet Estonia and Russia; finally, it inspires pilgrimage, tourism, and exoticizing representations that drive economic, cultural, and religious development across differences. The acoustics and geopolitics of Orthodoxy in Setomaa register how particular musical practices are efficacious and make the region integral despite competing territorial claims made by the Estonian and Russian states and Orthodox churches. With this in mind, I examine the liturgical singing of choir members, congregants, and priests at parishes in Setomaa to document their critical, agentive, embodied engagement in Orthodoxy and the geopolitics of postsocialism.

By concentrating on sound in the making, experience, and expression of Christianity and the establishment of sacred, social, and moral orders, I expand upon salient themes in ethnomusicological work on global Christianities. These include the role of language and spiritual charisma in Baptist and Pentecostal musics (e.g., Lange 2003; Titon 1988), the place of music in conversion and missionization (e.g., Engelhardt forthcoming; Garcia 1998; Spinney 2006; Vallier 2003), Christian musics and socioreligious transformation (e.g., Rappoport 2004; Sherinian 2002, 2005), popular music and Christian ethics (e.g., Romanowski 2000; Rommen 2002, 2006, 2007), syncretism and ritual in South America (e.g., Mendonza 2000; Reily 2002; Scruggs 2005), the importance of performance in African Christianities (e.g., Barz 2003; Muller 1999, 2005), approaches to Christian hymnody, composition, and chant (e.g., Barz 2005; Gray 1995; Lassiter 2001; Lassiter, Ellis, and Kotay 2002; Lind 2003; Palackal 2004; Stillman 1993), and the role of Christian musics in migration and the construction of diasporic identities (e.g., Bohlman 2002; Chow 2006; Mazo 2006).

There is much about the acoustics and geopolitics of Orthodoxy in Setomaa that is particularly Orthodox, however. Hymns and singing create sacred territory because of the ubiquitous presence of heightened speech and singing in Orthodoxy and the ontology of Orthodox sound itself. Orthodox hymns are not "music" in an objective sense that divorces them from the synesthetic reality of Orthodox liturgy, its temporality and textual environment, and the embodied experience of worshippers. While the musico-textual integrity of much Orthodox singing and chanting points to historical developments addressing practical concerns of ritual and audition, Orthodox singing is prayer, sacralized language, and the aural rendition of divine prototypes. Estonian words like *teenima* (to serve) or *lugema* (to read), used to describe sung participation in Orthodox liturgy, reflect this ontology (see Bohlman 1999). Thus the human voice is the ideal sound in most Orthodoxies because of its close connection to language and prayer, its nature as a creation of God, and its relationship to the ceaseless worship of the angelic hierarchies. Conversely, musical instruments are traditionally proscribed in most Orthodoxies because of their artificiality as human creations, their association with worldly activities like dance and work, and their alienation from language, which makes them unsuited to prayer and worship.[3]

The acoustics and geopolitics of Orthodoxy in Setomaa are also shaped by the competing canonical and jurisdictional claims of the Orthodox Church of Estonia (OCE) and the Estonian Orthodox Church of the Moscow Patriarchate.[4] These claims are legitimated by the importance of autonomous and autocephalous local churches throughout Orthodox history and represent concomitant struggles with phyletism (the struggle between canonical Orthodoxy and ethnolinguistic or nationalist ideologies). Another particularly Orthodox aspect of the musical and social dynamics I explore here is the play between the "normative power" (Shils 1981: 1) of tradition and innovative or untranslatable local practices. While the conservative essence of Orthodoxy is faithful adherence to its apostolic message, patristic wisdom, and church canons, the local and lay practices that situate Orthodoxy and make it seemingly invariant are often interpreted as syncretic or canonically suspect. Such interpretations make perilous assumptions about agency and the authenticity of beliefs and practices. As part of a global community of Eastern Christians whose practices have been shaped by Russian Orthodoxy but are not "Russian" Orthodox, singers, congregants, and priests in Setomaa practice an Orthodoxy that is neither derivative, inauthentic, nor uncanonical. It moves, in Gregory Barz's words, "beyond syncretism towards consciousness" (2003: 3). The integral relationship of their Orthodoxy to a territory and religious imaginary enhances Orthodoxy's universal message and ideology through its very particularity. Finally, the acoustics and geopolitics of Orthodoxy in Setomaa interact with Orthodoxy's gendered hierarchies through the sounds and leadership of parish choirs. It is with these specifically Orthodox phenomena in mind that I return to Saatse.

## BORDER LIVES AND BORDER PRACTICES

Father Andreas traveled to Saatse that morning to celebrate Pascha at the Church of St. Paraskeva, which, according to Seto tradition, lies where the Holy Spirit placed a stone cross taken from the nearby Russian village of Krupp (Kuusing 2005: 244–45). Saatse was also where Saint Vassili (Solovski), canonized by the OCE in 2004, served as a priest and was martyred in 1919. In addition to the bustling, dramatic, joyous celebration of Christ's resurrection, Pascha in Saatse included rituals that reaffirmed the sacredness of community and bonds of kinship. Father Andreas blessed special Paschal breads and eggs that were prepared in homes, placed with candles and icons on a special table in the church, and shared among family and friends with other food and drink at ancestral grave sites. There, Father Andreas briefly recited prayers for the dead and accepted some food and drink. Children climbed the church's bell tower and took turns ringing the bells throughout the afternoon, extending the joy of the feast to the bells' audible limits.

The broadly cast pealing of bells and gathering of singers at the Church of St. Paraskeva sutured together in sound a community of Orthodox believers divided by a fraught, polysemic border. The border is an ideological locus of post-Soviet "transition" and the institutional renewal of the OCE. A few hundred meters from the church, it is the border between Estonia and the Russian Federation, the European Union West and the Russian East, NATO and its post–cold war counterparts, and the Orthodox worlds of the Constantinople and Moscow patriarchates. It is a border that traces, in Talal Asad's words, "a history whose unconfused purpose is to separate Europe from alien times ('communism,' 'Islam') as well as from alien places ('Islamdom,' 'Russia')" (2003: 171).

That the border is part of people's everyday experience and concern in Setomaa became obvious during my ride with Father Andreas. The twelve-kilometer gravel road from Värska to Saatse passed twice over a "line of control" (*kontrolljoon*) formed by the jagged border between Estonia and the Russian Federation.[5] Father Andreas commented that this "line of control" emerged following the most recent redrawing of borders in Setomaa in 1991, in one case influenced by the vodka a Russian farmer gave to surveyors in order to keep his farm in Russia. Father Andreas went on to explain that one is not permitted to stop a car or walk along these stretches of road, which are under electronic surveillance, and speculated that the course of the road might have to be altered following European Union accession. The metaphysics of the border or "line of control" and the meanings it engenders are fundamental aspects of life in Setomaa. However, our drive to Saatse also demonstrated that the exceptional significance I sense in the border is, for others, an unexceptional but not insignificant part of everyday necessity and Orthodox practice.

Arriving in Saatse and approaching the Church of St. Paraskeva, Father Andreas drew my attention to the abandoned buildings of the former *sovkhoz* (Soviet state-owned farm) that encroached upon the cemetery surrounding the church. Among these buildings is the altar area of another church whose construction began in 1939 but was never finished. While the fate of this unfinished church under the Soviet regime was not uncommon (it was converted into a tractor repair shop for the *sovkhoz*), its existence is the result of an earlier division of the parish into Russian and Seto/Estonian congregations during the Republican period. In 1935, the congregation was divided along ethnolinguistic lines, and plans were made to build a separate church for the Russian congregation. This was part of state-sanctioned Estonianization in Setomaa, carried out within the OCE, that reified and ideologized what were otherwise more fluid ethnolinguistic identities. However, such distinctions were previously manifest in separate Russian and Seto/Estonian choirs within the same congregation and through the introduction of Estonian-language liturgies in the 1920s (Kaljukosk 2003; Raag 1938). During the Republican period, the border was about twenty kilometers farther east and incorporated all of what is currently considered Setomaa, including the fifteenth-century Orthodox monastery in Petseri upon which the church was historically dependent.

The situation today is very different. Pointing out the people walking to the church from the northeast, Father Andreas estimated that on Pascha one-third of the congregation would come from Russia, crossing the border on foot through a nearby checkpoint. These congregants come from the villages of Gorodishche and Krupp on the Russian side for important feasts and to visit their relatives' grave sites. For them, the church is simply the closest Orthodox place of worship, a center in their religious and social lives, and the place where they commemorate departed relatives. Their border crossings actively constitute the multiethnic, bilingual Orthodox community that has existed in Saatse since 1679 and at the Church of St. Paraskeva since 1801 (Kaljukosk 2003). Despite this, the number of worshippers has decreased by one-half since the redrawing of borders in 1991, while the ideological significance of Orthodoxy in Setomaa has been magnified considerably.

These border crossings and the religious practices they enable displace or suspend the border that is an ideological locus of post-Soviet "transition" and the institutional renewal of the OCE. They reveal how those living in Setomaa "are able to develop their own specific identities and functional spheres in relation to separate national interests and other divisions" (Eskelinen et al. 1999: 3; Kaiser and Nikiforova 2006; Nikiforova 2003). At the Church of St. Paraskeva, liturgical celebration, paraliturgical rituals, and Seto village parties transcend (if only by refusing to recognize) differences between the Patriarchates of Constantinople and Moscow and the European Union West and Russian East.

These movements, celebrations, and rituals emphasize the power and ideological orientation of the Estonian state and the OCE by calling into question these institutions' territorial limits and their ability to control the border and the meanings it inscribes.

Singing is everywhere in these processes of displacement and suspension. Its presence reflects the power sound acquires at borders: "It is in the non-verbal domain," writes Martin Stokes, "that people are often able to embrace notions of hybridity and plurality which are often unsayable; this domain is consequently a vital cultural resource in the management of border lives" (1998: 264). At the Church of St. Paraskeva, the choir led by Anna Kõllamägi moves as fluently between Estonian and Slavonic as its members move between Estonian and Russian in their everyday lives. The oral traditions and extemporaneous practices in Saatse and at other parishes in Setomaa are distinctive within the OCE. They are unlike the musical practices at Estonian Orthodox parishes in urban centers, which rely upon notated, institutionalized musics redolent of Protestant or "Byzantine" influences and featuring vocal techniques more in line with the mainstream national choral tradition (see Engelhardt 2005: 201–6, 247–63). Singing at the Church of St. Paraskeva features traditional melodies from the Petseri monastery (now a dozen kilometers away on the Russian side of the border) and a style intensely bound to the local community, its experience, and the performative relationship of choir members and worshippers. It indexes how style and relationship emerge through decades of commitment to making singing right, the ways in which people and sounds circulated within the whole of Setomaa until the 1990s, and the long history and rich folkloric tradition of Seto Orthodoxy.

What makes singing right in Setomaa—the acoustics of Orthodox practices there—challenges the ethnolinguistic and geopolitical ideologies that animate and are naturalized in Estonian "transition," European integration, and the post-Soviet renewal of the OCE. Orthodox practices in Setomaa are being shaped by a constellation of forces: by the interests of the Estonian state, the European Union, and the Russian Federation, the interests of the OCE, the interests of Seto activists and transnational NGOs, the impact of cultural tourism and pilgrimage, and exoticizing representations of Setos within Estonian, Finno-Ugric, and global imaginaries. Orthodox believers in Setomaa respond to these forces through their singing by recasting and rescaling their Orthodoxy within a new social and political order. These processes create the "friction" Anna Tsing describes as "the awkward, unequal, unstable, and creative qualities of interconnection across difference" (2005: 4).

The choir at the Church of St. Paraskeva in Saatse has a sound and style that is distinctive within Estonian Orthodoxy. Their singing is the sound of urban, literate Estonian and Russian Orthodox musical practices being translated to rural margins, and of modern Estonian and liturgical Slavonic being translated into the speech worlds of Setos, older Estonians, and Russians. It is exceptional within the everyday soundscape of Saatse, and its sacrality is enhanced by some singers' and worshippers' less extensive access to or use of mass media and digital technologies. Their singing beckons Russian, Seto, and Estonian worshippers from the Russian side of the border and creates community and affinity, perhaps like no other local (and here, transnational) action can. When the choir sings familiar, simple hymns in both Estonian and Slavonic, many worshippers join in, however modestly, thereby lessening the distinction between congregants and choir members, enacting Orthodoxy's conciliar ideal, and constituting a religious territory through sound. Their singing also beckons pilgrims from Tallinn, Tartu, Finland, and beyond on important feasts and commands the enthusiastic admiration of Metropolitan Stefanus, the Cypriot leader of the OCE, other priests, non-Orthodox cultural tourists, and non-Orthodox fieldworkers like myself.

Anna Kõllamägi, who is in her sixties, is a remarkable singer. She leads the choir, reading from her 1922 *Hymnal of the Orthodox Church of Estonia* (which contains only texts) to melodies that she knows by heart from the Republican-era OCE, Russian *Obikhod*,[6] and Petseri monastery. At the feast of Holy Pascha in 2003, she led boldly and confidently, knowing that the other women in the choir and her late husband Nikolai Kõllamägi, who was a deacon at the Church of St. Paraskeva, would eventually join in singing their extemporaneous parts. What is so striking about Anna's singing is her approach to language and the unselfconscious presence of her voice. Almost every syllable she sings is an autonomous entity within her streaming recitation, consonants popping out from long vowels in her almost aggressive and always joyful manner of singing. Her voice has a characteristic throatiness and nasality, and she mollifies its sharp timbre with frequent slides between pitches. Anna's singing is unreserved. The vitality, confidence, and conviction with which she sings are signs of the depth of her belief and the spiritual nourishment she receives from singing. On a practical level, her voice penetrates the clamor of scores of worshippers, structuring the relationship of congregation and clergy and ensuring the authority of the liturgical order.

On Pascha, all of this was very much in evidence as the choir sang a concluding prayer from the Paschal *stikhiry*.[7] The quality of Anna's voice, her intimate knowledge of Orthodox liturgy and local tradition, her musico-religious persona and position within the parish community, and the fundamental significance of the texts she delivers coalesce and feed off one another; when she sings, Anna embodies the border lives and border practices of Eastern Christians in Setomaa. The following is a transcription of the first and fourth verses of one of the concluding prayers from the Paschal *stikhiry* (see the appendix to this chapter for the musical notation).

TABLE 4.1  Verses from a concluding prayer from the Paschal *stikhiry*

| | |
|---|---|
| *1. Täna ilmus meile pühitsetud Paasa,* | Today a blessed Pascha has been revealed to us, |
| *Uus, püha Paasa,* | A new, holy Pascha, |
| *Sala Paasa,* | A mysterious Pascha, |
| *Kõigeausam Paasa,* | A most glorious Pascha, |
| *Paasa Kristuse Lunastaja,* | A Pascha of Christ the Savior, |
| *Veata Paasa,* | A Pascha without fault, |
| *Uskjate Paasa,* | A Pascha of the faithful, |
| *Paasa, mis meile paradiisi uksed lahti teeb,* | A Pascha that opens the doors of paradise for us, |
| *Paasa, mis kõik uskjad pühitseb.* | A Pascha that all the faithful celebrate. |
| | |
| *4. Ülestõusmise päev!* | Resurrection day! |
| *Pühitsegem rõõmupüha,* | Let us celebrate the joyous feast, |
| *Ja hakakem ümber teine teise kaela,* | And embrace one another, |
| *Ja ütelgem ka neile, kes meid vihkavad:* | And say to those who abhor us: |
|    *"Vennad"!* |    "Brothers!" |
| *Andkem kõik andeks ülestõusmise pärast,* | Let us forgive all because of the Resurrection, |
| *Ja hüüdkem nõnda:* | And thus cry out: |
| *Kristus on surnust üles tõusnud,* | Christ is risen from the dead, |
| *Surmaga surma maha tallanud,* | Trampling down death with death, |
| *Ja neile, kes hauas olid, elu kinkinud.* | And upon those in the tombs bestowing life. |

From a canonical perspective, this is quintessential Orthodox singing: Anna is utterly fluent in adjusting a melodic formula to the phonetic and formal properties of a text in the moment of liturgical performance, lingering longer on stressed syllables and making sure the melodic contour aligns with important phrases. Anna's singing realizes the musico-textual unity that is an Orthodox ideal: singing is not "music" anterior to the text it communicates. Rather, it is the sounding beauty and affect of the word and an essential complement to its semantic meaning and truth claims; it realizes in practice the Orthodox synthesis of aesthetics and veracity. It goes without saying that this entails considerable ability and sophistication on Anna's part, without which Orthodoxy would not do the work it does in Saatse.

The way Anna's choir sings at the Church of St. Paraskeva is deeply connected to the rurality, marginality, and multiethnic character of Setomaa. Their singing indexes ways in which villages like Saatse are incompletely part of the Estonian post-Soviet "transition," which is oriented toward ethnolinguistic and geopolitical consolidation, secularism, and a cosmopolitan form of European "normalcy" (see, e.g., Rausing 2004). The status of the Church of St. Paraskeva as a center of pilgrimage, and the continuity and vitality of religious life there, in spite of significant social and material challenges, demonstrate some of the modern efficacies of Orthodox singing in the lives of Eastern Christians.

## ORTHODOXY AND ACTIVISM

Me oleme maarahvas, aga kummardame vene-värki jumalat.
*We are people of the country, but we worship a Russian-type god.*

Setomaa stands at the historical crossroads of Finno-Ugric, Slavic, and European cultural spheres and German, Russian, Polish, and Swedish political interests. Unlike the rest of Estonia, Setomaa was never part of medieval Livonia or Livland, the administrative units that included parts of southern Estonia and northern Latvia under Polish, Swedish, and tsarist Russian imperial regimes. The mapping of Setomaa was part of the territorial expansions and conflicts of Eastern and Western Christianity, and Setos were Orthodox centuries before their minority Orthodox Estonian compatriots. Like Karelia, Setomaa has long been economically marginal and culturally and religiously distinct. Although little is known about the indigenous Seto population until the middle of the nineteenth century, the impact of Russian culture is marked: "It is particularly recognizable in language, folk dress, architecture, and landholding patterns. Furthermore, the Orthodox religion and the church calendar played a major role in ordering Setu life" (Raun 1991: 516). Toivo Raun notes that the history of Setomaa "is analogous to that of East Karelia (where the Karelian and Russian worlds met) and Latgale in the tsarist provinces of Pskov and Vitebsk (where the Latvian and Slavic worlds met)" (1991: 514).

Despite their common Orthodoxy, Russians did not view Setos as sharing the same faith. Setos were called *poluvercy* (half believers), and the area of the Pskov province where they lived was known as the *poluvercheskii krai* (region of half believers). This characterization was due to the linguistic alienation of Russian clergy from Setos, the absence of a vernacular liturgy, and the apparent syncretism of Seto religious practices. At the same time, Orthodoxy and language also separated Setos from their Estonian neighbors to the north and west.

Language, which plays an important role in Seto identification and activism today, has long distinguished Setos from Estonians and Russians alike. Setos speak a Finno-Ugric language similar to the one spoken in southern Estonia (Võrumaa), which is variously classified as a dialect of Estonian or a separate language in its own right. Russian elements include cognates like *praasnik* (religious holiday or Orthodox feast) and *tsässon*, the Seto word for a village prayer chapel (coming from the Russian word *chasovnia,* derived from *chas,* "hour" or "prayer of the hour"). On the other hand, *kirmask,* the word for a Seto village party, derived from the German *Kirmesk,* reveals a Western, pre-Reformation Catholic influence.

The epigraph that begins this section reveals the in-between nature of Seto identity. Setos could perceive themselves as "people of the country" whose religious practices were of the "Russian type."[8] However, for nineteenth-century Estophile elites, Setomaa was a living folkloric archive upon which they could build Estonian national culture. This was very much in line with the Herderian orientation of the Estonian national project and, like Herder himself, drew heavily upon the systematic collection and instrumental use of folk song, including Seto *leelo*. Their collaboration with and appropriation by folklorists and nationalizing elites in the late nineteenth and early twentieth centuries perforce brought Setos into an Estonian national imaginary. However, by emphasizing the affinities among Estonians and Setos, Estonian elites effaced Seto Orthodoxy in favor of their essential Finno-Ugric identity as "the ideal original Estonians" (*ideaalsed ürgeestlased*) (Jääts 1998: 37). It was during this extended "period of national awakening" (*ärkamisaeg*) that civilizing discourses addressing Seto "backwardness" emerged. Furthermore, Setos shaped the burgeoning geopolitical ideologies and ambitions of Estonian nationalists. In 1912, for instance, the Estonian Progressive People's Party called for the inclusion of Setomaa within a unified Estonian administrative unit—an idea that carries tremendous weight with Seto activists today (Raun 1991: 519).

During the War of Independence in 1919, Estonian forces gained control of Petseri and the whole of Setomaa. A 1920 treaty between the Republic of Estonia and Soviet Russia signed in Tartu fixed the borders of Setomaa to the south and east of Petseri. This reflected the extent of Estonian military control and the importance ascribed to "the long-term ethnic Estonian [Seto] presence in the area" (Raun 1991: 522). Setomaa became the site for projects of social, cultural, and economic integration. These modernization programs addressed the "backwardness" and multiethnic character of Setomaa through infrastructure projects, institutional and agricultural reforms, and even a plan for "repatriating" ethnic Russians. Estonian and Seto priests began celebrating services in Estonian (but not Seto) for the first time, and parishes like the one in Saatse were divided into separate congregations along ethnolinguistic lines. In the late 1920s and 1930s, the OCE enacted reforms in the spiritual and financial administration of the Petseri monastery, which included the establishment of an Estonian congregation, adoption of the Gregorian calendar, and celebration of services in Estonian. Many of the Petseri monks, most of whom were Russian or Russified Setos, passionately resisted these reforms, which they understood as heresy.

Overall, the state-sanctioned integration, modernization, and Estonianization of Setomaa during the Republican period improved the region's infrastructure and the level of education. While Raun believes these projects "constituted nothing less than a cultural revolution" (1991: 530), others note that they were undertaken through measures "too radical" for such a "delicate sphere" (Lõuna 2003: 139). Indrek Jääts observes that an increased emphasis on secular schooling transformed the "religious concretism" of Seto Orthodoxy. By the end of the 1920s, for instance, believers no longer venerated icons as actually living entities capable of influencing their world (Jääts 1998: 49).

The Soviet occupation of Estonia in 1944 had profound effects in Setomaa,[9] some of which continued processes of social and cultural transformation already underway during the Republican period. In January 1945, the border between the Estonian SSR and the Russian SFSR was moved to its pre-Republic position, thereby dividing Setomaa symbolically and administratively. Negotiating this border in everyday life, however, was not difficult. Unlike today, Setos, Estonians, and Russians moved with relative ease across the border to visit relatives, conduct trade, or visit the Petseri monastery. Using the term "Setomaa" in journalism or scientific writing, however, was "ill-advised," as it made geopolitical and national-ist claims that went against those of the Soviet regime (Jääts 1998: 58). The nation-alization of land and collectivization of agriculture had a much more concrete impact, dissolving traditional social and economic units. These changes trans-formed kinship relations, subjectivities, and ways of life, not least in the obser-vance of Orthodox and Seto calendric festivals. To the south and east of the border, rural life was heavily Russified, while in the Estonian SSR the Estonianization already underway in the Republican period continued. From the mid-1950s onward, many younger Setos from both sides of the border moved to Tartu and Tallinn. Setos were categorized as a distinctive Estonian ethnographic group fol-lowing Soviet nationality policy (see Hirsch 2005), thereby reproducing Republican ethnolinguistic ideologies, albeit for very different reasons. The only official iden-tity available to Setos was Estonian. There was no Seto-language education during the Soviet period, and the use of Seto retreated into the private realm of family and close friends. By the 1960s, the older Seto generation viewed themselves as Seto, but their children and grandchildren as Estonian.

As an integral aspect of traditional Seto identity, Orthodoxy remained impor-tant, by and large, only to older generations. Throughout Setomaa, village prayer chapels fell out of use and into disrepair. The transformation and secularization of Seto life was also visible at village parties, calendric festivals, and ritual meals at grave sites. Although multiple generations and entire families participated in these Seto practices, their association with Orthodoxy and traditional forms of ancestral veneration were largely lost, supplemented instead by notions of official ethnicity promoted by Soviet cultural ideologies (see Jääts 1998; Lõuna 2003).

Another transformation in Seto life from the 1950s onward was the folkloriza-tion of Seto musical and material culture. As urbanization, secularization, and the loss of identity were coupled with Soviet ideas about ethnicity and the instrumen-tal representation and control of national culture, Seto music making became more visible and audible as it was transported to the stage of official culture. In the early 1960s, a number of traditional Seto singing (*leelo*) ensembles were formed in Setomaa with official sanction and support from the Soviet regime, many of which are still active today. Some of the women who sing in these *leelo* choirs are active in Orthodox choirs as well, although they have on many occasions emphasized to me that *leelo* and "church singing" are entirely different from one another.

Since *perestroika* and the Estonian "Singing Revolution" (*laulev revolutsioon*) in the late 1980s and early 1990s, Seto activists have become more intensively involved in national and transnational fora. These well-organized activists work to reclaim, renew, and protect Seto language and identity in response to their Soviet and post-Soviet experience and, in some cases, their Orthodox belief. One of the defining, most contentious, and most emotional aspects of their work has to do with the border. Since the restoration of Estonian independence in 1991, activists have pressed for Estonian and Russian citizens' rights to visa-free border crossings, Estonian-language education for Estonian citizens living on the Russian side of the border, and, most controversially, the restoration of the borders defined by the 1920 Tartu Peace Treaty, which encompass the whole of Setomaa.

While Seto activism engages the institutions that animate Estonian post-Soviet "transition" (the European Union, UNESCO, and the Patriarchate of Constantinople), it simultaneously constructs alternative concepts of place, sacred and social order, and identity. Through tourism, pilgrimage, and cooperation with transnational Finno-Ugric and indigenous rights organizations, Seto activism is a process of cultural and ideological mobilization with a globalist orientation. The public moral appeal of Seto activism emphasizes self-determination and autonomy in focusing on the border issue, regional economic issues, the preservation and teaching of the Seto language, and the renewal of Seto culture. Activists have successfully petitioned the European Union to support cultural and development projects, and a commission has been formed to seek UNESCO recognition.

Beyond these political issues, the relationship of Seto activism to Orthodoxy is ambivalent. On the one hand, over 80 percent of the Seto population is nominally Orthodox, and, as of the late 1990s, 55 percent were churchgoers of some sort (Jääts 1998: 86–87). Major Orthodox feasts are important religious, cultural, and social events to which Setos, tourists, pilgrims, and ethnographers flock. The nurturing and renewal of Orthodoxy in Setomaa is one of the institutional imperatives of the OCE. For the OCE, popular Seto Orthodoxy is a model of authenticity, and Setomaa a place where vital Orthodox practices inspire and legitimate Estonian Orthodoxy as a whole. On the other hand, Orthodoxy registers very little in the public discourse of Seto activists, although the OCE is often solicited for financial and institutional assistance. By and large, activists are reticent about Orthodoxy in their construction and promotion of Seto identity, and a marked turn to alternative religious practices has taken place.

Despite Seto activists' ambivalence toward Orthodoxy and the serious social, cultural, and spiritual problems affecting life in Setomaa, there are many ways in which Seto Orthodoxy accommodates activists' politics and participates in their social and cultural work. Seto Orthodoxy is deeply implicated in the cultural tourism, pilgrimage, geopolitics, and representations that transform life in Setomaa. On the one hand, Seto Orthodoxy is vital for the spiritual renewal of Estonian Orthodoxy and as symbolic capital for the OCE. However, Metropolitan Stefanus cautions Seto activists that, for him, Seto culture and Orthodoxy cannot be divorced from one another, and occasionally questions the religious bases of their petitions for financial assistance. In fact, much of the OCE's activity in Estonian Setomaa has to do with asserting an Orthodox presence and making territorial claims in ambivalent or secular spaces. On the other hand, the OCE's instrumental interest in Seto Orthodoxy rescales local practices by adopting them as manifestations of institutional renewal. These processes happen in more concrete ways as well. As the boundary between the Orthodox worlds of the Constantinople and Moscow patriarchates, the border that bisects Setomaa is of particular ideological significance to the OCE at the same time that it cleaves the region physically and spiritually.

As post-Soviet geopolitics and the renewal of the OCE inscribe a fraught border in Setomaa, Seto activists and Orthodox believers negotiate relationships to the border by sacralizing symbols of an integral Setomaa. While the OCE has instrumental interests and makes territorial claims, local congregants continue their border crossings and untranslatable worship practices. While the renewal of Seto Orthodoxy draws upon the goodwill of Orthodox Finns and assistance from the European Union, the pilgrimages Finnish and other Orthodox believers make to Setomaa locate a center of authenticity and spiritual power there. Finally, while the gaze and audition of pilgrims, cultural tourists, and ethnomusicologists transport Seto musical and religious practices into global routes of circulation, the ways in which Setos use language, song, and Orthodoxy to address social, cultural, and spiritual challenges reveal their efficacies and meanings. Thus the acoustics of Orthodoxy in Setomaa are necessarily involved in the secular geopolitics playing out across the border and resound with singing that is the performance of a territorially specific Orthodoxy.

## SINGING THE RIGHT WAY

Orthodox singing is efficacious in post-Soviet religious renewal, geopolitics, and Seto activism because it expresses local ideals, gives voice to beliefs about Orthodox canonicity and authenticity, and enables multiple forms of embodied experience and participation. This is a vital part of what makes singing Orthodox in the dual sense of Orthodoxy as "right belief" (*doxa*) and "right worship" or "right glory" (*praxis*). Right singing is at once right belief and right practice, and what makes singing right involves Orthodox doctrine, lay theologies, oral traditions, and beliefs about sound that are situated in a specific place or religious imaginary.

Orthodoxy is sustained in crucial, musical ways by clergy, singers, and laypeople through orthopraxy. At the same time, church canons, traditions, and hierarchies inform orthopraxy through discourses of authenticity and by distinguishing the truth claims of Orthodoxy, which is upheld as the originary Christianity, from other global Christianities. Within Orthodoxy, singing is believing when what matters is *doxa,* and being Orthodox is about singing the right way when what matters is *praxis.*

These dynamics of belief and practice, of doctrine and how it is articulated within particular sociohistorical conditions and through individual capabilities, reflect much of what is essential to Orthodoxy: its strong sense of tradition, its proprietary claims on the apostolic message and its transmission, its particular temporality, which Metropolitan Stefanus characterizes as "in time and in spite of time" (2002), and its ways of mediating between the prototypical and the histori-cal, between the conciliar and the individual , and between what is ecumenical in scope and what is intensely local and untranslatable. Therefore, communities of Eastern Christians (wherever they are geographically) are individuals brought together as much through the external veracity of correct practice when they fast, perform prostrations, venerate icons, make the sign of the cross, and especially when they sing, as through the internal state of correct belief (cf. Rappaport 1999: 119–24, 395–96). In this way, thinking about Orthodoxy means rethinking the conventional scholarly emphasis on Christianity as belief and questioning instead how correct practice might engender correct belief, or at least how orthopraxy performatively recognizes the authority manifest in ritual order, thereby limiting the threat of alternative truths and heterodox beliefs (cf. Rappaport 1999: 121–23). Ultimately, Orthodox singing has an ethical dimension that relates liturgy to social conditions in its worldly environment; right singing is right action, and this has particular urgency in the Estonian-Russian border region.

At the Church of St. George in Värska, choir members and congregants sing a special prayer from an *akathist* to the Theotokos (Mary, the Birth-Giver of God),[10] which, as Father Andreas Põld explained, uses a melody unique to Setomaa and originating from the Petseri monastery, the historical center of economic and spiritual life in the region, fifteen kilometers from Värska and across the border. This melody is part of the oral tradition of the Church of St. George and makes audible the parish's historical connection to and dependence upon the Petseri monastery. That this and other "Petseri variants" were transmitted to Värska from the fifteenth-century monastery is well known to singers and worshippers. Hymns like these forge the regional identity and integrate the religious imaginary that makes singing in Värska right. The following is a transcription of a concluding prayer from an *akathist* to the Theotokos sung at the Church of St. George in Värska (see the appendix to this chapter for the musical notation).

TABLE 4.2 Concluding prayer from an *akathist* to the Theotokos

| | |
|---|---|
| *Mu kõige helgem Kuninganna,* | My most gracious Queen, |
| *mu lootus, mu Jumalasünnitaja,* | my hope, Birth-Giver of God, |
| *Sa vaeste sõber ja koduta olijate* | You, friend of the poor and shelter of the homeless, |
| *varjupaik,* | |
| *kurbade rõõm ja rõõmutute kaitseja.* | joy of the troubled and protector of the joyful. |
| *Vaata mu häda, vaata mu viletsust;* | Look upon my distress, my misery, |
| *aita mind, kes abita olen.* | help me, who is without help. |
| *Lõpeta mu kurbus, nagu Sa ise pead,* | Bring an end to my sadness, as You will, |
| *sest peale Sinu ei ole mul teist abilist,* | because except for You, I have the help of none other, |
| *teist hoidjat ja nende trööstijat* | no other guardian or consoler |
| *kui Sina, oh Jumalaema.* | than You, oh Mother of God. |
| *Sina hoiad ja kaitsed meid igavesti.* | You will protect and defend us forever. Amen. |
| *Aamen.* | |

Today, singing this hymn at the Church of St. George reaffirms the spiritual, social, and imaginative connections that exist, however tenuously, between the congregation and the Petseri monastery. The monastery itself is dedicated to the Dormition of the Theotokos, and this petition addressed and sung to Mary locates her intercessory power in the space where Värska is situated and the Petseri monastery is central. By reaffirming their connection to the monastery, those who sing at the Church of St. George overcome the border whose physical and metaphysical presence has such a deep impact on life in Setomaa. In singing this hymn, they reconstitute and renew a multiethnic, bilingual, transnational Orthodox community and, in the process, their beliefs about right singing.

This *akathist* invites worshippers to focus their devotional energies and pleas for intercession as a univocal utterance—an active transition from the individual to the collective that is echoed in a shift from first-person singular to first-person plural in the text of the prayer (see Hann and Goltz, in this volume). Like the example from the Church of St. Paraskeva in Saatse, this, too, is quintessential Orthodox singing. Here, singers adapt flexible melodic formulae to the shape and intonations of the text, specific words are intensified through heightened diction, and men's and women's voices join together in extemporaneous harmonizations, breathing together and sliding between pitches in the same way. In realizing the fullness of the word (its semantic meaning, truth claims, and sounding beauty) and a community that aspires to salvation and right action, singers in Värska realize a principal ideal of canonical Orthodox sound.

This melody from the Petseri monastery is effacicious because it is both memorable and meaningful. Uncomplicated enough for all to perform, this *akathist* locates Orthodox practice within a specific territory and temporality in spite of post-Soviet geopolitics and competing Orthodox jurisdictional claims, thereby making Orthodoxy's apostolic message, soteriological doctrine, and teaching about personhood sensible and audible. My emphasis on practice is important here since issues of orthopraxy are immanent in this *akathist* in terms of Orthodox canonicity and its relationship to the religious landscape and soundscape of Setomaa as a whole. Amid changes in congregational life at the Church of St. George in Värska and the role of Orthodoxy in border lives and practices, this hymn is right both for the voice it gives to correct belief and for the meanings it engenders as correct practice. For the faithful, this hymn is a concise expression of Orthodox doctrine. For those with less conviction, who are only nominally Orthodox, or who are non-Orthodox, this *akathist* is significant as a practice of social and cultural memory and for its relevance to the border issue.

This kind of religious territorialization is happening in spite of the border dividing Setomaa, which is an ideological locus for post-Soviet geopolitics and the institutional renewal of the OCE. Through their worship practices, singers in Värska and elsewhere in Setomaa are transforming the territorial and ideological dimensions of Orthodox renewal and Estonian post-Soviet "transition." Through sound, they struggle to sacralize and make integral a world at the frontiers of secularism, resurgent nationalist Orthodoxies, and geopolitical retrenchments. These struggles may intensify in the future as the religious and cultural significance of the Petseri monastery is lost on a younger generation, for whom traveling to the monastery is becoming increasingly difficult and less important. Demographic crisis and a decline in active Orthodox participation in Setomaa figure in as well, since the efficacy of this *akathist* from the Petseri monastery derives from Setos, Estonians, and Russians knowing this special melody and recognizing its meanings.

## CONCLUSION

The acoustics and geopolitics of Orthodoxy in Setomaa reveal how Eastern Christians respond to and transform their world musically. Beliefs and teachings about right singing are what make singing Orthodox, and differences in terms of musical style, oral and institutional traditions, vocal techniques, and approaches to language are what distinguish Eastern Christianity both internally and in relation to non-Orthodox Christianities. At the Church of St. Paraskeva in Saatse and the Church of St. George in Värska, singing makes parish communities whole and establishes sacred territory, all the while conforming to local understandings of Orthodox canonicity and echoing Russian Orthodox traditions that are global in scale (cf. Hann 2003: 231 for a comparative case in Poland). Through sound, Eastern Christians establish or create relationships with physical and metaphysical borders. These include geopolitical and jurisdictional borders between states, national churches, and patriarchates; symbolic borders between ethnolinguistic and cultural identities; borders between other Orthodox communities and alternative Christian traditions; borders between nationalist, imperial, and subaltern histories; and borders between different social and ethical norms.

From an anthropological perspective, understanding Eastern Christianity as sound is invaluable, because in sound, the ideological, experiential, and affective dimensions of Eastern Christianity merge; orthodoxy and orthopraxy sanction each other and together manifest an ultimate religious truth. Eastern Christianity as sound does not exist apart from the bodies and singing of believers and the temporal and social world of local parishes. At the same time, Orthodox practices in Setomaa show that the "Easternness" of Eastern Christianities is increasingly contested, deterritorialized, ideologically charged, and sensible through interactions across difference (Tsing 2005), no less so in the Estonian-Russian border region than in the Balkans, the Old Believer diaspora, or among converts in Western Europe and North America (not to mention the very different "Easternness" of the non-Chalcedonian churches). These interactions intensify the contingent nature of Orthodoxy in spaces of plurality, conflict, or secularity and the "awareness and recognition of the possibility of different or antagonistic beliefs" (Bourdieu 1977: 164) inherent in its concept of "right belief" and "right worship" or "right glory." The global soundscapes, imaginative dimensions, and ideological terrains of Orthodox Christianities come into being through untranslatable local practices that reiterate ever-migrating formations and ever-transforming expressions of Eastern Christianity. Attending to the acoustics of Eastern Christianity means attending to what is essential in Orthodox Christian worship, theology, and soteriology.

## NOTES

This chapter is based on fieldwork in Estonia and Russia (2002–2007) supported by a Fulbright-Hays Fellowship, a Charolotte W. Newcombe Fellowship from the Woodrow Wilson Foundation, and Amherst College. All translations and transcriptions are my own. Here I commemorate and thank Father August Kaljukosk and Nikolai Kõllamägi, two men whose service to the community of Saatse, wisdom, and kindness made a deep impression on me.

1. Seto is the ethnonym of the linguistically distinct, traditionally Orthodox Finno-Ugrians numbering approximately 3,600 and living in Setomaa, a territory that includes parts of extreme southeastern Estonia and the Pskov region of the Russian Federation. The total estimated population of Setos in Estonia is 10,000–13,000 (source: Setomaa Union of Rural Municipalities). Setomaa is also known as Petserimaa because of its historical connection to the religious, social, and economic hub of Petseri (Pechory). Except when quoting, I use Seto rather than Setu; the latter is an Estonian term with pejorative historical associations. Throughout this chapter I refer to the Estonian-Russian border region as Setomaa, with the understanding that others have different names for this area with different political and ideological meanings.

2. A *troparion* is a short hymn specific to a given date, feast, or saint.

3. Exceptions include the Ethiopic, Coptic, and Armenian traditions, in all of which some musical instruments are used.

4. In 1993, the Estonian state recognized the right of the OCE to church properties in Estonia based on its autonomy during the interwar period, effectively disenfranchising the churches subordinate to the Patriarchate of Moscow in Estonia. In 1996, the Patriarchate of Constantinople restored the autonomy of the OCE, thus invalidating its liquidation and subordination to the Patriarchate of Moscow in the 1940s (see Sõtšov 2002). In the wake of this dispute, the Patriarchate of Moscow took the extreme measure of suspending Eucharistic communion with the Patriarchate of Constantinople. Later in 1996, representatives from Moscow and Constantinople met in Zurich to discuss the situation, which was in violation of Orthodox canons concerning the exclusivity of patriarchal jurisdiction within a given country. The two patriarchates agreed to an "economy" (a concession to the exact letter of a church canon) that would allow individual congregations in Estonia to choose their patriarchal jurisdiction. This took place in 1996 and (with only a few exceptions) reified the ethnolinguistic and economic difference that exists in Estonia.

5. Seto activists refer to the Estonian-Russian border as a "line of control" to emphasize its contingency and contested nature. As of this writing, Estonia and Russia have yet to ratify a border treaty.

6. An *Obikhod* (from the Russian word for "common") is a collection of chant formulae and liturgical hymns. The Russian *Obikhod* currently in widespread use took shape through the work of Aleksey Fyodorovich L'vov (1798–1870) and others at the Imperial Capella in St. Petersburg in the nineteenth century. It is worth noting that L'vov was born in Tallinn (then Reval), the capital of the Russian imperial province of Estland. Strongly influenced by secular Italian and German styles, the L'vov *Obikhod* was published in 1848 and became the official service book for all Orthodox churches in the Russian empire (see von Gardner 1980: 110; Morosan 1994: 78–83).

7. *Stikhiry* derives from the Greek *stikhira* and means "verses."

8. The section epigraph is a Seto self-definition recorded in 1848 by the Estonian physician and folklorist Friedrich Reinhold Kreutzwald (1837–1917) (Kuutma 2005: 134). Here *maarahvas* (people of the country) is used to distinguish Setos from neighboring Baltic Germans and Russians. The same term was used by Estonians prior to the introduction of *eestlane* (Estonian) as an ethnonym in the middle of the nineteenth century.

9. I use the term "occupation" here to represent the ethnographic voices from my fieldwork who think and speak this way. There are, of course, other terms that Estonians use that make different ideological claims and carry different historical meanings—"Soviet period" (*nõukogude aeg*) or "Russian period" (*vene aeg*), for instance.

10. An *akathist* ("not sitting" in Greek) is a hymn honoring a saint (most notably the Theotokos), a person of the Holy Trinity, or a particular Orthodox feast (see Hann and Goltz, this volume). This *akathist* is in honor of the Virgin of Smolensk icon.

## REFERENCES

Asad, T. 2003. Formations of the secular: Christianity, Islam, modernity. Stanford: Stanford University Press.

Barz, G. 2003. *Performing religion: Negotiating past and present in Kwaya music of Tanzania.* Amsterdam: Rodopi.

———. 2005. Soundscapes of disaffection and spirituality in Tanzanian *Kwaya* music. *The World of Music* 47, no. 1: 5–30.

Bohlman, P. V. 1999. Ontologies of music. In *Rethinking music,* ed. N. Cook and M. Everist, 17–34. Oxford: Oxford University Press.

————. 2002. Ethnic identities/Religious identities: Toward an historiography of German-American sacred music. In *Land without nightingales: Music in the making of German-America*, ed. P. V. Bohlman and O. Holzapfel,127–58. Madison: University of Wisconsin-Madison.

Bourdieu, P. 1977. *Outline of a theory of practice*. Trans. R. Nice. Cambridge: Cambridge University Press.

Chow, M. M. 2006. Reflections on the musical diversity of Chinese churches in the United States. In *Music in American religious experience*, ed. P. V. Bohlman, E. Blumhofer, and M. Chow, 287–309. Oxford: Oxford University Press.

Engelhardt, J. 2005. Singing in "transition": Musical practices and ideologies of renewal in the Orthodox Church of Estonia. Ph.D. diss., University of Chicago.

————. Forthcoming. Right singing and conversion to Orthodox Christianity in Estonia. In *Conversion after socialism: Disruptions, modernities, and the technologies of faith*, ed. M. Pelkmans. Oxford: Berghahn.

Eskelinen, H., I. Liikanen, and J. Oksa. 1999. Introduction to *Curtains of iron and gold: Reconstructing borders and scales of interaction*, ed. H. Eskelinen, I. Liikanen, and J. Oksa, 1–8. Brookfield: Ashgate.

Garcia, M. A. 1998. Conversion religiosa y cambio cultural. *Latin AmericanMusic Review* 19, no. 2: 203–17.

Geraci, R. P., and M. Khodarkovsky, eds. 2001. *Of religion and empire: Missions, conversion, and tolerance in Tsarist Russia*. Ithaca, N.Y.: Cornell University Press.

Gray, C. 1995. Compositional techniques in Roman Catholic Church music in Uganda. *British Journal of Ethnomusicology* 4 : 135–54.

Hann, C. M. 2003. Creeds, cultures, and the "witchery of music." *The Journal of the Royal Anthropological Institute* 9, no. 2: 223–39.

Hirsch, F. 2005. *Empire of nations: Ethnographic knowledge and the making of the Soviet Union*. Ithaca, N.Y.: Cornell University Press.

Jääts, I. 1998. *Setude etniline identiteet* [The ethnic identity of the Setu]. Tartu: Tartu Ülikool.

Kaiser, R., and E. Nikiforova. 2006. Borderland spaces of identification and dis/location: Multiscalar narratives and enactments of Seto identity and place in the Estonian-Russian borderlands. *Ethnic and Racial Studies* 29, no. 5: 928–58.

Kaljukosk, A. 2003. Personal interview. June 2.

Kan, S. 1999. *Memory eternal: Tlingit culture and Russian Orthodox Christianity through two centuries*. Seattle: University of Washington Press.

Keane, W. 2007. *Christian moderns: Freedom and fetish in the mission encounter*. Berkeley: University of California Press.

Kivelson, V. A., and R. H. Greene, eds. 2003. *Orthodox Russia: Belief and practice under the Tsars*. University Park: Pennsylvania University Press.

Kuusing, K. 2005. Paraskeva pühastest ja reede kultusest Satserinna kiriklikus traditsioonis. In *Setumaa kogumik 3: Uurimusi Setumaa loodusest, ajaloost ja folkloristikast*, ed. M. Aun and Ü. Tamla, 238–81. Tallinn: Tallinna Ülikooli Ajaloo Instituut.

Kuutma, K. 2005. *Pärimuskultuurist kultuurisümboliks: Saami etnograafia ja seto eepose saamislugu* [Traditional culture as a cultural symbol: Sami ethnography and the story of the Seto epic]. Tartu: Eesti Kirjandusmuuseum.

————. 2006. *Collaborative representations: Interpreting the creation of a Sámi ethnography and a Seto epic.* Helsinki: Suomalainen Tiedeakatemia.

Lange, B. R. 2003. *Holy brotherhood: Romani music in a Hungarian Pentecostal church.* Oxford: Oxford University Press.

Lassiter, L. E. 2001. "From here on, I will be praying to you": Indian churches, Kiowa hymns, and Native American Christianity in southwestern Oklahoma. *Ethnomusicology* 45, no. 2: 338–52.

Lassiter, L. E., C. Ellis, and R. Kotay, eds. 2002. *The Jesus road: Kiowas, Christianity, and Indian hymns.* Lincoln: University of Nebraska Press.

Lind, T. T. 2003. *The past is always present: An ethnomusicological investigation of the musical tradition at Mount Athos.* Ph.D. diss., University of Copenhagen.

Lõuna, K. 2003. *Petserimaa: Petserimaa integreerimine Eesti vabariiki 1920–1940* [Petserimaa: The integration of Petserimaa in the Republic of Estonia 1920–1940]. Tallinn: Eesti Entsüklopeediakirjastus.

Mazo, M. 2006. Singing as an experience of American-Russian Molokans. In *Music in American religious experience,* ed. P. V. Bohlman, E. Blumhofer, and M. Chow, 83–119. Oxford: Oxford University Press.

Mendoza, Z. S. 2000. *Shaping society through dance: Mestizo ritual performance in the Peruvian Andes.* Chicago: University of Chicago Press.

Morosan, V. 1994. *Choral performance in pre-revolutionary Russia.* Madison, Conn.: Musica Russica.

Muller, C. A. 1999. *Rituals of fertility and the sacrifice of desire: Nazarite women's performance in South Africa.* Chicago: University of Chicago Press.

————. 2005. "Reading" the book, performing the words of *Izihlabelelo* zama Nazaretha. *The World of Music* 47, no. 1: 31–64.

Nikiforova, E. 2003. Contested borders and identity revival among Setos and Cossacks in the Estonian-Russian borderland. *Focaal: European Journal of Anthropology* 41: 71–82.

Palackal, J. J. 2004. Oktoēchos of the Syrian Orthodox churches in South India. *Ethnomusicology* 48, no. 2: 229–50.

Raag, N. 1938. Petserimaa kogudused [The parishes of Petserimaa]. *Usuteadusline Ajakiri* 1: 32–34.

Rappaport, R. A. 1999. *Ritual and religion in the making of humanity.* Cambridge: Cambridge University Press.

Rappoport, D. 2004. Ritual music and Christianization in the Toraja highlands, Sulawesi. *Ethnomusicology* 48, no. 3: 378–404.

Raun, T. U. 1991. The Petseri region of the Republic of Estonia. *Jahrbücher für Geschichte Osteuropas* 39, no. 4: 514–32.

Rausing, S. 2004. *History, memory, and identity in Post-Soviet Estonia: The end of a collective farm.* Oxford: Oxford University Press.

Reily, S. 2002. *Voices of the Magi: Enchanted journeys in Southeast Brazil.* Chicago: University of Chicago Press.

Romanowski, W. D. 2000. Evangelicals and popular music: The contemporary Christian music industry. In *Religion and popular culture in America,* ed. B. D. Forbes and J. H. Mahan, 103–22. Berkeley: University of California Press.

Rommen, T. 2002. Nationalism and the soul: Gospelypso as independence. *Black Music Research Journal* 22, no. 1: 37–64.

———. 2006. Protestant vibrations? Reggae, Rastafari, and conscious evangelicals. *Popular Music* 25, no. 2: 235–63.

———. 2007. *Mek some noise: Gospel music and the ethics of style in Trinidad.* Berkeley: University of California Press.

Scruggs, T. M. 2005. (Re)Indigenization? Post-Vatican II Catholic ritual and "folk masses" in Nicaragua. *The World of Music* 47, no. 1: 91–124.

Sherinian, Z. C. 2002. Dalit theology in Tamil Christian folk music: A transformative liturgy by James Theophilus Appavoo. In *Popular Christianity in India: Reading between the lines,* ed. S. J. Raj and C. G. Dempsey, 233–54. Albany: State University of New York Press.

———. 2005. The indigenization of Tamil Christian music: Musical style and liberation theology. *The World of Music* 47, no. 1: 125–65.

Shevzov, V. 2004. *Russian Orthodoxy on the eve of revolution.* Oxford: Oxford University Press.

Shils, E. 1981. *Tradition.* Chicago: University of Chicago Press.

Sõtšov, A. 2002. Achievement of and fight for independence of the Orthodox Church of Estonia in 1940–1945. In *The autonomous Orthodox Church of Estonia/L'Église autonome orthodoxe d'Estonie (Approche historique et nomocanonique),* ed. G. D. Papathomas and M. H. Palli, 285–305. Katérini: Editions Epekasis.

Spinney, A. M. 2006. Medeolinuwok, music, and missionaries in Maine. In *Music in American religious experience,* ed. P. V. Bohlman, E. Blumhofer, and M. Chow, 57–82. Oxford: Oxford University Press.

Stark, L. 2002. *Peasants, pilgrims, and sacred promises: Ritual and the supernatural in Karelian folk religion.* Helsinki: Finnish Literature Society.

Stefanus, Metropolitan of Tallinn and All Estonia. 2002. In time and in spite of time. In *The autonomous Orthodox Church of Estonia/L'Église autonome orthodoxe d'Estonie (Approche historique et nomocanonique),* ed. G. D. Papathomas and M. H. Palli, 35–39. Katérini: Editions Epektasis.

Stillman, A. K. 1993. Prelude to a comparative investigation of Protestant hymnody in Polynesia. *Yearbook for Traditional Music* 23: 89–99.

Stokes, M. 1998. Imagining "the south": Hybridity, heterotopias, and Arabesk on the Turkish-Syrian border. In *Border identities: Nation and state at international frontiers,* ed. T. M. Wilson and H. Donnan, 263–88. Cambridge: Cambridge University Press.

Stokoe, M. 1995. *Orthodox Christians in North America, 1794–1994.* Syosset, N.Y.: Orthodox Christian Publications Center.

Titon, J. T. 1988. *Powerhouse for God: Speech, chant, and song in an Appalachian Baptist church.* Austin: University of Texas Press.

Tsing, A. L. 2005. *Friction: An ethnography of global connection.* Princeton: Princeton University Press.

Vallier, J. B. 2003. Ethnomusicology as tool for the Christian missionary. *European Meetings in Ethnomusicology* 10: 85–97.

von Gardner, J. 1980. *Russian church singing*. Vol. 1, *Orthodox worship and hymnography*. Trans. V. Morosan. Crestwood, N.Y.: SVS.

———. 2000. *Russian church singing*. Vol. 2, *History from the origins to the mid-seventeenth century*. Trans. V. Morosan. Crestwood, N.Y.: SVS.

Werth, P. W. 2002. *At the margins of Orthodoxy: Mission, governance, and confessional politics in Russia's Volga-Kama region, 1827–1905*. Ithaca, N.Y.: Cornell University Press.

Znamenski, A. A. 1999. *Shamanism and Christianity: Native encounters with Russian Orthodox missions in Siberia and Alaska, 1820–1917*. Westport: Greenwood Press.

APPENDIX

EXAMPLE 4.1. First and fourth verses of one of the concluding prayers from the Paschal *stikhiry*.

EXAMPLE 4.1. *(continued)*

EXAMPLE 4.2. Concluding prayer from an *akathist* to the Theotokos sung at the Church of St. George in Värska.

ai - ta mind, kes a - bi - ta o - len.  Lõ - pe - ta mu kur-bus, na-gu Sa i - se pead,

sest pea - le Si - nu ei o - le mul teist a - bi-list,  teist hoid-jat ja nen-de tröö - sti - jat

kui Si - na, oh Ju-ma-la-e - ma.  Si - na hoi-ad ja kait-sed meid i - ga-ves-ti. Aa - men.

EXAMPLE 4.2. *(continued)*

# PART TWO

# Knowledge and Ritual

*Monasteries and the Renewal of Tradition*

# 5

# The Spirit and the Letter

## Monastic Education in a
## Romanian Orthodox Convent

### Alice Forbess

One striking aspect of my fieldwork in a Romanian convent was that, during all the time I spent in various monastic settings, rarely was any attempt made to teach me about God. This could perhaps be attributed to my Orthodox family background, which might have led the nuns to assume that I was already familiar with the faith. The fact that I had become a resident of the United Kingdom gave rise to concern that I might have lost the Orthodox faith. However, as I was sometimes told, it was expected that my prolonged exposure to the charisma-imbued physical space of the convent and the lives lived within it would effect a transformation from within. God, rather than individuals, would "convert" me.

An encounter during a visit to another monastery was also instructive. An elderly monk from P, a remote mountain monastery whose monks were reputed to have exceptional charisma, had begun telling me about God when I spontaneously interrupted him with a recollection of a dream I had had the night before, involving exactly the imagery he had just invoked: fish in an aquarium. Upon hearing it, the monk exclaimed: "Well! Then God's charisma [*harul domnului*] is already at work in you—no need to tell you about it in words that are imperfect!" After this incident the monks began allowing me freely to witness the more informal sides of their lives. The assumption was that being guided by charisma, I would not be misled by their idiosyncrasies.

This chapter examines how religious knowledge is produced and transmitted in the context of Orthodox monastic lives in contemporary Romania. It considers the use, by novices and those who train them, of notions of mysticism and charisma, in both discourse and practice, with particular reference to the use of texts. Cliché characterizations of Orthodoxy commonly emphasize a contemplative and mystical outlook. Such representations are not limited to Western observers. Orthodox theologians themselves speak of mysticism as the faith's central defining characteristic. For instance, a Romanian dictionary of theology (Bria 1981) defines two kinds of theological knowledge: (1) an inferior form referred to as negative (*cataphatic*) knowledge, which is intellectual and mediated through discourse, symbols, or images, and (2) a superior form called positive (*apophatic*) knowledge, which is nondiscursive, intuitive, direct, and possible only through the intervention of divine charisma. A theological textbook (Savin 1996) defines mysticism as the "highest" form of knowledge, inherent in the symbolic hidden sense of ritual actions and in the allegorical exegetical sense of scriptures. The term can be traced etymologically to the Greek μυστικός (*mystikos*), which in its pre-Christian usage referred to initiation cults. I. G. Savin suggests in the textbook that the word was borrowed from the writings of Plotinus (a philosopher much admired by Orthodox theologians), but stresses that in its Christian usage it came to imply the intervention of charisma, a connotation absent from its pagan meaning.[1] If mysticism is understood as a form of knowledge, divine charisma (Romanian: *har, harisma*)[2] is seen as the active principle that makes this knowledge possible. Often spoken of as an "energy" (*energie*), charisma is expected to transform those it enters in both a physical and a spiritual sense. Monks frequently acquire charismatic reputations as a result of unusual displays of intuition, mind reading, prophetic statements, and the perceived efficacy of their prayers. Having "graduated" to a higher stage in monastic life, such monks tend to be elderly, to live as hermits, and may practice stricter ascetic disciplines, such as a vow of silence.

A full discussion of charisma and related notions in light of the wealth of anthropological work on the topic would be beyond the scope of this chapter. Here I focus on the specific Romanian concept rather than the analytical term, and do so in a context of routinized charisma. Although most anthropological studies have concentrated on "pure" forms of charismatic activity (prophets, new religious movements), M. Engelke (2006: 68) is right to remind us that "charisma and routinisation are always present in one another" and that charisma is not incompatible with stable patterns for the transmission of religious knowledge (cf. Worsley 1968). Max Weber (1963: 47) opposed prophets to priests. The former are a source of creativity and innovation; the latter of stability, special knowledge, and fixed doctrines. This opposition contains the germ of Harvey Whitehouse's (1995) contrasting modes of religiosity. My argument will be that such dichotomies need to be reconsidered in the light of the role of charisma in monastic vocations.[3]

Fenella Cannell (2006: 39) suggests that Christians are preoccupied with salvation and share a feeling that God's "withdrawal" has left man in "a state of incompleteness that can be resolved only at death." The monastics I knew, however, were more concerned with *îndumnezeirea* (divinization)—the feat of becoming God-like while still in the flesh, as the saints are thought to have done. Holy relics, possessed by almost every monastery and convent, are considered the ultimate proof that *îndumnezeirea* is a real possibility. Thus Orthodox monks and nuns are less keenly afflicted by the "unhappy consciousness" of God's withdrawal, which in other forms of Christianity has resulted in a keen sense of the irreconcilable divergence of spirit and matter. Whereas the opposition between spirit (God's substance) and sinful flesh (aimed at reducing the flesh's demands upon the spirit) provides the impetus for self-mortification in many of the Western Christian traditions, this impetus is lacking in the Orthodox practices I witnessed. In the minds of these monastics, God has not retreated in transcendence but is very much capable of immanence. Charisma is the medium through which this occurs.

## MYSTICISM IN THE ROMANIAN
## SOCIOPOLITICAL CONTEXT

In the first half of the twentieth century, the theme of mysticism became so popular in Romania that it was appropriated by mainstream political discourse and portrayed as a central element of national identity. A group of intellectuals known as the "Orthodoxists" argued that the essence of the national soul was mystical (see Verdery 1991). Nae Ionescu, the mentor of Mircea Eliade, for example, argued that Western political and economic institutions were incompatible with the Romanian soul, which was essentially Orthodox. In Ionescu's view, to the "divisive" rationality of the Western Enlightenment, the Orthodox East opposed a "mystical synthesis," exemplified in the ideal of the union of church and state. In his programmatic early writings the young Eliade also saw mysticism as central to the unique "spiritual itinerary" of his generation, which he defined as the "actualization of religious reality inherent in true Orthodoxy" (Eliade 1992: 51; my translation). Later, some of the Orthodoxists developed fascist sympathies, and the idea of mysticism as a political platform was discredited.

The collapse of socialism was accompanied by an intense revival of popular interest in spirituality, and mysticism came to be seen once again as the "authentic" face of Romanian Orthodoxy (see Naumescu, this volume, for discussion of a similar process in the Ukraine). Cheap editions of texts by and about Orthodox mystics filled sidewalk book stands, and thousands of pilgrims began seeking out monks reputed to have charismatic powers. In particular, a form of contemplation called the *hesychast* prayer (or the prayer of the heart) emerged as a symbol of Orthodox spirituality.[4] The word *hesychast* (Romanian: *isihast*) derives from the Greek *hesychia* (ἡσυχία), meaning "stillness, rest, silence." Several of the novices at my convent and many pilgrims I interviewed said they had been attracted to monastic life by the *hesychast* and mystical vogue.

The themes popularized by the Orthodoxists—the critique of modernization and technology, the totalizing opposition of Eastern and Western forms of spirituality and thought, the influence of mystical theologians, and a visionary faith in Orthodoxy's potential for fostering a different kind of relationship between man and the world, thereby providing a genuine alternative to Western hegemony— might seem familiar to those acquainted with the Neo-Orthodox movement in Greece (see, e.g., Herzfeld 2002). Romania even had its own Heideggerian philosopher in Constantin Noica, who, like Christos Yannaras (1973, 1984), explored the points of rapprochement between a Romanian tradition of thought drawing on Orthodoxy and the Western phenomenological tradition that culminated in Heidegger. Noica almost outlived Nicolae Ceauşescu, and although he was a philosopher rather than a theologian, his ascetic lifestyle, in a small whitewashed cell in the mountains, caused him to become an underground symbol of Romanian spirituality.[5]

Given such precedents, one might have expected these mystical currents to flourish once more in the turbulent conditions of postsocialist political and economic change. This has not happened, however, and Greek Neo-Orthodoxy has had little impact in Romania to date.[6] The Romanian Orthodox Church has found itself in a relatively weak position vis-à-vis both the state and large sections of society, because of accusations of collaboration with the communist regime. It is far less self-confident and assertive than its Greek counterpart (see, e.g., Stewart 1998) in its relations with both the political establishment and the faithful. Attempts to exercise political influence have been largely unsuccessful,[7] and although the church viewed the European accession with suspicion and opposed changes such as the legalization of homosexuality, it has been remarkably restrained in its expression of these views. Unlike Serbia, Greece, and Russia, in Romania Orthodox sentiments did not, generally, translate into a militant anti-Western stance. At the time of my research, both believers and monastics, including senior clerics I interviewed informally, had remarkably positive views of the West and actively sought opportunities to travel abroad and acquaint themselves with all things Western. Thus, although Romanian Orthodox monasteries did, for many, become sites of reenchantment, away from the pitfalls of modern life, as well as markers of a version of authentic "Romanianness," monastics were also instrumental in expanding church organization and contacts abroad.

## CHRISTIANITIES AND THE TRANSMISSION OF RELIGIOUS KNOWLEDGE

This chapter draws on two principal strands of the vast anthropological literature concerning religious knowledge and its transmission. The first focuses on the role of religious knowledge in processes of cultural transmission and transformation.

With respect to this topic, in addition to the work of Whitehouse (1992, 1995), Fredrik Barth's article "The Guru and the Conjurer" (1990) is particularly interesting. Barth argues that religious knowledge is transacted according to the culturally specific rules that guide transactions of valuables in a given society, and links these transactions to the form and transmissibility of this knowledge itself. While the Melanesian conjurer seeks to obstruct access to his knowledge, a valuable that should be traded only "upwards" with the ancestors in exchange for health and fertility, the knowledge of the South Asian Muslim "guru" increases in value the more it is taught to others, resulting in a verbalized, abstract, and logically integrated body of knowledge. The second strand focuses on the historical transformation of religious knowledge following the introduction of new methods and techniques of codification and transmission (e.g., Eickelman 1992; Goody 1968, 1986; Olson 1977; Ong 1982). In response to "universalist" arguments, such as Goody's (1986) literacy thesis, critics have pointed out that "technological potential never explains the uses to which a technology is put" (Bloch 1998: 69). As with the first strand, culturally specific assumptions regarding knowledge and its uses determine or at least influence the socioreligious outcomes (cf. Kulik and Stroud 1990).

Anthropological studies of Christianity have so far tended to fall into two discrete areas, each with a rather separate research agenda. Work carried out in traditionally Christian settings and dealing with forms of Christianity more or less similar to "our own" has explored themes such as religious revival, inter- and intrachurch politics, religious practice and subjectivities, and syncretism and the construction of authenticity. Meanwhile, the second body of work has concentrated on Christianity's contribution to cultural transformation in non-Western settings, and on its links with modernity and modernization, including the rise of imagined national communities. The fall of socialism has created unique situations where both kinds of Christianity expertise are required—as, for instance, in the case described by Catherine Wanner (2003) of a rapidly expanding Evangelical church founded by a Nigerian pastor in traditionally Orthodox and white Ukraine. In today's "globalized" world, this separation between Christianity "at home" and "abroad" has become increasingly untenable.

"Christians," Joel Robbins (2003b: 192) has pointed out, "almost wherever they are, appear at once too similar to anthropologists to be worthy of study and too meaningfully different to be easily made sense of by the use of standard anthropological tools." They are too similar "by virtue of drawing on the same broad cultural tradition as anthropologists," and too different because they draw on a part of that tradition that "has arisen in critical dialogue with the modernist ideas on which anthropology is founded." Christians thus are at once continuous and discontinuous with the heritage of Western social science research. Both continuity and similarity constitute problems researchers of Christianity must address, albeit perhaps for those concerned with postcolonial settings continuity is the more obvious problem (see Robbins 2003a), while for those working "at home," a tendency, on the part of both ourselves and our audience, to assume the similarity of different types of Christianity poses greater problems in terms of communicating what is distinctive, unique, and characteristic about the specific object of one's study. This chapter attempts to circumvent these difficulties by seeking a balance: while focusing on how and why Romanian Orthodox monastics see themselves as distinctive, I also consider possible platforms for making similarity judgments. It is in this context that I turn to the work of Whitehouse (1995), which also provides an opportunity to engage across the two branches of Christianity studies.

In defining his modes of religiosity, Whitehouse takes as a starting point the role of technologies of codification and transmission in cultural change. He argues that Goody (1968, 1986) was right in distinguishing between two types of religious knowledge, but wrong to do so in terms of dependence on texts versus dependence on memory. Shifting the focus from technologies of codification (i.e., literacy) to cognition, Whitehouse argues that the really crucial distinction is made in the codification of religious knowledge into different types of memory—either "autobiographical" or "semantic." The knowledge encoded in autobiographical or "flashbulb" memory tends to be of a highly subjective kind, incorporating information that is difficult to verbalize because it integrates multisensory data linked with individual experiences. When confronted with a unique new experience we do not fully understand, we tend to store everything about it in our memory. This corresponds to the "analogic" mode of religiosity, in which the "persuasiveness of religious insights derives from an intense but confusing experience of partial recognition and mystery" (Whitehouse 1992: 781). By contrast, experiences we have routinely are not stored in such detail, but rather assimilated to a general schema of what should happen. Such knowledge is stored in long-term "semantic memory." It is easily verbalized, logically integrated, abstract, and general, leading to what Whitehouse terms the "doctrinal" mode of religiosity, which is "more deeply rooted in a sense of logical comprehension and intellectual revelation" (781).

Thus if the codification of religious knowledge and experience takes place primarily in the doctrinal mode, transmission of the message to believers must be frequent, and this leads to routinization. In this case, recall, rather than personal or autobiographical experiences, would bring to mind these general cultural schemas. Whitehouse argues that this "impersonal" doctrinal mode of encoding religious knowledge creates a "universalistic orientation," making it possible for people to imagine abstract national communities, for instance. It cultivates logical coherence, uniformity, disciplined behavior as a moral virtue, revelation through

intellectual persuasion, widespread dissemination, and doctrinal rigidity. The analogic mode is dichotomously opposed in all these respects. It is predominantly
nonverbal, emotional, and sensual rather than intellectual. It encodes "shocks,"
unique personal experiences (including intense religious revelations), producing
unique schemas and promoting a departure from normal routines and constraints.
Transmission is infrequent, and knowledge does not travel well, as the case of the
Baktaman shaman described by Barth (1975) demonstrates. Religious groups
worshipping in this mode tend to be small and localized, radically innovative,
resistant to organization, and prone to disintegration (Whitehouse 1995).

Whitehouse (1995, 1998) does not claim the two modes correspond to oral
and literate societies; in fact, he claims both modes existed within the Pomio
Kivung movement of Papua New Guinea, the subject of his field research. Yet he
does establish a clear link between modes of religiosity and the successful transmission and reproduction of religious knowledge. The analogic mode is characteristic of unstable "splinter movements," while the doctrinal mode defines the
enduring mainstream. Linguistic expression and logical elaboration are, in this
sense, privileged. While the analogic mode is assigned to limited, ephemeral, and
unstable movements, the predominantly linguistic doctrinal mode is "superior"
in terms of its stability, routinization, and universal appeal. In the light of this
reasoning, it would be odd for a form of Christianity with a well-developed doctrine and institutional structure to fall within the analogic mode.

Nevertheless, I will argue that the Orthodox Christians discussed here belong
to this category. Like the Baktaman (Barth 1975), they prefer an analogic style of
religiosity, which places mystery at its center and values a knowledge that is by
definition impossible to verbalize. Yet, like the mainstream Pomio Kivung
(Whitehouse 1995, 1998), these Orthodox Christians rely on written texts, institutional organization, routinized practices, and a church monopoly on religious
knowledge. They claim that true religious knowledge is mystical and nonverbal,
and yet training takes place in an institutionalized, literate environment. Engelke's
(2006) work on a group of Zimbabwean Apostolics reveals similar attitudes toward
different types of knowledge. Although fully acquainted with the biblical text, they
distrust it and prefer to receive their Christian message "live and direct" through
their prophet/preachers. In this postcolonial instance of a group of believers who
choose an analogic style, even though the doctrinal style is fully within their grasp,
as among Orthodox Christians "at home," charisma and its associated ambiguities
play a key role. Texts are the cornerstone of the doctrinal mode of religiosity, but
these two groups' distrust of textual sources as vehicles for meaning (on the
assumption that their "true" meaning is either hidden or corrupted) points to the
need to problematize and investigate notions of clarity and meaning, rather than
to assume their universality (Engelke 2006: 64).

## A NUN'S EDUCATION

Orthodox monastic structures differ from Catholic monasticism in several aspects. First, the Orthodox churches have no monastic orders as such, but rather monasteries with their own Typikon (Book of Rules), which are tightly integrated into the church hierarchy under the authority of their respective bishops. Second, nonmonastic priests are ineligible for higher clerical positions because they are required to marry prior to ordination. Since monasteries do not perform life-cycle rituals for the laity and leave such matters entirely to parish priests, situations of acute competition and conflict such as those described by Mart Bax (1983, 1995) in Catholic Brabant and Bosnia are far less common. At the same time monasteries are in a very real sense the training ground for all clergy. Although nuns are not able to take up appointments that require ordination, my fieldwork suggested that they can and do exercise a substantial degree of behind-the-scenes influence within the church, particularly as abbesses of important convents or secretaries to higher clergy. Monks are much more likely to acquire individual renown for their charismatic powers, partly because of the role they play as confessors, as I shall explain later. Few nuns acquire individual reputations, but convent collectives do, from time to time, gain spiritual renown.

This chapter is based mainly on fieldwork carried out in the convent of Zoreni,[8] but it is also informed by data gathered during shorter stays at another convent and at a monastery. The picture of monastic training offered here is not comprehensive, nor is it necessarily typical. What I hope to achieve by using this particular case is to pinpoint some of the dilemmas and contingencies that affect how knowledge is valued and transmitted in monastic settings, with special reference to notions of mysticism. I explore how ideas about charisma and mystical knowledge are inserted in the context of everyday interactions in convent life, the key encounters or situations in which nuns acquire religious knowledge, the nature of this knowledge, and how it changes.

Zoreni is a convent with sixty nuns, located only a three-hour drive from Bucharest. Its relative proximity to the capital, and the convent's renown as an architectural monument on the UNESCO World Heritage list, make it a popular destination for visitors, including prominent members of the political elite. During socialism the convent continued to function, albeit with reduced personnel because recruitment was almost impossible.[9] Apart from ten nuns, who were employed by the state as keepers of the historical monument, all nuns between the ages of eighteen and fifty-five were expelled in the early 1960s. In the 1990s many novices were admitted, and several of the expelled nuns returned to live their final years at the convent. However, the consequences of the twenty-year recruitment gap remained visible: most nuns were either very young or elderly, and the few in between were too busy with administrative tasks to be able to

sponsor and train the novices. This meant that the traditional system of apprenticeship, in which each novice was overseen and trained by a senior sponsor, could
not be revived in the 1990s. During my stay at the convent, intergenerational
communication was very limited, and most younger nuns showed little interest
in the experiences of older ones.

One of the first things that struck me was the superficiality of most nuns'
knowledge of the history and traditions of the convent. The fortresslike compound
with thick, tall walls and high, iron-clad gates impressed the visitor with its medieval atmosphere, and yet almost none of the nuns knew what had happened there
before the 1950s. Even the nun who acted as a historical guide to visitors knew
only the "official account" of the convent's early history and could say very little
about life there in the nineteenth and early twentieth centuries.[10] As I researched
the convent's history it became apparent that such discontinuities were not unusual
and that its two-hundred-year history had seen at least four radical changes
of population.

Mother Eftimia had been a nun at Zoreni for eighty years (having been given
by her parents "as a gift to the convent" at the age of two), and she was able to tell
me how monastic training had changed during her lifetime. Most of the nuns of
her generation had joined as children, often war orphans. She was brought up in
a family-like "household" of nuns, who were actually her maternal aunts. At the
beginning of the twentieth century, such households (seldom, in fact, related by
blood) were the norm, but soon after Eftimia arrived, community life became
more strictly regulated. The system of apprenticeship fostered close relations
between old and young nuns, producing continuity and integrating the community across generations. However, Eftimia also remembers her convent childhood
as surprisingly lonely and deprived of warmth:

> I would sit alone on the stairs, rocking back and forth and singing to myself "God
> have mercy on me," as I heard them do in church. . . . When I was old enough for
> school, they sent me to Braga convent (fifteen kilometers away), where nuns ran an
> orphanage. The children all had lice, and the nuns would wash us with cold water,
> in an unheated hallway, even in the winter. When I got an eye ailment, I came back
> to Zoreni. I continued to teach myself, by reading from the papers left by the Greek
> monks [in the convent's archive]. Later, they appointed me as the visitors' historical
> guide, and I was the only one who knew what was in those documents.

It seems Eftimia's aunts gave her relatively little verbal instruction regarding the
vocation of a nun. She thought it would not have occurred to them that this was
necessary. She learned by example. The education of her generation stressed discipline through work rather than verbal teaching. When she was a teenager, the
convent had an abbess who sought to impose absolute equality upon the nuns and
saw education as a threat to this goal. Consequently, she turned away would-be

novices who were educated, and stressed obedience to the rules as a leveling device. Nuns were regularly assigned tasks, closely monitored, and required to wear special "obedience costumes" with cylindrical woolen hats pulled tightly over head scarves, long-sleeved woolen tunics, and long skirts—even when working in the fields in the hot summer months. Stories about this time stressed that life was labor-intensive and exhausting. The emphasis of this monastic training was neither on a theological education nor on ascetic practices,[11] but rather on obedience through the performance of physical work.

Like Eftimia in her time, novices today receive little verbal instruction but are expected to pick up knowledge by participating in ritual and working life; private reading and prayer are left largely to the individual. Here one sees a clear continuity with early monasticism, where obedience was always fundamental to the order. The dominant means of teaching discipline or obedience is work. Although the convent does not depend on this work for its income (which combines state funds, donations, and revenues from running a hotel for the convent's guests), maintenance tasks had to be performed, and their assignment was a key source of tension. Nuns objected forcefully to being assigned the same task (such as serving food or attending to guests) indefinitely. They complained of the monotonous, repetitive, and unexciting nature of such work, which left them little time for prayer and meditation. As Sister Vera put it, "For the first few years, convent life is beautiful, but then you start to realize that you will be doing the same thing, like a robot, year after year. Then it hits you that you will never ever leave here." The resurgence of popular literature on Orthodox mysticism, and the visibility of charismatic monks, whose books and audiotapes are widely available, had led many of Zoreni's new recruits to expect that monastic life would center on mystical revelations and extraordinary experiences of the analogic mode type (see also Naumescu, this volume). Younger nuns felt disappointed by the routinized reality. "We are just unpaid labor," Vera once exclaimed; but elder nuns decried the novices' disobedience and habits of indulging in "too much food and laziness." Mother Marcia, the convent's administrator, sometimes hired help from the village, because she was afraid that if she made the novices work too hard they would all leave.

Relations between elders and novices occasionally became very strained—for example, when accusations of sorcery were made against an unpopular elderly nun. An outbreak of demonic possession that had taken place five years prior to my arrival was only rarely and guardedly mentioned. During a religious service five novices had suddenly started cursing and grunting like pigs. They had been forcibly restrained and carried off to one of the convent's hermitages, where they were kept in isolation. They had calmed down but relapsed whenever they heard the name of the Virgin Mary (the archetypal image of the nuns) or saw holy objects. One had managed to escape and jumped into a well, but she had been rescued before drowning. She had later blamed Mother Marcia, saying it was fear of her overbearing personality that had made her attempt suicide. The nuns had sought help from the monk-priests of a monastery famed for its charismatic powers, who performed two exorcisms before the problem subsided (for a discussion of exorcism, see Naumescu, this volume).[12] The incident was attributed to various causes. Some novices had blamed the black magic of an elderly nun, while others blamed Mother Marcia. Whatever the explanation, the novices clearly saw their relations with their elders as the cause of the disturbance. The nun relating the story interpreted the possession (with the benefit of hindsight) as a protest against the rules of convent life.

Generally, novices were not encouraged to excel in intellectual or artistic pursuits. A few had hobbies such as painting icons, learning church music notation, or reading theology and philosophy. These activities were facilitated by the convent's leaders, but an excessive attachment to these pursuits was condemned as indicative of the sin of pride. Since pride was the cause of Satan's fall from grace, such attachment was considered exceedingly serious. Thus the novice who was the most skilled at musical improvisation stopped singing altogether after being admonished that her skill had become a cause of rivalry. Another novice, Sister Raluca, was told to give up reading theological books because she had become too attached to them. A daughter of academic parents and herself possessing an MA in economics, she felt that convent life was far from intellectually challenging and bought religious books whenever she could. On one occasion she and another nun wanted the same book, and she was unable to give in. Witnessing her inner conflict, the priest who was selling the book advised her to give up reading books altogether. She obeyed, saying that she felt his advice showed an intuitive insight into her mind and must therefore be right (the implication being that this was a charismatic insight). All these seemingly local stories are archetypal for early Oriental monasticism, beginning with the first Egyptian and Palestinian monasteries. The danger of pride was also invoked by convent leaders and confessors when they warned nuns not to take ascetic practices too far, and not to confess too often (confession, I was told, should take place at most once a month, and ideally only a few times a year). As one renowned monk put it, "I think a constant wakefulness or self-awareness [is] more important [than *nevoinţele,* ascetic practices]: *do what your conscience tells you, not what reason says*" (Papacioc 1994; emphasis added). This distrust of reason was a recurring motif. The nuns read the work of a Greek theologian who argued that the Enlightenment, with its claim of the infallibility of reason, was the brainchild of a Masonic elite. Within the Romanian Orthodox Church there is a current of opinion that condemns education as a vain quest fueled by pride.[13] The desire to excel through one's own abilities, even if the activities are entirely innocent, was thought to contain the germs of hubris, excess, and danger.[14]

Given their dissatisfaction with convent life, why did the novices nonetheless take their vows and turn convent life into a positive experience? The routine disappointed them because it often seemed to lack the charismatic and miraculous character that they had read about in books or experienced during visits to other monasteries. However, charismatic knowledge was not just a myth for them. It had real effects on their lives, because it caused them to expect profound, analogic-style experiences, and to actively search for these. An important part of learning how to become a nun was to find and cultivate sources of charismatic knowledge and power in one's own life. For a novice, one such source was reading the lives of saints, and another her relationship to a confessor who shared her assumptions regarding mystical knowledge.

Prayers to each day's patron saints, and accounts of their lives, written in archaic language that made them sound particularly poignant, formed a prominent part of the evening service (*vecernia*). At Zoreni this service began with about an hour of prayers and psalms, read in a singsong voice by one or two nuns, and gradually built up momentum as more nuns joined in. The nuns were organized around two singing stations (*strane*) located opposite one another at either side of the altar. The audience, mostly elderly nuns, listened, kneeling or sitting, often peering up at the walls, which are painted throughout with scenes from the scriptures and images of the major saints. Occasionally they would perambulate in the church, bowing and kissing the icons and relics. The service culminated in the late evening when the nuns converged upon the icon of the Holy Virgin—their protectress—to whom they addressed a very moving hymn. The ambience of such rituals is reminiscent of a theatrical performance. In the words of Kain Hart (1992: 121), "The church, with performative roots located in the Roman imperial ceremony, intends to be an exemplary center, or metaphysical theatre, designed to express the ultimate nature of reality and at the same time shape the existing conditions of life to be consonant with that reality." The *vecernia* always had an intimate quality (outsiders were rarely present), and one felt a blurring of the distinctions between supernatural beings and human beings. Being remembered, discussed, and addressed directly, the Virgin and saints became an immanent, tangible presence.

Readings from the lives of saints had also been a key source of verbal instruction for Eftimia and her cohort. For the elder nuns these stories had helped to naturalize their vocation and to provide the means to imagine an outside world that they would never experience. In conversation, Eftimia frequently cited these stories, for instance, explaining the conflict in the Middle East in terms of a topography made memorable by incidents from various saints' lives, or recalling how she urged a group of Communist Party cadres to emulate a saint who had abandoned his great kingdom to join a monastery.[15] For her, the lives of saints provided precedents for moral decisions and suggested solutions to everyday dilemmas. For instance, when a neighbor came to the convent to ask what to do about her daughter's incestuous dreams, the advice she received was expressed in terms of saints' lives: the nuns gave her a book about Saint Marina, and Mother Eftimia illustrated her advice with the story of Saints Justine and Cyprian. Younger nuns were similarly interested in the lives of saints. For some of them the stories of saints highlighted the romantic, extraordinary potential of an otherwise rather drab way of life—such as, for instance, in the case of the often-told story of a beautiful young nun who was kidnapped and sequestered by a communist who had fallen in love with her; eventually she prevailed and converted him.

The relationship between nuns and saints was one of mimesis: the saints illustrated what the nuns aspired to become, and provided reassurance that all their suffering would not be in vain. The idea of aspiring to or identifying with an archetype was a familiar one to the nuns. They often spoke of their church "face" or persona as being that of an angel. This was the "essence" they were striving toward. Their position within the church hierarchy was homologous to that of angels within the greater divine hierarchy.[16] Whenever they were assailed by doubts, confusion, and disillusionment regarding convent life, these texts validated their experiences and restored belief in their chosen vocation. In contrast with the interest lavished upon saints, sermons at Zoreni were kept to a minimum. The abbess used to read brief (fifteen-minute) texts written in archaic language, formulaic and remote.

I was told that I would not be able fully to understand the experiences of nuns because, by having left the world, they had become extraordinary people, and their lives extraordinary projects, outside normal human experience. The saints were their exemplars. As in the Mongolian case described by Caroline Humphrey (1997), the focus of personal ethics resided not in a set of rules but rather in the relations between humans and cultural heroes from whose lives guidance was to be taken when making ethical decisions. Whereas Western Europeans tend to think of morality as rule centered, with rules consistently applicable to all members of a designated category, the ethics of exemplars constructs a different kind of individuality. Exemplars "can be used to support a variety of 'right' ways of life, rather than a single one" (Humphrey 1997: 34). A person can choose which exemplars to emulate, and ponder the meaning of these personally. I suggest that the lives of saints worked for the nuns in a similar way.

The lives of saints are used here very differently than doctrinal texts, which emphasize clarity, logical integration, and intellectual revelation. These texts are effective precisely because they are ambiguous, multivocal, and pliable. Elaboration may be essential in missionary situations, or wherever there is strenuous competition in the religious field, making it necessary to present the Christian message in a coherent and doctrinally clear form, but this is not the case in Romania, where the church has a dominant position and engages in almost no missionary work.

This situation may change with the influx of missionaries from the West, and I have heard of some Orthodox priests developing a more Protestant preaching style. However, my experience in the convent was that logically integrated, intellectual knowledge was devalued in favor of mystical knowledge, which was by definition nonverbal. It was considered dangerous even to try to verbalize it, lest one fall into the sin of pride.

## CONFESSORS AND THE DEVALUATION
## OF VERBAL KNOWLEDGE

The lives and training of the nuns who entered the convent before socialism were mainly influenced by relations with women, whether their spiritual sponsors, members of their cohort, or the novices they themselves adopted. Closeness between individual nuns and the convent's confessor was condemned. However, the novices who joined in the 1990s relied heavily for spiritual advice and support on the confessors they had had prior to entering the convent. These relationships compensated both for the gap between the realities of the convent and their expectations, and for the lack of senior nuns capable of training apprentices. This was particularly the case at Zoreni, where the resident confessor was disliked by many of the nuns (they said he had a stutter and a bad temper).

Many of the novices were inspired to enter the convent by the spiritual relationships they had developed with their confessors, usually elderly monks. The same was true for many of the nuns of the previous generation, now the convent's leaders. The confessor had been the first to interpret, on the basis of his intuition, the signs of a genuine monastic calling. This had usually started as a depression, which developed into a "madness for Christ," a deeply personal, "analogic-mode" experience. Arsenie Papacioc, a well-known charismatic monk, describes it as follows (1994):

> If it is a calling and a madness for Christ, where do you go? What does a convent mean? A losing of yourself in order to find yourself, a final transformation, to give up your position, your human personality for the angelic one, giving up your will.[17]

The charismas, or gifts, received by the apostles at Pentecost (*harismele*), including *duhovnicia,* the gift of the confessor, were thought to have been transmitted within the church in an unbroken line, through ordination. Nuns could confess only to monks who had been ordained as confessors, from which they themselves were disqualified. This link between charisma and office was in tension with the more popular understanding of charisma as an energy (*har*) that can enter anyone, layman or monastic, depending on God's will (for instance, in the 1920s several peasant "prophets" attracted huge followings; they were never repudiated by the church). The nuns did not explicitly distinguish between these different types of charisma; the charisma of office was not considered less powerful than that based on merit or reputation, and it continued to work even if the priest behaved in immoral ways.

A good confessor was very difficult to find. It took many visits and an outstanding show of commitment for Sister Elena, while she was a theology student, to persuade her confessor, a senior cleric at the Metropolitan See, to accept her. This was partly because the best confessors were in great demand, and partly because they did not grant absolution until, after many sessions of confession, they had satisfied themselves that the confession was complete and there was a genuine commitment to change. Confessors stressed that they were invested with great power and responsibility, combining two contradictory roles: that of judge, standing in for God, and that of scapegoat, who took upon himself all the sins of those he absolved. As a judge, the confessor's power to absolve was absolute: "I want the one who comes to me to truly see the unlimited power of the confessor." However, exercise of this power could be dangerous: "We kill as many souls as we allow to condemn themselves." The danger resided in the transfer of all sins, both confessed and unconfessed, to the confessor once absolution had been granted. Hence the confessor's art lay in his ability to convince the sinner that "the sin must be told with its taste and its essence; it must be deeply felt" (Papacioc 1994).

The gift of confession (*duhovnicia*) depended on following the spirit rather than the letter of the rule. Respected confessors played down rules in favor of intuition and an individually tailored approach. Following rules would often have entailed harsh penances and a focus on sin, but confessors preferred to use their discretion and to nurture a long-term relationship reminiscent of psychotherapy. The close conceptual link between charisma and intuitive understanding was the basis of their approach. Strict adherence to rules and rigorous penance was deemphasized in favor of the "spirit of the task": "I am not partial to form [*tipic*] but I preach a state of continual self-awareness, of presence, of living in the moment" (Papacioc 1994).[18]

I underwent one such confession session with the confessor of Sister Elena, a senior cleric whose job included settling monastic disputes and hearing the confessions of nuns in the Metropolitanate. First, I was asked to read a formulaic confession from a brochure printed for nuns, which acknowledged an entire range of sins, including seeing oneself naked and having fantasies in the altar enclosure. After this, the priest read a prayer over my head and then for over an hour we discussed my life in a relaxed fashion, focusing on key relationships and events. Sins were never mentioned, and the discussion reminded me strongly of the psychotherapy techniques I had encountered in courses for a behavioral science degree. I do not mean to draw a parallel with psychoanalysis here (his approach lacked the past-centeredness and unrelentingly investigative character of the psychoanalytical approach), but this confessor did use a range of techniques well known to Western therapists: empathetic listening, sensitive probing for areas of conflict and for the possibility of closure, prompting remarks, recapitulations, and so forth. When he finished he said that many more sessions would be necessary before absolution could be given.

Foucault has argued that Christianity occupied a crucial position in the creation of the modern self, making possible a form of interiority that foreshadowed and enabled the growth of modern psychological and psychoanalytical regimes:

> Each person has the duty to know who he is, that is, to try to know what is happening inside him, to acknowledge faults, to recognise temptations, to locate desires; and everyone is obliged to disclose these things either to God or to others in the community and hence, to bear public or private witness against oneself. The truth obligations of faith and the self are linked together. This link permits a purification of the soul impossible without self-knowledge. (Foucault 1997: 242)

Total obedience dominates the life of the monk. Foucault cites Cassian, one of the main architects of Western monasticism, invoking "an old principle from the oriental tradition": "Everything the monk does without permission of his master constitutes a theft" (Foucault 1997: 246). This kind of obedience, Foucault argued,

> is complete control of behaviour by the master, *not a final autonomous state.* It is a sacrifice of the self, of the subject's own will. This is the new technology of self. . . . The self must constitute itself through obedience. (Foucault 1997: 246, emphasis added)

I find it necessary to balance this stark and compelling account, built upon programmatic texts, with the following observation by Talal Asad:

> Programmatic texts relate to performances in a variety of ways—inspiring, recommending, prescribing, authorizing, justifying. Strictly speaking, however, program and performance do not stand alone in relation to each other. Essential to both are the mediating practices concerned with interpreting programmatic texts, applying their principles and regulations to the running of the monastic community, judging and assessing performances and in general teaching novices to carry out the program. (1993: 140)

In examining the meaning of confession in a given ethnographic context it is essential to problematize how monastics relate to their ideal and how texts are used. For instance, were one to read the Rule of St. Basil, used by Orthodox monastics, one would find his ideas more similar to those of Cassian than to those of contemporary Romanian Orthodox confessors. Yet in the Orthodox context I have presented the emphasis was not on a strict observance of rules (as one might expect on the basis of Foucault's reading of Cassian), but rather the opposite. For the nuns I knew, monastic education emphasized not the repression of desire or blind obedience, but rather learning to transform worldly desires and feelings to make them compatible with monastic life. Their education seemed more similar to Bernard de Clairvaux's pedagogical techniques for incorporating into his order monks who had already experienced life in the world: "The overall aim of this monastic project was not *to repress* secular experiences of freedom but *to form religious desires out of them*" (Asad 1993: 143; emphasis added). Like the nuns of Zoreni, these monks "stayed in the cloister because they creatively exercised virtue not because they were beaten into submission" (161–62). Notions of charisma acted as the lubricant of this process, making it possible for nuns to seek new potential and assert a more creative involvement in their own training.

According to Papacioc (1994), the dogma acknowledges a subtle distinction between the strict observance of practices and genuinely enlightened understanding of their meaning: *what matters is to understand and act according to the spirit rather than the letter of the rule.* Orthodox monastics do not even possess a rule in the Western sense, but rather a set of general ethical guidelines. Rules are not considered to be self-explanatory, and their application is subject to intuition rather than reason. Charismatic monks are sought out because they possess this art or gift of interpretation to a greater extent than priests. Charisma is the source of "true" knowledge, which by definition is revelatory and intuitive. Thus strict observance of rules is not necessarily a virtue, and their transgression is not necessarily such a serious offense.[19]

At Zoreni I found that religious knowledge was spoken of in terms of a hierarchy, but also in terms of a series of oppositions. The oppositions were strikingly similar to those proposed by Whitehouse's modes of religiosity theory, but the types of knowledge were valued differently than in the Pomio Kivung case. As Whitehouse rightly observes, the doctrinal and imagistic modes of religiosity have different strengths. Semantic, textual, logically integrated knowledge is superior to analogic knowledge in terms of its stability and success in reproducing itself, while analogic knowledge is superior through its vivid, intense, extra-ordinary quality. However, while the Pomio Kivung seemed rooted mainly in a doctrinal mode from which they occasionally strayed into analogic territory, Orthodox believers seem to enjoy the benefits of both types of knowledge by valuing them hierarchically. They rely on dogma and doctrinal elaboration (understood as an inferior knowledge) to provide a stable framework in which the more highly valued but vague and ambiguous analogic knowledge, which involves all the senses and is difficult to verbalize, can be pursued. Mystical knowledge is characterized in terms of dichotomies:

| | | |
|---|---|---|
| Source of knowledge: | Human | Divine |
| Faculty responsible: | Reason/Intellect | Intuition |
| Complexity of knowledge: | Two-dimensional | Multi-dimensional |

| Nature and effects of | | |
|---|---|---|
| knowledge: | Divisive, analytical | Holistic, synthetic |
| Means of expression: | Discoursive, explicit | Nonverbal, implicit |
| Relation of knowledge | | |
| to God: | Indirect | Direct |
| Separated from God | United with God's charisma | |

Such oppositions are routinely mentioned in theological texts, and they are consistent with what I heard in the informal talk of nuns and monks, who took it for granted that levels of knowing closer to divine truth were more difficult to access or were hidden.[20] The idea that some kinds of knowledge were more valuable than others seemed natural to my informants in light of Orthodoxy's hierarchical understanding of the proper order of the world.[21]

How then did this charismatic knowledge become relevant in the lives of the novices? Performances of charismatic insight provided a social space for deliberation about morality, about ways of life and personal ideals. Humphrey (1997: 26) observes (reiterating Foucault) that all morality comprises both codes of behavior and forms of subjectivation, but that societies vary in their emphasis on one or the other. The confessors' approach was more exemplar- than rule-centered, emphasizing forms of subjectivation rather than a code of behavior. In such situations, "the core of morality is primarily referred to the self, adjudicating one's own actions as good and bad for oneself" (33).

I found that monks and nuns had an explicit theory of the self and how divine power ought to work upon it. The metaphor most commonly used to explain the self was that of a vessel. At baptism, the point of highest purity, since this ritual absolves the young child of original sin, leaving him without blemish, the vessel of the soul was full of divine charisma. As the child grew, personal contents (memories, desires, thoughts, emotions, etc.) filled this vessel, and the pure grain, conscience, would shrink. Many novices made an earnest effort to follow the process of self-transformation described in books as a series of successive stages defined in terms of the mastery of specific, discrete components of the self, accompanied by gradual progress to purer forms of knowledge. One monk from Mount Athos (Gheron 1996) explained this as follows. In the first stage of monastic life, called purification, the senses had to be "crucified" (illustrated in Orthodox monastic iconography in the great composition of the monk crucified) by turning oneself inward and gradually being overtaken by a deep apathy toward all sensory experience. Detachment from the knowledge of the senses helped one to avoid temptation and entrapment by the world. There followed the "night of intellectual thinking." The three main faculties of the soul—consciousness, memory, and will—had to be emptied of all personal contents. One had to empty one's mind of all presuppositions and intellectual reasoning:

God was none of the things our intellect tells us he is. The purification of memory meant ridding oneself of all worldly memories. The purification of will meant detachment from any kind of feeling, affect, or passion, except the love of God. The second stage was called enlightenment and symbolized the descent of the Holy Spirit and bestowal of seven charismas, or gifts: devotion, strength, fear of God, knowledge, understanding, faith, and wisdom. When this stage was reached, divine charisma began to manifest itself in the person, and purification (refinement) continued with its help. This resulted in the seven capital sins being replaced by the seven capital virtues (prudence, justice, strength, self-control, faith, hope, and love). Finally, in the third stage, the person would achieve mystical union with God and become a permanent part of Christ's mystical body, being "divinized" (*îndumnezeit*).

In the struggle to live up to such obscure instructions, nuns relied upon the insights of others whom they believed to be inspired by charisma. Without the confessors' guidance they felt at sea, unable to know how they were progressing. Confessors' instruction, like the saints' lives, worked because of an openendedness, which allowed insights to be tailored to each individual's needs. This was consistent with the notion that truth was too complex for words, and that the best one could do was use analogies, or hint at an intuition of deeper truths. Charismatically gifted monks or nuns skillfully chose the terms of their analogies so as to produce the impression of unusual insight.

## CONCLUSION

In his article "What Is a Christian?" Robbins (2003b) makes the point that in order to have an anthropology of Christianity driven by a successful comparative project, it is important to pay close attention to the ways in which the adherents of different streams articulate their distinctiveness. He makes this point while remarking upon the difficulty of doing justice to differences and discontinuities between forms of Christianity, given the tendency, in light of the Christian background shared by most researchers and their audience, to privilege similarities.

In this chapter I have sought to bring into sharper relief the distinctive aspects of Romanian Orthodox Christianity by discussing them in terms of Whitehouse's modes of religiosity theory. I have argued that one important source of distinctiveness in this Orthodox case resides in a notion of knowledge that distinguishes clearly between different types of knowledge, placing them in a hierarchical relation to one another, and assigning them specific roles in the context of religious life. Romanian Orthodox monastics belonging to the stable mainstream church privilege an analogic style of religiosity, although all the elements of a doctrinal mode of religiosity are fully within their grasp—contrary to what we might assume on the basis of Whitehouse's typology. Although rules and texts are pervasive in the monastic environment, the ways in which these are understood and deployed is shaped by cultural assumptions. As Asad (1993) has pointed out, texts can be used in a variety of ways. Thus, in the Orthodox monastery of Zoreni, the strict observance of rules is downplayed, and sometimes discouraged as a potential source of hubris. Obedience to the spirit rather than the letter is stressed. Texts such as the scriptures are not understood as being explicit and self-referential, but rather as containing hidden meanings that can be grasped only through divine inspiration. Other commonly used texts, such as the lives of saints, are effective precisely because of their ambiguous, multivalent character. Yet a third type of text, the prayers and incantations used during rituals, act as performative utterances (Austin 1962). None of these uses of texts privileges the clarity or intellectual elaboration that characterizes the supposedly dominant doctrinal mode.

The modes of religiosity theory link cognitive faculties with two types of religious movements whose characteristics are specifically defined (Whitehouse 1995). Although they constitute a helpful backdrop against which to explore various contrasts with the Orthodox case, the centrality of the doctrinal mode in text-based religious traditions should not be uncritically assumed. In the Orthodox case, this would lead one to overlook what is most distinctive. The modes of religiosity theory can be useful in setting a comparative agenda focusing on how ritual and text are integrated in the context of religious practice, but it should not be assumed that the doctrinal mode of religiosity is the inevitable result of rationalization processes. As Cannell put it (2006: 38), "It may be that the history of modernity is inextricably bound up with the history of Christianity, but this does not mean that the meaning of Christianity is sufficiently explained by the history of modernity."

## NOTES

I carried out research in 2000–2002 with assistance from the Ernest Gellner Memorial Fund (London School of Economics). An Alfred Gell Memorial Studentship from the LSE Anthropology Department and a British Academy Postdoctoral Fellowship have contributed to the writing of this essay. I would particularly like to thank Deborah James and Peter Loizos for their comments on earlier versions. My research focused on postsocialist reconfigurations of power as expressed in political and religious activities at a well-known convent. I lived first inside the convent and later in the adjacent village, from which I could visit the convent and, as a result of my close friendship with some of the nuns, stay overnight on an informal basis.

1. Savin 1996 and Bria 1981 are not specialist theological texts but address themselves to the general public. These are mainstream doctrines.

2. Although often used interchangeably, the two words have slightly different meanings: *har* refers in a general sense to divine charisma, while *harisma* (pl. *harisme*) refers to the specific gifts bestowed by the Holy Ghost upon the apostles, which are thought to be passed on within the church through ordination.

3. It is important to note that the celebration of the Divine Liturgy, word and sacrament, is at the heart of the Orthodox "mystic theology," which is not to be confused with the Western concepts.

4. *Hesychasm* is a doctrine developed by the Athonite monk Saint Gregory Palamas (fourteenth century) that centers on an elaborate theory concerning the nature and attributes of charisma. The *hesychast* prayer is a technique consisting of the continual repetition of a set formula, such as "Lord God, save me, the sinner," so that it eventually becomes a constant refrain of the mind, repeated effortlessly and unconsciously. One has to learn how to focus one's energy, using the rhythm of breath and mentally concentrating on one's navel, in order for the prayer to take root and grow in the heart.

5. His son became an Orthodox monk and acquired a charismatic and intellectual reputation.

6. Yannaras has visited the country, and his works are available in Romanian; however, he is considered controversial, and relatively few people are well acquainted with his ideas.

7. These include the demand for the status of state church and for a quota of parliamentary seats to be assigned to clerics.

8. All names of places and persons are pseudonyms.

9. This was not the case everywhere in Romania. Some Orthodox convents flourished during socialism, notably that of Agapia.

10. For example, she did not know that in the 1920s the Romanian royal family frequently used the convent as a summer retreat and even added new buildings to the compound—facts known to older villagers and elderly nuns.

11. Ascetic technique includes two means of purifying the soul: contemplation and the practice of *nevointe,* or ascetic disciplines. The Romanian word could be literally translated as "nonwanting." It is linked both to the concept of will (*a voi, voință*) and, secondarily, to the idea of desire. In common language, the related word *nevoie* means "need." I have only ever heard the word *nevoință* used by monks and nuns (it is rather archaic), as both a noun (*nevoințe*—"non-wants," "desires") and a reflexive verb (*m-am nevoit*—"I made myself practice the 'nonwants'"). Orthodoxy frowns on excessive mortification of the flesh, because the body is not considered evil, but rather neutral, merely a vessel for the soul. Ascetic disciplines in addition to prayer (which is considered the most important, as it maintans vigilance of the mind) include fasting, foregoing sleep, and repeated prostrations called *metanii,* starting from a kneeling position and touching the ground with one's forehead. These last are often given as penance by the priest, usually during confession. (For example, when two nuns misbehaved during the liturgy, the priest ordered them to do a hundred *metanii* each.)

12. These monks were considered especially powerful because their monastery followed a stricter regime of work and prayer. It was associated in the local imagination with Mount Athos. No females were allowed to enter the monastery grounds.

13. From time to time nuns would warn me not to study so hard, because they had heard of a young girl who became insane after finishing at the top of her class.

14. Yet Zoreni was by no means an environment averse to learning and intellectual pursuits. Mother Gabriela, the abbess who had run the convent for thirty-five years during the socialist period, was proud of her efforts to introduce a more intellectual atmosphere by inviting scholars to study the convent and encouraging nuns to pursue theological training. She had joined in the early 1940s as a teacher at the convent's theological seminary for nuns. Sadly, this school was closed a few years later by the communist authorities. At the age of ninety-two, the abbess complained that, despite her attempts to encourage younger nuns to study theology or any other useful subject, they did not seem interested.

15. For a more thorough account of the multivalent role of saints in Orthodoxy, see Hart 1992.

16. Direct knowledge of divine beings is the central criterion in the structuring of both celestial and earthly hierarchies. The charisma of understanding (*harul cunoașterii*) is conveyed from higher to lower ranks, passing from God to various angels, and then to the church hierarchy and mystically enlightened monks, who act as intermediaries, conveying charisma to laypeople through rituals and personal relations such as confession. Thus monks are a step on the ladder down which divine

charisma is conveyed. Within the church, their persona or "face" (*chip, chipuri*) is that of angels, which are thought of as "essences" with a simple, intuitive knowledge of divinity. Unlike this kind of knowledge, human knowledge is mediated through symbols, analogies, and metaphors, which make it more like guesswork (*ghicitură*). The notion of the *bios angelikos* (angelic life) is classical for Eastern monasticism (see Frank 1964).

17. In discussing the art of confession (*duhovnicia*), I quote mainly from an interview with Arsenie Papacioc, because he makes a number of points that tally with what I was told in various fieldwork contexts (see also Cleopa, Părăian, Popescu, Galeriu, Popa and Pârvulescu in Magdan 2001).

18. The term *tipic* stems from Greek *Typikon*, which, as noted above, refers to a collection of the traditional rules of a monastery.

19. This observation corresponds with the Orthodox principle of *oikonomia*, realized on the basis of God's extraordinary grace, as expressed in his incarnation, which is the peak of God's *oikonomia* and *philanthropia*.

20. This theological point is often attributed to the influence of the Neoplatonist Alexandria school of scriptural exegesis, which flourished in the second and third centuries A.D. These theologians believed that while scripture had a literal, historical meaning that could be understood by all, it also had a deeper, allegorical meaning reflecting eternal truths. This true meaning (in the Platonic sense) was hidden and could be understood only through mystical revelation, which occurred when one was infused with the charisma of the Holy Spirit (Savin 1996).

21. The word for this in Romanian is *rînduială*; the term has a strong moral connotation (i.e., each thing should be in its proper place).

# REFERENCES

Asad, T. 1993. *Genealogies of religion: Discipline and reasons of power in Christianity and Islam.* Baltimore: Johns Hopkins University Press.

Austin, J. 1962. *How to do things with words.* Oxford: Clarendon Press.

Bălan, I. 1988. *Convorbiri duhovnicești.* Vols. 1–2. Roman: Editura Episcopiei Romanului și Hușilor.

Barth, F. 1975. *Ritual knowledge among the Baktaman of New Guinea.* New Haven: Yale University Press.

———. 1987. *Cosmologies in the making: A generative approach to cultural variation in inner New Guinea.* Cambridge: Cambridge University Press.

———. 1990. The guru and the conjurer: Transactions in knowledge and the shaping of culture in Southeast Asia and Melanesia. *Man* 25, no. 4: 640–53.

Bax, M. 1983. "Us" Catholics and "them" Catholics in Dutch Brabant: The dialectics of a religious factional process. *Anthropological Quarterly* 56, no. 4: 167–77.

———. 1995. *Medjugorje: Religion, politics, and violence in rural Bosnia.* Amsterdam: VU Uitgerverij.

Bloch, M. 1998. *How we think they think: Anthropological approaches to cognition, memory, and literacy.* Boulder, Colo.: Westview Press.

Bria, I. 1981. *Dicționar de teologie Ortodoxă.* Bucharest: Editura Institutului Biblic și de Misiune al Bisericii Ortodoxe Române.

Cannell, F. 2006. Introduction to *The anthropology of Christianity,* ed. F. Cannell. Durham, N.C.: Duke University Press.

Cleopa, I. 1996. *Ne vorbește Părintele Cleopa.* Roman: Editura Episcopiei Romanului.

Eickelman, D. 1992. Mass higher education and the religious imagination in contemporary Arab societies. *American Ethnologist* 19, no. 4: 643–55.

Eliade, M. 1992. *Romantism Românesc.* Bucharest: Nemira.

Engelke, M. 2006. Clarity and charisma: On the uses of ambiguity in ritual life. In *The Limits of Meaning: Case Studies in the Anthropology of Christianity,* ed. M. Engelke and M. Tomlinson. Oxford: Berghahn Books.

Foucault, M. 1997. *Ethics: Subjectivity and truth.* Trans. R. E. A. Hurley. The Essential Works of Michel Foucault 1. New York: The New Press.

Frank, K.-S. 1964. *Angelikos bios.* Münster: Aschendorff.

Galeriu, A. 1997. *Duhovnici Români in dialog cu tinerii.* Vol. 2. Bucharest: Editura Bizantină.

Gheron, I. 1996. *Mărturii din Viața Monahală.* Bucharest: Editura Bizantină.

Goody, J. 1968. Introduction to *Literacy in Traditional Societies,* ed. J. Goody. Cambridge: Cambridge University Press.

———. 1986. *The logic of writing and the organization of society.* Cambridge: Cambridge University Press.

Hart, K. L. 1992. *Time, religion, and social experience in rural Greece.* Boston: Rowman and Littlefield.

Herzfeld, M. 2002. Cultural fundamentalism and the regimentation of identity: The embodiment of Orthodox values in a modernist setting. In *The postnational self: Belonging and identity,* ed. U. Hedetoft and M. Hjort, 198–215. Minneapolis: University of Minnesota Press.

Humphrey, C. 1997. Exemplars and rules: Aspects of the discourse of moralities in Mongolia. In *The Ethnography of moralities,* ed. S. Howell, 25–48. London: Routledge.

Kulik, D., and C. Stroud. 1990. Christianity, cargo, and ideas of self: Patterns of literacy in a Papua New Guinean village. *Man* 25, no. 2: 286–304.

Magdan, L. 2001. *Ortodoxia în Mărturisiri contemporane.* Bucharest: Ed. Sf. Alexandru.

Olson, D. 1977. From utterance to text: The bias of language in speech and writing. *Harvard Educational Review* 47, no. 3: 257–81.

Ong, W. 1982. *Orality and literacy.* London: Methuen.

Papacioc, A. 1994. Despre Duhovnicie. http://www.brics.dk/~danher/Old/OC/Texts/despre_duhovnicie_carte4.doc.View interview: http://www.ortodoxtv.ro/media/pr-arsenie-pr-vasile-despre-duhovnicie.wmv.

Robbins, J. 1998. Becoming sinners: Christianity and desire among the Urapmin of Papua New Guinea. *Ethnology* 37, no. 4: 299–316.

———. 2003a. On the paradoxes of global Pentecostalism and the perils of continuity thinking. *Religion* 33: 221–31.

———. 2003b. What is a Christian? Notes toward an anthropology of Christianity. *Religion* 33: 191–99.

Savin, I. G. 1996. *Mistica și ascetica Ortodoxă.* Sibiu: Tipografia Eparhială.

Sf. Vasile cel Mare, Sf. Paisie Velicikovski, Nichifor Theotokis. 1998. *Sfaturi la intrarea în monahism.* Bucharest: Ed. Anastasia.

Stewart, C. 1998. Who owns the rotonda? *Anthropology Today* 14, no. 5: 3–9.

Verdery, K. 1991. *National identity under socialism: Identity and cultural politics in Ceausescu's Romania.* Berkeley: University of California Press.

Wanner, K. 2003. Advocating new moralities: Conversion to Evangelicalism in Ukraine. *Religion, State, and Society* 31, no. 3: 273–87.

Weber, M. 1963. *The sociology of religion.* Trans. E. Fischoff. Boston: Beacon Press.

Whitehouse, H. 1992. Memorable religions: Transmission, codification, and change in divergent Melanesian contexts. *Man* 27, no. 4: 777–97.

———. 1995. *Inside the cult: Religious innovation and transmission in Papua New Guinea.* Oxford: Clarendon Press.

———. 1998. From mission to movement: The impact of Christianity on patterns of political association in Papua New Guinea. *Journal of the Royal Anthropological Institute* 4, no. 1: 43–63.

Worsley, P. 1968. *The trumpet shall sound: A study of "cargo" cults in Melanesia.* 2nd ed. New York: Schocken Books.

Yannaras, C. 1973. Orthodoxy and the West. In *Orthodoxy, life, and freedom: Essays in honour of Archbishop Iakovos,* ed. A. J. Philippou, 130–47. Oxford: Studion Publications.

———. 1984. *The freedom of morality.* Crestwood, N.Y.: SVS.

# 6

# Exorcising Demons
# in Post-Soviet Ukraine

## A Monastic Community
## and Its Imagistic Practice

Vlad Naumescu

In this chapter I explore the making and unmaking of a monastic community in post-Soviet Ukraine. The postsocialist revival of religion took place within a ferment of unrest that saw the splintering and emergence of many religious communities. This process of religious restructuring has often been attributed to sociopolitical transformations, the emergence of competitive markets of religion, and the rise of nationalism. There has been little systematic inquiry into the transformations each religious tradition underwent in terms of content and modalities of expression, and little engagement with the anthropological literature addressing processes of cultural transmission. Here I approach the religious tradition of western Ukraine, a local variant of Eastern Christianity as a living tradition, a "cosmology in the making," in Fredrik Barth's terms (1987). My account is based on a search for correlations between the social organization, forms of religious transmission, and variation in religious knowledge in this tradition. The recent literature on religious transmission inspired by naturalist approaches to culture focused on the cognitive mechanisms that lie at the basis of transmission and distribution of religious representations (Sperber 1985; Boyer 1994). Such approaches privileged cognition over culture and context, studying mind outside culture and then using the cognitive models to explain how religion works in specific cultural contexts (see Bloch 1990 for a critique). Implicit in these approaches is the idea that religious thought and behavior are a by-product of human cognition, "a quaint but useless excrescence of a cognitive system that was designed for other, more useful purposes" (Harris 2000: 158).

Among cognitive models of religious transmission, Harvey Whitehouse's modes of religiosity theory (1995, 2000, 2004) focuses on processes of religious transmission and the codification of religious knowledge based on the specificity of human cognition without neglecting social context. His theory proposes a general explanation of religious evolution based ultimately on distinct mechanisms of memory retention: semantic and episodic. These distinct mechanisms give rise to two sets of psychological and sociopolitical features structured around contrasting modes of religiosity, the imagistic and the doctrinal. The "imagistic mode" involves nonverbal, highly emotional rituals. They take place within small-scale, cohesive communities, and their innovative forms are not easily disseminated outside the group. In contrast, the doctrinal mode is based on verbalized, textual doctrine and develops frequent and routinized ritual performance. It is characteristic of large-scale, hierarchical communities with diffuse membership. Whitehouse constructs the modes as ideal types or "attractor positions" (2004: 75). He argues that the imagistic and the doctrinal coexist within all religions in a dynamical tension, and it is their interaction that determines their particular evolution. In a religion operating primarily in the doctrinal mode, people tend to lose interest and motivation through boredom (Whitehouse 2000: 44). Some start to look for a reinterpretation of the dogma and to discover novel forms of religious practice closer to the imagistic mode. They typically become a splinter group from the mainstream doctrinal tradition. Yet if reintegrated the splinter group can serve to reinvigorate a religion that has become too "doctrinal." Whitehouse links the modes of religiosity to the specific patterns of social organization. In his view the doctrinal mode gives birth to enduring, universalistic religious movements (Christianity), while the imagistic is restricted to unstable small groups (New Guinea cults).

Elsewhere I have undertaken a more general analysis of patterns of reproduction and change in Eastern Christianity based on the interaction of the two modes of religiosity (Naumescu 2007). I argue that both imagistic and doctrinal are essential for the evolution of the religious tradition and that, by maintaining revelation at the core of its doctrinal corpus, Eastern Christianity presents a unique case of equilibrium between imagistic and doctrinal. In this chapter I will focus on the revival of an imagistic practice, exorcism, that has a long tradition in Eastern Christianity. The ethnographic case I propose comes from fieldwork undertaken in 2003–2004 in the monastery of St. Theodore Studite in Kolodiivka, western Ukraine.[1] This monastic community separated from an established monastic order following a reinterpretation of their doctrine. The splinter group had the characteristics of a spontaneous *communitas,* and its short history exhibited certain parallels with Victor Turner's analysis of the evolution of the Catholic Franciscan order from a spontaneous to an ideological *communitas* (Turner 1996: 47). Their story is not unique. In the religious effervescence that characterizes postsocialist Ukraine, countless splinter groups have emerged: for example, when a parish splinters due to competing factions of the Orthodox churches and the

Greek Catholic Church (Naumescu 2006). Most splinter groups are quickly integrated into the religious structures already available. Sometimes, however, an
autonomous community can flourish on the basis of an imagistic ritual rediscovered within the very same religious tradition. But, as I shall show, this phenomenon is likely to be short-lived, since it is bound to disturb the above-mentioned
equilibrium.

## MAKING KOLODIIVKA: THE EMERGENCE
## OF A SPLINTER GROUP

The monastic community at Kolodiivka began as a spontaneous movement made
up of a small number of people who tried to implement a shared monastic ideal.
It came into being as a splinter group of a monastic order well established in
Ukraine, the order of St. Basil the Great. The ascetic rules of the Cappadocian
Saint Basil the Great stem from the Eastern Orthodoxy of the fourth century, but
the order of St. Basil the Great is a monastic institution of the Greek Catholic
churches and is regulated according to Western monastic principles. Basilians
follow the centralized model of Catholic monastic orders: they reproduce one rule
and one structure in all their monasteries. In the early days of postsocialist religious revival in Ukraine, monastic orders were among the first to recreate religious
institutions. Emerging from the underground where they had been active since
the banning of their order in 1945, Basilian priests helped to lay the groundwork
for the reconstruction of the Ukrainian Greek Catholic Church.[2] Many young
people joined the order, attracted by the example of "underground" survivors, who
were living paragons of both Christian and national Ukrainian commitment.
Novitiate houses had to be built quickly to accommodate the monastic boom,
and the Basilians were the first. However, within a decade many houses were
almost empty, as interest in monastic life among young people waned as rapidly
as it had waxed.

In the 1990s the Basilian order found itself caught in between the general move
to modernize the Greek Catholic rite and the attempt of some of its members to
hold on to the ritual customs developed in the underground. Church leaders
argued that the Greek Catholic Church had to rediscover its Eastern roots and
eradicate centuries-old Latin influences. Hryhoryi Planchak, then teacher in the
Basilian seminary in Krekhiv, was at the forefront of this "Easternizing" trend
among Basilians, urging a return to the spirituality of the early church fathers. He
also called for a contemplative monastic life, based on withdrawal from the world
and concentration on prayer and mystical experience. He reinterpreted contemplation in the spirit of Orthodox monasticism, as the solitary exploration of inner
spirituality. Many students of Planchak at the novitiate house in Krekhiv were
excited by these ideals. Since the Basilians were historically oriented toward an

active life of missionary activity, education, pastoral care, publishing, and church politics, Planchak's aspirations were hard to accommodate within the order. Without wishing to separate from the order, Planchak's group set out to transform a Basilian monastery in Lavrir into a contemplative monastery. However, they were soon forced to leave the order. As Roman, one of Planchak's students, explained to me later, "[Planchak] wanted to go deeper into spirituality and return to the sources our early Fathers proposed. He wanted to live more absorbed in prayer and an inner [spiritual] life (*vnustryshnyi*). And when he couldn't do this in the Basilian [order], he received the blessing to leave it and form a new community."

Planchak's departure was also motivated in large part by his interest in reviving the ritual of exorcism in the church, a move that was unpopular among Basilians. Ten monks left with him, and together they moved provisionally into an apartment in Ivano-Frankivsk, where Planchak started to teach in a local theological seminary. In Ivano-Frankivsk, they organized themselves into a monastic community, observing a spiritual and communal program. The group soon received a tempting proposal to settle in a newly established monastery in the village of Kolodiivka, near Ternopyl. The birth of the new community in Kolodiivka was not unusual at that time of religious unrest, but its spiritual orientation tested the limits of the Easternization trend within the Greek Catholic Church. None of the existing monastic orders recognized their rule (*typikon*), so the community remained on its own.

Planchak's group forged the new monastery in the spirit of the "ideal community"; it would be an "island of spirituality" (*oseredok dukhovnosti*) set apart from the mundane world. The hardships of establishing a new, independent community were slowly overcome.[3] The monks concentrated on contemplation and spiritual self-accomplishment following the hermits' model, as the early church fathers had done. Their path to God was to be experienced in community rather than in individual seclusion. They also opened two "deserts" (*pustynjia)* in the mountains—small hermitages where monks and nuns could go for short periods of time to live a solitary life. The experience of seclusion was highly esteemed in the community and extremely challenging for those undertaking it. The hermitage was a place for "mystical experiences," providing the hardest spiritual challenge for each monk. There, "one is tempted by the devil at every step, and you can easily go insane if you don"t pray incessantly," one nun told me after returning from two weeks' seclusion.

Inside the monastery monks set a strict spiritual program: to the basic monastic division of the day into three periods (eight hours of sleep, eight of work, and eight for prayer), they added further obligations. Two days out of each week were governed by a desert within the community, including fasting and solitary prayer. One night per week was dedicated to continuous prayer, and monks took hour-long shifts during the night.

From ten monks at its founding in 1995 the monastery grew to forty-five members in 2004: seven monk-priests, two monk-deacons, and thirty-six monks. The rule of the monastery was influenced by Mount Athos monasticism.[4] However, the community in Kolodiivka continuously redefined itself. The exact status of some monks was unclear, particularly those not living in the monastery. Some pursued theological studies in L'viv and traveled only infrequently to Kolodiivka. This was the case for Brother Arseny, who eventually graduated from the Ukrainian Catholic University and became a missionary. Arseny, who had lived in several monasteries and was familiar with the mystical traditions of Orthodox monasticism, epitomized the figure of the wandering monk. Greek Catholic monasticism was in his view an incomplete tradition that did not pay enough attention to its Eastern roots. For Arseny, the beginnings of Kolodiivka were promising because of the emphasis placed on contemplation and on personal spiritual development (*pratsija nad suboiu*).

The permeable borders of Eastern churches, the mobility of priests, and the instability of parishes characteristic of the postsocialist revival all affected monastic life in the 1990s. In Kolodiivka, monastic rule was strict with regard to religious obligations but less rigorous in organizational matters. Planchak's public lectures and spiritual teachings attracted numerous theology students from all over the region, along with other young enthusiasts who wanted to experience monastic life in these distinctive conditions. Yet the newly founded monastery could not offer a proper novitiate under the guidance of a confessor, as is usually the case. The rules for novitiates were neither strictly Catholic nor Orthodox, and the period of probation, an in-between status between secular and monastic life, became a permanent state for some monks. Few of those in the monastery had made their minor vows, and only two had made permanent vows.[5]

Visiting monks attracted by Kolodiivka's devotional life could remain in the monastery for a while; and departing monks could postpone their official separation endlessly. The monastery retained its institutional flexibility, being open to novel opportunities and experiences that continuously reshaped the community. Besides monks hoping to realize their spiritual ideals, there were novices for whom the choice of monastic life was made for more pragmatic reasons, as an alternative to daily struggle and social obligations. For others who were social outcasts it was an opportunity to reintegrate into society, since being a monk was a highly respectable social role in postsocialist western Ukraine. People not accepted into other monasteries because of their past were welcomed in Kolodiivka and given a second chance.

Jaroslav converted while in jail and decided to become a monk after long discussions with Arseny, at that time a missionary monk providing pastoral care in prisons. He had searched for a monastery, but all, except Kolodiivka, refused him because of his past.[6] Inevitably, the initial ascetic and spiritual ideals of the founders of the monastery were affected by the actual functioning of the community. Planchak's charismatic teachings provided some guiding principles and a cohesive force, but since he was often absent, the community lacked permanent guidance. As the monastery expanded, it became more difficult to maintain the bonds that the original group had sustained.

Rather than follow the path of institutionalization—involving stricter rules and hierarchical authority—the monks in Kolodiivka sought a third way. They tried to preserve their initial *communitas* and thus avoid both more rigorous organization and the strict pursuit of a doctrinal mode of religiosity. They did so by following the abbot's inspiration and cultivating an imagistic ritual that, through its compelling emotional content, maintained the cohesion and increased the motivation of the group. Exorcism, brought to the monastery by Planchak, shaped both the practice and the beliefs of the community to such a degree that it became the focal point of the monastery and the key to its continued existence.

## EXORCISM IN KOLODIIVKA

The cognitive theory summarized above distinguishes between imagistic and doctrinal rituals by differentiating the psychological and social characteristics associated with each mode of religiosity. In Whitehouse's ethnographic examples, taken mostly from male initiation rituals in Papua New Guinea (Whitehouse 1995, 2000), imagistic rituals are linked to terror and violent emotions. However, their primary characteristic is not violence but the emotional intensity triggered by the ritual and its potential revelation (or "spontaneous exegetical reflection" in Whitehouse's words). With its violent enacting of a symbolic fight, possession trance, and powerful imagery, exorcism clearly falls into the imagistic category (Kapferer 1991; Goodman 1988). Yet the ritual also has a venerable doctrinal tradition in Christianity, where it has been regulated and controlled by ecclesiastical authority since becoming an established liturgical rite in the third century. Exorcist prayers were later incorporated into the baptismal service, which remains today the basic form of exorcism in Christianity (Stewart 1991: 207). The exorcisms of the early church fathers were transmitted through the hagiographical tradition of the church and supply models for exorcism rituals to the present day.

The Eastern and Western Christian traditions developed distinct forms of the exorcist rite and different mechanisms of control over its practitioners. Theological conceptions of the devil diverged, and attitudes toward exorcism were shaped by contrasting models of authority and dogma in the two Christian traditions. Yet all churches have tried to contain the practice of exorcism by standardizing the ritual form and integrating it into orthodox practice.[7] With the rationalization of aetiologies of illnesses in the medical sciences, churches partially accepted the psychopathological aspects of previously defined "evil afflictions."[8] Belief in evil was condemned as mere superstition, and some exorcist practices were accordingly rejected. However, by personifying collective anxieties the devil and demons remain important actors in many religions, especially in contexts of social fluidity and change (Clough and Mitchell 2001; Kapferer 2003; Parkin 1986; Meyer 1999). In the case of Orthodoxy, too, the persistence of the devil in the religious imaginary has caused exorcism to retain its role as the most appropriate response of the church (see Stewart 1991). The ritual is performed only where the influence of the devil can be clearly recognized, and so the main difficulty lies in the correct identification of evil as the source of an affliction, thus indicating a case of "possession" by the devil.[9] Thus the exorcist has first to identify the possession and to choose the best means of intervention among the church rituals available. Monks in Kolodiivka follow the religious tradition of discerning the spirits, a spiritual issue with a long past in the history of spirit possession in Christianity (Caciola 2000). In the words of Brother Roman, "The proof that people have a spiritual problem is that they are afraid of religious objects! Mentally ill people should not be afraid of crosses, holy water. . . . The first criterion is that the person reacts strangely in the presence of religious objects. They have a fear of icons, crosses, water. The second is that they are conscious of someone else living in their body."

The diagnosis is always relational: the priest, the person afflicted, and those around her (usually the family) act together. The anticipation of this moment is created earlier when the family decides to bring the afflicted to the religious specialist. If the possessed is not capable of speaking to the priest, a brief interrogation of her relatives serves instead. This usually includes a question about whether other specialists, such as other priests, doctors, or alternative practitioners, have already recognized that the person has "problems with the nerves." "Nerves," then, represent the cultural idiom in which a person can express distress and anxiety in relation to the social environment (Low 1994).[10]

The first meeting between the possessed and the exorcist is crucial for choosing the right treatment: an exorcism (*ekzortsyzm; vychytka*) or a healing prayer (*molitva za ozdorovlennuia*), depending on the gravity of the case. Only two monks in Kolodiivka have the special "gift" of discerning the spirits, by recognizing the signs of possession through divinely inspired intuitions. They are usually called to decide whether a religious experience, an unexpected event, or a personal affliction is divinely or demonically inspired. Their spiritual gift is responsible for their "mystical knowledge"; it is also the measure of their charisma (see also Forbess, this volume). Exorcists lacking the gift pursue a more conventional path of interrogation to establish which demonic agent is responsible. Since the monastery is the site of much highly animated imagistic activity, monks are constantly confronted by evil forces, and those with the gift often "visualize" demons or decipher their presence in certain signs. For the others, demonic presence is harder to bear because of the uncertainty surrounding it. They must constantly check and corroborate their personal experiences with the exorcist-priests, and this spiritual relationship enhances the authority of the latter.

In the church tradition, exorcism, unlike the more routinized healing prayers, which anyone may recite, is an extraordinary ritual performed only in special conditions by authorized priests. In practice exorcism always falls somewhere between standardized forms of the Orthodox rite and highly spiritual forms of personal devotion performed by mystics. Its practice is restricted to religious specialists and to particular places, notably monasteries. It usually includes an exegetic part in which the exorcist underlines the specific cosmology of the ritual, which is centered around the paired oppositions within the Christian salvation idiom: God and devil (Stewart 1991: 11). Whereas exorcists work within the cosmology of exorcism, persons in search of a cure switch between alternative explanatory frames that propose different diagnoses and their respective cures. Monks are aware that for some of those who approach them an exorcism is but one of the many possible therapies available. Arseny remarked in a realistic tone:

> Today there are many spiritual problems because people don't know what spiritual life is. For them it is the same to go to witches or to go to a priest. This is why [exorcism] is practiced in the monastery and not in churches, [so that] through those [exorcist] prayers we can teach people the basic truths of Christian faith; and tell them: "Spiritual problems exist and we all have them. They come from the fact that the human nature is corrupted by sin. To cure it, you should do this and that. . . ." This has always been the role of the monastery, like a bank where money gathers. Those who need money go to the cash machine. We have to live our spirituality, otherwise we don"t have [enough], and we cannot give to others . . . like an empty bank.

Since the community formed in Kolodiivka, Abbot Planchak persuaded his followers, including some who were reluctant in the beginning, that exorcisms were a legitimate part of the early church's tradition, and that the monastic ideal they were following required them to rediscover it. He mobilized the entire monastery to support this goal, and the imaginary of the community was gradually shaped around the cosmology of the exorcist ritual. "It is the duty of every priest to be an exorcist!" Planchak declared; it is a spiritual gift that every priest receives when ordained. In 2004 the community in fact contained seven exorcists who had discovered and nurtured their "gift" and two deacons who exercised their potential gift of expelling spirits. The monks often drew a parallel between exorcism as a spiritual gift received at a priest's ordination, and baptism as the spiritual gift received automatically with the baptism ritual. This analogy challenged the authority of the church to appoint exorcists and contradicted the marginalization of this practice by the church and monastic tradition. Hence the manner in which the ritual is usually performed in all Christian traditions, with a direct and controlled interaction between the exorcist and the victim, was reversed in Kolodiivka. Exorcism in their view has "opened up" and become accessible to any priest. Cultivation of "the gift of exorcism" (*dar ekzortsyzmu*) thus becomes a legitimate quest for all priests.

Soon after its establishment the monastery built up a reputation as a "nursery for exorcists" (*rozsadnyk ekzortsistiv*). Kolodiivka started to be visited by priests from Ukraine as well as Poland. Sometimes visitors could perform exorcisms themselves, with the abbot's blessing, in a public ritual performed monthly. Confronted with an increasing number of requests to perform exorcisms, the monastery decided to set a special date for public exorcisms.

## THE "LAST TUESDAY" SERVICE

On the last Tuesday of each month between Easter and Advent, large numbers of pilgrims come to the monastery early in the morning and stay until late at night. This is also one of the rare occasions when the entire monastic community comes together. Monks set up the entire program of the day based on a succession of liturgical rituals culminating in the exorcist ritual. In most monasteries where exorcism is practiced, the ritual takes place in an intimate setting involving very few people and just one priest. In Kolodiivka, however, the public exorcism performed on the last Tuesday of the month becomes the central aspect of the religious service for the entire community of pilgrims and monks. Both groups prepare intensively for this day. The monastic program consists of intense prayer and fasting. The community has to become spiritually strong enough to incorporate and process all the problems to which it will be exposed on the last Tuesday, and be able to "fight the evil forces" brought by pilgrims. Pilgrims fast on the day before their pilgrimage, and during the journey they recite the rosary and listen to the sermons of the abbot available on tape. Apart from its collective dimension, the last Tuesday pilgrimage is also a private spiritual quest. During the trip, newcomers are initiated into the specificity of Kolodiivka's rituals, in a socialization into exorcism, through which they become aware of the ritual's force even before attending it. This creates an individual predisposition and preparation for accepting the workings of the exorcism and the symbolic healing, and an easier integration into the ritual context (Csordas 2002).[11] The regular visits of those afflicted turn into a lengthy therapeutic process that helps them achieve the maximum spiritual benefit from Kolodiivka. The practice of last Tuesdays creates a routine out of an extraordinary ritual.

The sequence of ritual actions starts at 7:00 a.m. with the great vespers, followed by the morning prayer (*utrenia*). The Orthodox hymn service, or *akathist*, which combines salutations to the Mother of God and praise of Christ, is held at 10:00 a.m. (see Hann and Goltz, in this volume, p. XX). At 12:00 p.m. the abbot preaches a sermon, which is followed by a lengthy liturgy and a general blessing. The unction (*miruvania*) of pilgrims takes place at 4:00 p.m., and from 6:00 p.m. onward exorcism prayers continue until late into the night. Throughout the day more familiar, routinized practices are interspersed with devotional moments of intense emotion, with the religious fervor reaching its climax during the exorcism prayers.

Unlike pilgrimages to other devotional sites in Ukraine, pilgrims to Kolodiivka are not accompanied by their own parish priests. These priests prefer not to visit the "exorcist monastery" because of its controversial status and practice, while pilgrims come precisely because they expect to find "better priests" at the monastery than they would at home. Lengthy queues of those waiting to confess form outside the church. The monks and nuns who circulate between the monastery and the church are often stopped and asked for blessings.

Planchak's sermons utilize a very emotional rhetoric to create an interaction with the pilgrims, reminiscent of the preaching used in Charismatic churches but also of the liturgical dialogues and antiphones of the Eastern churches:

> *Abbot:* [Do you] Hear me!? Say it!
> *Congregation:* We hear! [*People answer.*]
> *Abbot:* Say: Love is power!
> *Congregation:* Love is power! [*They repeat after him.*]
> *Abbot:* Repeat after me: Love is power!
> *Congregation:* Love is power! . . .
> *Abbot:* Do you hear?
> *Congregation:* We do!
> *Abbot:* And what do you hear? Do you hear how the Holy Spirit works in you?[12]

At the end of the liturgy the abbot reemerges from the church to bless objects pilgrims have bought during their visit or brought from home. Pilgrims form two rows in front of the church and hold up the objects (e.g., icons, rosaries, family pictures, books, posters) they want to be blessed. Many hold pictures of the relatives for whom they have come to pray or to ask for healing. The abbot moves through the group and sprinkles holy water on people and objects. At this moment the first manifestations of possession appear. Contact with the holy water causes some people in the audience to start to shout and shiver.

In the unction ritual that follows, pilgrims approach the altar one by one to be anointed by a priest with blessed oil on their foreheads. Some ask for other parts of their body (such as the eyes, ears, hands, or nape) to be anointed as well. When the anointing has been completed, the monks propose a break to prepare for the exorcism prayers, and the abbot may ask those who are healthy to go home. This is consistent with the church's distinction between exorcisms that are part of standard rituals and effective for the general spiritual well-being of pilgrims, and those exorcism prayers that are addressed particularly to those afflicted by evil spirits. All rituals performed to this point—confession, blessings, communion, and the anointing —are already familiar to pilgrims from the common liturgical service. What follows from this moment on is the startling part, even for those already familiar with the exorcism ritual.

Pilgrims and nuns gathered in the church start singing continuously the famous Jesus prayer of the Orthodox *hesychasts* (see Forbess, in this volume, p. 133): "Jesus, son of God, have mercy upon us!" During this long moment of waiting for the ritual to start, people showing signs of possession shriek loudly from time to time and struggle violently to escape from their relatives' hands. When the exorcism begins, the church is crammed. Priests gather at the altar, and those who are possessed are brought forward. Some stand, while others sit in chairs or wheelchairs, agitated or completely numb. Their stories are extraordinary diverse: I observed young girls brought by their parents or friends, middle-aged women with their husbands, some older women and men, a few mentally and physically handicapped children, and teenagers of both sexes with their parents.[13]

The exorcists start the healing prayers at the same time, placing their hands on the head of each person. Some hold a cross; others use only their hands to bless while praying in silence or whispering prayers. When the person in front of them reacts by starting to shiver, scream, and shout, the exorcists touch the cross on certain parts of the body: the head, neck, chest, belly, back, or palms. As the exorcists place the cross on these spots, responses of anger and aggression are provoked from their temporary victims. Some priests blow air over the exorcised person, which has the same effect. Exorcists circulate, selecting pilgrims arbitrarily and praying for them in the same manner. Thus each person in the church may potentially reveal a hidden affliction. The exorcist "discovers" the presence of evil through something akin to an act of divination. Here again the ritual in Kolodiivka differs from other exorcisms in the way it reveals the possession and uncovers the evil spirits behind it. The exact form of the ritual has remained an object of contention, and each exorcist developed his own style, sometimes deviating greatly from the written forms extant in the church tradition.

Two monks walk around continuously, one carrying a censer, and the other sprinkling large quantities of holy water. The "possessed" display similar reactions: shrieking and shivering, with the eyes closed. They are held strongly by those around them. At times they try to attack others with their hands, groaning, growling, and spitting all the while. The groans become very deep, guttural sounds, and some burst into a voice that sounds unlike their own. Eventually they enter a possession trance (Bourguignon 1973), falling to the floor, wracked by waves of convulsions. Exorcists do not cease until the possessed gives signs of fatigue, at which point they will move on to another of the possessed. Those who are still not fully exorcised breathe deeply and slowly and become numb, barely reacting to blessed water or the people around them.

A second part soon follows when the priest returns to interrogate the possessing spirit. This time a dialogue takes place between the priest and the possessed, who speaks in a modified voice, that of the evil spirit within (sometimes it takes several performances before the possessed begins to speak with the spirit's voice). The aim is to identify the evil spirit and determine how difficult it will be to exorcise it. Apart from the "gifted" exorcist who "sees" the affliction and acts immediately, the others must discover demons by asking the possessed person and his companions questions. This is a joint effort to recreate meaning from a person's suffering and life experience by setting them within the networks of meaning proposed by the ritual cosmology (see Obeyesekere 1981: 106; Csordas 2002).

Identifying the demon and calling it by name are the most important and difficult parts of the exorcist ritual (see also Stewart 1991: 214). By using the name of the demon, the exorcist can directly ask him to leave the body of the person. There are hierarchies of demons, and sometimes several demons may possess a single person. Usually the demons exorcised in Kolodiivka reflect attributes of the person who is possessed: an older man from Transcarpathia has been possessed by the demon of the Carpathians, while a teenage girl brought by her parents because of her hypercritical attitude to everyone she encounters has the demon of criticism. A demon's name can also indicate the specific place of affliction: the demon of the womb, the demon of the throat, etc. Once the demon has been identified the exorcist has to make him leave. A typical dialogue proceeds as follows:

> *Exorcist:* Let me introduce you to God!
> *Demon:* Ah, you shouldn't!
> *Exorcist:* Come out in the name of God!
> *Demon:* I don't want to! No! No! No!
> *Exorcist:* Irineus [the name of the spirit], separate from her, go away from her!

Those who are not possessed or exorcised continue to sing and pray in the crowded church, gathered around the spots where exorcisms are performed. Loud cries and screaming induce fear in those in the back of the church who cannot see. Only those close to the possessed try to help them, while most of the audience looks on in terror. Many persons hold up pictures of their children or relatives for the exorcists to see. This symbolic healing reaches outside the monastery walls and shows how the imaginal field of the ritual (Kapferer 2003: 119) involves more people than those directly participating in it.

The Tuesday ritual in Kolodiivka incorporates into its performance major and minor rites of common religious practice. Thus it takes a compound ritual form (Kapferer 1991: 110). Both monks and pilgrims see the entire Tuesday ritual as an integrated sequence, a continuous prayer for healing the soul, the spirit, and the body. The exorcists demand of all those who subject themselves to the healing prayers that they complete the stages of confession, communion, blessing, unction, and exorcism. The abbot's homilies during the day provide an exegesis of the ritual, constituting an introduction into the meaning of exorcism.

While most of the day's rituals are familiar from everyday religious practice, the exorcism at the end is a shock. Its performative aspects are extremely important: the repetitious singing, pungent aromas, the almost imperceptible movement of the crowd in the church, the initially sporadic cries that later transform into unbearable shouting, and the dramatic struggles between exorcists and possessed. The aesthetics of the ritual create the drama that substantiates the cosmology of the exorcism and its imaginal reality (Kapferer 2003: 118). "You watch the exorcism, and it reminds you how close the devil is," remarked Brother Roman after one performance. The audience measures the gravity of a possession and the success of the exorcism by evaluating the degree of performativity of the ritual. The violence of the ritual comes from the enactment of the symbolic fight between God, made present by the priests-exorcists, and demons. This elicits strong emotional responses and sometimes disorientation from the audience. I had the impression that few if any members of the congregation were unmoved by the ritual and failed to share in its imaginary.

Despite the anticipation of the drama among participants, the actual enactment of the drama violates their expectations every time. The ritual generates high levels of emotional arousal, both collective and individual, which challenge the rational expectations of participants. Exorcism catalyzes individual fears and channels them into accepted cultural forms. Through analogic imagery it triggers multiple sensuous connotations and multiple public and private interpretations. Each act or word is interpreted by the exorcist within the imaginary of the ritual, but it is individually reflected upon by all the other participants. Their subjective interpretations or spontaneous exegetical reflections, often experienced as personal inspiration or revelation (Whitehouse 2004: 70–74), are later adjusted to collective interpretations. Like the Sinhalese exorcism rituals studied by Bruce Kapferer in Sri Lanka, these Eastern Christian exorcisms create a "dynamic field of force in whose virtual space human psychological, cognitive, and social realities are forged anew, so that the ritual participants are both reoriented to their ordinary realities and embodied with potencies to restore and reconstruct their lived worlds" (2005: 51).

Exorcism, an imagistic ritual par excellence, builds on metaphor and the vagueness and multivocality of symbols. Yet it does so in a specific context, which brings together familiar and routinized practice and highly tensional, intense emotions. In this sense, exorcism ritual in Kolodiivka combines imagistic and doctrinal practices in an effective yet counterintuitive way. The persistence of the representations constitutive of the ritual cosmology, among both monks and pilgrims, is due to the counterintuitive ritual context in which they are transmitted. As Carlo Severi has argued, "The persistence in time, and success, of notions of this kind are not explained by their 'counterintuitive' content, but rather by their insertion within very precisely defined, and yet counterintuitive, contexts of ritual communication" (2004: 817). However, doubt and estrangement may set in later when these representations are disconnected from the performance, and the ritual "reality" is challenged by the outside world.

## SHAPING THE MONASTIC IMAGINARY

So far I have shown how the exorcism ritual practiced in Kolodiivka has become central to the dynamics and cohesion of the community. A cosmology that emphasizes the continuous struggle between God and the devil has come to determine the monks' reactions to the changing world. Evil spirits attack not only those who are spiritually weak but also those who aspire to a higher degree of spirituality, such as the monks of Kolodiivka. The life of the community is seen as a continuous attempt to overcome evil forces. Monks cultivate imagistic practices to support their belief, and this reverberates in their daily lives.

Taras, a nineteen-year-old novice in the monastery when I lived there in 2004, enjoyed painting icons, although he had no prior training in this craft. His work was highly valued by the other monks. His talent was explained in terms of "divine inspiration," as in the old tradition of Orthodox icon painters. While painting and concentrating intensely, he occasionally began to shiver and would fall to the floor, unconscious. Once or twice he had destroyed the icon on which he was working, but upon waking he remembered nothing. Losing consciousness was seen in the monastery as a sign of being touched by the Holy Spirit. During the exorcism ritual, younger nuns and monks often fainted for short periods of time. The others left them alone, since it was assumed that it was the Holy Spirit who "took them over. " Taras, however, had recently had a minor accident that affected his hand. The accident was explained in the community as having been caused by evil, in the same way that temporary loss of consciousness was seen as a gift from God. Both were understood as normal steps in the spiritual life of any monk, part of his spiritual struggle to overcome evil. The source of evil was said to lie in a sinful act of the victim or one of his family members, and it was the confessor's duty to investigate it. In the case of Taras, the abbot determined that his older brother, also a monk in the monastery, was the source of the sin.

In many cases the source of affliction as well as salvation lies in family genealogies. Physical and psychic afflictions can result from sins committed by previous generations or close kin, and moral fault is transmitted intergenerationally. In recognizing possession, the priest restores the social status of the afflicted, and the family reintegrates him or her by accepting the interpretation and thus their own past faults as well as those of the afflicted. It has been argued that this latter aspect is particularly important in the postsocialist context, where new moralities are formed through massive conversions to Evangelical Protestantism (Wanner 2003). The exorcism ritual heals the person by reinforcing social bonds, restoring the wholeness of the individual in both the family and the larger community. Thus its influence extends beyond the world of the monastery into pilgrims' lived reality. However, it has little effect on the village of Kolodiivka, the inhabitants of which avoid the exorcism prayers. Their use of the monastery is limited to simple religious functions. It is left to the pilgrims to carry the messages of the monastery into the world. Transformed by the experience of the exorcism, some pilgrims do indeed become transmitters of the monastery's cosmology, feeling themselves empowered to spread its message and imagistic practice.

One example is Volodea, who began coming to the monastery in 1999 from his home in nearby Ternopyl when he was a boy of thirteen. He was brought by his mother, who was in search of a cure for his convulsions and asked Father Planchak to pray for him. The boy was extremely tired after that day but felt better, so his mother decided to bring him again. Over the next five years they attended almost every last Tuesday, and he was completely healed, as the two attested to me. Volodea decided to join the monastery, since he had already learned to pray "like the Kolodiivka monks." He prayed for others in his neighborhood who were ill, and his efforts were said to be helpful. The power of his prayers and the spiritual strength he and his mother had received every time they came to the monastery had recently saved them from a car accident. The two interpreted this event as a miracle, and it convinced them that Volodea must join the monastery.

For some pilgrims Kolodiivka is their last hope after a stay in a psychiatric hospital. Some try the healing prayers of the church first and opt for exorcism only as a last resort. The Kolodiivka exorcists are aware that some of those who visit them have mental problems, being "psychoneurotic" (*psykhonevrotychnyi*). Yet in their view a problem of the body or mind is first of all a spiritual problem. Their role is to heal "the whole person" through their exorcist prayers. The monks do not refer believers to psychiatrists, although psychiatrists from Ternopyl do sometimes send patients to the monastery. A successful cure confirms the cosmology of the exorcism ritual, whereas repeated failure produces mistrust, and religious healing is eventually abandoned. When the nineteen-year-old daughter of a university professor in L'viv began to behave strangely at home, her mother took her to a psychiatrist for a checkup. She was diagnosed with an advanced form of schizophrenia and prescribed medicine to slow the progression of the illness. The expensive medicine did nothing to improve the young woman's state. The mother had her doubts about the diagnosis; she thought her daughter's problem was more an illness of the soul (*dushevna balnoi*) than a psychological illness (*psykhichna balnoi*). Her suspicion, deriving from the daughter's excessive interest in spiritual literature, already placed the girl's affliction in the possible realm of spiritual healing. The parents began to seek alternative ways to challenge the medical diagnosis and find a cure for their daughter. When they learned about Kolodiivka, they decided to give it a try. The monks prayed for the young woman the first time the family came, and her condition improved. Encouraged, the family visited Kolodiivka two more times. After each visit the daughter felt better for a short time but later slumped back into deep crisis. For her parents it required a great effort just to come to the monastery, and the exorcism prayers brought only a temporary improvement in their daughter's health. Eventually they gave up the exorcism and began looking for another form of healing.

Alternative explanatory frameworks are at work in every society, and exorcism has always been one curative procedure among others. While the ritual form varies significantly, depending on period and religious tradition, the cosmology of exorcism has been remarkably constant over time (Grey 2005; Goodman 1988; Levi 1988). In this sense, exorcism is always modern, because the ritual process first destroys social meaning and then creates a new meaning following its own cosmology (Kapferer 2003). James Dow (1986: 56) suggested that the healing of a successful exorcism happens because "the culture establishes a general model of the mythic world believed in by healers and potential patients." The acceptance of possession creates a symbolic dissociation in the afflicted person: he or she is no longer one but two, the self and the evil spirit. The exorcism ritual proposes a symbolic reintegration of the self in which one has to get rid of the evil identified during the ritual. I have already stressed the role of the ritual context in the successful transmission of the ritual message; yet success is also dependent upon a certain predisposition toward imagistic practice and its conscious cultivation by monks.

Father Artemie, one of the exorcist priests, joined Father Planchak's community in Kolodiivka soon after its establishment. He came from an extremely religious Roman Catholic family; his three sisters were nuns in Byrki, the female branch of the monastery, and his brother was a Roman Catholic priest. He had studied theology with the Roman Catholic Franciscans in Poland but after four years had switched to the Eastern rite and entered the Basilian order. Determined to get closer to the Eastern Christian tradition, Artemie became interested in Planchak's community as soon as the news spread that a group was splitting off to start a new community. In Kolodiivka, Artemie found the environment he was looking for and became a priest and later an exorcist. Later, with Abbot Planchak's blessing, Artemie moved to the village of Dzhublyk to launch a small community of nuns and monks that was to be the basis for two new monasteries. Artemie believed in the veracity of the Marian apparition reported at Dzhublyk, but he soon became embroiled in a conflict between the local priest and the church hierarchy over the validity of the apparition. He had to abandon the project and return to Kolodiivka.

After his return, the Mother of God made her presence felt in Kolodiivka, too, in an event that is revealed to pilgrims only indirectly, through the messages read by Father Planchak to pilgrims on last Tuesdays. One of the younger nuns in Byrki, the associated convent, began to have visions of the Mother of God in 2001. Her private visions were first tested by the abbot and then accepted and even encouraged by him. She was asked to accept her gift, and while her influence on the abbot grew, her visions became increasingly important to the monastery. The community's inclination toward imagistic practices and the overwhelming presence of the Marian cult in the local religious tradition facilitated the acceptance of the visions by most monks and nuns. Other kinds of visions also manifested themselves among monks and sometimes among pilgrims. They involved trance (fainting), hallucinations (seeing or hearing), and sensorial experiences (turning numb, cold, or warm; suffocating). Some of the monks underwent such experiences more often, which were rendered meaningful with the help of their confessors, the exorcist priests. They thereby entered into the world of meaning of the exorcism and were encouraged to cultivate this kind of imagery (Noll 1985: 445) in order to increase their charisma. Visions and dreams were also favored as means for transmitting religious messages, as in classical accounts of shamanism (Stephen and Suryani 2000; Noll 1985) and certain movements within Roman Catholicism (Christian 1996; Csordas 1994).

The two modes of religiosity—the imagistic, as represented by visions and exorcisms, and the doctrinal, as represented by the monks' daily devotional routine—could coexist in the community as long as one mode was not accorded higher normative authority. But the visionary nun and the group around her began to impose imagistic practice as the most authentic form of knowledge for the monastery. The community found itself split between those who believed in her visions and cultivated a strongly imagistic mode of religiosity, fully expressed in the practice of exorcism, and those who questioned the authenticity and religious efficacy of such practices. With Abbot Planchak's support, the imagistic mode became the norm of the community, but this led to major conflicts and, in the end, to the departure of several monks from Kolodiivka in 2004–2005.

## CONCLUSION

In this chapter I have examined the interaction of Whitehouse's two modes of religiosity within a single monastic community. Breaking away from a traditional religious order, the splinter group reinterpreted doctrine in search of alternative models rooted in an ideal Orthodox spirituality. In Whitehouse's terms they migrated from doctrinal to imagistic, not because of boredom as he puts it, but in a constant search for self-improvement and expression, a typical feature of religious life in the turbulence of the postsocialist period. The spontaneous *communitas* that formed around Father Planchak was brought together around an ideal initially uttered by the founder and expressed above all in the practice of exorcism. The establishment of a community at Kolodiivka began to undermine the natural, ideologically based cohesion of the group and to replace it by monastic structure and standardized practice, as is usually the case with any normative *communitas*. However, this community's turn toward doctrinal went only halfway, as it increasingly took the shape of the imagistic ritual it was practicing.

The community stayed together for the best part of a decade thanks to the imagistic ritual that monks placed at the core of their monastery. Exorcism and the imaginary generated by it became a cohesive force legitimating the distinctiveness of the community. By cultivating the empowering discourse of spiritual gifts the community opened the exorcism ritual to pilgrims and priests, making them aware of its potential. Much as in Charismatic Christianity, which preaches a theology of spiritual gifts (Cox 1996; Csordas 1994), the monks in Kolodiivka experienced God through these gifts, the external measure of personal charisma. Discerning the spirits and exorcising them through the ritual performance was both an enactment of the monks' gift and the means for counteracting demonic presence in the monastery. "Seeing" was a spiritual gift of a few—the more experienced, charismatic monks—who were also the main sources of authority within the community.

The revelatory potential of exorcism was a sign of divine presence for the Kolodiivka monks. The imagery related to the devil was continually reinforced by the performance of the ritual. I argued that transmission of the religious message was successful because of the particular context of the ritual, which combined imagistic practices with standardized ritual forms. The emotionally powerful imagery triggered by the exorcism ritual forced new meanings into previous interpretations of illness and distress. The strength of the imaginary derived from the ritual performance and permeated the lived reality of monks and pilgrims in concrete ways. The healing aspect of the Kolodiivka ritual became more important than its theological meaning, developed by the church over the centuries. In the turbulent years of post-Soviet transformations, exorcism, like conversion, became a means for self-transformation and the creation of moral selves. Transformed by the experience of being exorcised, participants come out of the ritual as better persons, reconciled with both past and present and empowered to act according to a new moral order. The monastic community in Kolodiivka and its collective exorcisms participate in their own way in the vast enterprise of "converting

Ukrainian society," in which Evangelical Protestantism has been the driving force (see Wanner 2007).

In the postsocialist context, where political, economic, and social factors often have a very direct impact on religious dynamics, the conflicts that spark the emergence of religious splinter groups can rarely be reduced to a single cause. The ideal interaction of the modes, according to which imagistic religiosity emerges in a doctrinal tradition in order to revitalize it, is amplified by the imagistic proliferation characteristic of moments of social fluidity. According to the modes theory, a religious tradition succeeds through the dynamic interaction of imagistic and doctrinal modes; but this tension may not always be productive. As Pascal Boyer remarks, keeping the two modes separate may actually be a political move determined by religious specialists (Boyer 2002: 11–12). In cases where the modes coexist within one religious tradition or community of practice, conflicts are almost inevitable if one of the two modes is entirely repressed by the other. Kolodiivka emerged as part of the imagistic response to social transformations and created a complex ritual drawing on both doctrinal and imagistic modes. I have shown that in the monastery contestation intensified when one mode, the imagistic, was imposed as the sole normative form of religious practice. The monks who left Kolodiivka opposed the imposition of the imagistic mode and thereby denied the religious imaginary of the monastery, which had been shaped so decisively by the exorcism ritual. Thus the minority monks found themselves outside the world of meaning of their own community, and the community fissioned.

## NOTES

1. Kolodiivka was my third field site at that time, and I lived intermittently in the monastery in spring–summer 2004 and during a subsequent visit in 2005.

2. The Ukrainian Greek Catholic Church was banned in the Soviet Union in the period 1945–1989. After a period of intense repression in the 1950s, its surviving members organized themselves into an underground church that survived socialism.

3. The monks took over the village church and a nearby building that had previously been a school. This irked the villagers, who had hoped to see the school converted into a small food-processing factory.

4. From the beginning of Orthodox monasticism in medieval Rus' the multiethnic Orthodox monastic communities of Mount Athos were the basic source of Eastern Slavic monastic rules.

5. In Catholicism and Eastern Christianity, religious vows are promises made by members of monastic orders or brotherhoods to follow the evangelical commands that form the core of monasticism. After accomplishing a period of novitiate of usually one to two years a monk can take minor vows that are temporary and need to be renewed. Permanent vows are taken after several years to confirm the full commitment of the monk to the order.

6. The abbot's acceptance of the convict could have been motivated by the Eastern Christian tradition, which provides many examples of integration of convicts into monasteries. In Orthodox theology the thief crucified on Christ's right became one of the most important exemplars of salvation.

7. Recently, fear of abuse led to strong regulations and to a medicalization of the ritual. The Catholic Church enacted new guidelines for exorcists in 1999, as did the Anglican Church in the 1990s (Milner 2000).

8. For example, the medicalization and curing of *klikushestvo* (shrieking), a widespread phenomenon of possession and mass hysteria in nineteenth-century Russia, was a matter of importance for the modern science of psychiatry rising at the time in a traditional Orthodox society. Modern psychiatry was instrumental in changing the category of "soul illnesses" to "mental disturbance," thus posing a challenge to the traditional monopoly the church held over possession (Worobec 2001).

9. Possession by evil spirits as cause of a personal affliction is one among various aetiological systems; Janice Boddy (1994) offers an extended review of the literature. In Orthodoxy we encounter a form of involuntary possession in which an evil spirit takes over the body of a person, usually without the person's knowledge. I briefly illustrate the diagnosis of possession in this chapter, but a systematic analysis goes beyond the purpose of the chapter.

10. As Setha Low (1994) argues, the cultural construction of nerves as illness derives from a combination of factors related to social suffering. These include the breakdown of families or social networks, the loss of an intimate person, distress, and violence.

11. In his work on Charismatic Catholics Thomas Csordas describes this process of preritual socialization as bodily and mental preparation of the participant to accept the rhetoric of transformation proposed by the ritual, and thus to accept healing (Csordas 1994; 2002).

12. This exchange was recorded on 29 June 2004.

13. One could interpret the overwhelming presence of women and "weak" people among the possessed as an enactment of the power relations of a male-dominated society (cf. Lewis 1990). However, such an approach does not take account of exorcism's wider social, cultural, and aesthetic implications (Boddy 1994) and its particular role in the religious tradition.

# REFERENCES

Barth, F. 1987. *Cosmologies in the making: A generative approach to cultural variation in inner New Guinea.* Cambridge: Cambridge University Press.

Bloch, M. 1990. Language, anthropology, and cognitive science. *Man* 26: 183–98.

Boddy, J. 1994. Spirit possession revisited: Beyond instrumentality. *Annual Review of Anthropology* 23: 407–34.

Bourguignon, E., ed. 1973. *Religion, altered states of consciousness, and social change.* Columbus: Ohio State University Press.

Boyer, P. 1994. *The naturalness of religious ideas: A cognitive theory of religion.* Berkeley: University of California Press.

———. 2002. Book review forum: Arguments and icons: Divergent modes of religiosity. *Journal of Ritual Studies* 16: 8–13.

Caciola, N. 2000. Mystics, demoniacs, and the physiology of spirit possession in medieval Europe. *Comparative Studies in Society and History* 42: 268–306.

Christian, W.A. 1996. *Visionaries: The Spanish republic and the reign of Christ.* Berkeley: University of California Press.

Clough, P., and J.P. Mitchell. 2001. *Powers of good and evil: Social transformation and popular belief.* New York: Berghahn Books.

Cox, H.G. 1996. *Fire from heaven: The rise of pentecostal spirituality and the reshaping of religion in the twenty-first century.* London: Cassell.

Csordas, T. J. 1994. *The sacred self: A cultural phenomenology of charismatic healing.* Berkeley: University of California Press.

———. 2002. *Body/meaning/healing.* Basingstoke: Palgrave Macmillan.

Dow, J. 1986. Universal aspects of symbolic healing: A theoretical synthesis. *American Anthropologist* n.s. 88, no. 1: 56–69.

Geertz, C. 2000. *The interpretation of cultures: Selected essays.* New York: Basic Books.

Goodman, F. D. 1988. *How about demons? Possession and exorcism in the modern world.* Bloomington: Indiana University Press.

Grey, C. 2005. Demoniacs, dissent, and disempowerment in the late Roman West: Some case studies from the hagiographical literature. *Journal of Early Christian Studies* 13, no. 1: 39–69.

Harris, P. 2000. On not falling down to Earth: Children's metaphysical questions. In *Imagining the impossible: Magical, scientific, and religious thinking in children,* ed. Karl Sven Rosengren, Carl N. Johnson, and Paul L. Harris, 157–78. Cambridge: Cambridge University Press.

Kapferer, B. 1991. *A celebration of demons: Exorcism and the aesthetics of healing in Sri Lanka.* Explorations in Anthropology Series. Providence, R.I., Oxford, and Washington, D.C.: Smithsonian Institution Press.

———. 2003. *Beyond rationalism: Rethinking magic, witchcraft, and sorcery.* New York: Berghahn Books.

———. 2005. Ritual dynamics and virtual practice: Beyond representation and meaning. In *Ritual in its own right: Exploring the dynamics of transformation,* ed. D. Handelman and G. Lindquist, 35–54. New York: Berghahn Books.

Levi, G. 1988. *Inheriting power: The story of an exorcist.* Chicago: University of Chicago Press.

Lewis, I. M. 1990. Exorcism and male control of religious experience. *Ethnos* 55: 26–40.

Low, S. 1994. Embodied metaphors: Nerves as lived experience. In *Embodiment and experience: The existential ground of culture and self,* ed. T. Csordas, 139–62. Cambridge: Cambridge University Press.

Meyer, B. 1999. *Translating the devil: Religion and modernity among the Ewe in Ghana.* Trenton, N.J.: Africa World Press.

Milner, N. 2000. Giving the devil his due process: Exorcism in the Church of England. *Journal of Contemporary Religion* 15: 247–72.

Naumescu, V. 2006. Religious pluralism and the imagined Orthodoxy of Western Ukraine. In *The postsocialist religious question: Faith and power in Central Asia and East-Central Europe.* Chris Hann and the Civil Religion Group, 241–68. Berlin: Lit Verlag.

———. 2007. *Modes of religiosity in Eastern Christianity: Religious processes and social change in Ukraine.* Halle Studies in the Anthropology of Eurasia. Berlin: Lit Verlag.

Noll, R. 1985. Mental imagery cultivation as a cultural phenomenon: The role of visions in shamanism. *Current Anthropology* 26, no. 4: 443–61.

Obeyesekere, G. 1981. *Medusa's hair: An essay on personal symbols and religious experience.* Chicago: University of Chicago Press.

Parkin, D. 1986. *The anthropology of evil.* Oxford: Blackwell.

Severi, C. 2004. Capturing imagination: A cognitive approach to cultural complexity. *Journal of the Royal Anthropological Institute* 10: 815–38.

Sperber, D. 1985. Anthropology and psychology: Towards an epidemiology of representations. *Man* 20, no. 1: 73–89.

Stephen, M., and L. K. Suryani. 2000. Shamanism, psychosis, and autonomous imagination. *Culture, Medicine, and Psychiatry* 24: 5–40.

Stewart, C. 1991. *Demons and the devil: Moral imagination in modern Greek culture.* Princeton Modern Greek Studies. Princeton, N.J.: Princeton University Press.

Turner, V. 1996. *Drama, fields, and metaphors: Symbolic action in human society.* Symbol, Myth, and Ritual Series. Ithaca, N.Y.: Cornell University Press.

Wanner, C. 2003. Advocating new moralities: Conversion to Evangelicalism in Ukraine. *Religion, State, and Society* 31, no. 3: 273–87.

———. 2007. *Communities of the converted: Ukrainians and global evangelism.* Ithaca, N.Y.: Cornell University Press.

Whitehouse, H. 1995. *Inside the cult: Religious innovation and transmission in Papua New Guinea.* Oxford: Clarendon Press.

———. 2000. *Arguments and icons: Divergent modes of religiosity.* Oxford: Oxford University Press.

———. 2004. *Modes of religiosity: A cognitive theory of religious transmission.* Walnut Creek, Calif.: AltaMira Press.

Worobec, C. D. 2001. *Possessed: Women, witches, and demons in imperial Russia.* DeKalb, Ill.: Northern Illinois University Press.

# 7

# Monasteries, Politics, and Social Memory

## *The Revival of the Greek Orthodox Church of Antioch in Syria during the Twentieth Century*

### Anna Poujeau

Since the beginning of the twentieth century, the Greek Orthodox Church of Antioch and all the East,[1] the largest Christian denomination in Syria, has been a supporter of pan-Arabism. This ideology was born out of reactions to foreign domination by the Ottoman empire and later France and Great Britain. It was originally founded on the collective idea that anyone who lived in an Arab territory and spoke Arabic was de facto a member of the Great Arab Nation, and that this allegiance took precedence over religious, regional, or tribal ties and identities. During the first half of the twentieth century, the idea of a pan-Arabic unity gave birth to different nationalist political positions in the region, such as Nasserism in Egypt and Ba'athism in Iraq and Syria (see Carré 1991, 1993; Amin 1976). The Ba'ath Party has ruled Syria under various presidents since 1963. The coup d'état of Hafez al-Assad in 1970 marked the beginning of the "Assad era." Bashar succeeded his father in 2000. For the current regime, pan-Arabism is more than a background political ideology. It is the major political fact used by the government to justify the possession of power by the Alawite minority.[2] Hafez al-Assad prepared his coup d'état with great care, manipulating the communal solidarities not only of his own community but also of other religious minorities, such as the Druze and the Greek Orthodox, some of whose members were given key positions in the army and the Ba'ath Party. In the name of the "laic" ideology of Ba'athism, Hafez al-Assad introduced various laws to separate religion from the state and legitimate his own accession to the presidency (Picard 1980, 1996, 1997, 2005).

In defending an Arab nationalism judiciously accommodated to the local Islamic context, the Syrian Ba'ath has enabled the Alawite community to maintain unbroken dominance for almost four decades without having to encounter strong opposition (see Lesch 2005; Ma'oz, Ginat, and Winckler 1999; Van Dam 1996; and Seale [1988] 1989). The Greek Orthodox Church of Antioch (hereafter GOCA) has complied with the regime and been an important vehicle for spreading the Arab nationalist message. Although the present government remains authoritarian, Ba'athist power has cultivated carefully differentiated links with each of the country's diverse religious groups. My aim in this chapter is to analyze the present political position of the GOCA in this Syrian sociopolitical context, with particular attention to the monastic revival of the last thirty years, during which the Syrian government has encouraged the Greek Orthodox Church to acquire and develop new lands. It has given prompt authorization for building and offered construction materials at the same discounted prices as are charged for government projects. The patriarchate has responded by extending the church's presence over the entire territory of the country. Many places that the community considers to have been the scene of miracles and saintly apparitions in the past have been restored, and new monasteries have been built to welcome monastic communities and pilgrims (Poujeau 2007).[3] Obviously the church's early alliance with the Ba'ath Party facilitated this religious mission. Without the support of the Syrian government and the Alawite community, this renewal would surely have attracted accusations of imperialism and worse. Thanks to its adherence to the ideology of the Great Arab Nation and Greater Syria, the Greek Orthodox Church of Antioch was even able to extend its influence to Lebanon. When the presence of the Syrian army in Lebanon was hotly contested, Greek Orthodox bishops shared platforms with militants of the Shi'ite party Hezbollah, united in the defense of their pan-Arab community, as they perceived its convictions.

The Greek Orthodox Church is, then, clearly subordinate to the power of Damascus. How has its patriarch succeeded in reconciling this profane subordination with a mission of monastic revival? This chapter focuses firstly on the historical commitments of the church to pan-Arabism and shows why it was not able to be more politically engaged in the past. Secondly, it outlines the reconstruction of the church during the twentieth century and shows how monasticism, which represents a kind of authentic tradition, has been constitutive for the entire community. Finally, it inquires into the further implications of this religious phenomenon for relationships between the Greek Orthodox community and the Syrian state.

## HISTORICAL BACKGROUND

The Greek Orthodox Church of Antioch was not always as well integrated in its sociopolitical environment as it is today. The decision to embrace the pan-Arab political position was the brilliant political strategy of a previously weak church.[4] The first expression of this pan-Arab orientation was the work of Gregorius

Haddad (1859–1928), who became patriarch of Antioch and all the East in 1907. He took advantage of the opportunity presented by the Arab Kingdom of Faisal to reject the French Mandate and to demonstrate that his community belonged to an Arab state. Patriarch Haddad affirmed the rooting of the GOCA in the Arab world, and his great interest in Islamic history and law, together with his involvement in Arab nationalism, made him a very popular figure both in his own community and among Muslims. (After his death he was often called the "Patriarch of the Muslims.") Within a few years of the collapse of the Ottoman empire it was no longer necessary to be a Muslim in order to participate in the political struggle, and the patriarch realized that to embrace Arab nationalism would present advantage for members of minorities confined under Ottoman domination to *dhimmi* status (see Braude and Lewis 1982).

The GOCA had been in decline since the second half of the seventeenth century, partly because of the massive impact of Roman Catholic missionaries. Torn between the Roman Catholic Church and the Russian Orthodox Church's aspiration to control the churches of the Middle East, many priests, bishops, and even some patriarchs had converted to Catholicism (in the form of Uniatism, which allowed them to maintain their rite), and the GOCA had strengthened the old conciliar bonds with the Ecumenical Patriarchate of Constantinople.[5] In 1917 the Russian Revolution had deprived the Greek Orthodox community in Syria and Lebanon of the protection of the Russian Orthodox Church. With the collapse of the Ottoman empire in the following year, the Greek Orthodox authorities made the decisive political choice to support the establishment of a Great Arab Nation, in opposition to the ruling European powers. From the beginning, this choice involved a subtle game of encouraging the "secularization" of society as part of the struggle to establish an unifying Arab identity. As an institution the GOCA was politically and economically too weak in this era to be an effective leader of Arab nationalism. Although some of the founding members of the Ba'ath Party, such as Michel Aflak, and the Popular Syrian Party (PPS), such as Antoine Saade, came from the Greek Orthodox community, they made their mark as individuals rather than as representatives of their community. In any case these politicians tended to present themselves as atheists. The church gradually consolidated its position after the independence of Syria and Lebanon in 1941.

The establishment in 1942 of the Orthodox Youth Movement by fifteen young students of the Faculty of Law and Medicine of the University of Saint Joseph in Beirut was a major step in the strengthening of the church's position. Metropolitan Georges Khodr (as he was later known) was elected general secretary. He declared to the other founding members: "We have kindled this flame in the Antiochian Church; if the day shall come when we wish to give up our mission, a new generation will rise up to take our place. This is how the flame will keep burning, from one generation to another."[6] In 2004, he recalled: "Full of Christ's spirit, burning with the Gospel we invented a new language . . . yes in our Church the old were resuscitated through their children."[7] This religious movement spread rapidly by utilizing the existing network of parishes and dioceses. It promoted a range of social activities all over Lebanon and Syria, as well as more specifically religious groups such as Bible study classes. In 1945, only three years after its creation, the Orthodox Youth Movement was recognized by the Holy Synod as a "major spiritual movement." Its books and the magazine *An Nour* (The light) are still widely read. Since 1970 the church has improved education for priests through the creation of the Saint John of Damascus Institute of Theology in the ancient monastery of Balamand in Northern Lebanon. In 1988, two years before the end of the Lebanese civil war, three new faculties were created to form the University of Balamand. In the second half of the twentieth century the church had consolidated itself into a powerful institution.

## THE REBIRTH OF GREEK ORTHODOX MONASTICISM

From its foundation the Orthodox Youth Movement encouraged its members to engage with monastic life. Until the 1950s, Syria had only three small ascetic communities: nunneries dedicated to the Virgin and Saint Thekla in the villages of Saydnaya and Maaloula respectively, close to Damascus, and the monastery of Saint George, near the city of Homs. Monks and nuns prepared publications for the Orthodox Youth Movement, such as the volume published in 1999 by the mother superior of the new monastery of Bloumana in western Syria, which laid out the steps in becoming a nun. Children, teenagers, and young adults are now welcomed several times a year at the various monasteries of the region. Whether alone or with their families, friends, or groups of scouts, visitors can stay and participate in religious life for up to a few weeks. The Orthodox Youth Movement also organizes summer camps and spiritual retreats for its members, which emphasize the role of the monastic communities in representing and passing on tradition.[8]

The church's authorities have carefully nurtured the recent expansion of monasticism. In November 1977 Patriarch Elias IV Moawad declared:

> The creation of monastic communities is an indication of the spiritual maturity of the faithful. . . . The church needs both parish clergy and monks. A church that does not have these two complementary aspects is not complete. . . . Without the monasteries we are guided only by the bishops, and a bad bishop could drive his people toward evil. Herein lies the great importance of the monasteries. They have always been the history and the protection of Orthodoxy.[9]

Seven years later, in August 1984, Patriarch Ignace IV Hazim reaffirmed these ideas: "The monastic communities are an important element of my aim of revival.

Monasticism must be the purest element of the church."[10] Monasticism, with the vocation it creates, is considered by both patriarchs to be an authentic Eastern tradition and therefore a key element in the renewal of the community, going far beyond the acquisition of new land and the renovation of delapidated buildings. In the current context, the authenticity of a tradition is crucial to claims to modernity (see Couroucli, this volume). Less explicit but, as I shall argue, just as important is the way that monasticism allows the patriarchate to engage in different kinds of political concerns, all of them "impure." Whereas ascetics establish links with the saints and God, priests, bishops, and patriarchs deal with the political men of the country. Both relationships are necessary for the constitution of the religious community (Weber [1922] 1996: 329–486). The Patriarchate of Antioch and all the East can develop its lay political role only if it is perceived as the authentic representative of a united community, strongly rooted in Syrian history and territory. This community is reaffirmed in rituals at the country's various monasteries.

## THE INVENTION OF MONASTIC TRADITION

In order to revive the tradition of Eastern monasticism in Syria, the GOCA has built and restored several monasteries, notably that in the village of Saydnaya, only thirty-five kilometers from Damascus. The proximity of this village to the ultimate location of political power is consistent with the church's political aspirations. Damascus cannot ignore this presence, which is rendered concrete when the monastery marks major feast days with very public celebrations.

The creation of a monastery is always supported by a local story about an event that happened a very long time ago (*men zaman*), which gives the site its sacred character. The subject might be a saint's apparition, miracles on the grave of a saint, or a sermon he is thought to have given there. Whatever the detail, the saint and his action have marked the space and transformed it into a sacred place. Sometimes a small chapel or shrine was built in the distant past and maintained by the inhabitants of the closest village. In founding new monasteries, the Greek Orthodox Church exploits these circumstances and accounts. By producing for all visitors, Christian and Muslim, diverse hagiographies and illustrated narratives of the sacred events that took place in Syrian territory, the ancient presence of the GOCA in Syrian territory is confirmed. Large crowds take part in an annual pilgrimage to commemorate the founding miracle or the feast of the saint to whom the monastery is dedicated (for instance, 'aid mar taqla is celebrated on 24 September at Saint Thekla's feast in the monastery of Saint Thekla, located in the village of Maaloula, sixty kilometers from Damascus). Such a pilgrimage lasts for several days and consists of two categories of activities. First, each pilgrim, Christian or Muslim, comes to ask for the *baraka* (benediction) of the saint in order to be protected, according to the saint's specialty, from illnesses, infertility, and so on. Second, activities that evoke the collective memory of the GOCA take place. The two categories of ritual are observed in two different parts of the monastery. Although their size and locations vary (some are situated on top of a hill, others in a valley or the desert), each monastery contains an ancient section and a new section. The ancient section is usually a chapel or a shrine where the saint appeared or a source of water with which the saint was supposedly baptized or which he or she used to heal the population. These places are the object of individual pious visits. The rest of the monastery is physically separate and consists of modern bedrooms for the pilgrims, a kitchen, living rooms, dining rooms, and gardens. Pilgrims circulate between these two sections of the monastery. In the ancient section the atmosphere is calm. People pray, light candles, kiss the grave, make votive offerings, and drink sacred water. In the new section, pilgrims meet to evoke the history of their community, from its origin to the present. The tone here is very relaxed: men and women play music, sing, and dance traditional folk dances *(dabke),* while old women recite poems celebrating the saint, the monastic community, and God.

Pilgrims often talk about other monasteries and recommend their favorite. For instance, a middle-aged woman from Damascus whom I met during a visit to the monastery of Saint George in the village of Saydnaya spoke about another monastery situated close to Homs and the Lebanese border:

> My God, you have to go there, it is like heaven, everything is green, there is a lot of water, and you can see Lebanon from this place, it is on the top of a mountain. There are so many fruits on the trees that you just have to pick them; the food is very good and not expensive. The monastery is very big. . . . My God, when you pass the door it is heaven.

This kind of discourse does not use everyday speech but rather "extraordinary" language. The monastery is compared to heaven, and the abundance of nature is emphasized. If the monastery in question is situated in the desert the pilgrim is likely to evoke its quietness and the simple life of its community, in contrast to the luxury of the patriarchate in Damascus. Such discourse always glorifies the monasteries and opposes them to the cities, especially the capital, and the parishes.

Monasteries are open to visitors throughout the year. To justify her frequent visits to another monastery, a woman explained:

> Each time I go there, it is like the first time. Everything is enhanced; the faith is much more important than in the churches of Damascus. I like this place, the mountains. . . . It is so quiet. I like to work with the monks and the other pilgrims. We cook for everybody, we share everything, we pray together. Whenever I am not feeling well in Damascus I come here. God gave us the monastery. But I do not want

to become a nun; I have a good job in Damascus. . . . But sometimes God pushes me to come here. In the churches in Damascus, the priest says Mass and that's all, while in the monasteries, the monks and the nuns devote their entire lives to God.

Another woman who came with ten members of her family during a pilgrimage explained that though she was very proud of all the monasteries in Syria, in the course of the year she and her family regularly visited a monastery close to their village:

> All Christian people visit the monasteries because they are the first Christian places, the most ancient ones.. . . It is true that sometimes the monastery is new, but the place has been sacred for a very long time, and before, when the monastery was in ruins, people still came and prayed.. . . In the end it is the same thing. Of course currently it is very nice because we can sleep here and there are some monks, but even before the people still came here.

The monasteries represent a refuge for people who feel the need to leave their worldly life temporarily. The practices and discourses associated with them have changed significantly over time. The eldest people (about eighty years old) I interviewed had no memory of such huge pilgrimages. They can recall only a few small shrines in the entire region that were dedicated to saints and looked after by local people. People living in the surrounding countryside visited these places to make vows only on the occasion of the saint's annual feast day, when a mass was celebrated by the priest of the closest village. These holy sites were referred to generically as *mazar*, and they were seldom if ever home to monastic communities. Today, however, members of both majority and minority religious traditions are encouraged to see these sites as the remnants of ancient large monasteries, presumably destroyed by the Ottomans. This is an invented tradition, or even a blatant falsification, since there is no archaeological research to support such an interpretation of history, but its dissemination enables the GOCA to erect imposing new buildings, which are much more visible in the landscape than the small shrines.

In order to renew an ancient way of "living Christianity" the new monastic communities may draw creatively on various cultural elements. For instance, at the monastery of Saint Serge, which is also located in the village of Maaloula, a monk who is originally Lebanese claims to revive the Aramaic language. According to scholars, Aramaic was spoken by small numbers of Christians and Muslims in this region (Qalamoun) until the beginning of the twentieth century (Reich 1937). In the village of Maaloula, whose population is predominantly Christian, the revival of this ancient language offers villagers a way to assert their Aramaic origins and their close affinity with the ancient Christians, since Aramaic is presented as the language of Jesus Christ. As part of his strategy to present his

FIGURE 7.1. Youth enact the scene represented on the icon of Saint George, Monastery of Saint George at Saydnaya, Saint George's Day, 6 May 2004. Photograph by Anna Poujeau.

monastery as perpetuating an authentic Christian tradition and culture, the monk prays in Aramaic in front of the visitors to the monastery and presents them with a small Aramaic alphabet as a souvenir.

The feasts organized within the monasteries for the saints to whom they are dedicated have also changed considerably. Young people from the closest village are invited to play an important role in the feast. For instance, for the feast on 6 May at the monastery of Saint George, which is located near the village of Saydnaya (thirty-five kilometers from Damascus), local youth enact the scene represented on the icon of Saint George, in the main court of the monastery after Mass. One young man dresses as Saint George, mounts a horse (see fig. 7.1), slays the dragon (played by another young man), and frees a young girl dressed as a princess. Crowds gather to watch this spectacle and applaud the feat of the saint. Afterward, a group of young men carries the icon of Saint George in a lengthy procession through the streets of the village to the larger Greek Orthodox monastery dedicated to Our Lady of Saydnaya. Villagers throw rice, flowers, and rosewater at the young men, who dance and sing behind the icon. When the procession arrives at the larger monastery in the late afternoon it is crammed with pilgrims from all the country. The nuns there bless the young men with flowers, sweets, and rose-

FIGURE 7.2. Nuns bless the young men who carried the icon of Saint George in procession, Monastery of Our Lady of Saydnaya, Saint George's Day, 6 May 2004. Photograph by Anna Poujeau.

water (see fig. 7.2), and the villagers and pilgrims dance the local *dabke* until late into the night.

A priest from Aleppo whom I met in a monastery offered this concise summary of the experience of Syrian Christians:

> The monasteries are the most important places for Christians in Syria. For the people monasticism represents a constructive symbol to live their Christianity each day. After visiting a monastery they are able to have a normal life; it is essential. But having these monasteries also means that we feel good, here in Syria, we feel at home, and the monasteries are the representation of this feeling.

Patriarch Ignace IV Hazim continues this theme, arguing that the history and the revival of the community is built by and in the monasteries through the monastic communities. This history seems to take root in a very remote past that cannot be dated. Only a few marks can be traced through the imprints of the saints, around which the larger monasteries have been built. Visitors are encouraged to perceive monasteries as witnesses to the Christian past. Pilgrims are allowed a glimpse of how Christian life was in the past, before the Islamic conquest. The desert monastery of Saint Moussa is particularly appreciated because the comforts of life are scarce there, and the food very simple. The ascetics have no personal possessions, and they do a lot of manual work in the monastery, in addition to daily meditation and silence. Pilgrims are invited to emulate the monks, even though they may stay in the monastery for only one or two days. For a short time they enjoy a very distinctive *communitas* and reflect on the lives of those who constructed the first Christian communities in the region.

Internal monastic discourses emphasize that Christianity is older than Islam, and the Christian origins of Muslims are regularly evoked by all, from the humblest parishioners to Patriarch Ignace IV Hazim. In an interview in the Damascus daily newspaper *al-Joumhouriya* in 1984 the patriarch observed:

> The Arabic world is not Muslim; the leaders of the Arabic countries are Muslims, but among the people there are some Christians. . . . I already remarked in the past that the Muslims are guests, for us Christians. God put us in this part of the world to stay, and we will stay.[11]

In this context monasteries are religious landmarks, and the Christian collective memory would be impoverished without them. The ritual that takes place within them is the construction and commemoration of the community itself. At the same time through the discourses of the patriarchs they have become new symbols for the political affirmation of the group's presence in the Syrian state. Within the monasteries the members of the GOCA can revive their sense of their historical place in Syrian territory. The realization of these links, especially during a pilgrimage to a place inscribed by a saint, makes the community itself sacred. The patriarchs are then able to inscribe the community in the general political dialogue, since monasticism proves indisputably that GOCA members belong to the region and to the state. As the representative authority of a community, the patriarchate is considered by Syrian leaders to be an essential partner in political dialogue.[12]

## NUNS AS MARTYRS

Patriarchs Elias IV Moawad and Ignace IV Hazim have argued that monasticism unites the whole community, both lay and religious members, and creates and sustains tradition. To understand how this takes place it is necessary to untangle the links between the laity, the parish clergy, and the patriarchate, on the one hand, and the monasteries and their ascetic communities, on the other. While the former are involved primarily with worldly affairs, ascetic men and women form a separate order, which is nonetheless essential to the construction of the whole community (Weber [1922] 1996). Monasteries are physically and imaginatively remote from the various parish churches in the cities and from the patriarchate in Damascus. As Antoine Guillaumont (1979) has argued, monastic life stands in opposition to political life, just as asceticism contrasts with practical life more generally. Monks and nuns pursue a contemplative life away from society and all its practical concerns, including those of their own families. My analysis of the nunnery of Saint Thekla, situated in the village of Maaloula, only sixty kilometers from Damascus, has shown that while the nuns devote their lives to the saint and to the worship of God and Jesus Christ, their internal organization as a separate community permits the whole of the Greek Orthodox community to reproduce itself. The nuns use particular discourses to explain and justify the turning points in their lives, all of which are somehow linked to Saint Thekla, the famous disciple of Saint Paul. Saint Thekla is venerated as a virgin and a martyr, "the equal of the apostles," for it is she who controls the nunnery. The nuns look upon themselves as Saint Thekla's daughters.[13] Their decision to enter the nunnery is usually dictated by the saint, who appears to them in a dream or speaks to them during their prayers, convincing them to join this particular nunnery. Saint Thekla continues to help them during difficult periods of their lives through dreams or various revelations. Although it is the mother superior who decides who is to be admitted as a novice and later to stay as a nun, she says that her decisions are inspired by the saint. After about thirty years in residence the nuns are allowed to watch over the shrine of the saint for the entire day, thereby establishing very intimate relations with the saint. Some of the nuns affirm that they have spoken with her (see also Hanganu and Forbess, this volume).

The nuns' lives revolve around two additional elements. They present themselves as fiancées of Jesus Christ, and they plan for a supernatural life after death. In fact, death must celebrate their wedding with Jesus Christ, and their ultimate aim is to create an alliance with "Him." According to the entire Greek Orthodox community, the death of a nun marks the best Christian alliance. Now, in the context of a minority in the Middle East, marriage is not merely a question of alliance between two groups of kin for political or economic reasons, it is above all an alliance within the community to strengthen the community. Only such an alliance can preserve the dynamic of community construction ad infinitum. In Syria, as elsewhere in the Arab Middle East, children take the religion of their father. A Christian man cannot marry a Muslim girl without becoming Muslim himself. Mixed marriages jeopardize the whole group and the honor of the daughter's family members. They lose a girl and a descendant, and they cannot hope for anything in return. However, when a nun marries Jesus Christ she weds the first of the Christians. She remains within the community in an unproductive marriage that preserves her virginity. This exceptional alliance with the founder of the community inscribes the nun into a realm of perfect purity. From it, unlike all other alliances, the nun's family members gain special prestige. This in turn inscribes these kin into the field of "sacred" and confers on them a privileged position within the community as good Christians.

Within the community the nuns are presented as martyrs. They have voluntarily excluded themselves from society, sometimes for fifty years or more, in order to become, firstly, the daughters of the saint, and secondly, the fiancées of Jesus Christ, and finally, upon dying, His wives. The whole community can then respect them and even pray to them as intermediaries, even though within the monastery their memories are not celebrated, and their graves are scarcely visible to visitors. Only the mother superiors are commemorated by having their photos displayed on the walls of the big room used for pilgrim visits. Yet everybody agrees that all deceased nuns are martyrs. Outside their own lineages they become anonymous, but their individuality is not important, since they are not specific role models. Following Weber ([1922] 1996) we can argue that the nuns are the witnesses of the religion that founds the whole community. In this way nunneries as well as monasteries symbolically participate in the continuous re-creation of the whole Greek Orthodox community by enabling a perpetual return to the community's origins in the region.[14]

Because of their social exclusion, monks, too, are considered martyrs by the wider community. The main difference between monks and nuns is that the former can aspire to play an important role in the church hierarchy, which is exclusively male, whereas nuns cannot occupy positions outside their convents. Bishops and patriarchs are chosen from among monk-priests, while priests who do not belong to a monastic brotherhood (even in the Greek Catholic churches) are required to marry and are then ineligible for high office. Hence, as with nuns, the family members of monks can gain prestige through their association with the sacred. But for the nuns' family members this prestige accrues through the relative's death as a "virgin" and "wife of Jesus Christ," whereas in the monks' case high prestige is gained by family members only when their relative is promoted within the church hierarchy.[15]

CONCLUSION

In this chapter I have sought to show how the establishment of monastic communities has contributed to the construction of the collective memory of the Greek Orthodox community in Syria. The capacity of the GOCA to implant new monasteries in the Syrian landscape has allowed the community to claim stronger historical roots in Arab territory and to blend seamlessly into an pan-Arab community. The representation of the renewal of monasticism as the perpetuation of an authentic tradition has been a successful strategy to legitimate the church's action within the Syrian political context. The GOCA owes its success to its skill in persuading all Syrians that it is merely renewing a tradition and in no way jeopardizing the country's political balance. Monasteries, monks, and nuns are associated with a very ancient past, which might appear irrelevant in the contemporary political context. I have shown, however, that monasticism is more than a religious order structuring the GOCA community internally; it is also a key factor in the accomplishment of state-level political integration, which is exemplified by the patriarchate's role in the Syrian government. Through the rituals performed during feasts for the saints to whom the monasteries are dedicated, and through the continuing stream of pilgrims throughout the year, the GOCA demonstrates its strength. Without this visibility it would be difficult for its priests, bishops, and patriarch to relate as the representatives of a community to politicians at all levels. From this point of view, monasticism, ostensibly oriented toward the other world, is central to the political construction of the GOCA and provides legitimation for the patriarchate's political engagement.

## NOTES

1. The Patriarchate of Antioch and all the East has been based in Damascus since 1342. Today it has authority over Greek Orthodox Christians of Syria and Lebanon and their respective parishes in the worldwide diaspora.

2. The al-Assads belong to the Alawite minority, which, like the Shi'ite, Druze, and Ismailite minorities, are considered nonconformist by the Sunni majority in Syria.

3. We shall see how the establishment of monastic communities has contributed to the construction of a kind of collective memory for the Greek Orthodox community in Syria. The restoration and construction of large monasteries undertaken by the Greek Orthodox Church of Antioch demonstrate the church's will to impose its own historical stamp on national territory. The construction of this particular historiography must be considered in the general context of goverment policy, which has allowed and indeed fostered the Greek Orthodox community's social inscription in the national landscape and its political inscription in Syrian society.

4. This can be appreciated when one compares the strategy followed by the Greek Catholic Church of Antioch with that of the Maronite Church in Lebanon, which chose to support the French Mandate.

5. In 1774, the Ottomans granted Russia the right to protect all Christian Orthodox members of the empire. After their arrival in the region in 1831, the Jesuits created the francophile University of Saint Joseph (USJ) in Beirut, and British Protestant missionaries founded the anglophile Syrian Protestant College (now the American University of Beirut). Catholic and Protestant missionaries helped to train a clergy that was educationally far superior to the clergy of the Orthodox Church.

6. See the Web site of the Youth Orthodox Movement: www.mjoa.org.

7. See the Web site of the Greek Orthodox Church of Antioch: www.ortmtlb.org.

8. For instance, at the monastery of Saint Thekla in the village of Maaloula the Orthodox Youth Movement has a house for young members wishing to spend a few days there in the company of the nuns or to take part in a spiritual retreat. Sometimes the OYM's members help with farmwork or maintenance tasks at the monastery. It is a way "to be actively involved in the renewal of Christian monasticism in Syria and through that carry on an ancient tradition" (interview with young member of the OYM, Monastery of Saint Takla [Thekla], Syria, June 2004).

9. Patriarch Elias IV Moawad, speech, SOP 22 (1977); my translation. SOP is an Orthodox monthly news bulletin published in Courbevoie, France.

10. Patriarch Ignace IV Hazim, interview given to the Lebanese daily al-Nahar, reprinted in SOP 90 (1984); my translation.

11. Patriarch Ignace IV Hazim, 1984 interview given to the Damascus daily al-Joumhouriya, reprinted in Proche Orient chrétien 35 (1985): 381–84.

12. A similar structure can be noted in state relationships with the Maronite Church, especially the Patriarchate of Bkerke in Lebanon. The twentieth-century revival of the Coptic monastic movement in Egypt can be viewed analogously.

13. The first convent of St. Thekla was founded in early Christian times near the Cilician settlement of Seleukia (present-day Silifko, Turkey); it is still an important destination for pilgrims, now mainly Muslims.

14. See also Valter's (2002) analysis of how the government has sought legitimacy by emphasizing the territorial rootedness of the Syrian people.

15. It should be noted that the principle of virginity in monastic life is nonetheless independent of a person's sex. Monks, too, may qualify as "wise virgins," those who are waiting for Christ as their "bridegroom." Both nuns and monks are exemplars for laypeople, for all Christians are called upon to follow the examples of the wise virgins (see the hymns of Orthodox Holy Week).

## REFERENCES

Amin, S. 1976. *La nation arabe: Nationalisme et luttes de classes.* Paris: Éditions de minuit.

Botiveau, B. 1998. The law of the nation-state and the status of non-Muslims in Egypt and Syria. In *Christian communities in the Arab Middle East,* ed. A. Paci, 111–26. New York: Clarendon Press.

Braude, B., and B. Lewis. 1982. *Christians and Jews in the Ottoman empire: The functioning of a plural society.* New York: Holmes & Meier Publishers .

Brown, P. 1988. *The body and society: Men, women, and sexual renunciation in early Christianity.* New York: Columbia University Press.

Carré, O. 1991. *L'Orient arabe aujourd'hui.* Coll. Historiques. Brussels: Éditions Complexe.

———. 1993. *Le nationalisme arabe.* Paris: Petite Bibliothèque Payot.

Davie, M. 1993. Les orthodoxes entre Beyrouth et Damas: Une millet chrétienne dans deux villes ottomanes. In *State and society in Syria and Lebanon,* ed. Y. M. Choueiri, 32–45. Exeter: University of Exeter Press.

Escolan, P. 1999. *Monachisme et église: Le monachisme syrien du IV au VII siècle: Un ministère charismatique.* Théologie Historique. Paris: Beauchesne.

Frazee, C. 1983. *Catholics and sultans: The church and the Ottoman empire (1453–1923).* London: Cambridge University Press.

Guillaumont, A. 1979. *Aux origines du monachisme chrétien: Pour une phénoménologie du monachisme.* Spiritualité Orientale et Vie Monastique 30. Bégrolles en Mauges: Abbaye de Bellefontaine.

Hechaïmé, C. 1998. The cultural production of Arab Christians today: An expression of their identity in a predominantly Muslim society. In *Christian communities in the Arab Middle East,* ed. A. Paci, 155–71. New York: Clarendon Press.

Herrou, A. 2005. *La vie entre soi: Les moines taoïstes aujourd'hui en Chine.* Recherches sur la Haute Asie 15. Nanterre: Société d'ethnologie.

Hourani, A. 1947. *Minorities in the Arab world.* London: Oxford University Press.

Kedourie, E. 1992. *Politics in the Middle East.* New York: Oxford University Press.

Khawaga, D. el. 1998. The political dynamics of the Copts: Giving the community an active role. In *Christian communities in the Arab Middle East*, ed. A. Paci, 172–99. New York: Clarendon Press.

Khoury, P. S. 1983. *Urban notables and Arab nationalism: The politics of Damascus, 1860–1920.* Cambridge: Cambridge University Press.

———. 1987. *Syria and the French Mandate: The politics of Arab nationalism, 1920–1945.* London: Princeton University Press.

Lesch, W. D. 2005. *The new lion of Damascus: Bashar al-Asad and modern Syria.* New Haven: Yale University Press.

Maʾoz, M., J. Ginat, and O. Winckler. 1999. *Modern Syria: From Ottoman rule to pivotal role in the Middle East.* Brighton and Portland, U.K.: Sussex Academic Press.

Papadakis, A. 1988. The historical tradition of church-state relations under Orthodoxy. In *Eastern Christianity and politics in the twentieth century*, ed. P. Ramet, 37–58. Durham, N.C.: Duke University Press.

Picard, E. 1980. Y a-t-il un problème communautaire en Syrie. *Monde arabe Maghreb Machrek* 87: 7–21.

———. 1996. Fin des parties en Syrie. *Revue des mondes musulmans et de la Méditerranée* 81–82: 207–9.

———. 1997. La Syrie de l'après guerre froide: Permanences et changements: Présentation. *Monde arabe Maghreb Machrek* 158: 3–4.

———. 2005. Syrie, la coalition autoritaire fait de la résistance. *Politique étrangère* 4: 757–68.

Poujeau, A. 2007. Les monastères de Syrie: Ancrage sacré des églises et inscription politique dans le territoire national. *Théologiques* 15, no. 1: 95–112.

———. 2008. Églises, monachisme et sainteté: Construction de la communauté chrétienne en Syrie. PhD diss., Université Paris X Nanterre.

———. 2009. Partager la baraka des saints: Des visites pluriconfessionnelles aux monastères chrétiens en Syrie. In *Religions traversées: Lieux saints partagés entre chrétiens, musulmans et juifs en Méditerranée*, ed. D. Albera and M. Couroucli, 295-319. Études Méditerranéennes. Arles: Actes Sud.

Ramet, P. 1988. Autocephaly and national identity in church—state relations in Eastern Christianity: An introduction. In *Eastern Christianity and politics in the twentieth century*, ed. P. Ramet, 3–19. Durham, N.C.: Duke University Press.

Reich, S. 1937. *Étude sur les villages araméens de l'Anti-Liban.* Documents d'Études Orientales 7. Damascus: Institut français de Damas.

Rivoal, I. 2000. *Les maîtres du secret: Ordre mondain et ordre religieux dans la communauté druze en Israël.* Paris: Éditions de l'École des Hautes Études en Sciences Sociales.

Seale, P. [1988] 1989. *Asad of Syria: The struggle for the Middle East.* Berkeley: University of California Press.

Seurat, M. 1989. *L'état de barbarie.* Paris: Seuil.

Turner, V. 1969. *The ritual process: Structure and anti-structure.* Chicago: Aldine.

Valensi, L. 1986. La Tour de Babel: Groupes et relations ethniques au Moyen Orient et en Afrique du Nord. *Annales ESC* 4: 817–38.

Valter, S. 2002. *La construction nationale syrienne: Légitimation de la nature communautaire du pouvoir par le discours historique.* Paris: CNRS (Moyen Orient).

Van Dam, N. 1996. *The struggle for power in Syria: Politics and society under Asad and the Ba'ath Party.* London: I. B. Tauris.

Voile, B. 2004. *Les coptes d'Égypte sous Nasser: Sainteté, miracles, apparitions.* Paris: CNRS (Moyen Orient).

Weber, M. [1922] 1995. *Économie et société.* Vols. 1–2. Agora. Paris: Plon.

———. [1922] 1996. *Sociologie des religions.* Bibliothèque des Sciences Humaines. Paris: Gallimard.

# PART THREE

# Syncretism and Authenticity

## (Shared) Shrines and Pilgrimage

# 8

# Orthodox-Muslim Interactions at "Mixed Shrines" in Macedonia

Glenn Bowman

In his profoundly influential article "The Clash of Civilizations?" Samuel Huntington asserts that "Islam has bloody borders" (1993: 35). Throughout all but the first three centuries of its existence, Orthodox Christianity has shared borders with Islam across immense stretches of territory extending at times from North Africa to the steppes of Asia. In this paper I focus on Muslim-Christian interaction in one small portion of that shared borderland, examining intercommunal inter-action in the context of religious shrines used by both communities in Macedonia. This investigation of Orthodox communities in their encounters with "their other" reveals aspects of Orthodox belief and practice that are less notable in more homogeneous settings. It also, by making visible the rich diversity of interactions possible between Muslims and Christians, highlights the necessity of discarding facile generalizations about intercommunal hostilities and of instead committing ourselves to fastidious and open-minded research into the contexts that promote neighborliness, the conditions that foment antagonism, and the forces that trans-form one into the other.

## ANTAGONISTIC TOLERANCE

In 2002 I was asked by the editor of *Current Anthropology* to comment on Robert Hayden's ideas concerning "antagonistic tolerance" (Hayden 2002). Hayden con-tended that the acceptance of others in a shared holy place is "a pragmatic adapta-tion to a situation in which repression of the other group's practices may not be possible" (219). His presumption, made explicit throughout the paper and in the reply to discussants that followed, was that the presence of another—unless that other represented an insignificant and powerless minority—is necessarily perceived by communities with which it shares the relevant site as a threat that must, wherever possible, be obviated. In Hayden's construction the other, if it cannot be converted to sameness, reduced to relative impotence, or driven out, has to be "tolerated. " At the heart of that tolerance, however, is a fundamental potential for violence that can be activated by the slightest shift in the balance of power.

Hayden's observations did not concur with my own experience of intercommunal interactions around shared sites in Palestine, whether at Mar Elyas (the Monastery of Elijah) outside Bethlehem, at Bîr es-Saiyideh (the Well of Our Lady) in Beit Sahour, or at the Church of Saint George in nearby 'Khadr (see Bowman 1993: 433–39, 450–51). At these sites local Muslims and Christians had gathered and, rather than making explicit their sectarian affiliations, had identified situationally, discovering and connecting with whomever they were speaking through shared webs of association pertaining to locality of origin, connections through kin, friends, or neighbors, common or associated occupations or employers, and the amity-inducing like. The focus of their interest, nominally various wonder-working elements contained within the sites, seemed for the most part to be the pleasure of communal mixing per se. Antagonisms tended to come to the fore—unifying Palestinian Muslims and Christians— only when others (for instance, Greek Orthodox priests or Israeli police) aggressed against them as "Arabs." I consequently argued against Hayden's conception of a fundamental antagonism, observing:

> Identities at syncretistic shrines can function with relative unfixity, only being forced towards aggressive articulation, closure and mobilisation by the perception of an other setting itself against the inchoate identity it focusses and brings to expression. That perception can be propagated by political and/or religious elites, or can result from antagonistic activities by another community or people. More often, however, identities are unfixed and contingent with certain circumstances bringing one element of the field of identifications which constitute the social self to dominion and other circumstances overturning and reshaping that hierarchy. (Bowman 2002: 220)

To me identities were contingent and as capable of being aggressively mobilized against other groups as of being subsumed within other forms of identification, such as, in the Beit Sahouran instance, pan-sectarian nationalism. The antagonism Hayden stressed as foundational in intercommunal relations was for me a contingent result of situations and the powers and inequities at play in those situations. Mixing was thus neither necessarily a consequence of "antagonistic tolerance," nor of amicable syncretism. Close attention to the context, and the dynamics operative therein, seemed vital to any understanding of what was going on at shrines where communities mixed.

## SYNCRETISM AND ANTISYNCRETISM:
## TELEOLOGIES OF CULTURE CONTACT

It is impossible to avoid the term "syncretism" in discussing intercommunal mixing at shrines. Syncretism is defined by the *Oxford English Dictionary* as the "attempted union or reconciliation of diverse or opposite sets of tenets or practices" (the *OED* furthermore notes that usage of the term is "usually derogatory"). As Charles Stewart and Rosalind Shaw point out in their introduction to *Syncretism/Anti-Syncretism: The Politics of Religious Synthesis* (1994: 1),

> 'Syncretism' is a contentious term, often taken to imply 'inauthenticity' or 'contamination', the infiltration of a supposedly 'pure' tradition by symbols and meanings seen as belonging to other, incompatible traditions.

They locate the roots of this pejorative usage of the term in the reaction of both Catholic and Protestant theologians to seventeenth-century efforts to reconcile Lutheran, Catholic, and Reformed denominations. Such ecclesiastical reactions were themselves examples of "antisyncretism," defined as "antagonism to religious synthesis shown by agents concerned with defence of religious boundaries" (Stewart and Shaw 1994: 7). Stewart and Shaw and their contributors demonstrate how it, and the charges of "inauthenticity" and "pollution" it mobilizes, have opposed syncretism in academic, political, and popular debate to the present day. Nonetheless, Stewart and Shaw also discern a laudatory approach to syncretism in modern anthropology, initially emerging in Herskovits's portrayal of syncretism in *The Myth of the Negro Past* (1941) as a mode of assimilation in "melting pot" America and visible today in postmodern celebrations of "the invention of tradition" and "cultural hybridity" (see Stewart and Shaw 1994: 5–6 and 1).[1]

This "war of words" between syncretists and antisyncretists tends to efface the original sense of syncretism, and, when extended to the analysis of "shared shrines," distracts attention from what actually happens at those sites. Is a shared shrine necessarily "syncretistic"? Hayden certainly does not believe it is; for him sharing serves—since the presence of the other appears to threaten the integrity of self—to fortify further the frontiers between sectarian communities. He writes that "processes of competition between groups that distinguish themselves from each other may be manifested as syncretism yet still result, ultimately, in the exclusion of the symbols of one group or another from a religious shrine" (Hayden 2002: 228). If, however, we take up Herskovits's assessment of syncretism as instrumental in the progressive "acculturative continuum" (Herskovits 1941, cited in Stewart and Shaw 1994: 6) proceeding from culture contact to full cultural integration, then syncretistic "sharing" at holy places forges new and irremediable "hybrid" or "creole" identities. In the first instance there is, despite appearances, no sharing; in the second there is, after sharing, no going back. Identities are either fixed or irrevocably transformed. Neither approach adequately encompassed what I had observed in the shared shrines I had studied in Palestine.

The term *syncretism* first appears in *Peri Philadelphias* (On Brotherly Love), one of the seventy-eight essays of various dates that make up Plutarch's *Moralia*. Here the Roman historian (46–120 A.D.) describes "the practice of the Cretans, who, though they often quarrelled with and warred against each other, made up their differences and united when outside enemies attacked; and this it was which they called 'syncretism'" (cited in Stewart and Shaw 1994: 3). This definition, which Stewart and Shaw note "anticipated Evans-Pritchard's concept of segmentation" (4), circumvents the issue of identity transformation. Plutarch describes a situational assumption of a shared identity that, subsuming those that preceded it, can nonetheless be shed when the assault that brought it about has been overcome. Although Plutarch's usage does not explicitly pertain to religious practice or refer to sites constituted as "syncretistic" by shared practices, his definition easily extends to sites where common interests give rise to shared practices and even shared identities. Identities are mobile without being either fixed or amorphous; amity is possible but neither necessary nor binding. Here issues of agency, and of those things that restrain or impel it, come to the fore. Unbinding the discussion of mixed shrines from the constraints of particularly "loaded" definitions of syncretism enables us to navigate between the Scylla of fixed, conflictual identities and the Charybdis of "evolutionary" transformations to blended identities. Shared practices at mixed sites may entail antagonism and may forge novel identities, but neither is necessary; sharing may just as well be the practice of a moment engaged by persons who return, after that "communion," to their traditional selves and ways.

That passage through definitional straits does not, however, simplify the approach to mixed shrines; rather, it complicates it. If syncretistic shrines are neither arenas for "competitive sharing" nor sites of a "mechanical mixing" (Stewart and Shaw 1994: 6), then we need to know much more of what goes on in particular sites if we are to characterize them at all. What is the character of that mixing or sharing if engaging in common practices at the same site neither necessarily solidifies identities antagonistically nor opens them to transformation? The presence of agency necessitates close attention to what people are doing, and what they say they are doing, while they are in the process of doing it. It is vital to attend to *who* is saying *what* to *whom* and *who* is listening; long-term historical processes are characterized by silencings as well as debates. It is important to examine both if we want to really know what goes on in "sharing."

Hayden's study examines historical accounts as well as court records of an extended struggle over a shrine at Madhi in Maharashtra revered by Muslims and Hindus alike. He compares this case with the historical and ethnographic record of struggles between Muslims, Catholics, and Orthodox Christians in the Balkans, leading up to the frenzy of expulsions and destructions that marked the Yugoslav "Wars of Secession. " In all the cases he discusses he extrapolates the character of previous in situ intercommunal interaction around the respective shrines from processes taking place after legal or literal conflict had become the sole form of interaction. If, however, we do not assume that "end results" are predetermined by the initial moments of mixing at shrines, then we must attempt to see what happens on the ground *while* syncretistic practices are occurring. Only close attention to the discourses operating around shared or mixed sites allows us to know which of the multiple positions around the issue of sharing are occupied and how one of those (if that will prove to be the case) will overcome others and become hegemonic.

## FIELD AGENDA

My encounter with Hayden's arguments in the pages of *Current Anthropology* led me to examine contemporary instances of communal mixing around religious shrines. As such interaction has, for the most part, ceased in West Bank Palestine as a consequence of political developments there (see Bowman 2007), I turned to Macedonia (also known as the Former Yugoslav Republic of Macedonia), where I had, during earlier field excursions, witnessed such "sharing." Macedonia, like Palestine, has a mixed Muslim-Christian population that uses the same holy places, often concurrently,[2] but the new nation is also very different in having a dissimilar confessional demography, a "national minority" (Albanian-speaking Muslims), that took part in a nationalist uprising in 2001, and a government that has a history of being aggressively pro-Orthodox in practice and policy.[3]

For my fieldwork in 2006, I programmatically abandoned the term "shared" in the delineation of shrines, replacing it with "mixed." While I could not abandon the term "shrine" (by which I mean a place associated with a divinity, sacred figure, or relic and usually protected or signified by some sort of edifice) without extending the matter to be examined to absurd dimensions, "shared" already seemed too strongly to connote an amity that I would be wrong to presuppose. I knew from an earlier exploratory visit that Muslims came to Orthodox sites and that at one site Orthodox Christians worshipped in a disused mosque. Prejudging such interaction by labeling it "sharing" seemed problematic, while categorizing it as "mixing"—a term capable of embracing interaction ranging from antagonistic mobilization to amicable mutuality—allowed the nuances of each case to emerge.

Within Macedonia I chose to look at three sites, two in western Macedonia and one in the northeast. The first, Sveti Nikola (Saint Nicholas), is a tiny Macedonian Orthodox church on the outskirts of Makedonski Brod, a rural municipality of approximately six thousand inhabitants (all Christian). The church contains a *turbe* (tomb) of a Bektashi saint, Hadir Bābā, which is visited by Bektashi and members of other Sufi orders as well as by Macedonian Albanian Sunni Muslims from neighboring mixed villages and also from more distant sites. The second site was Sveti Bogoroditsa Prechista (Holy Mother of God Most Pure) outside of Kicevo, a mixed city in a region with a profoundly mixed Muslim-Christian population. Sveti Bogoroditsa Prechista is a large active Orthodox monastery whose spectacular nineteenth-century church contains within it a well over which is a pierced stone through which both Muslim and Christian visitors crawl prior to taking away water. The third site, the Husamedin Pasha mosque, is an empty early sixteenth-century mosque overlooking Štip, a city with an Orthodox majority that nonetheless contains significant populations of Sufi Roma as well as Macedonian-speaking Sunni Muslims. The mosque contains within its grounds a Halveti Sufi *turbe* where Ashura celebrations are carried out by the town's Sunni and Halveti Muslims, and the mosque itself is opened on 2 August for a priest-led celebration of the Orthodox feast of the prophet Elijah. The three sites, respectively, represent a popular mixed shrine with evidence of both Christian and Muslim objects of reverence, a Christian church in which Muslims and Christians alike engage in rituals that appear to be markedly Christian, and a Muslim place of worship that both Christians and Muslims seek to expropriate, ritually and physically, as their own. The three allow for observations of what at least formally seem to be "mixing of practices," "sharing of practices," and "antagonistic tolerance. "

### First Scenario: Sveti Nikola

Sveti Nikola is a small Orthodox church hidden within a grove of trees overlooking the town of Makedonski Brod. One approaches up a long flight of stone steps that carry visitors from the old Ottoman-period houses at the base of the hill, past concrete communist-period housing blocs, to a gateway flanked on the left by a niche containing a simple painting of Saint Nicholas—worn around the mouth from continuously being touched—and surmounted by an eight-inch-high cross surrounded by simple iron scrollwork. The church itself is a small square building (six and a half meters on each side) with an apse on the south wall that appears to be a later addition. There is no cross on the roof, but a small, indented cross has been worked into plaster above the narrow window of the apse. The interior is simple, with a stone slab floor covered with a multitude of diverse and overlapping pieces of carpet. The wooden iconostasis is covered with pictures of saints, apparently painted locally. On the right of the church, running parallel to the south wall, is a flat-topped platform approximately two meters long by three-quarters of a meter wide raised about forty centimeters above floor level and covered with multiple layers of cloth. The top covering is green, with a gold piece beneath it. Closer observation reveals that, particularly in the vicinity of this platform, the carpets and the pictures on and leaning against the wall are Muslim and represent Mecca, Ali, Hussein, and moments of Shi'a history.

There are two ways to approach the Sveti Nikola church and its function as a mixed shrine. The first is to perform an archaeology of its history. This is not something that can easily be done from the shrine, or even the town, itself. Local Christians, asked about the shrine, related stories of how an old bearded man "in the past" saved the townspeople from plague by having them kill an ox, cut its hide into strips, link them together, and mark out as much land as could be contained within the resultant rope for dedication to a monastery (see Stahl 1986: 178 on magical boundaries). People often say that the old man—Sveti Nikola—is buried beneath the raised platform within the church. Visiting Muslims told exactly the same story, except that in their version the old man is Hadir Bābā, a Bektashi saint, who is buried within the *turbe* (tomb) in the church. Other stories told of the local pasha, who, during the Ottoman period, found as he attempted to build his house at the bottom of the hill that each evening everything erected during the day collapsed. He then—depending on who was telling the story—dreamed of either the Christian or the Bektashi saint who told him to build either a monastery or a *tekke* (Sufi monastery) on the hill above. When he did he was able to complete his house, which still stands at the foot of the stairs.

Makedonski Brod today is completely Christian, and local people, talking in and around the church, speak as though it has always been. A local historian, formerly a communist and still a secularist, speaking in town (not at the church), told me, however, that until the early twentieth-century Balkan Wars Makedonski Brod had been a hub of Ottoman administration known as Tekkiya because of the Bektashi monastery built above the town. This version of history, suggesting that the Sveti Nikola church is in fact the *turbe* of the founder of the Bektashi *tekke,* is supported by an archaeological note in a Skopje museum newsletter asserting that "on that place today can . . . be seen the *turbe,* in which, according to the stories of the local population, was buried the founder of the *tekke, Haydar Bābā*" (Stojanovski 1979: 53). Other conversations in the town (*not* on the grounds of Sveti Nikola) included mention of the 1994 consecration of the building as a church by the local bishop and the removal, "some while ago," of a triangular frame that had for years sat on top of the tomb of Saint Nicholas (see fig. 8.1). This "archaeological" approach seems to indicate that the church of Sveti Nikola was, at one time, the central feature—the founder's tomb—of a Bektashi monastery, and that, in the wake of the flight of "Turks" from the town after the Balkan Wars and then through the long period of post-1945 state disapprobation of formal religion, it had sat, "disenfranchised," above the town, approached by different communities who remembered it in different ways, until, in the nationalistic fervor following the collapse of Yugoslavia and the formation of "Orthodox" Macedonia, the church expropriated it.

FIGURE 8.1. Turbe of Hadir Bābā in Sveti Nikola, 2006. Photograph by Glenn Bowman.

The diachronic analytic suggests an inexorable movement toward expropria-
tion of the site by one of the communities that currently seem to "share" it.
Another way of examining Sveti Nikola is to look synchronically at the relations
taking place at the present time within the shrine. That approach, while not
denying the trajectory indicated by the archaeological or historical view, offers
insights into forms of interaction between communities around a mixed site that
a "teleological" interpretation would render invisible. I would like here to offer
two vignettes that indicate, respectively, the symbiosis involved in "sharing" a
shrine, and some of the forces that work to dissolve that sharing.

Dragina is the Orthodox caretaker of the Sveti Nikola shrine. As she is getting
old, she is assisted in keeping the place clean and functional by her son Boge, who
works as a schoolteacher in the town, as well as by a number of men who make
up the "Church Committee." On 5 May, the day preceding the Orthodox feast of
Saint George, Dragina, Boge, and those with time to help work to prepare the
church for the "pilgrimage" to the site that local people will enact for the feast.
Preparation involves rendering the site much less like a mosque and more like an
Orthodox church, and thus the carpets are taken up from the floor, and the various
Muslim images and objects are hidden from the view of visitors. Green "Muslim"

ox tallow candles and the Muslim prayer beads (*sibhah*) that visitors step through for blessings are removed from the "tomb" of Saint Nicholas and replaced with white "Christian" candles and a smaller rosary.[4] Thus "Christianized," the site is ready for the hundreds of visitors, all but a few Orthodox, who visit that evening and throughout the following day. At dawn on 7 May, however, Dragina and Boge are busy in the church "returning" the site to its normal mixed state. Carpets are carefully relaid, and intense discussion takes place around where exactly the image of Ali with his sword Zulfiqar should be placed and how to arrange the cloth that partially covers it. Prayer rugs are laid around the *turbe,* the *sibhah* are replaced, and the tallow candles are lit because "they" are coming and must be made to feel at home.

There is, of course, an economic explanation for this: "the others" leave generous gifts, and Dragina points out that "we benefit from it." Nonetheless, the affection she shows for visitors and the easy generosity with which she and others, including the priest, give red "Saint George" eggs to, and fill the water bottles of, Muslim visitors belie a purely economistic reading. Women Muslims ask Dragina to pass the *sibhah* over them for blessings, and when a respected Sufi dervish from Kicevo comes to the shrine (praying with his wife in the direction of the iconostasis rather than toward the *turbe*), Dragina—concerned about her son's continuing failure to find a wife—asks the man to pass the beads over Boge so as to read his fortune (fig. 8.2).

Whereas the description above suggests an easy sharing of the site, and an institutional and personal openness on the part of Orthodox caretakers toward the presence of Muslim "others," there are ways that, without even being provoked by "higher" powers, such sharing might disintegrate. When I visited Sveti Nikola a week before Saint George's Day, the gate to the grounds of the church was surmounted by a small metal cross surrounded by ornamental scrollwork. While interviewing people who were gathered on the grounds I asked about the absence of a cross on the roof of the church itself. One man responded aggressively "I'll show you the cross" and left the grounds, returning twenty minutes later with a six-foot-high gold-colored anodized cross. This, it turned out, was a gift he, a *Gastarbeiter* who had returned to his hometown for a vacation, was presenting to the church.[5] A week later the small cross had been angle-ground off and thrown aside, and the gold cross had been welded in its place, overwhelming the entryway and the icon of Saint Nicholas (see fig. 8.3).

On the day following Saint George's Day an Albanian-speaking man and his wife came to Sveti Nikola to pray at the *turbe,* leave gifts, and take water from the shrine. They were clearly uncomfortable, and while the woman left quickly, returning down the stairway to their car, the man stayed behind and insisted on speaking to me, evidently a foreigner, about the "insult" of the cross over the gateway. He told me that the site is a Muslim holy place and that local people have no right to

FIGURE 8.2. Boge having his fortune told, 2006. Photograph by Glenn Bowman.

FIGURE 8.3. Entryway and cross at Sveti Nikola, 2006. Photograph by Glenn Bowman.

erect that cross over a place that has "been Muslim for centuries." I asked him what form of Islam he followed, and he responded: "It doesn't matter; I am a Muslim." I asked him to speak to the members of the Church Committee who were gathered nearby, and he went to them, politely commending whoever had been generous enough to make a gift to the shrine, but suggesting that person should, if he wanted to make a present, instead have helped pay for a better road to the place:

> This cross separates us; no Muslims will feel comfortable coming to this big and historical place that we used to come to visit. We have been here for years and have felt good to come here, but this is a barrier to us. . . . How would you feel if I came to your church, to your home, and put a minaret there? I will never put a mosque in a church.

The men responded apologetically, saying that they understood the problem and would talk with the man who paid for the cross. They claimed he was not around at the time, although he was in fact a member of the group addressed. After the Muslim left, the group was clearly discomfited, acknowledging that there was a problem but seeming uncertain how to address it.

### Second Scenario: Sveti Bogoroditsa Prechista

There is no doubt that Sveti Bogoroditsa Prechista is an Orthodox monastery, but this does not prevent a continuous flow into it of Muslims, Sufi and Sunni alike (the Albanian-speaking man discussed above claimed to be a frequent visitor). After entering its chapel, circumnavigating its icon-dense interior, and crawling three times through the small passageway beneath the icons of Mary and Jesus, they collect water from the well beneath to take back to their homes (see fig. 8.4). While Muslim visitors to Sveti Nikola occasionally speak of coming to the shrine for healing, they generally claim to come to pay respect to the saint, or because they have forged a bond with, or been called to visit, Hadir Bābā in a dream. Muslim and Christian visitors to Sveti Bogoroditsa Prechista, however, claim to come explicitly for healing; the shrine, through its well water, is renowned for inducing fertility in the sterile, returning sanity to the mad, straightening bent limbs, and other thaumaturgic cures. Even the imam in the central mosque of nearby Kicevo sends members of his congregation to Sveti Bogoroditsa Prechista when he feels they are afflicted by "Christian demons" that can be driven out only by beneficent Christian powers.

At Sveti Nikola, Muslim visitors carry out Islamic forms of worship around a *turbe* they see as that of Hadir Bābā, not that of Saint Nicholas.[6] At Sveti Bogoroditsa Prechista, Muslim visitors appear to carry out the same sorts of ritual activities as the many Christian visitors to the site. Like the Christians, the Muslims light candles and approach the icons throughout the interior of the church, particularly

FIGURE 8.4. The pierced stone with the icon of the Introduction of the Holy Virgin to the Temple at Sveti Bogoroditsa, 2006. Photograph by Glenn Bowman.

those lining the iconostasis, leaving before them small gifts (sometimes money, often towels or new, packaged articles of clothing, such as socks or shirts). Then, like the Christians, they go to the rear left of the church, where an east-facing icon of Mary's introduction to the temple and a west-facing icon of Jesus' healing of the paralytic at the Pool of Siloam (John 5:8–10) surmount an artificial hole through a wall. To the left of the icon Mary is hung a long string of cross-inscribed beads (the mother superior claims they were left by a Russian predecessor) that are passed over supplicants three times before they crawl, again three times, through the hole, in the direction of the west wall of the church. Having done this, they collect, or have given to them, water that has been drawn from the well below, which they first splash on their faces three times and then take to their homes to drink or to give to those who are ill (when the water runs out, the sickness returns, and people come back for more). Some visitors, both Muslim and Christian, decide to stay in the monastery, where they do work to support the church and are healed by their residence.[7]

Closer observation of Muslim visitors and interviews with them revealed that, although they appear to follow the same practices of approach and deportment as Christians, by holding back from Christian groups while moving through the church they introduce small but significant differences. In approaching icons they do not kiss them. They do not cross themselves, and in praying they silently mouth Muslim prayers and hold their hands open and palm up.[8] Nonetheless, they have no hesitation in acknowledging that the powers they approach are Christian; this is a healing place that is known to work, and therefore when one is ill or in need of help it is one of the preeminent places to approach (many of those inter-viewed—Muslim and Christian alike—said they had visited several places, both Muslim and Christian, in search of cures, fertility, etc.).

An intriguing practical logic is operative here: people visiting sites whose powers are renowned as efficacious (particularly for healing) will, at those sites, carry out the rituals appropriate to those powers as far as is possible to do so without explicitly violating the dictates of their own religions (Muslims, for instance, will not cross themselves). Knowing that certain visits and the rituals involved therein have worked for neighbors of other religions, they mimic those activities as far as possible without "self-harming" in the hope that such copying will produce the same effects for them, despite confessional differences. This is not a syncretism, as identities are not transformed, but it is a sharing. It is also a sharing acknowledged and legitimated (perhaps because they know people will do it regardless of whether or not they approve) by religious leaders, like the imam of the Kicevo mosque, who themselves would never think of entering the holy places of another religion.

In the Church of the Apostles Peter and Paul in Kicevo (which is half Muslim) we were told by the priest that many local Muslims come to the church not only for holy water and to ask for blessings but also, to provide specific examples, when a Christian man has converted to marry a Muslim woman but nonetheless wants to have their child baptized,[9] or when Muslims want priest-blessed icons to keep in their houses.[10] The priest prays over Muslims with a special prayer—that designated in the prayer books as appropriate to the unbaptized—and instead of laying his cope over their heads raises it in front of them.

This "space" for the unbaptized, and the non-Orthodox, is interestingly paralleled in the legendry and architecture of Sveti Bogoroditsa Prechista. The mother superior of the monastery told us that "in the past" the superior of the monastery and a pasha once discussed the respective virtues of Christianity and Islam. They decided to test whose faith was the right one by filling two glasses with water and dropping them some five meters off of a balcony, whereupon the glass of the pasha broke, while that of the superior remained intact, and its water did not spill. The pasha consequently decided to donate 120 hectares of land in the vicinity of Brod to the monastery, and the superior, in appreciation, promised that part of the church would be built for Muslim use.[11] Although the current superior stressed that the narthex was not "intended" for Muslims, she stressed that it was the part of the church "they can come to." It is not clear what the superior meant by this, as it was clear that Muslims frequented the whole of the church, but this part of the church, like the analogous part of the prayer book, was evidently deemed "appropriate" to those who were neither Orthodox nor Christian.

The "sharing" that occurs in the church is, however, vulnerable precisely because of the space that is designated as open to the other. While none of the Muslims I interviewed at Sveti Bogoroditsa Prechista mentioned this, one of the nuns—a novice recently graduated from university in Skopje—stressed vehemently that "Muslims" claimed that the undecorated narthex of the church belonged to them, and asserted that they were preparing to "steal" it from the church. When asked for water by Muslim visitors, she would tell them either that there was none or that they could get it themselves from the fountain outside.

### Third Scenario: Husamedin Pasha Mosque

In the previous two scenarios, we have observed forms of mixing and forms of sharing, both potentially threatened by tendencies toward fission. In the case of the Husamedin Pasha mosque we observe a site in which there is no mixing and all that is shared is the same site at different times.

The mosque, now fairly derelict, is an early sixteenth-century "central" mosque that was seriously damaged during the Balkan Wars yet functioned as a mosque for the minority Muslim population until 1945, when it was closed (fig. 8.5). At that time the local Halveti Sufi community, an order quite close to Orthodox Sunni Islam, began to celebrate the feast of Ashura on the grounds of the mosque where the *turbe* of Medin Bābā stands. In 1953 the mosque was reopened as a

FIGURE 8.5. The Husamedin Pasha mosque, 2006. Photograph by Glenn Bowman.

secular building and used as a gallery space for the Stïp Museum. In 1956 it closed and has scarcely been used since, although for a while the "Children"s Embassy," a Macedonian NGO established in 1992, held events in and around the building. At the same time (1992), allegedly because of the intervention of the nationalist Christian Democratic VMRO (Democratic Party for Macedonian National Unity) government, access to the mosque was given to the local Orthodox church, which began celebrating the feast of the prophet Elijah inside the mosque. This celebration, based on the idea—for which there is no firm evidence—that the original mosque was built over an Orthodox church, uses the mosque's interior for a liturgy, with icons set in the *mihrab,* and for a subsequent communal meal. Christians inscribe crosses on the front of the exterior of the mosque and burn candles on the porch around the entryway throughout the year. I was told that local Halveti Muslims until recently referred to the mosque as "St. Elijah's church."

The Islamic community, strengthened by substantial financial contributions from diasporic Stïp Muslims in Turkey, as well as from other Islamic sources, has been revitalized, not only restoring the only operative mosque in the town but also building an Islamic school. Members of the Islamic community have also been discussing the desirability of restoring the Husamedin Pasha as the central mosque. They have gained access to a document issued by the Macedonian Institute for the Protection of Cultural Monuments announcing that the mosque is a protected monument, which they interpret as indicating that it belongs to them as the appropriate cultural minority. As a result they have stopped calling it St. Elijah's church and begun referring to it as the Husamedin Pasha mosque. One activist in this movement told me that the Christian celebrations as they were currently being carried out were "inappropriate for a place of worship." The year before he and a friend had walked by during the feast and, afraid to enter the mosque, had seen through the door "Christians eating and drinking *rakia* [a distilled fruit alcohol] around a table they'd set up in the middle." Despite his sense of the mosque's desecration, he asserted that when the mosque was turned back to "what it should be" he would "share it with Christians on the day they want to use it."

I also spoke with a priest from the Church of Saint Nikola, the town's main church, who told us that Sveti Elia (the mosque) was built over the foundation of a destroyed church, as the cruciform shape of the mosque shows.[12] The priest explained:

> According to the ground-plan, this is a church, but when the Osmanli Turks came, they turned it into a mosque. The foundation is still a church. We want to make it a church again, but from Skopje they would not give us permission. Otherwise, it would have been a church by now. Now we don't know what it is any longer: neither one nor the other. We want it to be a church, and we will make it a church. We are asking for a permission to dig inside and see what will be revealed, but they know it is a church in the foundations, and that's why they deny us the permission. It will be a church. Why should it be a mosque? They have one already.

For the priest the mosque is no more than a historical excrescence occluding access to the real holy site that lies beneath it.[13] According to his description the Christian worship that takes place there proceeds as though the Muslim intervention was invisible: "During the ceremony a prayer is sung, a *panagia* is raised in the air,[14] and everything takes place inside. . . . Outside the anointment takes place." When it convinces the government to allow it to carry out the archaeological survey that will in its eyes legitimate its "restoration" of the church, the Orthodox priesthood, which is powerful in Stïp, intends to tear the Husamedin Pasha mosque down and build over it "a new and more beautiful ancient church."

In February 2006 members of the Macedonian Roma community, for the most part Halveti Sufis, had unofficially gained temporary access to the mosque during preparations for the Ashura feast at the neighboring *turbe* of Medin Bābā. These Muslims, who as a community had not had access to the mosque since its closure in 1945, removed accumulated rubble from the mosque (leaving Orthodox ritual artifacts, including icons of Elijah, in place in the niche in which they were stored between feasts), swept and washed it, and laid carpets on the floor. They then, with members of the Islamic Religious Community of Stïp who they had notified by mobile telephone, held a *namaz* (prayer) inside the mosque. Afterwards the delegation of the (Sunni) Islamic Religious Community left, and the Halveti had their Ashura feast inside the mosque. Subsequently the key to the mosque, normally kept by the curator of the Stïp Museum, was found to have gone missing. Little was thought of this until the eve of the feast of the prophet Elijah (2 August) when, as local Christians gathered for the two-day celebration and began setting up on the grounds their booths for selling food and candles, it was discovered that a second lock had been welded to the doors of the mosque. Late in the afternoon, as the priests from the Church of Saint Nikola arrived to prepare the interior of the mosque for the *panagia* and the saint's day liturgy, it was discovered that no one present had the key for the second lock. It was soon realized that that lock had been mounted by the Islamic Religious Community organization. Its members, when contacted, refused to remove it, claiming that the site was a mosque and theirs. Amid muted muttering and assertions that the site had been used for the feast since time immemorial, the *panagia* and the anointing were held on the portico while local people leaned candles against the doors and piled small gifts of cloth and flowers in front of it. Throughout the evening and over the following day locals came, prayed before the locked door, and left angry.

## CONCLUSION

In the three cases set out above I have attended to the boundaries between Orthodox Christians and their Muslim neighbors and have considered the ways in which these boundaries are variously reinforced, opened, and transgressed. In Macedonia, as in Palestine, the close proximity of communities that are not Orthodox strongly influences the ways in which Orthodox Christians and Orthodox institutions deal with heterodoxy. Laypeople here are used to interacting in various contexts with others who are not of their religious persuasion, and they are less prone to xenophobia (in the literal sense of "fear of strangers or foreigners"). Religious authorities find it more difficult to impose conceptions of ritual purity on sites traversed by the beliefs and practices of heterogeneous peoples. Furthermore, although such authorities may strive to influence state policies, the marriage of church, state, and people discussed by Renée Hirschon in this volume is bound to face objections (often militant) from populations threatened with disenfranchisement by such a union. This is not to say that moves toward expelling alterity and homogenizing shrines and communities are not being made at present and will not be made in the future; the fate of much of the rest of what is now "Former" Yugoslavia, as well as that of early twentieth-century Greece and Turkey (Clark 2006), testifies to the fragility of intercommunalism.

Nonetheless, it is important to observe and note, in situations where intercommunal mixing continues to occur, the ways in which such mixing takes place and the structures of belief and practice that support such interaction. In concluding I want to focus on the ways in which lay Macedonian Orthodox Christians and their clergy relate to the presence of Muslims in shrines they consider their own.

A straightforward response of denial and exclusion is evinced toward Muslims at the Husamedin Pasha mosque by the Orthodox priest of Stïp. His attitude, which may or may not be echoed among his parishioners, is theologically correct: Muslims are doctrinally defined as followers of a false prophet and are thus, in ontological terms, either heretical or null entities. In the religious context of the "Sveti Elia church" the works of Muslims are effectively obliterated, both in the imaginary (the mosque counterfactually "is a church") and in the attempts to block access of Muslims to the interior. There is, furthermore, a surtext. The second of August is not only the feast of the prophet Elijah in the Orthodox calendar; it is also the anniversary of the Ilinden (from the Slavic *Ilin den,* meaning the Day of Elijah [Elias]) Uprising of 1903, during which the Internal Macedonian Revolutionary Organization orchestrated a revolt against the Ottoman state, which, though rapidly crushed, resulted in the establishment of provisional governments in three localities and the declaration of the Krushevo Republic, an icon of subsequent Yugoslav and then Macedonian nationalism (see Brown 2003: 1–21 and passim; and Poulton 2000: 48–62). The Christian occupation of the semi-ruined mosque and the displacement of its Muslim users here replays the religio-nationalist victory of Orthodox Macedonians over Muslim oppressors. It is this resonance that, one suspects, not only prompted the 1992 appropriation of the Husamedin Pasha mosque by the Orthodox Church—supported by a Macedonian nationalist government—but also leads the priest to believe, perhaps rightly, that in time the government will abandon its concessionary attitudes to the Muslim Macedonian population and allow the full erasure of an emblem of past Muslim sovereignty. The move by local Muslims to reassert their rights of possession over the mosque has great potential to reignite a history of intercommunal violence that has fitfully smoldered over the past century.

The second possible response is that of the abbess of the Sveti Bogoroditsa Prechista monastery and the priests of the Church of Saints Peter and Paul in Kicevo. Whereas for the Stïp priest the mosque has to become—in both space and time—fully Christian, for the abbess of the monastery and the priests of the church Christians and Muslims can coexist separately—performing parallel rituals—in contiguous spaces within the holy places. The narthex, which in early Christian church architecture is the part of the church to which the catechumens and the unbaptized (those literally not part of the congregation) were restricted, becomes "the place" for Muslims, just as a general prayer for the unbaptized is substituted for the particular daily prayers said over Orthodox Christians and the priest's cope is raised before Muslims rather than laid over their heads. These diacritical settings and gestures are observed more in discourse than in practice; the abbess, who claims that Muslims restrict their attentions to the narthex of the church, knows from observation that they circulate throughout it, just as the priests who claim that Muslims and Christians are addressed with different prayers will nonetheless baptize the child of an Orthodox man who has converted to Islam to marry a Muslim woman.[15]

The Orthodox theology of the icon, so central to belief and practice, provides a means of understanding this seeming contradiction (see Hann and Goltz, Luehrmann, and Mahieu, this volume). For the Orthodox, Adam and Eve's original sin of being devoted to the world rather than to its creator insinuated a breach between the human world and the divine. This breach can be bridged by various sacra, among which the icon is preeminent but which include as well the liturgy and the churches in which icons are displayed and liturgies performed (Galavaris 1981: 5). Fundamental to relations with these sacra is faith. As numerous interviewees have made clear to me over my years of working with Orthodox communities, an unbeliever looking *at* an icon sees nothing more than an image made from pigment on wood, while a believer looking *into* an icon will see the saint looking back at him or her (Bowman 1991: 103–4, 108–12). Muslims in this sense do not participate in the same world as Christians when they move through a church, approach the icons, and carry out seemingly identical rituals; the Orthodox Christian here stands at the gates of paradise looking in, while the Muslim remains enmeshed in the corporeality of the world.

This "inclusive exclusion" does not prevent Orthodox hierophants from appreciating and benefiting from the presence of Muslims at their holy sites; the abbess of Sveti Bogoroditsa Prechista spoke at length of how she had come to love the Muslims, appreciating their honesty as well as their dedication to and generosity toward the monastery. These virtues were, however, very much of this world, and the abbess's appreciation of them was neighborly and pragmatic; when it came to "the final things," Muslims and Christians did not, in any way, occupy the same places.

Orthodoxy seems to be far more situational at Sveti Nikola. The preparation of the shrine for the feast of Saint George is certainly indicative of this tendency to render a shared space "properly Christian" for feasts, but perhaps more telling is the anomalous hanging—in the wake of that cleaning—of Bektashi devotional pictures (of Ali and of the tombs of Sufi holy men) around and above the altar behind the iconostasis (in the holiest domain of the church) and the placing of the Muslim rosary on the altar. Despite the frequent presence of the priest and of members of the Church Committee in the apse in the twenty-four hours between the time I noticed the placement of these objects and the commencement of the feast day liturgy, they were not removed until that liturgy—which is believed to transform the space behind the iconostasis into an icon of paradise—commenced. Such situational sanctification was duplicated by visiting Bektashi and Halveti *bābās* who would, before inviting those accompanying them into the shrine to perform prayers, ask everyone to leave the building, and then close the door and carry out an (unobserved) preparatory ritual. While such oscillation between sacred and secular moments serves to keep the Christian liturgy free of the Muslim elements that crowded around it in this mixed shrine, the boundary between Christian and Muslim practice seems far less prophylactic on the popular level. Orthodox Christians, observing Sufi visitors circumambulating the *turbe* for blessings, themselves followed the practice even while believing they were asking a blessing from Sveti Nikola rather than Hadir Bābā. Muslims visiting the shrine seemed as likely to pray toward the iconostasis, as Christians did, as toward the *turbe* of Hadir Bābā.

In his fascinating study of popular conceptions of *exotika* on the Greek island of Naxos, Charles Stewart shows how "doctrinal religion draw[s] upon local concepts and transpose[s] these into its own more literate terms" (1991: 244). He also demonstrates how islanders, in formulating responses to local afflictions and dilemmas, draw elements from Orthodox Christianity and reshape these into popular beliefs, representations, and practices suited to their particular needs and situations. On Naxos both doctrinal and popular religion appear profoundly "Greek":

> Consistencies between doctrinal and local religion are perhaps to be expected in a culture such as the Greek, where Orthodox tradition has been elaborated over the centuries by Church fathers, many of whom were themselves members of a Greek-speaking society and who were reared in culturally Greek local communities. (244)

The Naxions use Orthodox forms and elements in elaborating their spells and superstitions because these are available in everyday life; Macedonians, in working their cures and prognostications, use both Christian and Muslim beliefs and practices for the same reason. In Macedonia, where a multiplicity of communities jostles in everyday life and occasionally meets around sites variously deemed holy, locals will draw practices of approaching "powers" from those they perceive as having been efficacious in their approaches to the sacra. In mixed communities and mixed shrines the persons emulated will not only be priests and other Christians but also, when "Orthodox" approaches have proved ineffectual, Muslims.[16] In a rural postsocialist community with this mixed heritage, "confidence" and "authority" are not necessarily vested in the Orthodox clergy. Dragina, growing old and—despite her prayers—watching her son remain unmarried, was not uncomfortable asking a renowned Sufi dervish to do for Boge what she had witnessed and heard of him doing for many others. Here Orthodox Christianity engages with the heterodox, and we see something distinctly akin to sharing.

Nonetheless, the trajectory evident in these three scenarios indicates that mixing and sharing are at increasing risk of being replaced by separation and antagonism. The contemporary tendency, promoted by discourses of nationalism and resurgent scripturalism, is to mark intercommunal activities such as those described at Sveti Nikola and Sveti Bogoroditsa Prechista as at best unorthodox and at worst blasphemous; there is a possibility that in bringing them to wider attention by describing them I will expose them to forces analogous to those that have worked to extinguish similar manifestations elsewhere.[17] However, insofar as both intercommunal amity and intercommunal antagonism are discursively constructed, it seems vital, in the midst of the war of words evident in debates over the "clash of civilizations" and "antagonistic tolerance," to show that there is nothing natural or necessary in hating your neighbor, and that people, when they perceive interaction and amicability as working for rather than against them, are fully capable of mixing with, and embracing, the other.

## NOTES

1. This polarization around syncretism appears to be related to larger "culture wars" (see Rena Lederman's comments on "the fault line, which cleaves contextualist and essentializing ways of knowing, [which] runs through American culture," Lederman 2005: 50; see also 74 n. 2); the rhetoric of antisyncretists often shares ground with that of ethnic nationalists and religious fundamentalists, while those who see syncretism as a good thing tend to sound like advocates of federalism, globalization, and secularism.

2. Shrine sharing characterized much of the Balkans prior to the recent wars and dislocations: see Duijzings 1993 and 2000; Hawkesworth, Heppell, and Norris 2001; Norris 2006; and Stahl 1979/1980.

3. Keith Brown has provided a splendid ethnographical record of the fractious play of history and contemporary identity in Macedonia (see particularly Brown 2003 and 1998). Poulton 2000 is a useful sketch of the players and field of play in the Macedonian contests, and Brunnbauer 2005 critically examines the role of history, and historians, in the construction of a Macedonian people. Neofotistos 2004 discusses the lability of ethnic distinction in the contemporary setting.

4. Initially these objects and images were "hidden" behind the iconostasis on the floor of the apse, but I noticed, in the period leading up to the feast day, that someone (perhaps a Bektashi visitor) had later hung them on the apse's eastern wall amid the icons surrounding the altar (and had placed the green ninety-nine-beaded *sibhah* on the altar). These remained there until the town priest (who had seemingly ignored them while in the apse on the previous day), coming to the church on the morning of the feast day to perform the liturgy, removed them, placing them again on the floor, with the images turned to the wall.

5. Another wealthier economic migrant, who returned from Australia annually with his family for summer vacations, had given the town a ten-meter-high cross to be mounted, like those being erected all over Macedonia, on the mountain above the town.

6. There is, however, little uniformity in the Muslim practices; some pray toward the iconostasis of the church, others toward the *turbe* from its foot," while others perform *zikir* (a devotional choral chanting of Islamic texts), kneeling at each corner of the platform. Most Muslim visitors, like most Christians, circle the *turbe* one to three times.

7. A disused room near the monastery's main gate was formerly used for holding mad persons who were thought to be healed by that incarceration—a practice identical to that described by Taufik Canaan at the monastery of St. George at Khadr near Bethlehem (1927: 79–80).

8. Orthodox Christians pray by standing simply and respectfully with their hands at their sides or adopting the classical posture of the *orans.*

9. The priest indicated that according to church law both parents must be baptized, but that local priests baptize such children anyway "so as not to damage the marriage community of the couple."

10. There is an echo here of the practices of "Crypto-Christians" in the Balkans under Ottoman rule (see Skendi 1967: 234 and passim).

11. Whether there was truth to the legend, or whether the legend was generated to explain the architectural anomaly, the narthex at the western end of the church is undecorated and the only part of the church not adorned with frescoes.

12. The mosque is square and, according to a cultural survey, "typical of early sixteenth century Osmanli sacral architecture." Architectural Heritage 2005: 170.

13. As Islam historically follows Christianity and, in Islamic thought, corrects and clarifies Christian interpretations of revelation, Muslims are able to attend Christian sites that, although manifesting an imperfectly understood divine revelation, are nonetheless informed by revelation. For Christians, Islam is a heresy or deviancy, and attendance at a Muslim site is effectively blasphemous. As Hasluck noted, "A mosque, unless it has been (or is thought to have been) a church is rarely, if ever, taken over as a church by the Orthodox" ([1929] 2000: 104).

14. A small loaf of bread (*prosphora*), when stamped with an image of Mary as Mother of God, becomes the *panagia,* which is blessed over the altar during the Divine Liturgy.

15. During the Halle conference Renée Hirschon and I discussed whether or not Orthodox priests would baptize Muslims. The Kicevo instance, like a case in Beit Sahour of a Muslim chicken vendor who had an ill child baptized in 'Khadr, leads me to believe that, while in mixed communities religious officiants may find ways of allowing for exceptions, the ecclesiastical rules in homogeneous communities will be far more strictly observed.

16. Marcel Mauss ([1935] 1979: 101–2) discusses the central role of "prestigious imitation" in enculturation: "The child, the adult, imitates actions which have succeeded and which he has seen successfully performed by people in whom he has confidence and who have authority over him."

17. See Bastin 2008 for a description of a Sri Lankan mixed shrine "purified" by a papal visit.

## REFERENCES

Architectural Heritage. 2005. Joint restoration project-plan/Estimation of the architectural and archaeological heritage of southeastern Europe (2003–2006). Component C: Preliminary technical evaluation of the architectural and archaeological heritage, vol. 1. Skopje: Skopje Ministry for the Protection of the Cultural Heritage.

Bastin, R. forthcoming. Saints, sites, and religious accommodation in Sri Lanka. In *Sharing the sacra: The politics and pragmatics of inter-communal relations around holy places,* ed. G. Bowman. Oxford: Berghahn Books.

Bowman, G. 1991. Christian ideology and the image of a holy land: The place of Jerusalem pilgrimage in the various Christianities. In *Contesting the sacred: The anthropology of Christian pilgrimage,* ed. J. Eade and M. Sallnow, 98–121. London: Routledge.

———. 1993. Nationalizing the sacred: Shrines and shifting identities in the Israeli-occupied territories. *Man* 28, no. 3: 431–60.

———. 2001. The two deaths of Basem Rishmawi: Identity constructions and reconstructions in a Muslim-Christian Palestinian community. *Identities: Global Studies in Culture and Power* 8, no. 1: 1–35.

———. 2002. Comment on Robert Hayden's "Antagonistic tolerance: Competitive sharing of religious sites in South Asia and the Balkans." *Current Anthropology* 43, no. 2: 219–20.

———. 2007. Nationalising and denationalising the sacred: Shrines and shifting identities in the Israeli-occupied territories. [In Arabic.] *Chronos: Revue d'Histoire de l'Université de Balamand* 16: 151–210. Forthcoming in English in *Confrontation and co-existence in holy places: Religious, political, and legal aspects in the Israeli-Palestinian context,* ed. M. J. Breger, Y. Reiter, and L. Hammer. New York: Routledge.

Brown, K. 1998. Contests of heritage and the politics of preservation in the Former Yugoslav Republic of Macedonia. In *Archaeology under fire: Nationalism, politics, and heritage in the Eastern Mediterranean and the Middle East,* ed. Lynn Meskell, 68–86. London: Routledge.

———. 2003. *The past in question: Modern Macedonia and the uncertainties of nation.* Princeton: Princeton University Press.

Brunnbauer, U. 2005. Ancient nationhood and the struggle for statehood: Historiographic myths in the Republic of Macedonia. In *Myths and boundaries in south-eastern Europe,* ed. Pål Kolstø, 262–96. London: Hurst and Co.

Canaan, T. 1927. *Mohammedan saints and sanctuaries in Palestine.* London: Luzac and Company.

Clark, B. 2006. *Twice a stranger: How mass expulsion forged modern Greece and Turkey.* London: Granta.

Duijzings, G. 1993. Pilgrims, politics, and ethnicity: Joint pilgrimages of Muslims and Christians and conflicts over ambiguous sanctuaries in Yugoslavia and Albania. In *Power and prayer: Religious and political processes in past and present,* ed. M. Bax and A. Koster, 80–91. Amsterdam: VU Press.

———. 2000. *Religion and the politics of identity in Kosovo.* London: C. Hurst.

Galavaris, G. 1981. *The icon in the life of the church.* Iconography of Religions 24.8. Leiden: Brill.

Hasluck, F. W. [1929] 2000. *Christianity and Islam under the sultans.* Vol. 1. Istanbul: The Isis Press.

Hawkesworth, C., M. Heppell, and H. T. Norris, eds. 2001. *Religious quest and national identity in the Balkans.* Studies in Russia and East Europe. Basingstoke: Palgrave.

Hayden, R. 2002. Antagonistic tolerance: Competitive sharing of religious sites in South Asia and the Balkans. *Current Anthropology* 43, no. 2: 205–31.

Herskovits, M. 1941. *The myth of the Negro past.* New York: Harper and Brothers.

Huntington, S. 1993. The clash of civilizations? *Foreign Affairs* 72, no. 3: 22–49.

Lederman, R. 2005. Unchosen grounds: Cultivating cross-subfield accents for a public voice. In *Unwrapping the sacred bundle: Reflections on the disciplining of anthropology,* ed. D. Segal and S. Yanagisako, 49–77. Durham, N.C.: Duke University Press.

Mauss, M. [1935] 1979. Body techniques. In *Sociology and psychology: Essays,* trans. B. Brewster, 95–123. London: Routledge and Kegan Paul.

Neofotistos, V. 2004. Beyond stereotypes: Violence and the porousness of ethnic boundaries in the Republic of Macedonia. *History and Anthropology* 15, no. 1: 47–67.

Norris, H. T. 2006. *Popular Sufism in Eastern Europe: Sufi brotherhoods and the dialogue with Christianity and heterodoxy.* Routledge Sufi Series 20. London: Routledge.

Poulton, H. 2000. *Who are the Macedonians?* 2nd ed. London: Hurst and Company.

Skendi, S. 1967. Crypto-Christianity in the Balkan area under the Ottomans. *Slavic Review* 26, no. 2: 227–46.

Stahl, P. 1979/1980. Croyances communes des chrétiens et des musulmans balkaniques. *Buletinul Bibliotecii Române* n.s. 7, no. 11: 79–126.

———. 1986. *Household, village, and village confederation in southeastern Europe.* Trans. Linda Scales Alcott. East European Monographs 200. New York: Columbia University Press.

Stewart, C. 1991. *Demons and the devil: Moral imagination in modern Greek culture.* Princeton Modern Greek Studies. Princeton: Princeton University Press.

Stewart, C., and R. Shaw, eds. 1994. *Syncretism/Anti-syncretism: The politics of religious synthesis.* European Association of Social Anthropologists. London: Routledge.

Stojanovski, A. 1979. One legend affirmed. *Newsletter of the History Museum of Macedonia* 4: 53–57.

# 9

# Empire Dust

## *The Web of Relations in Saint George's Festival on Princes Island in Istanbul*

### Maria Couroucli

Every year on 23 April, the monastery of St. George on Prinkipo (Princes Island), less than two hours by boat from Istanbul, attracts some 100,000 visitors. As at other Eastern Mediterranean Christian holy places,[1] all visitors, Christian and Muslim alike, are welcomed as pilgrims by the local monks and priests who offer prayers for health and well-being. A leaflet published by the monastery informs visitors to the island: "Almost none [of the pilgrims] are Christian. Many of them will come back to thank Saint George by offering a bottle of olive oil for his lamp, because their prayer was heard and their wish fulfilled."[2] Saint George's festival is a modern syncretic phenomenon belonging to an old tradition. The sanctuary at Prinkipo is one of a number of Christian holy places in the ex-Ottoman lands that continue to attract great numbers of Muslim pilgrims, and one of many shrines and holy fountains in Istanbul with a reputation for healing and "making vows come true."

While anthropology is just beginning to put together a comparative grammar of such experiences in shared sacred places, most analyses to date have focused primarily on issues of tolerance and antagonism in situations of crisis and conflict between religious social groups (on former Yugoslavia, India, and Palestine, see Bax 1995, 2000; Claverie 2003; Hayden 2002; and Bowman 1993). My research, however, was focused on times of peace and addressed the issue of the coexistence of more than one religion as a traditional feature of the Eastern Mediterranean through the study of ethnographic material on "mixed" celebrations around Saint George's shrines in Ottoman and post-Ottoman society. The method used was ethno-historical, combining ethnographic observation with the study of archival material on this type of practice at the beginning of the twentieth century.

By "empire dust" I mean the relics of a long-gone Byzantine society. The Greek Orthodox community in Istanbul is a living example of the experience of religious plurality characteristic of both Byzantine and Ottoman traditions. Here, as elsewhere in the Eastern Mediterranean, one can study diachronically one of the most important features of the Eastern Christian heritage: coexistence, cohabitation, cultural and religious diversity as a way of life. Greek Orthodoxy today can be observed in two different contexts: (a) within the Greek national territory, where it is dominant (see Hirschon, this volume), and (b) outside the national territory, where Orthodox Greeks are a minority, either among other Christian denominations (as in the United States, Canada, Australia, or Germany) or among other religious majorities (as in Turkey, Israel, Egypt, etc.). The first context resembles the situation of Orthodox churches in the Balkans and Eastern Europe (Bulgaria, Serbia, Romania, Russia), while the second can be compared with other Christian communities (not only Greek Orthodox) living in minority situations in the Near and Middle East. Istanbul belongs to the latter category, albeit with a particularity: the everyday life of the Rum (the local Orthodox Greek community) is closely related to the political scene in Greece itself, because of the political and symbolic importance of the community for the larger population. The minority situation of native Orthodox Christians within the larger Ottoman world is a *longue durée* historical phenomenon that can be traced to the last years of the Byzantine empire (Runciman 1968).

Mixed practices in Istanbul and in Anatolia are by no means a novelty; sacred fountains in or near Christian churches have attracted Muslim visitors since Byzantine times (Couroucli 2009). But genuine sharing in the daily experience of mixed practices has not been a general rule. Rather, it is characteristic of moments, points in the vast Ottoman space/time where different logics meet to enable communication between social (religious and cultural) groups. It is important to underline that these practices are not symmetrical: it is usually Christian shrines, those belonging to the minority group, politically subordinate, that are visited by members of the Muslim majority.[3] This research has shown that while the mixed practices related to Saint George's shrines constitute an example of syncretism, of a positive manipulation of the symbols of another religious tradition, there is no ethnographic or historical evidence to corroborate the idea that they took place in a spirit of "togetherness." It would be anachronistic to characterize these phenomena as expressions of a spirit of "tolerance" in the sense of the multicultural ethics of the most liberal section of the population in today's Western world.

Saint George's celebrations on Prinkipo reflect a growing fascination with the Ottoman past, and this nostalgia for "old Istanbul" builds on what is taken to be an imagined collective memory and identity in contemporary Turkish society. One way to unfold some of the intricate overlay of meanings in this context is to compare today's data with archival information about similar practices during the Ottoman period, when larger Christian communities were living alongside the Muslim majority in both Anatolia and Istanbul. It is also useful to consider the association between religious tolerance and the "cosmopolitanism" of the Ottoman heritage as an example of "structural nostalgia, a collective representation of an Edenic order, characteristic of both official narratives and contemporary intellectual discourse" (Herzfeld 1997: 109, 115-16), a longing for a time when social relations among the Muslim majority and the Christian and Jewish minorities were peaceful and balanced. Henk Driessen (2005) has challenged the use of the term "cosmopolitanism" in relation to Mediterranean port cities of the Ottoman empire. He points out that the link between the two is "often assumed but rarely demonstrated" and that "tolerance of otherness as a key cosmopolitan value is double-faced." In fact, "cosmopolitanism" was not characteristic of the lifestyle of the majority of the population but "seems to have been largely the result of the encounter between the non-Muslim Ottomans and the different communities of Western Europeans" (138). With this critique in mind I propose to analyze an ethnographic example of mixed religion practices in Istanbul today.

Syncretic practices similar to the festival on Prinkipo can still be observed at other Christian holy places in Istanbul.[4] Saint George's Day is extraordinary chiefly because of the numbers of people who attend, which have been rising continuously. Three factors help explain its popularity. First, 23 April is a public holiday in Turkey— Sovereignty and Children's Day—and the island possesses obvious attractions for the inhabitants of the overcrowded megalopolis. Prinkipo is a quiet, beautiful town with seaside cafés, horse-drawn carriages, and green hills a few minutes' walk from the pier. Second, the inhabitants of Istanbul have become increasingly interested in their heritage, and specifically the late Ottoman period, when the city still had a mixed population of Muslims, Christians, and Jews (Örs 2002; Özyürek 2006). The third and most important factor is the syncretic tradition of Istanbul: Christian chapels and shrines have always attracted a wide range of Muslim visitors, and well-to-do multilingual Muslim elites have frequently attended Christian churches (Millas 1988).

The first quarter of the twentieth century was a watershed for modern Turkish society: in 1913–1923, following the Balkan Wars, massive "population exchanges" took place, allowing the formation of ethnically and religiously homogeneous nation-states (Mazower 2002). But just before this turning point, before Constantinople became definitely Istanbul, the great city experienced its cosmopolitan zenith (Yerasimos 1992; Georgeon and Dumont 1997; Anagnostopoulou 1997; Örs 2002).The neo-panygeris that takes place on Prinkipo on Saint George's Day can be seen as validating a certain representation of the past, the tradition of multiculturalism and "tolerance" in Ottoman society.[5] The festival exemplifies metanationalist discourses on identity and nationhood in the Balkans and in modern Turkey. One such narrative concerns the cosmopolitan character of Istanbul at the turn of the twentieth century, when Christians and Muslims lived together in peace. At that time the monastery, like the rest of the island, was a favorite destination for the leisure class (Millas 1988). There are practically no Christian residents on Prinkipo now, but the island is still an exclusive place where rich families own beautiful villas and patronize the local clubs. Here the privileged can practice a lifestyle quite different from the more traditionalist ways of popular Istanbul. The crowds who visit the island on 23 April also come from an urban tradition; few recently arrived migrants from eastern Turkey find their way there. Prinkipo continues to stand for modernity and secularism, in opposition to rural Anatolian modes of living.

From the Orthodox point of view, Saint George's festival brings to light a complex web of identities of the Orthodox Greeks of Istanbul, a once numerous and prosperous social group that underwent dramatic changes during the twentieth century, from *millet* to nation and from elite to almost extinct minority.[6] Three groups interact today, each partaking of Greek identity in a different way. First there are the few (between one and two thousand) remaining Rum, Greek Orthodox natives of Istanbul who have become Turkish citizens and whose conditions since the 1920s have depended closely on the state of relations between the Greek and Turkish nation-states. Their point of view has become almost inaudible because of their demographic demise. They remain, however, politically important for the other two groups, who often speak and act in their name. The second group, also in decline, consists of the Orthodox clergy attached to the patriarch's see. Its members have a dual identity: vis-à-vis the Orthodox, they constitute the clergy around the ecumenical patriarch, while vis-à-vis the Turkish authorities they have been, since 1924, the spiritual leaders of the remaining Rum. The third group consists of the staff of the Greek Consulate in Istanbul, who strictly speaking have almost no "Greek" community to look after but who nevertheless express the "Greek" point of view in matters concerning the Rum.

These three groups have different, often diverging agendas in their relation to the Turkish authorities, but they are interdependent. They have no political power but possess a symbolic importance for both national states. The Greek state, via its diplomatic mission, sometimes tries to promote the causes of Orthodox Greeks in Istanbul to the Turkish authorities, but for the latter they are Turkish citizens who belong to a specific minority. Their gradual disappearance has made them vulnerable, yet they are remnants of a cosmopolitan past that has become more highly valued as Europe has drawn nearer. Their token presence helps sustain a fantasy about an ideal past of "living together," in both Greek and Turkish narratives (Örs 2006; Millas 2006; Theodossopoulos 2006). These narratives are prominent in present-day political discourse and serve as counternarratives to stories of war and forced exile in the traumatic period 1912–1924. They are inspired by intentions of goodwill and pragmatic politics, but there is as yet little substantial historical research to undergird them.

## SYNCRETISM AND CALENDAR
## IN ANATOLIA AND ISTANBUL

In the late Ottoman period approximately one in four inhabitants of the capital was Christian.[7] Many travel books and memoirs mention the presence of Muslims at Greek Orthodox celebrations at the monastery of St. George on Prinkipo, but they usually stop short of relating mixed practices in detail. Most are written by the more learned and socially privileged and describe social events involving both Christians and Muslims, like picnics and Sunday receptions at the Kazino, the kiosk-restaurant at the foot of St. George's hill.[8] It seems that the wealthier inhabitants of the city organized mixed parties on social occasions but did not participate in religious celebrations. Mixed ritual practices seem to have been more common among the less privileged social groups, those who visited the sanctuary as pilgrims on the saint's day or on other special occasions.

Folklore sources concerning Saint George note the celebrations around Hidirellez, which are said to be pre-Islamic practices. Hidirellez is now celebrated on 2 May, and the link to Saint George has been lost, to the nonerudite at any rate. In fact, the two celebrations are closely linked (Bazin 1972: 727, 764). The traditional Anatolian and Ottoman calendar separates the year into two seasons: the cold season, which starts on 26 October according to the Julian calendar (8 November in the Gregorian calendar), and the good season, which starts on 23 April (6 May today). The first is called Kasim ("November" in Turkish) and corresponds to Saint Dimitrios's Day in the Christian calendar, and the second Hidrellez (Old Turkish: Hidir Ilyas), corresponding to Saint George's Day in the Christian calendar. The dates also coincide with the movement of the Pleiades, which appear at nightfall during the cold season and disappear in summer.

According to Louis Bazin the name Hidr refers to a prophet of Islam, whose Arabic name (from the root h-d-r) expresses the idea of "green." The Arab-Christian tradition has assimilated him to Saint George, and he is in fact a pre-Islamic figure expressing spring's renewal of nature.[9] Ilyas was, according to Bazin, the Arab name of the prophet Elijah, who was confused with Hidr (Turkish: Hizir) in popular Turkish tradition. Bazin thought that the prophet Elijah, who is not mentioned in the Koran as the harbinger of the good season, assumed this role thanks to the close homonymy of Elijah with the Turkish il(k)-yaz, meaning "first spring." He then concluded that Hidrellez was a Turkish custom (dating to at least the eighth century) disguised as an Islamic one, and that it was closely related to the Greek Christian tradition in which Saint George played the role of Hizir Ilyas (announcing the warm season), and Saint Dimitrios the symmetrical role (announcing the cold season). The dragon slain by Saint George was winter, while Saint Dimitrios was celebrated when it was time to sow grain. According to Bazin, the coincidences between dates in the Turkish-Muslim and the Greek-Christian calendars and traditions (both building on pre-Christian customs) were an indication of the syncretic character of Ottoman culture. F. W. Hasluck was the first scholar to establish a connection between Saint George and Hidr for the larger Ottoman area, and more specifically to identify the two figures in Anatolia. In Hasluck's view, "The functions and conceptions of Khidr are at once so varied and so vague as to adapt him to replace almost any saint, or indeed to occupy any site independently. . . . In Khidr there is no independent Moslem or pre-Moslem element. The Elias part can all be paralleled in Jewish tradition, while the George part is all Christian."[10]

Bazin did not offer any explanation as to why Hidirellez is now celebrated on 2 May in Turkey. The most plausible explanation would be that 2 May was "canonized" after the adoption of the Julian calendar by the Turkish republic in 1925 (Shaw and Shaw 1977: 385). After the Kemalist regime established a secular republic, it is possible that nonreligious aspects of the feast took over and its Muslim undertones were "forgotten." The way in which folklore was used as a "national" science in Turkey resembled the uses made of folklore in other Balkan countries. The key trait was the attempt to establish an uninterrupted continuity of customs from ancient to modern times by means of "survivalist theories" (Georgoudi 1979; Herzfeld 1982). Popular religion was believed to contain "pagan" elements from pre-Christian or pre-Islamic times. After the Second World War socialist regimes in the Balkans, like the Kemalist authorities in Turkey, opposed "popular" customs to official religious practices and promoted new rituals outside the control of the established religious hierarchy.[11]

## THE CONTEMPORARY PILGRIM'S TRAIL

The monastery and its church are situated on top of a hill on the southern part of the island. The usual approach is to take a horse-drawn carriage (phaeton) to the bottom of the hill and then walk up the steep path. From the harbor it takes a little over an hour, but on the day of the festival there is a long queue for the phaetons, and the total journey time is much longer. According to legend the monastery dates from the tenth century. It has been rebuilt many times and is not a grand place: the principal church, dedicated to Saint George, is only a hundred years old; it is surrounded by smaller chapels much more modest in size, one of which was the original church. These are situated next to the principal monastic building and around the holy fountain (*ayasma*).[12]

In the early twentieth century pilgrims used to come in great numbers from both the European and the Asiatic shores of Istanbul. According to the historian

Akilas Millas (1988: 484–92), the monastery attracted people who came for both pleasure and prayer:

> At every celebration, people came to the monastery on boats, bringing sheep as presents; they camped in the woods for a few days and feasted. Many people also came from Istanbul; one made a vow, to go up barefoot from the foot of the hill or even from the wharf. ... At least once a year, every local family went to the mountain to worship the saint, get sprinkled with water, [and] fill the bottles to be kept for hard times. While the masses visited on the day of the feast, the most wealthy families often went there for a picnic, and open-air receptions were common. On important occasions, a table was set up behind the monastery, and the abbey itself was the host. The Greek newspapers of Istanbul at the time often mentioned those gatherings. ... There were always people on Sundays at St. George's monastery.

The distinction between those present only on the feast day and the more distinguished visitors who might also come on other occasions is still a relevant one. Now, however, the "more popular" visitors are exclusively Muslims, while Christians (Armenian as well as Orthodox) are more likely to visit on other occasions. A group of Armenian girls offered this perspective:

> We have come for some fresh air, to enjoy the holiday away from the city. We don't go into the church today; there are too many people. We don't buy votive objects either; a candle is enough. On 23rd April it's mainly for the Muslims. The other Christians go on Sundays; there are fewer people.[13]

Those who gather on Prinkipo on 23 April are for the most part educated Muslims born in Istanbul, both Sunni and Alevi. They are not religious in the strict sense of the term: women wear Western-style clothes without head scarves, and the men rarely have beards. Two women describe why they visit:

> We have heard that this is a great place, so we have come, we don't know what to do exactly, we know nothing, we just go there, and we don't know what one should do. Last time I went to see the priest and told him what I wanted. What are the threads for? The candles? How does one do it? Do we have to pay for the prayer?[14]

With the dramatically increased numbers of visitors the presence of the authorities has become more visible. The police and fire-brigade are on alert and help organize the flow of pilgrims along the main road up to the monastery. Downtown, locals welcome the visitors, and shops around the main square sell water and snacks. In 2004, parents from the local school sold pastries to help finance a school project. One could also purchase a small pamphlet from the local cultural association explaining the historical interest of the monastery and the pilgrimage associated with it. The clearing at the bottom of the hill is packed with people and carriages. Cars cannot go beyond this point, except the car belonging to the monastery. At the beginning of the path, some twenty stalls sell votive charms, blue glass charms, small paper icons, bottles of water and oil, even scarves and clothes; many sell reels of thread, large and small. Attached to shrubs or fences, thousands of threads lead upward along the right-hand side of the path. Pilgrims believe that if their thread does not break, their vow will be heard, and help granted. People also tie shreds of cloth to shrubs and trees, so that by the end of the day thousands of pieces of cloth are hanging from the branches alongside the path. The ascent is usually accomplished in silence. A few pray while walking, while other pilgrims pause halfway to build small piles of stones on either side of the path: the vow will be realized if, despite its fragility, the construction holds together.[15] After a further ten minutes, pilgrims reach the point where they must wait in line to enter the church. The crowd is compact, and there is a waiting time of about thirty minutes. This area is cordoned off by police, and people wait their turn calmly. "People seem happy here," my young Turkish interpreter commented, impressed by the number of visitors and the peaceful order they maintained.

On my earlier visits, in 1992 and 1996, the pilgrims were not so numerous, and the visit lasted longer. There was a long queue to enter the church, but once there people could perform the rituals with less haste. Pilgrims lit a candle at the entrance, then proceeded into the church proper, knelt in front of the iconostasis, then again before Saint George's silver-plated icon; some put coins into the box next to it. Those who arrived early, during Mass or just after Mass, would also be offered a piece of blessed bread, the *antidoron,* which is distributed to the congregation at the end of the liturgy. They could approach the priest standing by and ask for a prayer to be read from the *Euhologion* (Book of Prayers) and for a blessing. The exchange would take place in Turkish, but the prayers were read in Greek. Some would deposit bottles of oil before leaving through the rear door, some would leave a paper on the *epitaphios* with their wishes written on it,[16] some would try to touch the frescoes and make coins stick to the walls,[17] some would try to turn a key in the keyhole of the rear door, and some would simply stand, watching what the others were doing before attempting to imitate them. Outside the church one could visit the *ayazma* in a chapel near the rear door and drink its water. Monks standing by would prevent pilgrims from using the water to wash themselves.

By 2004, the time one could spend inside the church had been reduced, and the visit limited to its bare essentials. Candles were still lit at the narthex; pilgrims then passed through the main church; the priest standing by the icon blessed only those nearest to him. After less than five minutes the visit was over. Outside some visitors would light candles next to or on the walls, some rubbed coins against them, and some prayed in the Muslim way, with outstretched palms. Access to the nearby chapel and holy fountain was closed. All around, people sat down to eat the food they had brought with them, though some waited in line for a seat in the self-service restaurant just behind the main building. Most took a short rest to enjoy the breathtaking view before starting their descent toward the Luna Park and the city center.

In the 1990s some pilgrims had made small constructions with bricks on the low dry stone walls surrounding the monastery grounds, for Saint George was said to assist those who asked for help with building their house. This particular custom had disappeared by 2004. The saint continues to cure all kinds of illness and to bring luck. In the stalls at the foot of the hill, visitors can choose from a large variety of charms corresponding to their vow: "chance," "love," "marriage," "house," "money," "baby," "job," "car," (protection against) "evil eye," (success in) "school," and "health" are the standard choices. Charms become effective after having been taken up to the monastery to be blessed by the saint. Traditionally, Saint George was also known for curing the mentally ill, and for this purpose incubations were practiced in the nineteenth and early twentieth centuries (Hasluck 1929: 693; Millas 1988: 468). Patients were taken up to the monastery to spend the night attached to special chains in the hope of seeing a healing apparition of the saint (cf. Bowman 1993). Finally, Saint George was known for protecting children. When Greeks lived on Prinkipo, the island was full of the saint's "little slaves" (*sklavakia*): parents would take their children to the monastery to "sell" them to the saint. As payment, they would receive a small bell to hang on the children's clothes, a protective amulet that they kept until they grew up. It was then returned to the saint, often plated in silver or gold, together with an altar candle, in thanks (Millas 1988: 490).

The average visitor to the monastery of St. George on 23 April has knowledge of a holy map of Istanbul, featuring both Christian and Muslim shrines. It is this sense of being autochthonous that Muslim visitors share with both the Rum and with the older priests, those born and educated in Istanbul. The syncretic practices are part of the Ottoman heritage, a traditional way of living side by side with other religious communities. As one of the older priests explained in 1996, "The Ottomans have faith; if I cheat them I am in sin, and I am blasphemous if I don't say prayers for their health, for their work, for their houses. These prayers are the same we pronounce for the Romii. When they come with faith, you cannot refuse." The imagined community that comes into being for a day in Istanbul thus appears to be built around traditional ways and habits dating back to Ottoman times. Let us now examine the historical context of a shared Ottoman past more closely.

## ARCHIVAL EVIDENCE

The phenomenon of shared shrines is an old one in the Ottoman world, and it has been variously interpreted. In 1913, Hasluck characterized as "ambiguous sanctuaries" those "claimed and frequented by both religions." He believed these to represent a "transitional" stage: "The ambiguous sanctuary, claimed and frequented by both religions, seems to represent a distinct stage of development—the period of equipoise, as it were, in the transition both from Christianity to Bektashism, and, in the rare cases where political and other circumstances are favourable, from Bektashism to Christianity."[18]

Shared shrines are plentiful on the Pontus, the Black Sea region of northern Anatolia, where many mixed villages and towns were still to be found at the turn of the twentieth century. The archives of the Centre for Asia Minor Studies in Athens contain rich materials concerning places of worship related to Saint George in this region.[19] According to these sources, there were two distinct kinds of celebration of St George's Day among the Pontic Greeks: rituals organized around a parish church within a village or town, and other celebrations held in the countryside. In towns where a parish church was named after Saint George, the service on 23 April was attended not only by the local Christian community but also by visitors from other villages. Sometimes a small fair was organized for the day.[20] Social celebrations took place after Mass: people gathered in each other's houses to share a meal, including guests from distant places who were offered hospitality by local families. The archives contain some rare mentions of "Turks" (i.e., Muslims) visiting Christian private houses; this was apparently part of the custom of exchange visits involving mostly local dignitaries on each side.[21] One testimony refers to Turks "standing by" as the saint's icon was taken in procession (*periphora*) around the neighborhood.

The second kind of celebrations took place in the countryside, either inside chapels or next to the "ruins" of old Christian shrines dedicated to the saint. These were the occasions for mixed ritual practices. The usual narrative explains: "Saint George is venerated by Turks, they call him Hidirellez, and they fear him, because he is a strong saint and punishes those who show disrespect." In the sample from the Black Sea area archives, with data from forty-two villages with churches or chapels or monasteries dedicated to Saint George, there are explicit mentions of shared practices in eight locations. All celebrations took place on 23 April outside the village or town. Both Christians and Muslims gathered. In two cases they practiced animal sacrifice (*kurban*).[22]

When these shrines no longer functioned as Christian chapels (i.e., there was no proper edifice with a roof), no priest was supposed to come, since no religious service could be held. However, local people still went to visit the saint on that day to practice incubation for healing, to hang pieces of cloth to a nearby tree to get rid of illnesses, or to try to make coins stick to a slab of stone from the ruins of the shrine. In Ladik, for example, St. George's church had become a *tekke* during the lifetime of the informant's grandfather:

> On Saint George's Day Turks were celebrating, too. They called the saint Hitirelez. On the door of the *tekke*, there was a slab of stone, upright. Next to it some trees

with no fruit. Turks and Greeks went there, tore off pieces from their clothes, and made knots on the branches. Then they asked for help [*hares,* lit. "favors"] from the saint of the *tekke*. They also took small stones or coins and tried to make them stick to the slab of stone. If they did, their wish would be fulfilled. The Turks kept a tomb inside the *tekke,* covered with a green cloth, and they said that inside there were bones.[23]

Most legends about Saint George were variations on a central theme about the saint: he traveled on horseback around the countryside and punished those who showed a lack of respect for his sacred places (by stealing from the chapel or felling a nearby tree, for example) or for his memory (by working on the saint's day). Such persons were liable to be struck down (much as one would imagine from the icon of Saint George striking the dragon), and they would recover only if they prayed and promised offerings. In the Asia Minor archives the Orthodox comments on Muslim visitors resemble those made in present-day Istanbul: the Muslims come to the shrines to make vows because Saint George/Hidirellez is a "strong"—and efficient—saint, able to cure and bring solace.

The two kinds of celebrations in the Pontus region can be related to the dual character of religion in the Ottoman empire. On the one hand, religion referred to a social domain, determining membership of a *millet* and conferring a distinct status on its members. No individual could belong to more than one such community, and conversion was one of the biggest taboos of Ottoman society. On the other hand, religion also referred to ritual practices. For the Greek Orthodox, when these practices took place within the parish structures—that is, within the organized *millet* system—they concerned solely the Christian community and were performed according to the official ecclesiastical rules and *doxas,* leaving no room for any mixing. Shared practices could take place only outside the villages and towns, beyond the local authorities' jurisdiction.

Glenn Bowman, who studied the Mar Elyas monastery in Palestine, also visited by both Muslims and Christians, suggested that "objects" of discourse were constituted through the meanings people attributed to them, and that the different meanings of the Mar Elyas celebrations were not unified, since they had not been stabilized by any religious authority (Bowman 1993: 456).[24] This also applies to the pilgrims to St. George at Prinkipo, since it is clear, given the political and demographic context, that the Orthodox clergy today are not an effective authority. Visitors manipulate symbols and meanings, which vary according to their different social and cultural backgrounds. Meanings and representations are often expressed as personal relations with the shrine among Christian pilgrims, both Rum and Armenian, whose strong sense of familiarity derives from the regularity of visits, generally taking place on the same date each year.

Celebrated on the two most important dates of the preindustrial calendar, the beginning and the end of the "good season," Saint George's festival was important for the regulation of economic activities (transhumance, navigation, and crop-sharing contracts) in Anatolia and the Balkans. It is no accident that these dates coincide with key dates of the old Turkish calendar (Bazin 1972; Gokalp 1980). The syncretic tradition associated with shrines dedicated to Saint George thus stretches well beyond "sharing practices" and the fact that a "strong" Christian saint attracts many Muslims.[25] "Religion" does not seem to be an adequate category to describe these practices, which are manifestly independent of ecclesiastical institutions. The Orthodox high clergy has always expressed hostility toward "pagan" practices and tried to stop them.[26] Those who nonetheless visit sacred places at specific times partake of a tradition that is both local and familiar and available to be shared by "others." Once near the shrines, visitors and pilgrims have their own agendas about how to employ symbols: attaching pieces of cloth to a nearby tree, rubbing coins on slabs of stone, taking oil to the priest celebrating Mass on that day, attaching threads that take the vow to the saint, "building" houses for new arrivals in Istanbul, and so on. It is clear that in this web of symbols no religious authority is pulling the main strings; rather, the syncretic tradition is a local phenomenon perpetuated by the transmission of ritual practices.

## ISTANBUL: BETWEEN NOSTALGIA AND MODERNITY

In Orthodox Christianity as in Islam, knowledge of tradition implies knowledge of a learned tradition (Yerasimos 1999). In the case of Saint George's festival on Prinkipo, the urban/rural gap also divides those who "know" from those who possess no memory of the Saint George/Hidirellez tradition. Descendants of the old Istanbul-born urban Muslim elites share this common culture, while migrants from the Anatolian provinces have no memory of the multicultural society of Ottoman times. Thus, while the crowds that gather on Prinkipo on 23 April are too large to be ignored, the event remains marginal and somehow disconnected from public life in Istanbul. Television coverage does not dwell on the religious character of the event, which is presented as just one of the many festivities taking place on the national holiday.[27] On the other hand, the pilgrims who gather on Prinkipo on 23 April each year can be said to partake in the imagined community of the natives of Istanbul, those who "remember" the times when the city was home to Turks, Greeks, Armenians, and Jews alike. These memories are nourishing present-day representations and discourses about the past as a lost Eden, a "structural nostalgia" in the sense in which the term is used by Michael Herzfeld.[28]

Istanbul's transformation from a cultural mosaic of one million people at the turn of the twentieth century into an all-Turkish megalopolis of ten million people within less than a hundred years has also informed self-representations and local narratives about national identity. Istanbul has always been a constantly changing topos. As G. Dagron (1992: 572) has pointed out, "Constantinople . . . seems laden with memories, reminiscences it does not really own, nor really knows how to deal with. It lives in the present. Fundamentally, it is a new city, and has remained such for the last thousand years." Today, Istanbul is also the focus of nostalgia for a long-gone past.

A. Soysal has observed that the basic characteristic of the literary movement in Turkish poetry called "the second renewal" was the opening to "others": that is, the "Judeo-Christian minorities of Istanbul" (1992: 700). Fascinated by the neighborhoods of Pera and Galata, where minorities used to live, these poets and novelists introduced the "Greek thematic" in their work. The minority characters "represented the proper space of Istanbul, that is at once Byzantium and the city that used to be the capital of the Ottoman Empire" (711). This literary movement was also an anticonformist political statement, a reaction to the official ideology of the 1950s and 1960s, when nationalism prevailed, even in scholarship. Historical narratives on both sides of the Aegean Sea had long avoided the last years of the Ottoman era (Mazower 2004; Herzfeld 1997; Couroucli 2002, 2005). The population exchanges between the Balkans and Anatolia in the late nineteenth and early twentieth centuries were a protean form of ethno-religious "cleansing," taking place when the old multicultural, multireligious, and multilingual Ottoman society gave way to monochrome, homogenized nation-states, with little contact across borders for the best part of a century (Lory 1996; Hirschon 2002; Keyder 2002; Berktay n.d.). Reconsidering nationalist historical narratives also involved revisiting the old historical model of "Oriental despotism," which had nurtured earlier perceptions of late Ottoman society. The Ottoman heritage has been widely viewed as a "cosmopolitan" experience, as if anticipating today's politically correct multiculturalism (Driessen 2005; Theodossopoulos 2006). Örs's ethnographic study shows how memories (re)collected among the Rum of Istanbul make reference to "an urban cosmopolitan legacy," a "grand past" when "the Istanbulite *Rum* acted as leading influential agents of Europeanization, and made their impact on the creation of an elite lifestyle with a unique mode of cosmopolitan modernity. . . . Being Constantinopolitan is equated with being cosmopolitan: connection to an imperial multicultural tradition is an essential feature of being from the City" (2006: 87).[29] Nostalgia is also the central theme of a study of Istanbul urban families, the Kemalist elite, among whom "nostalgic modernity is a political ideology, as well as a discursive and a sentimental condition" (Özyürek 2006: 19). Early republican days are remembered as "a joyous time in which individual citizens were ideologically and emotionally united with their state" (62). In fact, "Kemalist citizens and government officials have promoted a specific nostalgia for the foundational years of the republic in order to legitimize their lifestyle and position in society" (153).

Key issues of contemporary politics always inform historical and sociological discourses about the past, as "memory preserves the past so as to serve both present and future."[30] Representations of the Ottoman world as a social system characterized by peaceful coexistence and religious tolerance are shaping a new collective memory of cosmopolitan city life in the Eastern Mediterranean region. This transformation is taking place within a particular historical context: the collapse of the socialist regimes in Eastern Europe and the Balkans, the Yugoslav ethnic conflicts, and the ongoing war in the Middle East.

## CONCLUSION

Since the late 1980s many anthropologists have turned to historically informed ethnography in order to comprehend syncretic practices in many parts of the world (Stewart 1999; Bringa 1996; Bax 1995; van der Veer 1994). Adopting this practice in this chapter, I have compared ethnographic material on ritual practices in the Pontus area at the beginning of the twentieth century with what I observed in Istanbul between 1992 and 2004. Syncretic practices take place, then as now, outside parish territories, beyond the reach of religious authorities; one could even say beyond and in spite of the *millet* system, which kept communities separate. The symbolic transfers by means of which the relation of the pilgrim to the saint is established—the gestures performed (kneeling, praying, or receiving prayers from the priest), the objects manipulated (coins rubbed against slabs of stone or icons, pieces of cloth attached to a tree next to the shrine, piles of stones, threads pulled along the path leading to the sacred place), the practices attached to objects (drinking and sprinkling holy water, touching chains or icons, using keys on doors), and finally the gifts brought to the saint (oil for the lamps, candles) all point to continuities between early twentieth-century Anatolia and present-day Istanbul.

But it is important to insist once again that mixed practices represent moments: they are not (and were not traditionally) part of everyday experiences; they take place in special places on particular dates and often mark exceptional events in the lives of those who participate. Such shared practices were shaped within the Ottoman empire, where the coexistence of more than one religious group was organized according to the *millet* system. This was not a structure implying either equivalence or equality between communities. Each was organized according to its own principles, their members living side by side but not really together. Even in mixed villages and towns, neighborhoods (*mahalle*) were monoreligious social spaces. At the local level, social and religious divisions often coincided: in the mixed localities of the Black Sea, the dignitaries were Muslim pashas (civil servants and/or big landlords) and Greek Orthodox or Armenian priests and merchants. Another feature of traditional Ottoman space was the preponderance of churches over mosques, especially in small localities. As Muslim religious authorities were to be found only in big cities, the closest Muslim equivalent to the local

Christian clergy would be members of the different religious orders (*tarikat*), living in *tekkes* and not subject to any central authority.

Thus mixed religious practices taking place in Istanbul and in the larger post-Ottoman region cannot be reduced to local expressions of a "cosmopolitan" lifestyle. The use of overextended terms such as "cosmopolitanism" and "tolerance" involves ambiguous representations of the past (Berliner 2005; Driessen 2005). It is important to distinguish between cosmopolitanism, a spirit related to the lifestyle of the minority elites of Ottoman society, and the reality of religious plurality and tolerance in Ottoman society, which allowed shared practices at certain moments. In this chapter I have emphasized the contingent character of Saint George's festival in Istanbul and attributed part of its popularity to an increasing nostalgia for the *Pax Ottomana* on both sides of the Aegean. As Herzfeld has pointed out, structural nostalgia can also be a strategic resource (1997: 115). In both post-Ottoman societies, longing for a long-gone past has acquired postmodern global meanings, where nostalgia for the empire begins to take the form of a new, shared experience. This tendency is developing within a particular political climate in southeastern Europe, where the integration of the Balkan states and Turkey into the European Union is one of the major political stakes. In Turkey, remembering and celebrating the Ottoman multicultural past is very much bound up with efforts to promote minority and human rights. Similarly, recent positive images of Turks and things Turkish in Greece cannot be separated from the reorientation of Greek diplomacy, promoting Turkey's entry into the EU and pursuing constructive solutions to the Cyprus problem. The latter stance was adopted after Greece's own European credentials had been definitively established (Millas 2006; Theodossopoulos 2006; Couroucli 2002, 2007; Calotychos 2003). Within this new political climate and while the numbers of Greek tourists to Istanbul and Turkish visitors to the monastery of St. George continue to rise, a reimagined community seems to be emerging as the basis of post–cold war "political correctness." Greeks' recent infatuation with *baklava*, Istanbul cuisine, and baptism and marriage ceremonies at the patriarchate followed by receptions at the newly restored plush Ottoman palaces on the shores of the Bosporus are all part of the new reality of the reimagined community of the "authentic" inhabitants of Istanbul. This phenomenon also offers insight into one of the basic characteristics of Eastern Christian traditions: their capacity to survive alongside and beyond dominant alien cultural and ideological modes.

## NOTES

I wish to express my gratitude to Ayşe Baban and Altan Gokalp for taking me to the monastery of St. George on Prinkipo. Although both have helped me in my efforts to understand Saint George's festival within the context of contemporary Istanbul, they are not responsible for any errors in my interpretation and analysis. I am indebted to the director and staff of the Centre for Asia Minor Studies in Athens—S. Anestidis, V. Kontoyanni, D. Politis, E. Kapoli, M. Papayannopoulou—for their generous hospitality while I worked in the archives in October 2005 and May 2006. I would also like to thank Roger Just for insightful remarks on draft versions of this paper.

1. See Poujeau, this volume; Voile 2004; Mayeur-Jaouen 2005.

2. See *The Holy Monastery of St. George Koudounas, Prinkipo* (Oropos: Holy Monastery of the Paraclete, 2004); the 31-page brochure is published in Greek, Turkish, and English. An inscription in Ottoman and Greek over the iron gate of the monastery of St. George Koudounas indicated that Resul Efendi, a Muslim, had offered the gate after his wife's cure by the saint.

3. See Mayeur-Jaouen 2005. Archival material from the Black Sea region is explicit on this point: "Turks" visited Christian shrines in quest of healing, while in the only case in which "Greeks" were allowed to visit a *tekke* (not a mosque), it was because the particular holy place was originally built as a church, and so was a place that had once "belonged" to their ancestors. See also Mazower 2004: 79–86 on Saint Dimitrios church and Casimiye Mosque in Salonica, and also on the symbolic importance of the figure of Saint George in both Christian shrines and Sufi *tekkes*.

4. A large number of *ayazma* (from the Greek *agiasma*, "holy fountain") in and around churches and chapels in Istanbul attract visitors from all denominations, especially women: see Atzemoglou 1990; Örs 2006.

5. *Panygeris,* or *panigiri* in modern Greek: "traditional festival."

6. *Millet* referred traditionally to a religious minority of the Ottoman empire. Greeks constituted the Rum *millet,* whose head was the patriarch of Constantinople. The term Rum (Turkish) or Romioi (Greek) refers to the Byzantine origins of these Greeks, Byzantium being the ancient Eastern Roman Empire. The population exchange of 1923 resulted in the departure of all the Orthodox Greeks from Turkey, except those living in Istanbul. The latter comprised two distinct categories: the original Rum, who were Istanbul-born, ex-Ottoman subjects with Turkish citizenship since 1924; and those of Greek origin and Greek citizenship whose ancestors had settled in Istanbul after 1830, the last of whom were expelled from Turkey in 1964; see Alexandris 1983: 281. Both are referred to in Greece as Polites, but only the autochthonous consider themselves Romioi; see Anastasiadou and Dumont 2007: 34–66. In her ethnographic work (2002, 2006) Örs uses the term Rum Polites to refer to both groups as a whole.

7. The Greek Orthodox were the largest minority (see Shaw and Shaw 1977: 206, 240). The composition of the population changed dramatically within ten years, from 20 percent Christian in 1913 to 2 percent in 1923 (Keyder 2002: 43).

8. Millas (1988) mentions a number of such travel accounts from the nineteenth century: Charles Colville (1830), C. Strahlheim (1837), Frédéric Lacroix (1839), Alexandre Timoni (1844), Théophile Gautier (1852), Lady Hornby (1856), and Gustave Schlumberger (1884).

9. Bazin does not mention the Greek *nea chidra* (young shoots of wheat) and makes no connection to the Byzantine Christian custom of blessing these in church, probably around the same dates.

10. Hasluck 1929: 329, 334; for the relation of Hidr to other saints, see pp. 321–25.

11. See also Danforth 1989 on the negative attitude of the Orthodox Church toward fire-walking rituals in Greece; and Stewart 1991 and 1999 on the Orthodox high clergy's hostility toward "pagan" practices.

12. A large aisle of the monastery comprising cells for monks and for guests was destroyed by fire in 1986 and has not been rebuilt; the whole complex was renovated in 1997, after a fire in 1995 had severely damaged the abbot's house and part of the church.

13. Conversation with three Armenian girls in their twenties on the boat back to Istanbul, 23 April 2004.

14. Conversation with two women from southern Turkey on the boat from Istanbul, 22 April 2004.

15. In 2004 I met a group of Evangelical Christians about halfway up the hill. They spoke English and Turkish and were distributing Bibles, singing prayers, and giving blessings. They said that they did not "belong to a congregation" but were there "to help those in need." Very few people stopped, but most took the Bibles in Turkish that were handed out.

16. An *epitaphios* is a wooden representation of Christ's sepulchre used during ceremonies in the week before Easter. In 1992 and 1997 the *epitaphios* had remained inside the church. In 2004 a box where people could put their wishes was set up near the rear door; according to the curators it had to be emptied many times during the feast day.

17. Making coins stick to slabs of stone is also done on *türbe,* the tombs of Muslim saints. The prayer will be heard if the coin adheres.

18. Hasluck 1929: 564; for a recent study of Hasluck's work, see Shankland 2004.

19. The archives consist primarily of extensive interviews with refugees from Anatolia who arrived in Greece after the Lausanne agreement in 1923.

20. When the town had more than one parish, a *monokklisia* was organized: Mass was celebrated in St. George's church, where all the clergy of a town and all Christian inhabitants would be invited to participate.

21. Visit exchange is a highly ritualized custom in both traditional communities and has been described in detail by more than one ethnographer; see, for example, for Greece, Herzfeld 1987; Hirschon 1989; Couroucli 1997. Information on "mixed" visits, on the other hand, is harder to come by; it is mostly to be found in literary works about life in Istanbul at the turn of the century; see, for example, Iordanidou [1962] 2000.

22. Centre for Asia Minor Studies (CAMS), files PO177, PO 679.

23. CAMS, file 965.

24. Bowman follows Derrida in using the concept of a "floating signifier" to analyze objects of and in discourse.

25. The Greek refugee archives mention Bafra as the location of two churches of St. George. According to the Web site of the Turkish Ministry of Culture, 6 May (i.e., 23 April according to the old calendar) is still considered a "significant day" locally. http://www.kulturturizm.gov.tr.

26. For general discussions, see Stewart 1991, 1999. On *kurban* practices in contemporary Greece, see Georgoudi 1979 and Tsibiridou 2000. The ecclesiastical authorities of the Black Sea at the beginning of the twentieth century seem to have been equally hostile: the bishop of Trebizond intervened to stop priests from celebrating Mass outside churches on Saint George's Day, but he did not succeed in stopping syncretic practices.

27. I am indebted to Alexander Toumarkine of the French Institute of Anatolian Studies, Istanbul, for this personal communication.

28. For Herzfeld, "structural nostalgia" is "the collective representation of an Edenic order—a time before time—in which the balanced perfection of social relations has not yet suffered the decay that affects everything human." He observes further: "Structural nostalgia characterizes the discourse of both the state and its most lawless citizens" (1997: 109).

29. See also Georgeon and Dumont 1977; Örs 2006.

30. J. Le Goff, ed., *La nouvelle histoire* (Paris: Retz-CEPL, 1978), quoted in Todorov 2004: 7.

## REFERENCES

Alexandris, A. 1983. *The Greek minority in Istanbul and Greek-Turkish relations, 1918–1974.* Athens: Centre for Asia Minor Studies.

Anagnostopoulou, S. 1997. *Mikra Asia, 19ᵒˢ ai.—1919, Oi ellinoorthodoxes koinotites, apo to millet ton Romion sto Elliniko ethnos* [Asia Minor, 19th—20th Centuries, the Greek-

Orthodox communities, from the millet of the Rum to the Greek nation]. Athens: Ellinika Grammata.

Anastasiadou, M., and P. Dumont. 2007. *Oi Romioi tis polis* [The Istanbul Rum]. Athens: Estia.

Atzemoglou, N. 1990. *Ta thaumatourga agiasmata tis Konstantinoupolis* [The miraculous fountains (*ayasma*) of Constantinople]. Athens: Ressos.

Bax, M. 1995. *Medjugorje: Religion, politics, and violence in rural Bosnia.* Amsterdam: VU University Press.

———. 2000. Barbarization in a Bosnian pilgrimage center. In *Neighbors at war,* ed. J. Halpern and D. Kideckel, 187–202. Philadelphia: University of Pennsylvania Press.

Bazin, L. 1972. *Les calendriers turcs anciens et médiévaux.* Thèse Paris III. Lille: Service de reproduction des thèses, Université de Lille.

Berktay, H. 1998. *National "Memories": Understanding the Other, Taming your Own.* http://www.hri.org/por/Summer98/story3.html.

Berliner, D. 2005. The abuses of memory: Reflections on the memory boom in anthropology. *Anthropological Quarterly* 78, no. 1: 197–211.

Bowman, G. 1993. Nationalizing the sacred: Shrines and shifting identities in the Israeli-occupied territories. *Man* 28: 431–60.

Bringa, T. 1996. *Being Muslim the Bosnian way: Identity and community in a central Bosnian village.* Princeton: Princeton University Press.

Calotychos, V. 2003. *Modern Greece: A cultural poetics.* Oxford: Berg.

Claverie, E. 2003. *Les guerres de la vierge.* Paris: Gallimard.

Couroucli, M. 1997. Se rendre chez l'autre: La visite dans la société greque. In *Vivre dans l'empire Ottoman,* ed. F. Georgeon and P. Dumont, 335-48. Paris: L'Harmattan.

———. 2002. Le nationalisme d'état en Grèce: Les enjeux de l' identité dans la politique nationale, XIXᵉ–XXᵉ siècle. In *Nationalismes en mutation en Méditerranée orientale,* ed. A. Dieckhoff and R. Kastoriano, 41–59. Paris: CNRS Editions.

———. 2005. Du cynégétique à l'abominable, à propos du chien comme terme d'injure et d'exclusion en grec moderne. *L'Homme* 174: 227–52.

———. 2007. Identity, nationalism, and anthropologists. In *Between Europe and the Mediterranean: The challenges and the fears,* ed. P.S. Cassia and T. Fabre, 73–87. Houndmills, Basingstoke: Palgrave.

———. 2009. Saint Georges l'anatolien, maître des frontières. In *Religions traversées: Lieux saints partagés entre chrétiens musulmans et juifs en Méditerranée,* ed. M. Couroucli and D. Albera, 177–210. Arles: Actes Sud.

Dagron, G. 1992. Constantinople: Du bon usage de la mémoire et de l'oubli. *Critique* 48, nos. 543–544: 572–82.

Danforth, L.M. 1989. *Firewalking and religious healing: The anastenaria of Greece and the American firewalking movement.* Princeton: Princeton University Press.

Driessen, H. 2005. Mediterrannean port cities: Cosmopolitanism reconsidered. *History and Anthropology* 16, no. 1: 129–41.

Georgeon, F., and P. Dumont, eds. 1997. *Vivre dans l'empire ottoman: Sociabilités et relations intercommunautaires (XVIIIe–XXe siècles).* Paris: L'Harmattan.

Georgoudi, S. 1979. L'égorgement sanctifié en Grèce moderne: Les "Kourbania" des saints. In *La cuisine du sacrifice en pays grec,* ed. M. Detienne and J-P. Vernant, 271–307. Paris: Gallimard.

Gokalp, A. 1980. *Têtes rouges et bouches noires.* Paris: Société d'Ethnographie.

Hasluck, F. W. 1913–1914. Ambiguous sanctuaries and Bektashi propaganda. *The Annual of the British School at Athens* 20: 94–119.

———. 1929. *Christianity and Islam under the sultans.* Ed. Margaret M. Hasluck. 2 vols. Oxford: Clarendon Press.

Hayden, R. B. 2002. Antagonistic tolerance: Competitive sharing of religious sites in South Asia and the Balkans. *Current Anthropology* 43, no. 2: 205–31.

Herzfeld, M. 1982. *Ours once more: Folklore, ideology, and the making of modern Greece.* The Dan Danciger Publication Series. Austin: University of Texas Press.

———. 1987. "As in your own house": Hospitality, ethnography, and the stereotype of Mediterranean society. In *Honor and shame and the unity of the Mediterr*anean, 75–89. Special publication 22. Washington, D.C.: American Anthropological Association.

———. 1997. *Cultural intimacy: Social poetics in the nation-state.* London: Routledge.

Hirschon, R. 1989. *Heirs of the Greek catastrophe: The social life of Asia Minor refugees in Piraeus.* Oxford: Clarendon Press.

———, ed. 2002. *Crossing the Aegean.* Oxford: Berghahn Books.

Iordanidou, M. [1962] 2000. *Loxandra.* [In Greek.] Athens: Hestia.

Keyder, C. 2002. The consequences of the exchange of populations for Turkey. In *Crossing the Aegean,* ed. R. Hirschon, 39–52. Oxford: Berghahn Books.

Lory, B. 1996. Les Balkans, carrefour des peuples et des nations: Pour une approche historique renouvelée. In *Les Balkans, carrefour d'ethnies et de cultures: Les espaces éducatifs et culturels,* ed. M. Couroucli, 37–42. Strasbourg: Council of Europe.

Mango, C. 1992. Constantinople, ville sainte. *Critique* 48, nos. 543–44: 625–33.

Mayeur-Jaouen, C. 2005. *Pèlerinages d'Egypte: Histoire de la piété copte et musulmane, XVe-XXe siècles.* Paris: EHESS editions.

Mazower, M. 2002. *The Balkans.* New York: Modern Library.

———. 2004. *Salonica, city of ghosts: Christians, Muslims, and Jews, 1430–1950.* Harper Perennial.

Millas, A. 1988. *Prinkipos.* [In Greek.] Athens: Melissa.

Millas, H. 2006. History and the image of Turks in Greek literature. *South European Society and Politics* 11, no. 1: 47–60.

Örs, I. 2002. Coffeehouses, cosmopolitanism, and pluralizing modernities in Istanbul. *Journal of Mediterranean Studies* 12 (1): 119–45.

———. 2006. Beyond the Greek and Turkish dichotomy: The Rum *polites* of Istanbul and Athens. *South European Society and Politics* 11, no. 1: 79–94.

Özyürek, E. 2006. *Nostalgia for the modern.* Durham, N.C.: Duke University Press.

Runciman, S. 1968. *The Great Church in captivity: A study of the Patriarchate of Constantinople from the eve of the Turkish conquest to the Greek war of independence.* Cambridge: Cambridge University Press.

Shankland, D., ed. 2004. *Archaeology, anthropology, and heritage in the Balkans: The work of Hasluck.* Istanbul: Isis.

Shaw, S. J., and E. K. Shaw. 1977. *History of the Ottoman empire and modern Turkey.* Cambridge: Cambridge University Press.

Stewart, C. 1991. *Demons and the devil: Moral imagination in modern Greek culture.* Princeton: Princeton University Press.

———. 1994. Syncretism as a dimension of nationalist discourse in modern Greece. In *Syncretism/Anti-Syncretism: The politics of religious synthesis,* ed. C. Stewart and R. Shaw, 127–44. London: Routledge.

———. 1999. Syncretism and its synonyms: Reflections on cultural mixture. *Diacritis* 19, no. 3: 40–62.

Soysal, A. 1992. Prononcer aujourd'hui le "très ancien nom." *Critique* 48, nos. 543–44: 634–39.

Theodossopoulos, D. 2006. Introduction: The "Turks" in the imagination of the "Greeks." *South European Society and Politics* 11, no. 1: 1–32.

Todorov, T. 2004. *Les abus de la mémoire.* Paris: Arléa.

Tsibiridou, F. 2000. *Les Pomak dans la Thrace grecque: Discours ethnique et pratiques socio-culturelles.* Paris: L'Harmattan.

van der Veer, P. 1994. Syncretism, multiculturalism, and the discourse of tolerance. In *Syncretism/Anti-Syncretism: The politics of religious synthesis,* ed. C. Stewart and R. Shaw, 196–211. London: Routledge.

Voile, B. 2004. *Les coptes d'Egypte sous Nasser: Sainteté, miracles, apparitions.* Paris: CNRS Editions.

Yerasimos, S. 1992. Du cosmopolitisme au nationalisme. In *Istanbul 1914–1923: Capitale d'un monde illusoire ou l'agonie des vieux empires,* ed. S. Yerasimos. Paris: Autrement.

———. 1999. De l'arbre à la pomme: La généalogie d'un thème apocalyptique. In *Les traditions apocalyptiques au tournant de la chute de Constantinople,* ed. B. Lellouch and S. Yerasimos, 291–332. Paris: L'Harmattan.

# 10

# Pilgrimages as Kenotic Communities beyond the Walls of the Church

Inna Naletova

Orthodox religiosity in Russia, like much in contemporary European religion generally, challenges scholars to broaden the range of experience they study. Grace Davie (1993, 2000) and Danièle Hervieu-Léger (2000), for instance, have put forward a "mobile" model of religiosity that stresses social relations, memory, and the emotional high points of spiritual activities such as pilgrimages, in contrast to static approaches, which emphasize regular church practices and familiarity with religious dogmas. Characterizing European religiosity in general, Davie concludes that "religious belief persists, but becomes increasingly personal, detached and heterogeneous" (2001: 110). In this chapter I shall argue that Russian Orthodoxy provides an interesting context for examining the relationship between churchly religiosity and religion outside the church. The church is tolerant and supportive of various forms of religious activities taking place outside its own domain. I shall focus on pilgrimages in order to examine how Orthodox believers relate to the church and society, distinguishing between two kinds of pilgrimage: processions and the veneration of "traveling icons." By offering religious education and experience outside of the church, these kinds of pilgrimage demonstrate how the revival of Russian Orthodoxy continues to create kenotic communities of believers.[1]

Kenosis is a theological concept that concerns the Incarnation and the nature of God's self-sacrifice for the redemption and salvation of the humanity (the kenosis of the Son of God).[2] The concept is also applied to religious practices of "self-emptying" in seeking union with God. Kenosis is a mystery of transcendence of the world through imitating Christ's love and self-sacrifice. Kenotic communities are centered around a holy place and guided by a belief in God's suffering for humanity and His sacrificial death on the cross. Just as Christ "emptied Himself" for humankind, a believer can participate in the divine life by following the example of Christ through practice of a personal self-emptying (*kenosis*). A variety of kenotic communities exist outside the church. Like an altar, which is seen as an open grave of Christ in a church, holy springs, rivers, fields, and the graves of saints can also be seen as places to encounter the Holy. While traveling to a holy place pilgrims resemble a parish community performing a smaller pilgrimage to the altar for Holy Communion. By limiting their wills and desires through fasting, walking long distances, and voluntarily working in monasteries, pilgrims follow the example of Christ, who "poured Himself out" to the world and "made Himself nothing." If a person is viewed as made in the image or "likeness of God," then meeting up with people can also serve as a means to encounter the Holy in a broader social context. Through kenosis, liturgy becomes extended in time and space, and church teaching is experientially applied to life.

Kenotic communities are based on a specific ethics, defined by the ideals of self-limitation and service to God and people. The early church fathers viewed *kenosis* as a mystical transformation of man into an icon of God (*theosis*). The Russian Church made a special point of emphasizing humility, poverty, and hard work as a way to experience the grace of God in the world. Numerous Russian saints, from the first passion-bearers Boris and Gleb to the new martyrs of the Soviet era, resembled Christ in a passive way by taking on themselves the "internal cross" of moral duties, ascetic practices, obedience, and martyrdom. In characterizing the features of the Russian religious mind Georgy Fedotov argued that a very humane image of Christ was developed in Russian Christianity. Imagining Christ as weak, suffering, and obedient to his Father, the early Russian converts elaborated a different image of God than the more powerful and courageous image created by Byzantine culture. A weak and suffering image of the Son of God touched the hearts of the Russian Christians and became, as Fedotov put it, their "main religious discovery" (1996: 129). The Russian religious writers of the nineteenth and early twentieth centuries tried to grasp the nature of "Russian kenosis" by placing the ethical ideals of nonresistance, humility, and self-denial in a broader context of discussions about the Russian national character and culture. My argument in this chapter is that contemporary Orthodox pilgrimage serves as a context for the revival of kenotic practices outside the church. I will discuss the forms of self-limitation undertaken by pilgrims and will show how the experience of communal living during pilgrimages helps them socialize in the church and society.

I find Victor Turner's (1974) notion of *communitas* helpful for understanding how pilgrimage contributes to a restoration of social integrity and trust, in Russia. Following Turner, I will show how, on the way to a holy place, pilgrims are challenged to accept ascetic and collective conditions of living and become exposed to social realities to which they are not accustomed. If they succeed in coping with difficulties, explains Turner, they return home with the renewed strength to carry the burden of structure. While liberating people from structure, pilgrimages also help them readjust to it. Feelings of brotherhood and togetherness, and also national pride and pain for the fate of their country, are the central features of Russian pilgrimages and support Turner's insight into the capacity of pilgrimage to strengthen social bonds and networks of trust.

Turner's *communitas* is also helpful when we consider the mystical aspects of religious experience during pilgrimage. In line with Turner's views concerning the negation of structure and the embracement of *communitas,* Orthodox theology views the Holy as being encountered through restraining one's worldly desires and "emptying oneself" toward others. In both approaches, participation in the Holy requires individual self-limitation, which has to be unfolded within a community. "There is something magical about it," writes Turner. "Those who experience *communitas* have a feeling of endless power" (1978: 251). However, according to Turner the highest point in pilgrimage experience—*communitas* or the state of the "essential we"—is not a community of ascetic self-limitation, but rather a community of self-expression, a community of feelings that are primitive and unsophisticated (1974: 308). This does not seem to me to correspond to a reflective, conscientious, Christ-centered kenosis. Pilgrims themselves, even at the end of their journey, are often not emotional at all, because pilgrimages have more to do with inner reflection than outer emotion. Although many Russian pilgrims are insufficiently familiar with the teaching of the church, they receive guidance from priests or more experienced believers. They take inspiration from prayers and icons, as well as from Russian classical literature, which is so rich in religious ideas. However temporary and spontaneous pilgrim communities might be, they exist not in an exotic land but in the homeland, whose history is generally well-known to all citizens. These communities are formed within a larger network of communication, in which churches and monasteries contribute to shaping pilgrims' experience and understanding. In short, the Orthodox experience of *communitas* is far from being primitive and feeling-based; rather, it reflects and is guided by many sophisticated sources available in Russian society.

Contrary to Turner's critics, who present pilgrimage as an arena of conflicting interpretations (Eade and Sallnow 2000), I view the various sources of pilgrims' inspiration as working toward unanimity. Simon Coleman, reacting to the "postmodern playfulness" of John Eade and Michael Sallnow's approach, noted that pilgrimage has an ability to "fertilize" contesting cultural sources and to "convert them into sacralised forms which can then be reconsumed" (2002: 360). Turner's insight into the unifying and enlightening nature of *communitas* helps reveal the religious core of pilgrimage, which combines cultural trends, institutional power, and pilgrims' mundane interests. In the following sections, I will focus on the social background of contemporary Russian pilgrimages. Following a description of some of the most popular pilgrimages, based on survey data I shall outline pilgrims' demographic characteristics and social orientations. Then I will focus on the kenotic aspects of pilgrimage: the specific forms of self-limitation undertaken by pilgrims, and their experience of communal living, as well as the resulting experience of the miraculous. I will conclude by discussing pilgrimages' contribution to strengthening national identity and forging communal bonds in Russia.

## AWARENESS OF PILGRIMAGES
## IN CONTEMPORARY RUSSIA

After many decades of suppression, pilgrimages have once again emerged as a mass phenomenon in Russia. The interest in pilgrimages is growing so quickly that the senior members of the church have began to worry about the movement getting out of the church's control (Kirill, Mitropolit 2004). For evidence it is enough to inspect the announcements on public notice boards. It is hard to find a church that does not announce pilgrim trips. In Moscow such announcements also appear on the bulletin boards of libraries, student dormitories, museums, and even at the entrance to the Academy of Science. In summer 2004 an announcement titled "All Come to Bow to Our Father Seraphim!" invited Moscovites to travel to Diveevo, and dozens of posters placed all around Nizhnii Novgorod displayed the appeal "Father Seraphim, Pray to God for Us!" Whereas a few years earlier central TV channels had hardly ever mentioned Orthodox events, by 2004 the most popular pilgrimages received generous media coverage. Books about pilgrimages could be found in almost all bookshops. The Department of External Relations of the Moscow Patriarchate published a journal titled *Pravoslavnyi palomnik* containing historical and practical information about holy places (addresses, guesthouses, and means of transportation) and designed to help the church keep the rising popularity of pilgrimages "inside its walls." The Ministry of Tourism played its part by formulating the main principles to be observed by travel agencies involved in organizing pilgrimages—provide simple hotels, offer no secular entertainments, keep fasting rules, and allow sufficient time for pilgrims' participation in church services.

The increasing interest in pilgrimages could also be felt at regional historical museums. Such museums exist in every medium-size city and are usually supported by local government. Many of these museums have recently changed their Soviet displays to foreground materials concerning the religious history of the region, including the history of pilgrimages. Such materials are often incorporated in the curricula of public schools. The increased popularity of pilgrimages is confirmed in open polls. The question "Would you like to be present in Diveevo at the time of celebration of the anniversary of Saint Seraphim Sarovskiy?" was answered positively by 28 percent of respondents.[3] Responses to another question—"What *first* comes to your mind when you hear the word 'Jerusalem'?"—

showed that 3 percent of respondents associate Jerusalem with pilgrimages, and 19 percent with holy places.[4] Thus 22 percent could be seen as representing actual or potential pilgrims. This figure is almost twice that of regular church-attendees.

In interpreting such data it is important to appreciate the cultural background of pilgrimage in Russia. "Pilgrim-professionals" (*stranniki*) emerged as an institution in the eighteenth century, when "spiritual wandering" became recognized as a way of life. Such travelers were not punished by the state but were granted juridical rights. Unlike wanderer-professionals in India or Tibet, Russian wanderers did not belong to a spiritual hierarchy but represented society (mostly the peasantry). One spiritual quest was described in the famous nineteenth-century book *Sincere Stories of a Wanderer*, about the life of a peasant-wanderer (*strannik*) who was searching for the right way to do the Jesus prayer (Anon. 2001). In his novel *The Enchanted Wanderer* (1873) the writer Nikolai Leskov described the life of a peasant who had been thrown into exile but lived according to his convictions as an active, "practical Christian." Saint Maxim Grek, a prominent Greek figure in the cultural history of sixteenth-century Russia, saw the whole country as a female pilgrim "dressed in black, sitting, lost in thoughts, on her way. She feels herself at the end of times, she thinks about her future. She is crying" (Shchepanskaia 2003: 25). These ways of experiencing religion are fully encompassed by the old Russian word *poklonnik*, which refers not so much to spiritual wandering (from the Latin *peregrinato*), but more to bowing down before the Holy (Slavonic *poklonenie*, "kneeling down"; Greek *proskinitís*, "pilgrim"). *Poklonnichestvo* means "pilgrimage" in a broad sense. It is a state of being "before God's eyes," searching for God's grace. Such pilgrimage, like liturgy and penance, is essentially a kenotic practice, directed at God and society (Egorievskii 2004; Moklezova 2003; Romanov 1999).

Pilgrimages can also serve as a means of expressing opposition to the atheist state. A picture of a procession can be found, for instance, on an icon depicting the life of believers canonized as martyrs at the Church Council of 2000. In the traditional style of Orthodox iconography it shows a group of people walking with icons in front of soldiers with loaded weapons. Christian martyrdom of the Soviet era is the central feature of contemporary pilgrimages to the Solovki Islands in the far north and to Butovo to the south of Moscow. More than a million prisoners died in the Solovki camps, and hundreds were killed in Butovo. Unlike Solovki (an ancient monastery), Butovo (formerly a training ground) does not have a long religious history. Still, it too is visited by thousands of pilgrims annually. They participate in a grandiose liturgy held under the open sky, with several bishops officiating. Pilgrimage to such places differs radically from that at other, more tranquil locations. The meaning of the former is not encompassed by categories such as purity, simplicity, and antiquity (Kormina, this volume). A continuity of sacrifice, compassion, and community with those suffering on the cross—a kenotic core of the Christian faith—is what people experience at holy places where hardly a stone is not marked with blood.

It is a mistake to reduce pilgrimage to the experience of beauty in nature. While many holy places are indeed picturesque, one does not need to go on a pilgrimage to see their beauty. In Kasan, for instance, I was struck by a group of pilgrims praying at a place that did not look beautiful at all—in a back yard disfigured by the garbage of a factory. The site where the icon Kasanskaia Mother of God appeared in a deep forest centuries ago was, by 2004, part of a tobacco factory. In such locations people feel an acute sense of pain for the fate of their damaged country. Here is how one man remembered his walk in Viatka, one of the most beautiful, but also very poor regions of northern Russia:

> We walk through dozens of former villages. We recognize them by the cherry trees, lindens, abandoned wells, and remnants of stoves. Empty lands. This village is deserted and remains, like a skeleton, unburied. . . . Our pilgrimage is an uninterrupted prayer. With this prayer we will overcome the devil. He thought that Russia is dead, but we are alive. He thought that he would destroy villages, and people would leave. But we come and walk here and fill the devastated lands with our prayers. These prayers cover our Russia with a healing shroud. (Krupin 2004: 32, 64)

In such places, a sharp concern for the future dominates the pleasure of experiencing beauty and a villagelike antiquity. Pilgrimage to such places is an experience of prayer and an opening of the self toward all who lived there before and who will live there in the future.

## PROCESSIONS

Various types of procession evolved in Russia as a response to postsocialist political and cultural events. Many repentance processions were performed throughout the country after the discovery of the remains of the royal family in Ekaterinburg. I was able to accompany the annual summer procession on part of the journey from Ekaterinburg to Diveevo, in which an icon of the Tsar-martyr is carried from one village to another over a distance of 1,600 kilometers. In 2003, 150 people walked the entire distance, and many more accompanied them for shorter periods.[5] A tragedy such as the sinking of the submarine *Kursk* (1999) was marked by commemoration processions in Murmansk. Priests were invited aboard a submarine to travel together with the crew and perform an "underwater" procession—a modern interpretation of an old practice.[6] Protective processions were performed in Moscow in 2003 when terrorists took hostages in a theater. A group of believers took a bus around the city, making stops at all points of the compass to form a cross. At each stop they got out of the bus to pray, while the priest blessed "the city" with holy water. There were also protest processions, whose variety precludes summary here.[7] I will limit my discussion to processions that take more than one day to walk to holy places.[8]

The river Velikaia in the Viatka region is the destination of the "Velikaia River Walk" (*velikoretskiy krestniy khod*), which sets out from the city cathedral and proceeds to the village of Velikoretskoe some ninety kilometers away. Four hundred pilgrims participated in this procession in 1993; in 2000 the procession numbered almost six hundred, in 2005 about three thousand. The participants were welcomed in local churches and accommodated overnight in private homes and local schools. The procession celebrates a miracle that happened in 1378 when an icon of Saint Nikolay was found in the forest, near the village.[9] Although a night prayer and confession are the central events, pilgrims also engaged in other activities, such as walking under the roots of the trees growing at the river's bank while asking Saint Nikolay for healing. As they did so, they collected small stones on the bank, which, with a little imagination, could be taken to resemble the body parts in need of attention. These stones are taken home to be kept near icons or passed on to people who could not themselves attend. Finally, the procession walks back to the city, making a stop at the Trifonov monastery to venerate the relics of the saint Trifon Viatskii. Altogether the procession known as "Viatka's Easter" covers a distance of 170 kilometers in five days.

A similar tradition exists in Kursk, where a procession is devoted to the icon of the Mother of God "Korennaia." This procession was reviewed in 1990 on the grounds of the monastery Korennaia Pustyn (Kulagin 1998). Later it began at the city center and continued down the central avenue, still named after Lenin. In its festivity this event was reminiscent of the demonstrations performed during the Soviet era, when practically all residents would come out onto the streets to join or watch the marching columns. After leaving the city, pilgrims proceeded to the monastery on buses provided by the local government. Near the monastery there are numerous springs of crystal-clear water. Pilgrims drink, fill bottles with water, and bathe in specially designated places. Hundreds of people participated in these events in summer 2005, but only about sixty continued on to Diveevo the next day, after an overnight stay in the monastery. This walk took several weeks (June 11–July 31) and covered 1,200 kilometers. As I was walked alongside pilgrims, in each settlement through which the procession passed, I saw people coming out on the streets to watch, to join for short periods, and to participate in common prayers. Every year at the end of July, Diveevo is the destination for several processions from different regions of Russia (see fig. 10.1). In 2003 about ten thousand visitors attended "Diveevo's Easter." A huge camp was built to house up to three thousand pilgrims.[10]

In its demographic composition and structure, Orthodox procession has many similarities with a parish during a church service. Most participants are women,

FIGURE 10.1. A procession arriving from Ekaterinburg makes a ritual walk along the moat circling the monastery at Diveevo, July 2004. One pilgrim (left) carries a portrait of Tsar Nikolay II. Another (center) carries a banner with a quotation from a hymn: "Holy Russia, Keep Your Orthodox Faith!" Other pilgrims carry icons of the Virgin of St. Serafim Sarovskiy and of the Tsar-Martyr. Photograph by Inna Naletova.

middle-aged or older. Many are pensioners. There is also usually a group of students, intellectuals, and other urban residents. A typical procession consists of a column, with three or four persons walking in step in each row. As in church, men and women are separated. Men walk in the front rows, carrying banners and icons that are often heavy. When the procession goes through a forest the rows become disordered, but, as soon as it becomes possible, the structure is reestablished. The ethical rules of processions are also "churchly." Nobody tries to overtake other walkers, because the procession is not a competition: the group is expected to arrive at the destination together, as a unity. Not just walking, but walking *together* is encouraged. Splitting up into smaller groups is considered to be a mark of failure of the whole enterprise. It is believed that the grace of God is given to the whole group, rather than to separate individuals: "Only together will we overcome the devil," I was told by pilgrims in Viatka. Those bringing up the rear are accompanied by a priest or more experienced pilgrims, who provide encouragement to those who have difficulty keeping up with the rest of the group.

All pilgrims, including children, carry their own bags. Carrying bags is like carrying one's sins: one has to do it by oneself. While walking, pilgrims chant prayers constantly, though they do so with greater intensity when approaching the holy places. Sung prayer enables people to feel the rhythm of the group: "Lord Jesus, the Son of God, have mercy on us!" sing the men, and the women repeat these simple words of the Jesus prayer until they are too exhausted to sing any more. Often, however, prayers are silent. One hears nothing but feels their intensity by observing the believers.

I found that local governments usually supported processions by providing food and overnight accommodation. In Viatka, the authorities prohibited any public entertainment on the streets scheduled for the procession. In Diveevo, the government helped organize summer tents and provided police to maintain general public order. In Siberia, local authorities helped organize an additional train in order to transport pilgrims to a remote settlement during the days of a religious celebration. In Kursk, buses were provided to connect the city center to a monastery, thus uniting pilgrims, local residents, city authorities, and the church in one community, not so much "antistructure" as "beyond structure."

Occasionally, however, pilgrims feared government interference in their activities—for instance, by prohibiting singing hymns glorifying the tsar. In 2004 some pilgrims marching with an icon of Nikolay II along the streets in Viatka were afraid to sing these hymns. They remembered the persecution of religion in the past and thought that policemen might turn against them. The local authorities did not want to encourage the rise of political monarchism in the region and were indeed monitoring the activities of the so-called monarchist groups. These activists, using the image of the Tsar-martyr, were concerned to promote the idea of monarchy as the only true political order in Russia, and to use the pilgrimage as a demonstration against the current government. Although aware of these tensions, other pilgrims nevertheless joined in the singing of the hymns. The majority venerated the tsar as a martyr and a heavenly protector of Russia, not as a political figure. The procession ended peacefully, and no one was punished; even so, the fear of punishment gave the event an oppositional flavor.

Veneration of the Tsar-martyr has become a common component of many Orthodox pilgrimages. It originated from below long before the church approved it in 2000, thus playing the role of mediator between popular religion and the state. When people said "Russia needs a good tsar," they revealed their distrust of their political leaders, but such declarations should not necessarily be interpreted as opposition to democracy.[11] The tsar's self-sacrifice and martyrdom have impressed themselves on the religious imagination of Russian believers much more strongly than on mainstream political opinions. In this context, the "*communitas* paradigm," which emphasizes the socially binding functions of pilgrimage, seems more pertinent than the "contestation paradigm." However, Turner's classification of pilgrimage as antistructure does not take account of the way Eastern Christianity fuses political and religious domains, as exemplified in the veneration of the Tsar-martyr. A meeting with Russian pilgrims in Abhasia was memorable for me in this regard. The group had visited a site in the vicinity of the monastery of New Athos, where the relics of Saint John the Baptist were formerly kept. Although the relics are no longer there, the place is still believed to be holy. Because of the absence of infrastructure in the region, the site of the monastery was difficult to reach. Carrying the icon of the Tsar together with that of Saint John, one pilgrim commented: "Try to make him [the tsar] your own, personal saint. Pray to him. Then you will see how powerful he is." It was clear to me that there, in a foreign land, the Russian tsar was the pilgrims' protector, *their* saint, the one who had made their trip to Saint John possible. The pilgrims' devotion to Saint John merged with their reverence for the tsar and their feeling of national belonging. The holy place in Abhasia (to use Coleman's terminology) "fertilized" different components of structure in one sacralized form and united pilgrims as a community. The pilgrims' unity and religious enthusiasm resulted not from their negation of structure but from their selection and adaptation of those elements of structure that were the most meaningful and necessary for them at that time.

## TRAVELING ICONS

In the preindustrial past, especially in times of epidemic or war, it was common for believers in one region to borrow miracle-working icons from another region. One might say that pilgrimages, in this case, were performed by the icons, which traveled to "visit" people. In recent years such "visits" have usually been initiated by the church, often with the support of the government and the media. For instance, in summer 2004 the relics of Princess Elisaveta Feodorovna Romanova were brought to Russia from the Holy Land. The event was organized jointly by the Moscow Patriarchate and the Russian Orthodox Church Abroad (which derives from the "white" emigration after 1917). The relics were taken to dozens of cities, and thousands of believers came to meet them.

"Traveling icons" are venerated mostly by women, many of them elderly. In Moscow, I observed a line of people waiting to enter St. Panteleimon church, the church representation in Russia of the monastery of Mount Athos. They had come in a procession carrying the relics of the apostle Andrew from the Cathedral of Christ the Savior and were waiting their turn to venerate the relics at the church. In an orderly manner, with icons and prayer books in their hands, reading or singing prayers, hundreds of believers stood in a slowly moving line just to have a moment of personal contact with the holy object. There were clergy and laypeople, parents with children, and many women wearing long skirts and kerchiefs (i.e., traditional churchly dress). After taking their turn the pilgrims were eligible to receive a tiny bottle of oil, blessed at the relics. This busy Moscow neighborhood was apparently saturated with the sacred. I did not notice any loud conversations, music, eating or drinking, or other forms of everyday behavior, such as the quarrelling that was quite common in queues at supermarkets during the Soviet era. It was a queue of religiously motivated people ready to withstand discomfort, who did not really consider waiting to be a hardship. I met a family of pilgrims who had arrived in the city from a distant suburb. They were going to spend the night on the street in order to be able to visit the relics early the next morning, before catching a train home. I also met a family who had spent the summer wandering from one holy place to another, living and working in monasteries. One young man was standing in the line for the second time. He explained that since a sacred object of such great value seldom arrived in the city, one should make the most of a chance to venerate it.

Such gatherings differ from those described by Émile Durkheim in *The Elementary Forms of Religious Life*. For Durkheim, religion is born in "effervescent social environments," where people are gathered in a large concentration. People's feelings dominate over their intellect, making them think and act differently from mundane time (1958: 217–18). The feeling of sacredness, for Durkheim, comes from a contrast between profane, everyday life and the exceptionally intense environments created through communal singing, dancing, and ritual agitation. However, the religious gathering in Moscow described above did not generate much agitation. The emotions of the people were turned inside and betrayed few external expressions. Their attention was focused on the holy object, not on themselves. People were waiting patiently, devoutly, and in an orderly fashion, in contrast to the hectic environment all around them (see figs. 10.2 and 10.3). Although some pilgrims sang or talked to each other, I do not think that anyone there had "the impression of being himself no longer" (Durkheim 1958: 218, 223). It was not a situation where "collective consciousness dominates individual consciousness," but rather one in which individuals' religious feelings had transformed the secular environment of the modern city into a religious one. It was not effervescence, but kenosis, a "pouring out" from inside the church onto the secular surface of the city, which gave this gathering a churchlike atmosphere.

Queuing is an almost inevitable part of pilgrimage. Lines spontaneously form near springs when people wait their turn to bathe or to fill bottles with water, and in churches when people wait to kiss the cross or an icon, to receive anointing, or to make a confession. Accustomed to waiting, believers use the time for prayer. Many simply enjoy being there, in the church environment, together with others and at the same time alone. Such religiously motivated waiting is socially binding, invisibly connecting people in a group. Although these groups are non-Durkheimian insofar as they do not manifest any formal structure and have no clearly

FIGURE 10.2. A queue of believers waits to venerate the icon and relics of Saint Matrona Moskovskaia, which are exposed outside the church of the Pokrovskyi monastery, Moscow. Photograph by Inna Naletova.

defined membership, they nonetheless contribute to forming people's behavior and social orientations.

## PILGRIMS: DEMOGRAPHIC COMPOSITION
## AND SOCIAL PORTRAIT

The Orthodox pilgrimages described above are not specific to certain regions but are found all over Russia. Survey data give us further insight into the demography and values of participants. In 2003, of the 2,199 respondents in a Russia-wide survey carried out by the GfK market research institute, 1,737 identified themselves with a Christian denomination, and 59 chose the option "pilgrimages" as an activity in which they enjoyed taking part.[12] Statistically speaking, this is a small group; however, it allows us to compare pilgrims with other Christians and offers an idea of pilgrims' distinguishing characteristics.[13] The data showed that the majority of pilgrims were women, many of them pensioners. On average, pilgrims are well educated, as can be seen in table 10.1.

FIGURE 10.3. Pilgrims queue for water at Saint Seraphim Sarovskiy's holy spring near the monastery "Kurskaia Korennaia Pustyn," Kursk, Russia, July 2004. Photograph by Inna Naletova.

TABLE 10.1 General characteristics of Russian pilgrims, 2003

|  |  | Pilgrims (%) | Nonpilgrims (%) |
|---|---|---|---|
| Gender* | Male/female | 29/71 | 41/59 |
| Age | 18–29 years | 29 | 27 |
|  | 30–49 year | 25 | 38 |
|  | 50+ years | 46 | 35 |
| Location* | Village | 22 | 35 |
|  | Small- or mid-sized city | 59 | 46 |
|  | Large city | 19 | 19 |
| Education* | Elementary school | 20 | 20 |
|  | Middle school | 44 | 57 |
|  | At least some high | 36 | 23 |
| Occupation** | Professional | 29 | 12 |
|  | Manual laborer | 14 | 25 |
|  | Retired, disabled, working in the home, unemployed | 32 | 27 |

*$p < .05$, **$p < .01$.

TABLE 10.2  Belief and practices of Russian pilgrims, 2003

|  | Pilgrims (%) | Nonpilgrims (%) |
|---|---|---|
| Belief in God (yes/no)* | 92/8 | 83/17 |
| Attending church (yes/no)** | 39/61 | 14/86 |
| Fasting (all periods/some/none)** | (19/37/44) | (3/19/76) |

*$p < .01$, **$p < .001$.

Although no macroregion lacks pilgrims, some regions have more than others. In relation to the number of believers there are more pilgrims in central Russia and Viatka than in the Volga, Ural, or Far East regions. This finding supports the intuition that pilgrimages are likely to spread in those regions in which a tradition of pilgrimages has been already established (Viatka) and where Christianity has a longer history (central Russia). In other words, the incidence of pilgrimages seems to reflect the depth of religious memory and the richness of religious tradition in a region. As for the residential pattern, it can be understood in terms of the particular role that pilgrimages play in the life of residents of small or medium-size Russian cities. During the Soviet era, villages and large urban centers were better able to preserve religion in their collective memory, and they found it easier to rebuild churches in the postsocialist era, whereas sacred buildings were destroyed in hundreds of smaller cities (or they were built as new Soviet cities, without churches). Pilgrimages in such locations complement churchly religiosity by offering the residents an opportunity to participate in communal religious practices without requiring them to familiarize themselves with churchly life.

Exactly as I found in my fieldwork, the data show that the majority of pilgrims are believers who do not attend churches. However, 56 percent of pilgrims fast in one way or another, and 19 percent fast in a strict, almost monastic way (i.e., during all fasting periods laid down by the church) (see table 10.2). This suggests that pilgrimages might be effective as a "socializing mechanism" to integrate pilgrims into church life.

Table 10.3 shows that pilgrims have a more positive attitude to collective work and processions than do nonpilgrims. They also enjoy Russian national traditions and Orthodox holidays more. They have a greater interest in visiting Russia's historical cities, as well as a stronger inclination to be involved in political demonstrations and to be concerned about ecology. All together, the data show that pilgrims are more involved in the life of their society. Thus pilgrims are more positive in their attitude to state holidays (e.g., the Day of the Army, Victory Day) than nonpilgrims. This might be evidence of their strong patriotic feelings. At the same time, pilgrims show less enthusiasm for New Year's Day and 8 March (the all-Russia holidays). This can be explained by the memory of the atheist

TABLE 10.3  Attitudes of Russian pilgrims, 2003

| | Pilgrims (%) | Nonpilgrims (%) |
|---|---|---|
| "Do you like . . . ?" | | |
|     Russian national traditions | 80 | 69 |
|     Orthodox holidays** | 90 | 73 |
|     All-Russia (secular) holidays* | 27 | 84 |
| State holidays* | 48 | 32 |
| "Do you like to participate in . . . ?" | | |
|     Collective work*** | 42 | 21 |
|     Processions*** | 42 | 19 |
|     Tours to old Russian cities | 58 | 50 |
|     Political demonstrations*** | 19 | 4 |
| Concerned about ecology[a] | 76 | 66 |

$*p < .05$, $**p < .01$, $***p < .001$.
[a] This question was formulated as follows: "Do you think that ecology is the most important problem in our country or are there other more important problems that need to be solved?"

persecution during the Soviet time, when these holidays were promoted as substitutes for the religious celebration of Christmas and Easter.

## PILGRIMAGE AS A KENOTIC COMMUNITY

The notion of a kenotic community denotes a religious congregation centered around a holy place, the members of which participate in ascetic and communal practices intended to resemble Christ's self-sacrifice and love for humanity. Pushing oneself to one's physical limits is a key part of a kenotic experience. Pilgrims commonly told me that one should walk as long as "God will allow." Walking even a short distance was viewed as a sign of God's grace. One woman in Kursk said that she "gathered her strength" during the whole year in order to join a procession in July. Although pilgrimages were voluntary, they resisted the infiltration of modern comforts. By choosing to walk, even when easier ways of traveling were available, pilgrims showed their ascetic understanding. If they arrived at a monastery on foot, they were accepted as family members; if they came by bus, they were viewed as guests (Poplavskaia 1999). When pilgrims had overcome the exhaustion of a long walk, they often reported receiving a spiritual strength, which they perceived as God-given. An elderly woman named Margaritushka, who had walked to Velikaia seventy times, was greatly respected. "Eat less, drink less, talk less!" Margaritushka admonished her fellow pilgrims. "One has to pray more! And sleep less. When we pray, the Antichrist shrinks." Responding to pilgrims' complaints about insects, she said: "They too need to eat. And it's good for us to show some patience" (Krupin 2004: 28). In Diveevo I met a group of pilgrims who had just arrived at the monastery. "My whole life is worth this one moment," said a middle-aged man in profound contentment. Another pilgrim in Viatka remarked that a pilgrimage required great physical effort but the reward was an unforgettable spiritual experience: "Physically, it is very difficult. When you imagine that you have to get up at 2 a.m. and walk the whole day long, you begin to hesitate. But then you walk and feel it as a great happiness."[14] Even failures were given a divine interpretation. Walking back from the river Velikaia, one pilgrim felt so tired that he thought he would not be able to return home:

> I sat down to rest. Couldn't walk any more. But who would take me from here? No transportation. No one. And I lost strength. I slowly walked to the village. Saw a car there. I asked: "Where will you go?"—"To Kirov."—"Will you take me?" And they brought me to the city. How this could have happened, I don't know. My wife said: "St. Nikolay has helped you." This was such a happiness.[15]

The happiness felt in pilgrimages did not occur by itself but was *achieved* by self-limitation and by viewing hardships as God-given. "They intentionally sought out difficulties or desired them in their thoughts," wrote a historian about the pilgrims of past centuries (Balashova 1998: 64). A contemporary pilgrim said that difficulties were the signs of God's presence in the world: "Last year the snow was falling. This year is terribly hot. This means God did not forget us but is checking on us" (Krupin 2004: 29). "I wish I could walk there again," another pilgrim said to me, remembering his walk to Velikaia during the Soviet era. Despite the risk of punishment, "there was so much happiness then, so much." Among pilgrims preparing for departure in Kursk I saw several people leaning on sticks. Obviously, I thought, it will be difficult for them to keep up with the group. One elderly man explained that he did not expect the walk to be easy: "One should be ready to feel some pain. We do it not for ourselves, but for God." In Viatka, a middle-aged woman said: "I would rather go alone, slowly. But how could I go alone!" This exclamation highlighted the social character of the pilgrimage: if she were to walk independently or take a bus, then everything she desired to achieve during the pilgrimage would be lost.

Bathing in springs was another common practice requiring a lot of determination (see fig. 10.4). It was not easy to immerse oneself fully in nearly freezing water. Nevertheless, pilgrims confirmed that no one fell sick as a result of such bathing, and viewed this as evidence of the place's holiness. In Optina Pustyn I observed pilgrims bathing in January when the air temperaturewas −30°C. The ritual consisted of immersing the body fully three times "for the Father, the Son, and the Holy Spirit." No towels were allowed; water was to dry on the body "to preserve the Holy Spirit." No warm dressing room was available. Only a prayer recited by other pilgrims outside the bathing hut provided crucial encouragement to those

FIGURE 10.4. A group of pilgrims gathers to sing prayers before bathing in a holy spring, August 2004. The woman in a white kerchief holds an icon called Resurrecting Russia (Rus' Voskresaiuschaisa); the woman in a red dress, an apocalyptic icon with the Virgin and Jesus on a Russian two-headed eagle (cf. Rev. 12:14). Photograph by Inna Naletova.

who decided to bathe. The ritual ended with happy exclamations and hot tea prepared by the bus driver.

That pilgrims could experience intense joy in a social environment in which ethical norms are highly ascetic poses a challenge to the modern sense of pleasure, comfort, and individual freedom. It is possible and the norms can be fulfilled only because of the strength of the associated structures of meaning. Durkheim emphasized the importance of community in motivating participants and providing the meanings that, in his view, formed the very core of the society itself. Similarly, for Victor Turner the experience of communal living is a principal source of pilgrims' religious experience. Russian pilgrims provided much support for these views. For instance, one pilgrim compared the brotherhood of a pilgrim camp with spiritual enlightenment: "Fifty people were living in one tent. . . . Many experienced an almost forgotten sense of unity and commonality. This experience makes for remarkable changes in human life."[16] A visitor from England noticed that no one in a Viatka procession wore a "Viatka 2001" T-shirt or displayed any outward sign of personal achievement. The concept of personal achievement was meaningless: "There was the feeling that all were helping all. . . . Despite my exhaustion in the end, I felt that I would rather keep walking with these people than separate and return to my own life."[17] "All my life is the anticipation of the next walk to Velikaia," said another pilgrim. "Everything in human life is re-viewed through this walk. I am not outside of it but inside—all my life is measured from one walk to another."[18] These and other emotions expressed by pilgrims referred to more than the Durkheimian-Turnerian feeling of togetherness. Rather, such emotions were evidence of intense reflection on issues of personal and communal concern, involving a great deal of inner concentration and reasoning. Pilgrims were systematically encouraged to structure their internal quest for meaning and given convincing reasons why such a difficult walk had to be done: because together we will overcome the devil, because the grace of God is given to the whole group, because one has to carry one's sins, because we have to develop patience, because sins are like sickness and they stick to people, because the walk is like an uninterrupted prayer, because Russia has to preserve its traditional faith, and so on. The resulting inner concentration made the journey a collective reaffirmation of meaning-structures that were traditional and churchly and, indeed, constituted the deepest core of society itself but at the same time had to make sense to each individual participant. The ascetic and communal practices were the key mechanisms for intensifying reflection and led to feelings of joy and religious enlightenment.

Communal work during pilgrimages was also accorded a spiritual dimension. Usually pilgrims were invited to stay in monasteries as guests for up to three days; those wishing to stay longer were expected to help in the monastery's kitchen, garden, or restoration projects. But many pilgrims volunteered to work from the very day of arrival. Monastery works were often included in trips organized by pilgrim services. "They want to help," complained a Diveevo nun during a high pilgrimage season, "but I do not know what work there is to give them." Physical work was attractive to intellectuals and office workers, but volunteers came from other social strata as well. Parents found communal work valuable in the socialization of their children. Sometimes the duties were so time-consuming that a pilgrim barely found a free minute to visit the church. According to one publication, "The prayer of the heart [Jesus prayer] is recommended to those who are experienced enough; for others—singing is advisable; for newcomers—work and humility."[19] Just like communal praying or walking in a group, volunteer work for a monastery is an element of the kenotic practice of opening the self toward others.[20]

Miracles and healings were considered a divine response to the efforts made by pilgrims during the trip. Among the miracles reported by pilgrims were deep confessions, acknowledgments of guilt, and conversion (see fig. 10.5).[21] Pilgrims often told me that while on the road to a holy place they reviewed their entire

FIGURE 10.5. During an open-air church service at Diveevo in August 2004, several priests hear confession. Near the graves of saints buried at the monastery, some pilgrims (looking toward the right) are listening to the service, while others are waiting their turn for confession or simply walking around. Photograph by Inna Naletova.

lives and their connections to others, including relatives, neighbors, and colleagues. The writer Vladimir Krupin collected several such stories (2004). One of his informants had walked to Velikaia so many times that he could not recall the exact number: every year, he supposed. In the course of a year, he explained, sins stuck to people, like sicknesses. By walking to Velikaia one could purify oneself. Another pilgrim said: "I began walking to Velikaia because of my head. I had horrible headaches. A woman told me to go to Velikaia: 'Go,' she advised. 'Your head will be cleaned, and you will become a believer.' So I went and was healed. Now I walk there every year. I cannot live without it." In Diveevo, I talked to a middle-aged man who had just recently been released from prison. Explaining why he liked working for the monastery, he said that "in the world" he feels "weak," while in the monastery his "strength comes back" to him. Once having experienced religion at a holy place, believers were afraid that God's grace would leave them if they were to stop visiting the place. Thus a pilgrimage was not over at the end of the trip but had a long "echo" in a person's life. In Turner's terms, the experience of *communitas* during pilgrimage gave participants the strength to carry the burden of structure. For many, the pilgrimage opens up a broader meaning-structure, so that life prior to the pilgrimage appears sinful and generally inadequate.

The community is also a reference point in convincing other people of the reality of a miracle. Observing Catholic pilgrimages in France, Ellen Badone has noticed that published accounts of miracles are often characterized by contestation of spiritual authenticity. A similar contestation can be found in the Russian context. In one such story from a local brochure in the Ufa region, the anonymous authors described a miracle that had happened in their church in a "we language," and placed the event in a progressively wider social context as a device to convince skeptics of the reality of the weeping icons they saw:

> On 30 July 1993 at 12 pm in the prayer house of the village K. a copy of the icon of Tabynskaia Mother of God began to cry. The face on the icon was very indistinct, the colours having faded. But suddenly the face became full of oil. As if from a sponge, the oil began to drop down. A soft fragrance was coming from it, like a smell of forest. The same day, at 14:30, another copy of the icon began to cry. It was an old icon, small, unskillfully restored. It came to all of us as a surprise that this icon was crying, and so copiously. Its surface was covered with drops of oil, flowing down. We sang prayers. Next day, the icon was taken in a procession around the village. At the spring, we met pilgrims from Ufa and Orenburg. Everyone could witness the miracle. . . . On 1 August, the second icon stopped crying, but the first continued for 40 days. We noticed that the face of the Mother of God became more distinct. More pilgrims came to our village those days than ever before. Many pilgrims experience healing by the oil from the lamp that burns at this icon.[22]

The narrative progressively unfolds from a local level to larger social realms. At first one icon was observed to be weeping, then a second, then both were taken in a procession outside the church and shown to the neighborhood. After that, pilgrims came from nearby places, and finally the icons were seen by masses from farther afield. The meeting with the pilgrims is described in this account as an unexpected event—itself like a miracle. "One does not need to go to Kiev or Jerusalem, because they are all here"—these words of Saint Seraphim were often quoted by pilgrims when they wanted to stress the importance of Russia's own holy places. Thus the miracle witnessed in Ufa becomes just as important as those at the world's major pilgrimage centers. In contrast to what Jean Rémy (1989: 141) noted about Catholic believers' veneration of Saint Anthony, which was dependent on a particular empathy—"I know him, he knows me, I know how to act with him"—Russian believers emphasize the "we" component in their relation with the Holy—"*We* know him. He knows *us*." "O *our* wanderer Saint Nikolay, give *us*, sinful, Your helping hand!" pilgrims sang in an imaginary dialogue with the saint (Krupin 2004: 59–60; emphasis added). Describing the beauty of landscapes, they

FIGURE 10.6. The arrival of the icon Kurskaia Korennaia at Diveevo in August 2004, following a two-week procession from Kursk. Photograph by Inna Naletova.

express a common love for their country: "These places revive *our* historical memory and return *us* to the sources of the Holy Russia."[23] A conversation I had with pilgrims in Diveevo illustrates this communal aspect of religious devotion. When I heard from pilgrims that the famous icon Kurskaia Korennaia, carried by them all the way from Kursk, had been weeping, I went to see the icon and was disappointed not to see it weeping (see fig. 10.6). One pilgrim responded: "You cannot see it weeping because you did not walk with us." By walking, living, and praying together, pilgrims learned to put their personal feelings in the context of a community and to perceive miracles as events of communal importance.

The community formed during a pilgrimage also includes saints and deceased relatives. When a believer entered a sacred place, I was told, everything that happened was experienced as happening because of the will of the saints present there. During my first visit to Diveevo a person who had been living there for a long time asked me why I had come. "I simply wanted to visit," I answered. "No one comes here simply to visit," was his response. "If you came, it means that there was a need for that. The elder Seraphim [Saint Seraphim Sarovskiy] wanted you to come." My visit was placed, firmly and unquestionably, into a divine-human society. The stories about saints accompanying pilgrims were numerous.

Pilgrims said that the sacred path around Diveevo was unique because "all energies are focused there," and the world "opens up" to let light from the other world flow in.[24] One pilgrim felt the presence of her deceased parents intensely at this spot. A moat dug around the monastery was believed to have been initially commissioned by the Mother of God. During the Soviet era it was filled in, but by 2004 it had been fully restored by nuns digging mostly by hand. While walking clockwise along the moat, pilgrims were advised to recite the prayer to the Mother of God at least 150 times. The Mother of God, they said, was walking there, too, and one should not walk in the opposite direction so as not to disturb her. This circular path was viewed as giving protection against evil, and not only the monastery but the whole of Russia had to be protected. While walking along the path and praying, believers were advised to refer to their own problems only at the very end. "This path," one pilgrim said, "is like Russia in miniature, like the image of a future Russia. When this path is fully reconstructed, then Russia will rise."

The pilgrims of the twenty-first century did not have to walk to holy places but usually had recourse to a bus. They did not have to bathe in the cold water of holy springs, nor carry bags all the way to the holy place. Collective praying, walking, and working in monasteries were all optional practices, alternatives to more individualistic and comfortable models of being religious. Nevertheless, I found that kenotic communities, built upon self-limitation, discipline, and devotion to God and people, were flourishing. The voluntary nature of these communities is proof of their vitality and social authenticity.

## FORGING COMMUNAL BONDS

An account of pilgrimages is not complete without consideration of the forms of their interaction with the larger society. Pilgrimages are an opportunity to receive an informal religious education. For people who grew up during the Soviet era, joining a pilgrim group to learn about religion is preferable to attending church. Pilgrimages allow neophytes to share their thoughts and feelings with more experienced believers and to learn the basics of the church's customs and teaching— and thus gain the background necessary to feel comfortable in a church.

Pilgrimages also offer an opportunity to enter into an informal network of support and communication. I experienced the functioning of this network in Taganrog, where a nun showed me the way to the house of Saint Pavel Taganrogskiy and gave me a bag with blessed bread to take there. She took it for granted that I would do what pilgrims have always done: serve as a courier between spiritual centers. Such informal correspondence was considered to be more reliable than the mail and served as a way of introducing a pilgrim into a new community. People were drawn into a large network of support and communication, which enabled the circulation not only of religious messages but also of sacred objects and the mundane products of monasteries.

Pilgrimages' connection with Russian classical literature should also be mentioned. In my conversations with pilgrims I noticed that their interest in pilgrimage was often matched by their love of Russian literature. In church kiosks and private homes I observed that works of the Holy Fathers were placed on the same shelves as the novels of nineteenth- and early twentieth-century writers, as if both were written in the same spirit and imbued with similar or, at any rate, complementary meanings. Thus pilgrimage had the potential to reveal to people not only the depth of the religious tradition but also the richness of the literature.

Pilgrimage was also a way to reconnect with the past of the country. A guide at a pilgrim service recalled the pilgrimages organized in the early 1980s. These trips were led by a small group of enthusiasts trying to locate holy places on the map and reestablish pilgrim routes. With only one bus at their disposal and no supporting infrastructure, they traveled with only a vague knowledge of the route and of what they expected to see upon arrival. Nevertheless, there was soon a long waiting list of people wanting to join this group. Another guide remembered an episode when pilgrims had had to climb over a fence surrounding a factory in order to reach the grave of a saint. The desire to take part in such pilgrimages was reinforced by the sense of novelty and adventure. Pilgrims discovered religion through exploration of the unknown past of their country.

This study has examined Orthodox pilgrimages at a turning point in Russian history. In the 1990s Soviet institutions had vanished, but the new institutions were unreliable. Poverty and disorder were prevalent. "By the mid-1990s most Russians began to realize that the nation has headed down the road of self-destruction," wrote Vsevolod Chaplin, the spokesman for the Moscow Patriarchate (2003: 32). Pilgrimages provided one of the principal means through which people sought reintegration into society and new ways to communicate and congregate.

## CONCLUSION

In this chapter I used the theological concept of kenosis to describe communities of Russian pilgrims practicing elements of the kenotic ethic. Traditionally, kenosis (self-emptying) is understood as the mystical practice of following the example of Christ by accepting humility, suffering, and self-limitations and undertaking voluntary duties. Although many Russian pilgrims in the postsocialist era were unaware of theological concepts, the centuries-old tradition of building kenotic communities has been preserved in pilgrimage.

Kenotic communities are not individualistic. They allow participants to generate stronger connections to each other and to their nation. The major pilgrimages did more than this: they also forged links to nature and created specific networks of trust. When social structure is weak and institutions unreliable, as was the case in postsocialist Russia, people need to support each other within informal circles. The revival of pilgrim communities in Russia showed that people had a continuing need to be integrated into such informal networks. Pilgrim communities did not require of their participants that they be familiar with the life of the church, nor did they aim to recruit each individual into the church. The concept of membership was not applicable to these communities. Sensitive to individual autonomy, flexible and friendly to newcomers, these groupings bound their participants together and shaped their social orientations according to communal ethics inspired by the teaching of the church. They occupied a space beyond what Davie (2000) has identified as "static" and "mobile" models of modern religiosity.

Kenotic communities are difficult to describe with the theoretical tools of modern anthropology. The Durkheimian concept of effervescent gatherings does not seem to be helpful; its emphasis on the collective consciousness dominating the individual is erroneous. In kenotic communities, individuals' religiosity is directed ("poured out") toward other people, thus forming their communality. Neither is Turner's *communitas* fully applicable to a kenosis that is essentially based on the idea of care of other people and voluntary limitation of one's wills and desires. Emphasizing the irrational component in pilgrimage experience, Turner's theory does not consider the role of inner concentration and the reflection of pilgrims on their lives and on society, nor does it pay attention to theological and historical contexts. It cannot account for the religious meaning of suffering evident in the veneration of the new Orthodox saint martyrs of the Soviet era. The veneration of the Tsar-martyr is an additional challenge to the Turnerian paradigm, since the fusion of the political and the religious in the image of the tsar undermines the distinction between structure and antistructure, which is fundamental to Turner's approach. Finally, the contestation paradigm of Eade and Sallnow (2000) focuses on the mundane conflicts inherent in pilgrimage, thus dealing with discourses of secondary importance to the community. The Russian pilgrimages described in this chapter have the capacity to absorb different cultural influences and give pilgrims a feeling of community beyond contestation and beyond the walls of the church, but nonetheless rooted in church traditions of kenotic practices. It seems impossible to me to fully grasp the meaning of these religious experiences without using the underlying theological concepts, such as kenosis, kenotic communities, and kenotic ethos.

## NOTES

1. My analysis is based on fieldwork in Russia in 2002–2004, information from religious publications, and data from a survey conducted in May 2003 by the market research institute GfK Group into which I was able to insert several questions on religion.

2. The basic text of Christ's kenosis was an early Christian hymn; it was quoted by Saint Paul in his epistle to the Philippians, 2:5–11.

3. For the results of a national survey conducted by the research institute ROMIR in 2003 and presented at the XII Christmas Conference in Moscow on 28 January 2004, see Alexandr Musafarov, "The Year of the Orthodox Russia," http://www.pravoslavie.ru. The survey was based on a representative sample of 1,500 respondents (18+) controlled by age, gender, type of settlement, and region.

4. The report of the survey "Jerusalem in the Views of the Russian People," conducted by FOM (Foundation "Public Opinion") in April 2005, is available in the FOM archive at http://bd.english.fom.ru. The survey was carried out in 100 Russian settlements in 44 regions and was based on a representative sample of 1,500 respondents.

5. R. Mahankov, Vosvrashchenie k istoky, *Foma* 9 (2003): 3.

6. Editorial, *Rus derzhavnaia* 1 (2004).

7. For instance, many believers were worried that the introduction of electronic identification tags in 2003 would allow the state to gain greater control over their lives. Hundreds of people walked with icons in front of the Duma building behind a banner that read "We Are People, Not Numbers." In the same year a conflict arose around an art exhibition showing works that, in the view of believers, were disrespectful to their faith. Hundreds of believers gathered in front of the city court to protest against the exhibition. Individuals who tried to destroy the exhibition were prosecuted, but, after further demonstrations, the court freed the accused, and the exhibition was closed. *Blagovest* 21 (2003).

8. Such processions are considered to be of national importance; see Trifonov Pechengsky Monastery 2003.

9. Krupin 2004: 1–35; see also *Scat-Info* 1–2 (2004), a special issue devoted to the Viatka procession. In the following discussion I juxtapose my own materials with data drawn from a variety of published sources.

10. For additional information, see special issues 13 and 15 of *Tserkovnii Vestnik* (2003) and *Moscovskii Tserkovnii Vestnik* 14 (1991).

11. In 1992, 15 percent of Russians agreed that "the tsar should return to Russia" (WCIOM, the All-Russian Public Opinion Research Center, http://wciom.ru/); in 2006, 10 percent considered a restoration of the monarchy desirable, according to the 24 September 2006 WCIOM report "With a Tzar in Mind: Revival of Monarchical Tendencies in Russia," by M. Tarusin, available at http://wciom.ru/arkhiv/tematicheskii-arkhiv/item/single/3122.html?no__cache=1&cHash=d3067854cf. FOM reported that, in 1994, 18 percent viewed the restoration of the monarchy as desirable, and 15 percent as possible; see now the 19 June 2002 FOM report "About Monarchical Tendencies in Russia," by V. Chesnokova, available at http://bd.fom.ru/report/map/oz02061906.

12. The majority were Orthodox Christians. One person self-identified as Protestant, and two marked the option "other Christian denominations."

13. If the GfK sample is representative, it implies that some 2–3 million Russians participate in pilgrimages; church data provide a similar estimate (Kirill, Metropolitan 2004: 7).

14. Interview, *Vstrecha: Kulturno-prosvetitelnaia rabota* 5 (1996): 31–34.

15. P.I. Klepnikov, interview by E.N. Mokshina, 2001, http://vera.mrezha.ru/440/12.htm.

16. L. Lyinina, Serafimovskie torzhestva, *Tserkovnyi vestnik* 15 (2003): 12.

17. L. Holms, Velikoe duhovnoe ispytanie [A great spiritual trial], *Skat-Info* 2 (June 2004): 7.

18. V. Krupin, Bogom hranimaia Viatka, *Skat-Info* 9 (Sept. 2004).

19. From the introduction to Anon. 2001.

20. In an analysis of popular literature of the nineteenth–early twentieth century, Jeffrey Brooks points to an attitude toward wealth among Russian peasants that was governed by kenotic ethics. The characters of popular stories, according to Brooks, do not wish to enjoy material possessions and prefer sharing them with the community. Wealth achieved through commerce and business was condemned

as immoral (agricultural and physical work was granted a higher moral status); however, it could be justified religiously as a reward for long and passive suffering—an attitude that Brooks interprets as a reproduction of the religious tradition of kenoticism (1985: 288–89).

21. L. Belkina, Village Nikolskoe: Notes about a pilgrimage, *Blagovest* 20 (2003): 8.

22. *Istoria ikony Tabynskoi Bogomatery* (Ufa, 2003) 31.

23. V. Kurylev, Rodnikovoe koltso Rossii [Russia's circle of springs], *Desiatina* 7 (2003): 8; emphasis added.

24. K. Mialo and S. Savostianov, Diveevskia taina [The Diveevo's secret], *Moscow* 12 (1995): 165.

## REFERENCES

Anon. 2001. *The Way of a Pilgrim*. Trans. G. Pokrovsky. Woodstock, Vt.: Skylight Paths. This work was written by an anonymous Russian writer in the nineteenth century and was originally published as *Otkrovennye rasskazy strannika duchovnomy otcu svoemu* [The sincere stories of a wanderer told to his spiritual father] (Moscow: Lestvitsa, 1884).

Badone, E. 2007. Echoes from Keriyinen: Pilgrimage, narrative, and the construction of sacred history at a Marian shrine in northwestern France. *Journal of the Royal Anthropological Institute* 13: 453–70.

Balashova, E. L. 1998. Zemlia obetovannaia po izobrazheniam rysskih palomnikov 18–19 vekov [The Promised Land according to the description of Russian pilgrims of the 18th–19th centuries]. In *Collective works of the Museum of History,* 3: 64–73. St. Petersburg: Museum of History.

Brooks, J. 1985. *When Russia learned to read: Literacy and popular literature, 1861–1917.* Princeton: Princeton University Press.

Chaplin, V. 2003. Orthodoxy and the societal ideal. In *Burden or blessing? Russian Orthodoxy and the construction of civil society and democracy,* ed. C. Marsh, 31–36. Boston: Institute on Culture, Religion and World Affairs.

Coleman, S. 2002. Do you believe in pilgrimage? *Anthropological Theory* 2/3: 255–368.

Davie, G. 1993. You will never walk alone: The Anfield pilgrimage. In *Pilgrimage in popular culture,* ed. I. Reader and T. Walter, 201–19. Houndmills, Basingstoke, Hampshire: Macmillan.

———. 2000. *Religion in modern Europe: A memory mutates.* Oxford: Oxford University Press.

———. 2001. The persistence of institutional religion in modern Europe. In *Peter Berger and the Study of Religion,* ed. L. Woodhead with P. Heelas and D. Martin, and Peter Berger, 101–12. London and New York: Routledge.

Durkheim, E. 1957. *The elementary forms of the religious life.* London: Allen & Unwin.

Eade, J., and M. Sallnow. 2000. *Contesting the sacred: The anthropology of pilgrimage.* Urbana: University of Illinois Press.

Egorievskii, Bishop M. 2004. Pravoslavnoe palomnichestvo: soderzhanie poniatii [Orthodox pilgrimage: The contents of the motion]. *Orthodox Pilgrim* 6/19: 12–13.

Fedotov, G. P. 1996. *The Russian religious mind: Kievan Christianity.* Cambridge, Mass.: Harvard University Press.

Hervieu-Léger, D. 2000. *Religion as a chain of memory.* Trans. S. Lee. New Brunswick, N.J.: Rutgers University Press.

Kirill, Metropolitan of Smolensk and Kaliningrad. 2004. Problemy rasvitia sovremennogo pravoslavnogo palomnichestva [Problems of the development of today's Orthodox pilgrimage]. *Orthodox Pilgrim* 6/19: 5–11.

Krupin, V. 2004. Krestnyi hod [Procession with the cross]. In *Lovtsy chelovekov,* 3–111. Moscow: Russian Mission.

Kulagin, M. 1998. *Is istorii monastyrei Kurskoi oblasti* [From history of the monasteries in the Kursk region]. Kursk: Kursk University Press.

Moklezova, I. V. 2003. *Hozhdenia v russkoi kylture 10–20 vv.* [Going through Russian culture 10–20 centuries]. Moscow: Textbook.

Poplavskaia, C. V. 1999. Pravoslavnye palomnichestva [Orthodox pilgrimages]. *Istoricheskii Vestnik* 1: 23–41.

Rémy, J. 1989. Pilgrimages and modernity. *Social Compass* 36, no. 2: 139–45.

Romanov, G. A. 1999. Russkie krestnye hody [Russian religious processions]. *Istoricheskii Vestnik* 1: 20–23.

Russian Academy of Tourism. 1999. *Apostolstvo turisma* [Apostolate of tourism]. Moscow: Russian Academy of Tourism Press.

Shchepanskaia, T. V. 2003. *Kultura dorogi v russkoi miforitualnoi traditcii 19–20 vv.* [Culture of the way in the Russian mytho-ritual tradition]. Moscow: Indrik.

Trifonov Pechengsky Monastery. 2003. *Pilgrims' guidebook.* Moscow: Kovcheg.

Turner, V. 1973. The center out there: Pilgrim's goal. *History of Religions* 12: 202–23.

———. 1974. Pilgrimage and communitas. *Studia Missionalia* 23: 305–28.

Turner, V., and E. L. B. Turner. 1978. *Image and pilgrimage in Christian culture: Anthropological perspectives.* New York: Columbia University Press.

# 11

# Avtobusniki

## Russian Orthodox Pilgrims' Longing
## for Authenticity

Jeanne Kormina

"We got into such antiquity [*starina*]! Real Russia, Rus'! What I liked—it was simple folk standing there. They were selling pies for just three rubles each . . . everything on simple stools. The people were Seto.[1] There are only nine hundred of them left. And they also sold apples—only one ruble for a bowl. One could choose them oneself. . . . I was there on the 4th and 5th of October, only two days. I felt as if I had a week of vacation. Along the way one could see . . . nature, these smells, and our lopsided little grey village cottages [*izbushechki*] . . . I have learned that eyes relax very well while looking at our Russian landscape. . . . And when approaching the city, it seemed to me that we were driving into hell itself. Chimney smoke, advertisements, tobacco smoking. My God! Where did we drive, into a kind of a pit."

These were the words of Vera, a woman in her early fifties who was working as a cleaner in a small publishing house in St. Petersburg. I found Vera through a friend of a friend who worked at the same organization and recommended Vera to me as an experienced pilgrim and a person who loved talking about her travels and giving advice to people on religious matters. The recommendations proved worthwhile. Vera had indeed participated in more than two dozen pilgrimages since her first trip to the towns of Pechery and Izborsk (Pskov province) in 1996, the subject of the above recollections. She readily agreed to an interview, but there was a problem in identifying a place to meet. Vera did not want to invite me to her home because her husband ridiculed her religious activism and, as I heard later, was a heavy drinker. She did not want to meet at her working place, where she held a position of low prestige. I suggested that we met at her church, but she said she was not a member of any particular parish. Like many new Orthodox believers in Russia, she changed churches frequently, looking for a better priest, a more convenient location, and something else that she could not articulate. Eventually, I invited Vera to my home.

Where to conduct interviews was one of the major difficulties I faced during my research in 1999–2006 on organized pilgrimage in contemporary Russia. I also interviewed people in buses, once in the informant's own car, occasionally in their homes, but never on the premises of a parish. I participated in pilgrim trips to sacred sites in the provinces of Leningrad,[2] Pskov, and Novgorod. Some of my observations from 1999 were no longer valid by 2006, but the search for authenticity has remained one of the basic purposes of what I shall refer to in this chapter as Russian Orthodox religious travel.

Vera, unlike many of my informants who converted to Orthodox Christianity during the religious boom of the end of the 1980s and early 1990s, was baptized as a child in one of the few churches of Soviet Leningrad. Before the mid-1990s she did not practice her religion. She described herself as a blind person; during a tourist visit to the Russian Orthodox convent (Piukhtitsy) in Estonia during Soviet times she "for some reason could not see anything." This changed only in 1996 with her first pilgrimage, which in effect was a conversion experience. The pilgrimage boom was slow in starting. The organizers had to elaborate new routes and establish contacts with local clergy (mostly recent converts themselves) (see Kormina 2004). Pilgrims themselves helped to invent ritualized programs, which included reciting prayers collectively in the bus, bathing in holy springs, sharing a meal (*trapeza*) in a remote monastery or village parish, participating in the liturgy there, and so on. The first pilgrimage agency was founded in St. Petersburg in 1993 by Melitina Ladinskaya, a former English teacher. As in Soviet times, travel was mostly restricted to short trips of one or two days and took place within Russia. It was possible to visit holy sites abroad such as Mount Athos, Jerusalem, and Bari (where the relics of Saint Nicholas of Myra, the most popular saint in Russia, are kept), but most pilgrims stayed within their own region. Short trips were cheaper, took less time, and were easy to organize. There was also a strong ideological explanation for staying close to home. Small monasteries, stones marked by God's footprint, holy springs, and the graves of holy persons (*startsy*) were represented in pilgrimage discourse as containers of Russian Orthodox Christian tradition.

The bus pilgrimage was a new arena of popular religious practice.[3] Although bus pilgrims insist on the continuity of their religious tradition, in fact what they do is novel. It is popular in the sense that it is initiated by ordinary believers, often without even nominal control by the official church, and it is opposed to sophisticated forms of religion such as monastic life. It often stands in opposition even to regular parish life. Pilgrims themselves make such distinctions. They are mostly relatively poor people whose practices differ considerably from the demonstrative religiosity of Russia's new elites.

In this chapter I will explore both the production and the consumption of authenticity, which in the sphere of religious travel is an object of negotiation among different agents. The principal agents are the organizers of religious travel (both official pilgrimage agencies and independent activists); the participants; and the keepers of the shrines, including local clergy. Following John Eade and Michael Sallnow, I will try to "develop a view of pilgrimage . . . as a *realm of competing discourses . . .* brought to the shrine by different categories of pilgrims, by residents and by religious specialists, that are constitutive of the cult itself" (Eade and Sallnow 2000: 5). As we shall see, authenticity is central to discourses about the sacred in contemporary Russian pilgrimage. Although the discussion of this concept originated in tourism studies (MacCannell [1976] 1999), numerous anthropologists have begun to explore the affinities between tourism and pilgrimage both in ideology and in practice (Cohen 1992; Eade 1992; Badone and Roseman 2004; Coleman and Eade 2004). Both kinds of travel involve interaction between hosts and guests, a trip to some desired destination, and a search for the authentic. Moreover, the genealogy of contemporary Russian-organized pilgrimage shows that post-Soviet religious travelers drew directly on their Soviet experience of domestic heritage tourism.

Tourism studies tend to link mass Western secular tourism to the postcolonial order. According to Dean MacCannell, tourists are doomed to experience only simulated pseudo-events. Following Erving Goffman, MacCannell argues that hosts ("natives") put on special performances for guests and try to convince them that they are having an authentic experience by observing or participating in the performances (MacCannell [1976] 1999: 91–100). By contrast, in the case of Russian Orthodox pilgrimage the convention is that every Russian has the right to access the authentic, nonsimulated experience. Orthodox Christianity is understood by many Russians in a rather primordial way, as something naturally inherent in the national landscape and in people's minds and bodies. In theory at least the hosts and guests are interchangeable: pilgrimage is a form of heritage tourism where the natives are visited by the natives (or, as we shall see, by the former natives). I shall show that what is perceived as authentic depends upon the level of the pilgrims' involvement in religious life, their religious knowledge, and their role in the performance of authenticity.

It would be too easy to conclude that the religious knowledge of the bus passengers is low and that their travel is in fact highly secular. Yet the participants insist that they are looking for religious experience and that they do in fact manage to gain it. The task of the social scientist is then to analyze this new style of religiosity, and to show how prior spiritual and nonspiritual experiences of the neophytes, as well as a range of social and economic factors, influence their under-standing of religion and ways of practicing it. Pilgrimage in pre-Soviet times was obviously very different, yet the contrast should not be exaggerated. As early as the middle of the nineteenth century more secular (urban and educated) pilgrims developed aims and practices that differed from those of peasants (Chulos 1999). Traditionally (and in the Soviet period) pilgrims used to have an individual goal, a vow (*obet, zavet*—both nouns derive from the verb *obeshchat'*, "to promise"). The vow is a kind of a secret personal agreement with God based on the idea of reciprocity. A person did not ask advice from anybody, not even the parish priest, in taking the vow. Usually, a believer promised to make a pilgrimage to some sacred place and to give something (for example, towels) or to make something (for instance, build a chapel or restore a well) there. The promise had to be kept in return for God's help. Alternatively, the effort was expended as a request for such help.[4] The tradition of taking vows remained a popular religious practice in rural areas in the Soviet period. Since monasteries were mostly closed, people directed their vows to local sacred sites.[5] This practice has now become marginal-ized. Contemporary religious tourists are not familiar with such traditions, which if they persist at all are sustained by old village women. In their religious behavior contemporary religious tourists follow the instructions of the organizers of the trips, who are also neophytes. Traveling by bus, religious tourists might be seen as heirs of a Soviet habit, since, before the 1990s, collective shopping trips and excursions were commonly organized by trade unions or activists at factories, schools, and hospitals (in northwestern Russia, for example, people used to travel to Soviet Estonia for a better range of goods).

## THE QUALITIES OF AUTHENTICITY

Participants in religious travel themselves sometimes make a comparison between secular tourism and pilgrimage. "This time it was tourism rather than pilgrimage" was the negative comment of one pilgrim when the journey had not lived up to expectations. She complained that the group leader had not done her best to "make a pilgrimage of the trip" and that the places visited had not been holy enough to provide an authentic experience. "Tourism" (*turism*) for this woman as for many others means the inauthentic or false, while "pilgrimage" (*palom-nichestvo*) denotes some reality that is "true" in their eyes. They do not use the term *autentichny* nor the related terms *podlinny* (genuine) or *nastoyashchy* (real). As Regina Bendix has demonstrated in her work on folklore studies, authenticity is an etic, rather than an emic, concept. However, everybody knows what is authentic and can talk about it using a specific vocabulary (Bendix 1997: 36–44). The main tropes of authenticity for post-Soviet urban religious travelers are sim-plicity, purity, and antiquity. Let us look closely at each in turn.

*Simplicity*

In her story about her first pilgrimage experience Vera spoke enthusiastically about simple folk (*prostoy narod*) using simple stools (*taburetki*) as stands for their artless goods. The fact that the people selling food to the pilgrims belonged to a non-Russian ethnic group was seen as enhancing authenticity, because it rooted them in that rural locality. Their grey huts, and wonderful village smells, belonged to the landscape of the real Russia, Rus'.[6] Poverty made them even more authentic: they were living as if the new capitalist economic conditions did not yet exist, and represented a primeval state in which people were simple and life easy. The term Rus' evokes a poetic passage by Pushkin that is known to almost everybody in Russia: "Zdes' russky dukh, zdes' Rus'u pakhnet" (Here's Russian spirit, it smells of Rus'). Vera was following a Russian tradition that ties authenticity to sensual perception. Writers and painters began to promote the Russian landscape as an aesthetic object in the nineteenth century, as part of their contribution to the construction of national identity (Ely 2002). Vera sought authenticity in a rustic idyll, and she concluded her narrative with a list of the characteristic features of the opposite, nonauthentic world, with its chimney smoke (modernization), advertisements (commercialization) and tobacco smoking (decline of morality).

Although the authentic is located outside urban life, it is possible to live a decent life in the city, too. Vera constantly stressed that she herself lived frugally. When she narrated her autobiography she drew on representations of sanctity found in the popular booklets available in church shops.[7] Thus her bad relations with her husband and son-in-law, who mocked her religious activism and prevented her from taking her grandson to church, were interpreted as *gonenija* (persecution)—that is, she was suffering for her faith. As a cleaner she had no social esteem, but her simplicity and poverty rendered her sufficiently pure in the eyes of her superiors (*nachal'nikov*) to be entrusted to perform religious missions. God was in permanent contact with Vera, setting puzzles for her to solve. In one of her stories the chief accountant of the bank where she had worked previously asked Vera to pray for her to escape an onerous impending audit. Vera had made a pilgrimage to a small provincial town in Novgorod province where an ancient miracle-working icon of Theotokos (The Holy Icon of Our Lady of Staraya Russa) was kept. Initially she had not intended to comply with her superior's request. However, after she had visited the church and seen the icon, a priest in the church had asked her: "Where have you been?" Vera responded: "I've been to the church." "No," replied the priest, "you have visited Theotokos herself! You should ask for everything you want." "It was as if he reminded me about that request," Vera explained to me. She had then returned to the church and expressed the request of the chief accountant to the Theotokos (Bogoroditsa): "Do what the servant of God Galina [the name of the chief accountant] asks you" ("Vot prosit tebia raba

Bozhia Galina, vot tak i sdelai"). It helped: though dismissed from the office, she managed to avoid further punishment, and the audit did not take place. Vera represented herself in this account as an independent person who obeyed God and whose prayers were efficacious. The priest had served to mediate between God and Vera, with whom he wanted to communicate. She had been chosen by God, implicitly because of her simplicity.

In her interview Vera told me many stories of how she had helped her colleagues in different religious matters. She had interpreted dreams, prayed for her colleagues' children before their exams, informed others about the dates of church feast days, taken a secretary at the bank who suffered from eczema on her hands to the chapel of Saint Xenia of St. Petersburg where "the doctor whom you don't have to pay" had healed her, and so on. At her workplace Vera represented herself as a person endowed with deep religious knowledge and experience. She used her religious knowledge as cultural capital, to make herself an important person in the eyes of her superiors: "They [at the bank] always sent me to pray for somebody if needed." In other words, Vera considered her pilgrimages as a form of public service rather than a personal religious deed, very much in accordance with notions of public work developed in the Soviet period. As in that time, there was no reciprocity involved, just recognition that low-status workers might have authority in some nonwork sphere. We can conclude that Vera participated in at least two different performances of authenticity. The first performance included the simple way of life in the rural landscape, where Vera was a spectator who believed that she experienced something authentic. The second show of authenticity involved Vera deploying her religious knowledge on the urban stage, where her colleagues were both spectators and consumers of the authenticity that she performed.[8]

In addition to being a personal trait and the quality of a place, simplicity can refer to a particular time. Thus simplicity is a characteristic feature in narratives about the early 1990s, when monasteries and parishes were renovated and restored by simple egalitarian church communities. Those people represent themselves as resembling the first Christians or the protagonists of an etiological myth. Galina, a woman in her late fifties, told me about her family's connections with Konevets, an island monastery located in Ladoga Lake in Leningrad province. She recalled her baptism in 1991: "Father Superior N. baptized me on Christmas Day in the monastery refectory in an enamel basin, because it was too cold in the church." When Father N. later took up a prominent post in the church, Galina had hesitated to turn to him for confession and communion, viewing these church rituals as routine and unworthy of his attention. She dared to disturb him only when she had to make some important decision, about changing her job, for instance. When she lost her employment as a doctor she asked him for his blessing to work as a guide in the pilgrimage agency of her "native" Konevets monastery.

In the first half of the 1990s many residents of St. Petersburg, including Galina and her family (in 1991 she and her husband were forty-four years old, and their son and daughter were sixteen and twenty, respectively), participated in the rebuilding of monasteries by giving their labor in return for basic accommodations and food. Galina had heard an announcement on the radio by Father N. encouraging volunteers to join the effort. It had been a very hard time for her family; in addition to their daughter's mental disability, their son had left school and was experimenting with drugs. Later Galina thought that the work in the monastery had saved him: "manual labor in fresh air in such a holy place" had done the trick. In those years of mass conversion many people preferred to be baptized in a remote semidestroyed rural church or monastery. Galina did not like to go to church in the city. She preferred to confess and receive communion in the monastery: "My soul opens there, while in urban temples I feel myself as . . . in a crowd."[9] She recalled being often reduced to tears after confession in the monastery with Father N. "Nowhere had I ever felt such a sense of purification as in that temple on Konevets. I remember: I am standing . . . and on the floor, on the nonpainted batten, there is a dark spot. My tears are streaming."

The enamel basin and bare batten in Galina's narrative of "the time of creation" exemplify simplicity. She had helped Father N. to rebuild the monastery and thereby participated in the creation of an ideal Orthodox world, which later had gradually disintegrated. The spiritual purification experienced by Galina and her family harmonized with the idea of technological simplicity in the rural environment. The everyday life of a monastery in some ways resembled that of the traditional peasantry. as this was understood by urban pilgrims at any rate. There were no bathrooms, no flush toilets, no television. Monasteries kept animals and bees and made their own butter, cheese, and bread. In other words, in this religious discourse the economic backwardness of the countryside was converted into a positive quality; the village appeared as a kind of a preindustrial paradise and a guarantee of authenticity. Again, such attitudes have Soviet roots, in this case in recreational practices such as ecological tourism, which was a popular collective vacation among the Soviet "technical intelligentsia." This, too, was definitely a search for an antiurban experience, but ecological tourists escaped to nature without any serious engagement with rural life, just as dacha owners could live in a village for leisure without engaging with the local peasants (Zavisca 2003). Village life in the late Soviet period had no prestige. Yet in the early post-Soviet years many people of this sort spent their vacations in a monastery doing peasant work. This rather sudden idealizing of rural life can be understood only in the broader context of the demodernization that took place in the 1990s all over Russia, but especially in the provinces. The revival of Orthodoxy in its traditional antimodernist version was an organic dimension of this process. However, this period was short-lived. A few of the early enthusiasts joined monastic orders or became village clergy, but most resumed their secular urban lives as "the time of creation" gave way to routinization and institutional consolidation.

## Purity

A person wishing to participate in a pilgrimage has only to call one of the numerous pilgrimage agencies. The prospective customer will be informed of a few obligatory points. It is necessary to bring a vessel for holy water and a bathing costume for the holy spring. Although bathing is widespread in Christian pilgrimage, there are many variations. According to Eade less then 10 percent of pilgrims to Lourdes visit the baths (2000: 56–57). For Russian bus pilgrims bathing in holy springs and lakes or showering with water from a holy well is as essential as attending church services. In my experience almost every trip included this possibility, and almost everybody took advantage of it. In their narratives pilgrims liked to mention that although the weather was unsuitable for bathing, nobody got ill. Vera had bathed in a holy spring at the beginning of October during her first pilgrimage, although the temperature of the water was no higher than 10°C. Pilgrims, mostly women, neither young nor particularly healthy, washed their entire bodies, or at least their legs and hands, in the cold water. I once saw a small girl about six or seven years old crying from the cold, but her grandmother pushed her to get undressed and threw cold water from the holy spring over her. She explained that the girl was only crying because of the devil inside her, who did not like the holy water.

Bathing at holy places was common in Russia until the middle of the twentieth century: some elderly informants recalled that the sacred places in their villages had separate bathing facilities for women and men. However, local people living close to a sacred place no longer practice this custom. They call the bathers "walrus" or *morzhi* (winter swimmers), emphasizing the secular character of this practice in their eyes. Pilgrims themselves see bathing as another form of religious experience. Liudmila, a woman in her fifties who worked as an accountant at a shipyard in St. Petersburg, represented the results of her bathing as a miracle:

> It was the first time I plunged into the holy spring. It was cold. It was snowing even. However, I decided to try, to enter into that holy spring. Almost all the people in the group were from our factory.[10] All of us work in the accounts department. Then one woman, we work together, said to me: "Liudmila Efimovna, are you crazy? Do you really want to bathe?" You know, one must plunge one's head three times into the spring. And it is amazingly hard to enter the water for the first time. You feel as if your body is not yours. The water is icy. And you must plunge a second time, and a third time. And then—you hover as if you are in space! Those who were sitting in the bus became green and frozen, while those who plunged had red cheeks after bathing. While those who took the plunge did not get sick, those who did not—half of them got sick. And again: what is the secret? It is incomprehensible.

Small miracles of this kind can be experienced by everybody.[11] Dipping one's body into a holy spring is somehow associated in the pilgrim's mind with the practice of baptism. While dipping their bodies three times into the water the pilgrims, under supervision of a trip leader or of their more experienced fellow pilgrims, make the sign of the cross three times "in the name of the Father, and of the Son, and of the Holy Spirit." The performance resembles a baptism ritual performed without a priest. Another reason for the popularity of bathing is that it corresponds perfectly with the idea of accumulating grace in a human body, as I shall show below.

In the pilgrims' discourse the trope of purity is frequently articulated in secular language. Purity is understood as an ecological clarity of air, water, and the sacred landscape as a whole. The leaders of pilgrimages often pointed to signs of virgin nature as additional evidence of the holiness of a sacred site. During a trip to the Konevets monastery, pilgrims, encouraged by their group guide, tried to find seals living on the island. In Pskov province a pilgrimage agency guide, using religious and secular arguments simultaneously, encouraged pilgrims to buy houses in that region. First, she drew attention to the large stork population, which indicated ecological purity. Second, she explained that cities had a curse on them and every Orthodox Christian should escape to remote areas to increase his or her chances of obtaining salvation. Third, she noted the unique sacred objects that were to be found there. It is quite typical for urban dwellers to merge their obsession with ecology with religious eschatological discourse. Purification of both body and soul is one of the implicit aims of all religious travel, and bathing in clean and holy water is perceived by pilgrims as a practice of purification and a way to gain a personal religious experience. However, in contrast to many "traditional pilgrims," contemporary religious travelers seek recreation rather than miraculous healing.[12] Vera's first pilgrimage was a mere two days, but she felt as if she had had a week of vacation, and that was her small miracle. She also mentioned that her eyes could "relax very well while looking at our Russian landscape." Recovery from blindness was the most typical form of miraculous healing in pre-Soviet Orthodox culture. Vera's eyes did not just recover; they became relaxed.

### Antiquity (Namolennost')

When indicating the spiritual value of a site (a church, a monastery, or a village shrine with a stone bearing God's footprint on it) or an artifact, people often used the term *namolennost*,' which can be roughly translated as "antiquity." Pilgrims had difficulty explaining its meaning. Orthodox journalists stress the nonrational nature of *namolennost'*, which can be grasped only sensually, like a fragrance or like beauty (Suglobova 1996).

Unlike Muslim *baraka* (see Meri 1999), for contemporary Orthodox in Russia, the quality of *namolennost'* is attached to an object or place rather than to a person and his relics. Holy icons are the objects most often called *namolennye* (which literally means "absorbed many prayers"). However, the quality of "wonder working" does not correlate with *namolennost'*. The former derives from the biography of the particular icon, which is not relevant to the latter. While a person accumulates and spends his or her stock of grace (*blagodat'*), which requires replenishment, a church or a holy icon saves up the prayers of "many generations of people" (Zykov 2007). Material sacra do not lose their *namolennost'* even when it is transmitted from them to other physical objects by means of physical contact. When I asked whether an ordinary paper icon could be *namolennaya* I was told by an informant:

> Yes. Yes, of course. We have been to Tikhvin,[13] and all the icons in the church shop were made of paper. But all of them were *namolennye*. They were put on the icon [of Our Lady of Tikhvin]. . . . Some energy passed to them from this icon.

The word *namolenny* is a participle derived from the verb *molit'sya,* which means "to pray." The degree of grace concentration in a site or object depends on how many people used to pray at the place and for how long. Liudmila, like many others, used the word "energy" (*energija* or *energetika*) to explain the essence of *namolennost'*. For example, she recalled disputes about God at her workplace:

> I don't tell you [her colleagues] that God sits on clouds, dangling his legs, waiting for you to start praying to him. I tell you that there is holy energy (*sviataya energetika*). It's different. After all, one goes to a temple because, presumably, it concentrates there . . . perhaps they are constructed in a specific way . . . so that you feel something . . . something happens inside of you.

Presumably an echo of this idea is what prompts many pilgrims to collect all manner of souvenirs from each holy site they visit. They buy or take liters of water from holy springs, holy oil from local churches, candles, icons from church shops, homemade bread, honey, and other peasant goods produced in a monastery, flowers, sand, stones, rocks, and so on. I was told that in one village market the price for potatoes cultivated at the local monastery field was four times higher than the asking price for ordinary potatoes: a high premium for authenticity.

As we have already seen, the new believers need to translate religious ideas into their everyday language (see Ginzburg 1980). Exploiting the quasi-scientific metaphor of energy is a good example of such translation in religious speech of new Russian Orthodox Christians. The genealogy of this metaphor can be traced to Soviet urban beliefs in bio-energy healing and *extrasensy* (Lindquist 2001: 21–22; Panchenko 2006: 127). Later, in the early 1990s, healers like A. Kaspirovski generated mass hysteria (Lindquist 2001: 23). In many flats and houses at that time one could find a bowl of water standing close to the television to receive the healing energy Kaspirovski transmitted during his TV shows. It was believed that this energy could then be further transmitted to cure sick bodies. Similarly, many pilgrims believed that the human body could also be a container for grace or "holy energy." Unlike holy places and items, the grace in a person can decrease as well as increase: indeed, human energy has to be topped up from time to time. One pilgrim group's leader commented on this in a speech to pilgrims at the end of their journey: "Keep the *blagodat'* you have received during our trip as you keep heat after travel to the South." This is why it is considered good to participate in pilgrimage, communion, and other religious practices regularly.[14] Perhaps this is one of the reasons pilgrims insist on having communion in a monastery or a church on their trip. The liturgy performed at a remote holy place is more holy and hence more efficacious.

The degree of *namolennost'* of a material object corresponds directly with its authenticity. Here we have a creative process of inventing values and ascribing them to things and places. Places are also things in this logic; they participate in the market of religious tourism and compete with each other in their *namolennost'*. Russia as yet lacks a harmonious grand historical narrative, but the majority of Russians see Orthodox Christianity as somehow primordial, and the generations of believers who prayed at holy places were undoubtedly Russians. They filled the churches and monasteries with their holy energy, which can now be transmitted to the bodies and souls of modern visitors. Holy places and holy things provide continuity between the ancient inhabitants and those of today. Since the holy energy concentrated in a place cannot ever diminish, even the destruction of icons, their transfer to museums, and the conversion of monasteries into hospitals, storage facilities, military bases, or prisons did not pollute the holy places. This Soviet history can therefore be forgotten.[15] The appeal to Orthodoxy as a basis for national identity is a way to avoid history, or at least the traumas of recent history. At the same time, the need to ensure personal access to "holy energy," which is not under control of the church, is evidence of a mistrust of the current church as a religious institution. In short, traditions conceived as primordial are authentic, but history, along with the secular logic of economics and urban modernity in general, is not.

## AUTHENTICITY PERFORMED

As Regina Bendix points out, "The crucial questions to be answered are not 'what is authenticity?' but 'who needs authenticity and why?' and 'how has authenticity been used?'" (1997: 21). Let us now examine how authenticity was performed for visitors to holy sites and how it was understood by local inhabitants.

There were several categories of visitors to a sacred site such as a monastery. Monastery dwellers had their own emic classification, according to which the most alien were those who came in groups by buses. They were sometimes called *avtobusniki* (literally, "those who come by bus"). They were always in a hurry. During their short stay (from several hours to a couple of days at the most) they tried to collect as much "holiness" (*sviatost'* or *blagodat'*) as they could. Another type consisted of people who stayed in the monastery for several weeks, often their entire vacation. While these visitors devoted their free time to God, real monastery people lived their whole life for Him, and their entire identity was invested in the monastery.

A third category was that of the *trudniki*.[16] The word *trud* means "labor" or "work," and a *trudnik* is a "person who works in a monastery for free, because he or she has made a vow" (Dal' 1996: 437). In the first half of the twentieth century it was a common practice in Karelia (and not only there) to dedicate a sick child to a monastery for a certain period of time; "then having reached adulthood he or she would make a journey to a monastery and stay there for the duration promised to perform volunteer labor." A sick person could also promise that a relative would go and perform unpaid work in a monastery if he or she recovered (Stark 2002: 161–62). I found that the practice of making vows had almost disappeared, at least in big cities, and *trudniki* were those who lived and worked without pay in a monastery for a few months before returning to secular life. Normally they did not intend to become monks or nuns. People often pronounced this word as *trutnik,* which changed the meaning radically. A *truten'* is a drone, metaphorically a person who lives at the expense of others. This category of visitor included former alcoholics, drug addicts, prisoners, and others who had failed to socialize into "normal" life. As Marina, a girl in her early twenties who had spent half a year in a monastery two hundred kilometers from St. Petersburg when she was fifteen, explained to me, for many monks and nuns work was a substitute for prayer, but work by *trudniki* was of a lower quality.[17]

The hosts, to use MacCannell's term, were those who were preparing to take or had taken a monastic vow.[18] They performed a staged authenticity for guests, while their own backstage reality was "intimate and real" (MacCannell 1999: 94). Marina provided the following vivid account of how monastery people perceived their visitors:

> Pilgrims travel to communicate with the sacred. It is necessary (in their opinion) to bathe naked in the holy spring—otherwise they'll not be sanctified [*ne osviatiatsia*]. There is an obvious irony in the monastery against them. Normal monastery people understand that if there are village guys hiding beyond a bush and spying upon bathers, then you should wear a swimsuit or a shirt. But it is impossible to make pilgrims change their mind. . . . There are narratives there. . . that the Mother of God appeared at the spring at 4 in the morning. That's why monastery people bathe at night. . . and because they don't want to be seen by village guys.

Monastery people put on a show for their guests, treated them with ironic distance, and did not allow them to enter the "back stage" of monastery life. They guarded the boundary between the front and back stages of performance. In this example the narrative about the Mother of God was designed for internal use and served to consolidate the group. The same distinctions can be traced in different spheres of everyday life. Monastery people use water from the holy spring for mundane purposes, too, since it is the closest supply of water to the monastery, and they do not call this water "sacred." They do not use it for tea or cooking because it does not taste good. In general, monastery people and villagers living close to a sacred site and venerating it are less overtly respectful than pilgrims.

For monastery people, all three categories of visitor (*avtobusniki, palomniki, trudniki*) were pilgrims (*palomniki*), and this term did not have positive connotations. Pilgrims were outsiders, and even those who lived and worked in a monastery for months would remain strangers. Once on my way to Konevets monastery I asked the woman sitting next to me on the bus if she had ever met "real pilgrims," thereby implying that our obviously semisecular travel was not quite authentic. She looked surprised and said that in her opinion our group was just a normal pilgrim group. In fact it contained some people who did not know any prayers; almost nobody kept the fast (it was the time of the fast before the feast of the Assumption); many women used makeup and were clothed in trousers (the church forbids all cosmetics and the wearing of trousers for women); some had uncovered heads, and the group guide wore a cap instead of the head scarf prescribed by the church. At first I was puzzled by the reaction of my neighbor, but later I realized that she was herself a "monastery person," and for her the level of authenticity of the pilgrims was not relevant. No matter how carefully they might dress, for her they would remain aliens. This woman was given free transport by our group guide as a "native person" of Konevets. She had spent the previous "twelve winters" in the monastery carrying out different jobs, long enough to cross the boundary and become part of the monastic community, even though she had not formally taken vows.

The pilgrims performed the same actions and used the same standard narratives at every monastery or village shrine they visited. Their hosts simulated the "true experience" while concealing unique details of their local community. Students of tourism argue that there are no "real places" anymore and that the dramaturgy of tourist places has become so elaborate that nobody could imagine that there could be a real "back stage" (see, e.g., Rojek 1997: 60). However, as long as "locals" produce authenticities to be consumed by the visitors in special performances and narratives, it seems safer to infer the continued existence of backstage performances. Theoretically, every pilgrim can gain access to a "more authentic" experience by moving from the tourist stage to the back stage. He or she just has to become a "native," a long-term *trudnik,* the keeper of a local shrine, a member of clergy, and so on. Some might then be disappointed to find that their invasion into the authentic destroyed it totally. Authenticity is a matter of belief rather then an entity; it can be enjoyed, emotionally and physically, as we saw, but not appropriated. Vera once spent several days in a monastery as a *trudnitsa* and decided it was not her way. She disliked monastery life because of its strong hierarchy, heavy labor, and lack of freedom. She was satisfied with the variant of staged authenticity that she experienced during her pilgrim trips, which gave her respect and some hidden power over her colleagues and superiors. Monasteries and parishes receiving pilgrims also made some profit from their authenticity. Pilgrims brought food, clothes, and household goods.[19] They bought candles in the monastery and ordered prayers for their deceased and living family members, for which of course they paid.[20] They also bought local honey and milk products, oil, icons, CDs, and DVDs in church shops. In short, the inhabitants of the sacred places are just as interested in the pilgrims as the pilgrims are in their quest for authenticity.

## BELIEVING WITHOUT BELONGING,
## BELONGING WITHOUT BELIEVING

It was not unusual for people in their fifties or older to be unsure about the circumstances of their baptism. Galina told me that her husband had learned from his mother when in his forties that he had been baptized by his aunt as a child. Many baptized their children in deep secrecy because the practice had serious consequences, including the loss of one's job.[21] However, in some cases the "baptism narrative" had no solid factual basis. Liudmila and some of my other interlocutors preferred to think they had been baptized, knowing that theoretically it was possible and hence not a pure lie. One explanation of Liudmila's assertion is that she might have felt herself too old to be baptized together with the younger generation of her family. Another possible motivation was that to her mind she had a right to Orthodox Christianity as a part of the cultural tradition she belonged to by birth. She was a Christian because her ancestors had been Christians, and she did not need a priest and church rituals in her religious life. What mattered was to accumulate "holy energy" by traveling to sacred places.

For many city dwellers in Russia participation in an organized pilgrimage has become one of the most acceptable ways of practicing religion. It is seen as a "user-friendly" version of Orthodox Christianity. The pilgrim is taught how to convert her or his secular cultural experience and knowledge into something that, according to emerging convention, could be considered a religious experience. Although a pilgrim might believe that such a pilgrimage guarantees an authentic religious experience, nonetheless this type of religious traveler is better classified as a consumer in the religious market. Another category of pilgrims (Vera is one of them) consisted of critically minded individuals who were actively looking for God outside the institutional church. These believers wanted to be religious without having to accept any control over their religious life—whether the commands of a parish priest in his role as confessor or the social control exercised by a church congregation. Belonging to a parish would also take up time and other resources. Pilgrimage agencies by contrast offered their clients the chance to become anonymous members of a temporary religious community. Each trip usually included the Eucharist in a village church or remote monastery. While some travelers made confession and communion for the first time in their lives and saw this as the exotic highlight of a cultural program, for others the ritual was more meaningful. They confessed to a local priest whom few of them had seen before and whom they would never see in the future. The older and more locally rooted this priest was, the more authentic he was held to be.[22]

The guides and organizers of these bus pilgrimages cultivated the idea that it was possible to become religious not so much by accepting certain religious ideas but by coming into contact with a tradition that is as much cultural as it is religious. Everybody had a right to this tradition, and the mediation of the church was superfluous. This phenomenon might be called a democratic form of religiosity, as it stands opposed to the demonstrative religiosity practiced by Russia's postsocialist elites. The latter need institutionalized religiosity more than the common people.

In her study of the religious life of contemporary Britain, Grace Davie stated that "the majority of British people . . . persist in believing . . . but see no need to participate with even minimal regularity in their religious institutions" (Davie 1994: 2). This "believing without belonging" both resembles mainstream religiosity in Russia and differs from it radically. In Russia I found many believers who did not want to belong to a parish but were ready to join a temporary religious community that provided access to spiritual experience. Such believers needed to practice religion, unlike the British, who are content with their faith. The Russian religious travelers I have discussed received their religious experience collectively but anonymously. While bathing in holy springs, kissing holy icons, or just taking the air in a holy place they were accumulating something unconditionally "true" (*podlinnoe*), good, and efficacious. They *practiced* their religion, and for many participants these practices were a substitute for even minimal religious knowledge.

The organizers consciously represented their tour parties in terms of *communitas* (Turner and Turner 1978). Collective meals and prayers, equality of treatment, and the sharing of discomfort were all instruments to bind the group together. However, the pilgrims often differed so greatly in their religious backgrounds and in their purposes that efforts to create a *communitas*-group failed. A structure emerged in which positions depended on religious experience and sometimes on personal closeness to the organizer. Moreover, people resisted the forging of a collective. As we saw in the cases of Vera and Liudmila, the pilgrims' quest was for individual religious experience. Individualization must be recognized as one of the key features of what I call here the new popular Orthodoxy. At the same time, being part of a pilgrim group strengthened the sense that pilgrims were indeed participating in religious practice. I met pilgrims who had not been baptized, had not even a minimal knowledge of the liturgical life of the church, and only the vaguest ideas about how to behave in church. They might not even be sure that they believed in a Christian God, preferring instead to talk about "holy energy" (e.g., Liudmila) and to concede only that "probably there is something" (*chto-to est'*). However, by joining the bus pilgrimage they could convince themselves that they were living out the authentic life of an Orthodox Christian. In other words, "belonging without believing" has become a new variant of Orthodox Christianity in Russia.

## CONCLUSION

According to the 1999–2000 World Values Survey, 70.3 percent of the Russian public answered affirmatively when asked whether they believe in God, while only 9.2 percent attended church at least once a month (Agadjianian and Rudometov 2005: 14). Some inside observers state that scarcely 1 percent of the population participates properly in the liturgical life of the church and can be considered *prikhozhane* (those who belong to the parish, *prichod*); the majority are *zakhozhane* (those who drop in) or *prokhozhane* (those who go by) (for discussion of the wordplay here, see Chekrygin 2007). In other words, the average believer in post-socialist Russia is not a churchgoer and arranges her or his religious life outside the church. Instead of acquiring religious knowledge and language under the supervision of the church, the new believers have created their own mode of religiosity by drawing upon their previous experiences (such as heritage tourism) and beliefs (such as bio-energy healing, etc.). As we have seen, they have found abundant ways to gain personal religious experience, to make small miracles happen, and to articulate them in terms of everyday secular language. Overall, intensive recreation has come to substitute for miraculous healing in their pilgrim narratives. As the famous preacher and mission deacon Andrey Kuraev puts it, the credo of the majority of those in Russia who consider themselves Orthodox Christian can be boiled down to two simple statements: "There is something" and "We are Orthodox because we are Russian" (Kuraev 2006: 62). Against this background, the organizers of bus pilgrimages collude with "locals" to offer exactly what these religious travelers are looking for: an authentic Russian tradition dressed in the clothes of Orthodox Christianity.

The new, user-friendly, democratic style of religiosity described in this chapter is just one of a range of religious styles available within Russian Orthodox Christianity. It is most typical for the cohort of ex-USSR citizens born in the 1950s, who have their distinctive history of spiritual searching. Their children have had a different religious socialization and may in time gravitate to quite different orientations. All that can be concluded with confidence is that a longing for authenticity has been a central part of the construction of new identities in Russia, and that this process have been expressed in the language of Orthodox Christian tradition, as people know this language in their post-Soviet present.

## NOTES

Research for this chapter was supported by the International Association for the promotion of co-operation with scientists from the New Independent States of the former Soviet Union (INTAS). I am very grateful to Simon Coleman and Sergey Shtyrkov for their comments on a draft.

1. The Seto are an ethnic group living mainly in the borderland between Russia (Petchery region of Pskov province) and Estonia; in fact, they number about 13,000. See Engelhardt, this volume.

2. The name of the city of Leningrad was changed to its original name, St. Petersburg, in 1991, but its province has kept its Soviet name, Leningradskaya oblast'.

3. The emerging market for religious travel in Russia comprises many actors. First, independent pilgrimage agencies are organized and headed by a charismatic person, usually a woman, and not supervised by any official church representative. Some of these persons become leaders of pilgrimages and assume the roles played normally by priests. Second, parish-based pilgrimages are managed by parish priests who consider pilgrimages a valued activity for the church community. Third, some large monasteries, such as Valaamo (in northwestern Russia), provide their own pilgrimage services and organize special courses for people who want to work as pilgrim guides. They monopolize pilgrimages to the sites they control and have a "business" attitude. Fourth, diocesan pilgrimage operators have offices in the diocese administration and, compared to other service providers, are more tolerant of secular participants. Some of these guides wear caps instead of the Orthodox head scarf, and female pilgrims may wear trousers instead of a skirt. The diocesan operators double as specialists in heritage tourism.

4. The tradition of making obet or zavet in Russia is discussed in Shchepanskaya 1995: 118–20 and Panchenko 1998: 82. See also Stark 2002: 157–66.

5. For example, according to a report of the representative of the Council on Religious Affairs in Pskov province, in 1949 three thousand people came to venerate a village shrine in Gdov district, without clergy or any official permission. State Archive of Pskov Province, file 779, p. 33.

6. The term Rus' refers to the early centuries of the East Slav polity, before the rise of the Muscovite state.

7. For urban believers, booklets of this sort have become the main vehicle of religious self-education.

8. The efficacity of simplicity and humility is also a biblical tradition in Christian ethics and hagiography; cf. the Vita of the servant Euthymios, who served at the lowest level of a monastic kitchen but was more highly honored by God than the whole brotherhood that he served, and was taken every night to paradise from his lowly corner in the monastery kitchen.

9.. She borrows the word *khram* (temple) from church discourse in place of the usual *tserkov'* (church). The word *khram* has become a common speech marker for so-called church people (*votserkovlennye*), and Galina uses it to stress her identity as an Orthodox Christian believer.

10. The trade union of a factory used to organize collective pilgrim trips, just as it had arranged secular tours in the Soviet period.

11. It is a widely held view, disseminated through popular religious literature, that miracles are relatively common occurrences on the margins of the new, commercially oriented Russian society, namely, among the deprived. In Vera's case typical miracles were economic in nature: she had no money for a pilgrimage and suddenly received some; the cat food for which she had spent her last rubles doubled in quantity by the time she reached home. It seems that in the post-Soviet context a shortage of money and other resources became the main impetus for miracles.

12. Of course, there are exceptions to this rule. Fertility problems and children's diseases have been motives for pilgrimage in recent times, just as they were in earlier periods.

13. In 2004 the miracle-working holy icon of Our Lady of Tikhvin returned to the town of Tikhvin (Leningrad province) from the United States, where it had been kept after the Second World War. According to a legend supported by the Orthodox Church it is believed to have been painted by the evangelist Luke and appeared miraculously near Tikhvin in the fourteenth century. The government of the city of St. Petersburg and Leningrad province held splendid celebrations to mark the return of the icon.

14. Some devout Orthodox Christians explain that they receive communion every Sunday in order to replenish the grace diminished in them since their last Eucharist.

15. The relics of many saints were placed in museums as a result of atheistic campaigns in the 1920s through 1930s. But when these items are rediscovered they have lost none of their sacred power. For example, the relics of the famous Orthodox saint Serafim Sarovskiy were miraculously found in the attic of the Museum of the History of Religion in St. Petersburg in the 1990s and given back to the monastery in Nizhni Novgorod province.

16. Also sometimes called a *poslushnik*, "a person who carries out *poslushanie*" (derived from the verb *slushat'sya*, "to obey"). Usually, one performed the same job throughout one's stay at the monastery: for example washing dishes, cooking, or gardening.

17. It is true that some *trudniki* live in monasteries for many years and become "natives," yet they never obtain any official status in the monastic hierarchy.

Marina's religious biography differed from that of the older women I discuss in this chapter. She had decided to be baptized when she was eleven because many children in her school had crosses on their necks. Her parents and sister were baptized at the same time. Later she joined the Orthodox youth club and a group that spent some vacation time at the monastery, where she decided to prolong her stay. She eventually left the monastery after deciding that it was not her way. She had graduated from university and was enrolled in a PhD progam when I met her. She might be considered typical for a critically minded intellectual believer.

18. The guest-host division is by no means the only cleavage affecting the monastic community; other "political" divisions may be even more important.

19. I was told that no one ever brought underclothes or hygienic tampons, which are much needed in convents inhabited mostly by young girls and women of fertile age (but perhaps considered unsuitable as gifts from visitors). The "true life" of bodies was not consonant with the roles they played in performances of spirituality and authenticity for pilgrims.

20. The prayer for the dead and the living is one of the oldest functions of a monastery and one of the strongest ties between the monastic and mundane worlds.

21. My own father (born 1946) was secretly baptized by his mother's younger sister and without the knowledge of his mother, who was a convinced atheist and had an official position she could not afford to lose.

22. A priest in a village church in Novgorod oblast' was marketed by the pilgrimage leader as *blagodatny batiushka* (a priest full of divine grace) because of his authenticity: he was a local person, a tractor driver in the Soviet past, and the very embodiment of tradition.

## REFERENCES

Agadjanian, A., and V. Roudometov. 2005. Introduction: Eastern Orthodoxy in a global age—Preliminary considerations. In *Eastern Orthodoxy in a global age: Traditional faces in the twenty-first century*, ed. V. Roudometov, A. Agadjanian, and J. Pankhurst, 1–26. Walnut Creek, Calif.: AltaMira Press.

Badone, E., and S. R. Roseman, eds. 2004. *Intersecting journeys: The anthropology of pilgrimage and tourism*. Urbana: University of Illinois Press.

Bendix, R. 1997. *In search of authenticity: The formation of folklore studies*. Madison: University of Wisconsin Press.

Chekrygin, O. 2007. *Miriane: Pechal'neyshaya povest'* [The laity: A sad story]. Chapter 1. www.portal-credo.ru.

Chulos, C. J. 1999. Religious and secular aspects of pilgrimage in modern Russia. In *Byzantium and the north*, 21–58. Acta Byzantina Fennica 9, 1997–1999. Helsinki: Finnish Association for Byzantine Studies.

Cohen, E. 1992. Pilgrimage and tourism: Convergence and divergence. In *Journeys to Sacred Places*, ed. E. A. Morinis, 47–64. Westport, Conn.: Greenwood Press.

Coleman, M., and J. Eade, eds. 2004. *Reframing pilgrimage: Cultures in motion*. London and New York: Routledge.

Dal', V. I. 1996. *Tolkovy slovar' zhivogo velikorusskogo yazyka* [Explanatory dictionary of the live great Russian language]. Vol. 4. Reprint; St. Petersburg: Diamant, 1882.

Davie, G. 1994. *Believing without belonging: Religion in Britain since 1945*. Oxford and Cambridge: Blackwell.

Eade, J. 1992. Pilgrimage and tourism at Lourdes, France. *Annals of Tourism Research* 19, no. 1: 18–32.

———. 2000. Order and power at Lourdes: Lay helpers and the organization of a pilgrimage shrine. In *Contesting the sacred: The anthropology of pilgrimage*, ed. J. Eade and M. Sallnow, 51–76. Urbana and Chicago: University of Illinois Press.

Eade, J., and M. Sallnow. 2000. Introduction to *Contesting the sacred: The anthropology of pilgrimage*, ed. J. Eade and M. Sallnow, 1–29. Urbana and Chicago: University of Illinois Press.

Ely, C. 2002. *This meager nature: Landscape and national identity in imperial Russia*. DeKalb: Northern Illinois University Press.

Ginzburg, C. 1980. *The cheese and the worms: The cosmos of a sixteenth-century miller*. Trans. J. Tedeschi and A. Tedeschi. Baltimore: Johns Hopkins University Press.

Kormina, J. 2004. Pilgrims, priest, and local religion in contemporary Russia: Contested religious discourses. *Folklore* 28: 25–40.

Kuraev, A. 2006. *Pochemu pravoslavnye takie?* [Why are the Orthodox people special?]. Moscow: Podvor'e Sviato-Troitskoi Sergievoi Lavry.

Lindquist, G. 2001. Wizards, gurus, and energy-information fields: Wielding legitimacy in contemporary Russian healing. *Anthropology of East Europe Review* 19, no. 1: 16–28.

MacCannell, D. [1976] 1999. *The tourist: A new theory of the leisure class.* 2nd ed. Berkeley: University of California Press.

Meri, J. W. 1999. Aspects of baraka (blessings) and ritual devotion among medieval Muslims and Jews. *Medieval Encounters: Jewish, Christian, and Muslim Culture in Confluence and Dialogue* 5, no. 1: 46–69.

Panchenko, A. A. 1998. *Issledovaniya v oblasti narodnogo pravoslaviya* [Exploration in the field of folk orthodoxy]. St. Petersburg: Aleteya.

———. 2002. *Khristovshchina i skopchestvo: Fol'klor i traditsionnaya kul'tura russkikh misticheskikh sekt* [Khristovshina and skopchestvo: Folklore and traditional culture of the Russian mystic sects]. Moscow: OGI.

———. 2006. Novye religiosnye dvizhenija I rabota fol'klorista [New religious movements and the work of a folklorist]. In *Sny Bogoroditsy: Issledovanijapo antropologii religii* [The dreams of the Mother of God: Essays on anthropology of religion], ed. J. Kormina, A. Panchenko, and S. Shtyrkov, 119–29. St. Petersburg: European University.

Rojek, C. 1997. Indexing, dragging, and the social construction of tourist sights. In *Touring cultures: Transformations of travel and theory,* ed. C. Rojek and J. Urry, 52–74. London: Routledge.

Shchepanskaya, T. B. 1995. *Krizisnaya set': Traditsii dukhovnogo osvoeniya prostranstva. Russky Sever: K probleme lokal'nykh grupp* [The crisis network: Traditions of spiritual mastering of the landscape in the Russian north: Toward the problem of the local groups]. St. Petersburg: Musei Antropologii i Etnografii.

Stark, L. 2002. *Peasants, pilgrims, and sacred promises: Ritual and the supernatural in Orthodox Karelian folk religion.* Studia Fennica Folkloristika 11. Helsinki: Finnish Literature Society.

Suglobova, I. 1996. Dragotsennye moi [My precious you]. *Pravoslavny Sankt-Petersburg* [Orthodox St. Petersburg] no. 11 (53), November.

Turner, V., and E. L. B. Turner. 1978. *Image and pilgrimage in Christian culture: Anthropological perspectives.* New York: Columbia University Press.

Zavisca, J. 2003. Contesting capitalism at the post-Soviet dacha: The meaning of food cultivation for urban Russians: Tourism and travel in Russia and Soviet Union. *Slavic Review* 62, no. 4: 786–810.

Zykov, S. 2007. Sviashchennye veshchdoki [Sacred material evidences]. *Gazeta* no. 51, March 22.

# PART FOUR

# Person and Nation

*Church, Christian Community,
and Spectres of the Secular*

# 12

# Indigenous Persons
# and Imported Individuals

## Changing Paradigms of Personal Identity
## in Contemporary Greece

### Renée Hirschon

Religious change in Greece may lack the drama of transformations in the former socialist countries, but in fact European integration since 1981 has resulted in significant shifts, which challenge, both obliquely and directly, the long-accepted and deeply entrenched structures of church and state. Greece is one of the most homogeneous countries in Europe, where over 95 percent of the population are declared Orthodox Christians. It is still a country where church and state are not separated, and there are heated debates about whether this is a negative or a positive feature of the modern Greek nation-state. In this chapter, I focus on a rather specific aspect of life in contemporary Greece, that of personal identification, a feature that, I maintain, is undergoing radical though largely unperceived change. Since this phenomenon is linked to political, economic, and ideological transformations and refers to religious constructs of the person, its analysis necessarily bears upon much broader issues, such as secularization, modernization, and Westernization. My analysis covers some aspects of legislative modernization, particularly the revision of the Family Law code in 1983, and the hotly contested issue of a new form of ID card, where religious affiliation was deemed to be a private matter. At a more intimate level these forces for change are reflected in the changes in the emphasis on celebrations of personal identity. The ethnographic evidence suggests a shift in the construction of the human subject, from that of a socially embedded person to that of the atomized individual, expressed respectively through name day or birthday celebrations. It reveals the unobtrusive but intense forces driving a secular agenda in opposition to those behind what can be called a premodern worldview rooted in religious precepts and practices. In short, the argument covers some of the connections between macro-scale international pressures and those of the individual experience, in which configurations of personal identity are being redefined.

## RELIGIOUS AND CIVIC IDENTITY

Greece stands out among European societies with regard to the way in which religion relates to social life. According to a 2005 poll concerning religious devotion, Greece stands out among Western European countries for the proportion of its citizens who declare that they are "religious" (86 percent of those polled). It was among the top ten in a survey of sixty-eight countries on all continents.[1] People who are used to living in a secular society, both foreign visitors to Greece and diaspora Greeks, notice the frequency of outward signs of religious practice while they are in Athens. This kind of "diffuse religiosity" or what E. Prodromou (1998: 102) calls "religious vitality" (as distinct from institutionalized religion) is not self-conscious; it is simply common practice for people to make the sign of the cross when they pass a church, or to enter to light a candle and venerate the icons, taking a break in the course of other activities to interact with the divine. Although such actions can be dismissed as examples of unthinking habitual conduct, they represent how "close to the surface" religious practice is in everyday life. The city of Athens provides many places for such casual observances, in new and old churches and at small roadside shrines located throughout the urban landscape (Hirschon 2009).

Another striking characteristic of this type of religiosity is the inapplicability of a separation between "sacred" and "secular" or "mundane". The Durkheimian dichotomy is not appropriate for understanding Greek life in general, nor does the division between private and public accord with that of the religious sphere. At all levels, until very recently, church and state were inextricably linked at the institutional, official, and informal levels in education, politics, and personal life. This interweaving of sacred and mundane—generally separate spheres in the Western world—is further expressed in the coincidence of religious and civil identities for most of the population. Though changes are evident, some of which are charted in this chapter, this continues to be a salient feature of contemporary Greece, despite the legal reforms since 1983.

One of Greece's significant peculiarities arises from its historical trajectory and cultural heritage. In what can be seen as an extraordinary irony, the Greek nation-state, established in 1830 after a war of independence (1821–28) following centuries of Ottoman rule, has incorporated a central aspect of the heritage of that imperial regime. Under Ottoman administration, the primary basis of identification for those recognized as "people of the covenant" (*dhimmis*) was membership in a religious community, the *millet* (lit., "nation"). It is interesting to note that despite Greece's long engagement with Western ways, the early Enlightenment influence, its struggle for independence from Ottoman domination, and the development of nationalist thinking over the nineteenth century (Kitromilides 2006), the separation of civil and religious spheres in contemporary Greece has still not taken place.

In 1983, the socialist (PASOK) government's program of modernization introduced major reforms in the civil code, especially regarding family law. In particular, civil marriage and divorce were allowed for the first time as an alternative to religious marriage. Up to then, marriages were contracted and dissolved only through the church, or the equivalent religious authorities for Jews and Muslims. These reforms constituted a radical change, and the new civil code also consolidated previous civil reforms, reinforcing the measures for registration of a child specified in Law 344 of 1976, which established the procedures whereby a child's name should be recorded in the civil registry office, or *lyxiarcheion* (where individuals' personal records are kept). In doing so, the law clarified the distinction between name giving (*onomatodosia*) and baptism (*vaptisi*) (arts. 22, 26). In terms of legal specifications these are separate issues, but in practice issues surrounding registration and naming continue to be confused.

In particular, the procedures required to register a child's birth demonstrate the resilience of cultural patterns ("habitus" in P. Bourdieu's terms) in the face of legislative change. People have long believed that without a baptismal name a child could not be registered and therefore could not be enrolled in school. It continues to be widely believed that a person's full membership in Greek society requires an official affirmation of their religious affiliation, essentially in the form of a baptismal certificate or its equivalent for the recognized religions, which include Judaism and Islam (but not the Roman Catholic Church, whose members do not enjoy official legal status; K. Tsitselikis, personal communication; Frazee 2002; and for Orthodox Old Calendarists, see Ware 2002). Public consciousness apparently continues to hold that a child's registration at school requires the registration of a baptismal name or the production of a baptism certificate.

Significantly, though, this is a misapprehension, because it has long been legally possible to confer a child's name without baptism. It is a startling fact that the possibility of civil registration (without baptism) can be traced to the mid-nineteenth-century Greek Civil Code (*Astikos Ellinikos Nomos,* TZA' 1856). This measure apparently never took hold and is not even well known in legal circles. Reiterated in the statute books in 1976, civil registration has finally been strictly applied only since 1983 (see Lixouriotis 1986; Stathopoulos 2005; N. Alivizatos, e-mail message, December 2007). Nonetheless, it is striking that even today the religious rites of baptism and marriage continue to be practiced, and only a tiny minority of people use the civil registration alone: the vast majority continue to employ baptism as the means of conferring a name (N. Alivizatos, personal communication, 2006). The same is true with regard to marriage, where only a small proportion of couples (7 percent in 1983, increasing to 30 percent in 2006) prefer to legitimate their bond solely through a civil marriage, while the overwhelming majority of couples continue to marry in church, and, for a variety of reasons, many have both civil and religious ceremonies.

As already noted, it has long been possible to confer a child's name without a religious rite, but in practice this was seldom done. The 1983 law requires the immediate registration of the child's birth in the civil registry office (*lyxiarcheion*), but a name need not be specified. A child can still be registered in the civil registry without a name until the parents decide upon the name that will be officially registered; after that it cannot be changed. If a first name is registered at this time, it cannot be changed (*ametaklito*), even if baptism confers a different name later: for example, if Leonidas is the name given at birth, and the name Panayiotis is conferred at baptism, the only legal name is Leonidas. To facilitate the immediate registration of a birth, maternity hospitals in Athens provide the appropriate forms, which do not require a name to be specified, but only the child's sex and parents' names.

The significance of the distinction between civil and religious naming practices is profound and should not be underestimated, for it differentiates membership as a citizen in the state (i.e., nationality) from religious affiliation. Though this distinction might be a commonplace in Western Europe, from the Greek perspective it signals a radical break with the long-established equivalence of national and religious identities. The secularization agenda is promoted, too, by the introduction of civil marriage and divorce as legal alternatives to the religious rites (divorce has always been permitted in the Orthodox Church), and both possibilities are provided for equally as options in the 1983 law. In 2005 the Hellenic League for Human and Citizen Rights, a legal pressure group, proposed a radical draft bill aimed at the full separation of the church from the state, and including, among other measures, the stipulation that all civil procedures of family law would be compulsory, while religious rites would be optional. The bill's proponents argue that they are following a common Western European model; in fact, the bill is actually based on the French model and notably does not correspond with the situation in the United Kingdom, Denmark, or Greece, which can still be called "confessional states," in which there is an established religion.

## THE ID-CARD CONTROVERSY

Given this context, the issue of a new form of identity card (*taftotita,* also known as *astynomiki taftotita*) revealed the singularity of the articulation of religion in Greek society. The debate about ID cards lasted for more than two decades and was marked by total reversals in the law and a persistent controversy about whether or not to include religious affiliation.[2] ID cards were introduced early in the Second World War, when Greece was under Axis occupation. They are thus long established and do not in themselves provoke consternation. Greeks are used to being identified through a laminated card with a photo and thumbprint, basic personal data, and a specification of religious affiliation.

Since the mid-1980s, various proposals for a new type of ID card have been debated, and numerous laws and amendments passed. Among the PASOK government reforms was the 1986 Law 1599/86 *Skeseis kratous-politia, kathierosi neou typou deltiou taftotitas kai alles diataxeis,* which proposed that religious affiliation be omitted. It also proposed a single identifying number for each citizen (EKAM, *eniaio kodiko arithmo mitroou,* art. 2). This number would be used for all purposes, including ID and passport numbers, driver's license, local and national electoral rolls, health service registration—for all official records. Widespread objections centered on the assignment of a single identifying number to each individual, so that a person would no longer be identified by name. The use of a single number invoked great concern in relation to the new technology: it was also to involve an electronic chip, which many feared would open up the possibility of storing secret data and would permit widespread surveillance.

The law was eventually passed, despite vehement and widespread objections. Five years later, however, the government admitted that it had proved impossible to apply the law "for practical reasons", and also "because of the almost universal rejection by the people" of a single identifying number (Vlachos 2000: 31). Amendments were proposed that eliminated the use of the single number (EKAM), but the card was still to be readable electronically (31–32).

In 1993 the debate about the inclusion of religious affiliation was reviewed when the Holy Synod (College of Bishops), anticipating that the government would finally enforce the law, released two statements (*egkyklioi*). These asserted that the government was being subjected to external pressures, pointing out that the church would not allow "the bond (*dhesmos*) between Orthodoxy and Hellenism [sic] to be broken" (Vlachos 2000: 32–34), and called on the government not to proceed with the issue of this new type of ID, thereby "bowing to foreign pressure" (34). The main objection was tellingly expressed: "For us Greeks, the identity card is not simply a public document, but a document which declares our identity as a people/race" (38). There were no further developments until, early in 1997, the Data Protection Act (Law 2472/1997) was introduced in Parliament. Under this rubric, religion could now be classified as a private matter, a notion hitherto unfamiliar to Greeks. The key issue here was the public/private separation, a central characteristic of the secular state, but one that has an unusual and problematic articulation in Greek social life. The measure relegating religion to what was now being defined as a private sphere by the Hellenic Data Authority was not brought before Parliament, however; it was endorsed by the prime minister at the time, Costas Simitis, who ordered a change in the relevant administrative act. Thus the change in ID cards was passed in an unobtrusive way ("as a coup d"etat" (*praxikopimatika*), as one objector put it). This act thereby unobtrusively introduced the particular categorization of the Western world, heralding the advance of secularization.

This was not the end of the matter, however. The controversy continued from late 1999 through 2000. It reached a climax when the Holy Synod and the archbishop, wishing to demonstrate the church's power, used the mass media to rally support for their position. Negotiations with government ministers broke down, and finally the clerics suggested that the people should be consulted through a referendum. When the government ignored this proposal, the political clout of the church was demonstrated. Public meetings were called in the main cities, petitions were circulated, and a huge mobilization resulted in the collection of over 3 million adults' signatures (in a total population of less than 11 million). The petition demanded a referendum to decide whether the information on religion should be included voluntarily on the new ID card; for constitutional reasons, the government turned down this initiative. The expectation was that public opinion would reject the ID card as an external intervention in domestic affairs through an EU-driven initiative.

Certainly, one impetus of the church's support was political and nationalist, since the government was seen to be succumbing to pressure from outside. The public outcry shocked the liberal establishment. The populist wing of the church exploited the massive resistance and again brought into focus the problematic issue of church-state relations. Paradoxically, some of those who supported the church's petition were not themselves practicing believers (left-wing and atheist protesters objected to the electronic card and the threat of surveillance), while, among the more religious, not all supported the petition, as they felt that the church was overstepping its role and entering a political arena.

What all this boils down to is a puzzle and a challenge to simplistic conclusions about modernity and secularization in Greece. The short answer to why the vast majority rejected the government proposal to omit religious affiliation from the new ID cards is that religion in Greece is intimately bound up with national identity,[3] even today. In the face of the growing presence of other nationalities, races, and religions in the country, it is still widely held that to be a Greek is to be an Orthodox Christian. Though it would be a distortion to conflate the three categories, it is fair to say that contemporary Greek identity continues to be a complicated amalgam of national, cultural, and religious features. A clear illustration is provided by a historian colleague of mine, a self-proclaimed atheist, who does not attend church but appears at major church festivals, and explains: "I'm not a believer, but I'm Greek, so I'm Orthodox" (see a similar example in Ware 1983: 208). The entanglement of religious and national identity is a feature of Greece's modern history that has ramifications in all spheres of life, notwithstanding wide-

spread immigration since the late 1990s from the third world and from neighboring Balkan and Eastern European countries.[4] There are two points to underline
here: firstly, religion is so intricately bound up with national identity that it can
barely be disentangled, and, secondly, that religion is not commonly seen to be
an individual or a private matter. On the contrary, it has a high public profile,
religious ritual accompanies national celebrations, and everyday ritual (lighting
candles, venerating icons) flourishes.

This situation raises a question: How can secularization take place in a country
where religion and national identity overlap to such an extent? The removal of
religious identity from the new ID cards was apparently perceived as a fundamental threat to identity, both at the personal and at the collective level. This proposed
measure provoked such a public outcry that the government had to allow the issue
to lapse until it could be introduced "through the back door." For reasons of
Greece's particular historical trajectory and its cultural heritage, the process of
secularization has been delayed and differs from that in other Western states.

## PERSONAL CELEBRATIONS:
## ETHNOGRAPHIC OBSERVATIONS

At the everyday level, processes of religious and ideological transformation can
be observed in many areas of Greek social life. Over the period that I have been
studying Greek society (since 1969), I have noticed a significant change in the way
in which personal identity is celebrated. In the 1970s, the celebration of name days
was a striking social feature: people celebrated annually on the feast day of the
saint or holy person whose name they bore. The celebration usually included a
formalized visit to the celebrant's house, where simple, conventional, and predict-
able exchanges took place. The house was open to all comers; participation was
expected as a social obligation for the entire community. The general pattern was
recognizable throughout Greece with some variation by region and by social class.
In that period, birthdays were seldom marked in any way.

Today, however, birthdays are more widely celebrated. Increasing numbers of
Greeks, roughly those who are thirty years old and under, have had the experience
of celebrating their birthday. For children brought up today birthdays are a major
event. Personal celebrations may—and indeed often do —take place on name days
as well, but the manner in which name days are celebrated has also undergone
suggestive changes. Name-day celebrations have become more selective, highly
elaborate, and tinged with strong competitive overtones.

In summary, I have observed three tendencies: the increasing observance of
birthdays, a decline in name-day celebrations, and a marked difference in the way
the latter are observed. The changing patterns of personal celebration are undoubtedly the result of macro-scale economic and political forces, connected with the

legal reforms and modernizing program of the PASOK period. They are also obviously associated with the strong influence of European institutions on Greek society and with new styles of consumerism. But instead of simply concluding that these changes are part of the process of modernization or Europeanization of Greek society, and that attempts to create a Western secular state are finally becoming effective, I wish to inquire further into the significance of such changes. In my view, they must be viewed in a wider philosophical and religious context, since they express a deeper transformation of a worldview. These changes in patterns of personal celebration can be seen to produce—as well as to reflect—a paradigm shift in Greek society. What can easily be dismissed as a trivial social feature—the preference for birthdays over name days—is a sensitive index of a deeper conceptual change, with interesting comparative implications. Unlike the issue of ID cards, however, which provoked public and political controversy, the effects of these changes at the personal and informal level are insidious, and their significance is not readily perceived.

## INDIVIDUAL AND PERSON IN GREECE

It is often glibly remarked that Greeks are individualists. This cliché has some foundation in the quality and character of social relations in Greece, which are essentially volatile and eristic and have long been characterized in the anthropological literature as "agonistic" (e.g., Friedl 1962; Campbell 1964; Herzfeld 1985). The turbulent quality of social life, expressed so readily in interpersonal conflicts, *kavgades,* which stimulate and provide entertainment as well as necessary outlets for endemic frustration, can give the impression of untrammeled individualism. Certainly many of us who have known Greece for some time observe a people who explicitly extol the value of freedom, and who habitually contest the constraints on individual expression inherent in membership in the social polity.[5] This attitude is summed up in the rhetorical rejoinder *kai pios eisai esy?* ("And who are you?"), readily voiced whenever precedence is claimed. But does this constitute individualism in the Western understanding? A nuanced examination of the notion of individualism in the Greek context is essential: we need a more neutral analytical basis. The analytical category required for cross-cultural comparison, the ultimate end of the anthropological endeavor, should be culturally neutral as far as possible and not presuppose the indigenous typologies or terminologies. I therefore advocate using the term "human subject" as the analytical one with which others, such as "person," "self," and "individual," can be examined as culturally specific constructions.[6]

In his *Essays on Individualism* (1986) Louis Dumont presents a framework for considering larger comparative questions regarding social change, in which our examination of concepts of personal identity can be situated. Dumont is interested in pursuing "the origins of individualism," which for him constitute a mode of social organization and way of thinking. He asks how a transition has been possible between what he calls "two antithetic universes of thought," one where the paramount value is the individual ("individualism"), the other where the paramount value is vested in society as a whole ("holism") (1986: 25). He posits a polarity between the "individualistic" type of society and another type, which he calls "holistic" (the latter mode of organization is also referred to as "communal" or "collective"). I suggest that the Greek case provides a rare chance to examine a fundamental shift in orientation from holistic to individualistic. The Greek instance also alerts us to subtle variations within Western society regarding the constitution of the human subject. The contested issue of ID cards and the shift from name days to birthdays allow us to trace the way in which a society with a more holistic or collective emphasis is turning toward an individualistic focus.

I suggest that our understanding of the Greek way of thinking can be enhanced by recognizing the distinction between "individual" and "person" as indigenous categories which can only be appreciated in the general context of Greek social life. Many anthropologists have drawn attention to the central role of kinship in Greek society, pointing to the importance of the intimate realm of the family, the domestic realm, and the network of kinship relations. Despite major changes in the political and socioeconomic spheres, kinship continues to be the primary locus of individual identification and loyalty. No Greek exists outside of the kinship nexus that confers identity upon him or her. This observation is by no means unique, however, and holds for many other societies. In Italy and other southern European societies, similar patterns in which adult unmarried children remain in the parental home even into their late thirties provoke social commentary (M. Herzfeld, personal communication, 2007; also BBC Radio 4, Today programme, report on family life in Rome, 5 November 2007).

Even today in Greece, I would argue, the focus and point of orientation is family, and it is in family that the efforts and endeavors, aspirations and ambitions, and loyalty of every individual are invested. In my first fieldwork in Kokkinia in the 1970s and through experiences in provincial areas and more recently in Athens, I have found that the fundamental social bonds remain those involving the kinship group. I am constantly reminded that "individuals" have family obligations as a primary point of reference. My recorded observation in the 1970s that there was no expectation of the progression from dependent child in a family of origin to independent adult individual living separately from the family (Hirschon [1989] 1998: 107–9) is still largely true in Athens, though cases of independent living have certainly increased.

By contrast, according to the characteristic pattern of the West, children are expected to "leave home." In the American tradition, independence and autonomy are highly valued (Bellah et al. 1985: 56–57). Although in the Anglo-Saxon West there is an expected phase of independent unmarried adulthood, even today Greek youth do not have an acceptable period of unmarried independent existence "on their own." When it does occur, for example, during higher education, it is seen as a measure of expediency. Though there are undoubtedly signs of change in Greece as marriages are being delayed among middle-class Athenian youth and earning power allows for residence away from parents, this is not yet the norm, and examples are few and far between. This situation reflects the kinship-embedded character of personal identity in Greek society. The idea of a separate, individual existence as the criterion of adulthood is a foreign import. In the older Greek view, one is a member of one's family, either that of origin or that of marriage, and it is in the latter state that one achieves full adulthood.

A second feature of most Western societies (particularly the United States, according to Bellah et al. 1985) is the conceptual separation of individual from society, and the separation of private and public, an important concomitant characteristic of secularization. In the United States these features are central and critical. They result in a social context within which the individualism of American society can be specified and further categorized into "different modes" (such as "utilitarian" or "expressive," according to Bellah et al. 1985: 28). Together, these features provide interconnecting sets of ideas that constitute the human subject in a very different way from its composition in Greek society.[7]

## THE BAPTISMAL CONTEXT

To further our understanding of the shifts that affect long-established practices and perceptions in contemporary Greece, we must consider naming patterns, since names are the primary markers of personal identity. Anthropologists have demonstrated the associations of naming with kinship (Bialor 1967; Tavuchis 1971), with property and inheritance (Kenna 1976, 2008; Herzfeld 1982; Sutton 1998), and with international political tensions (Sutton 1997). My focus, however, is the ontological dimension of naming practices and various associated personal celebrations of identity. In the Greek case, therefore, examination of the significance of the rite and practice of baptism is necessary.

As we have seen, until recently, Greek public consciousness did not acknowledge civil registration of identity, even though it was possible by law. The widespread belief that a child could not be registered at school unless baptized (or the equivalent for Muslims and Jews) indicated that for most Greeks there was no social identity without a declared religious identity. Until he or she experienced the rite of baptism, a child was called *bebe/beba* and in some village communities might even be given the animal-like appellation *drakos* (noted on Naxos by Stewart 1992; cf. du Boulay 1974: 42). Consequently, the significance of the notion of the person and of personal celebrations in Greece can be comprehended only in the context of Orthodox Christianity and through recognition of the centrality of the practice of baptism within it.

The baptismal service contains a set of condensed symbols that convey the fundamental beliefs of the Christian life. For infant and adult alike, in Orthodox Christian practice, baptism takes place through total immersion. The rite signifies the burial of the old Adam and a person's rebirth, the raising into a new life with the promise of salvation from the fallen condition. Baptism confers a new identity on the initiate, through the passage from death to rebirth (Schmemann 1976). The infant receives new life through the regeneration of the whole person at the spiritual level: she or he becomes a full member of the church. Because the confirmation rite, in the form of the Holy Myron, is celebrated immediately after baptism, in Orthodox practice, the baptized infant is a full communicant in the liturgy, together with the adults. The baptismal or ecclesial name confers specific personal identity as well as total membership in Christian society. The anointing with the Holy Myron, symbol of the Holy Spirit, represents a second sacrament and is an integral part of the baptismal ritual, marking initiation into the Royal Priesthood. The combined sacraments of baptism and Myron thus confer a completely new personhood and full membership in the church, which according to the Greek Orthodox worldview itself constitutes society. Through baptism the newly redeemed ecclesial person is identified by a proper Christian name. (See Schmemann 1976 for a clear exposition of the symbolism of the baptismal ritual and an interpretation of the loaded significance of personal names in the Orthodox tradition.)

The bond of spiritual kinship created through baptism is another significant feature of Orthodox practice. It is believed that the blood itself changes during participation in the ritual of baptism, so that the children of co-godparents become "spiritual siblings" (psychadelphia), and a prohibition on marriage is applied to all involved. In a society where the family is the foundation of social organization, and kinship loyalties are the organizing principle for many activities, relationships with godparents, an extended quasi-kinship bond, are a major social force. This special bond is illustrated in the ritual of baptism itself, as the godparent takes the place of the natural parents and even has the acknowledged right to choose the child's name (Campbell 1964: 220; Bialor 1967; du Boulay 1974: 21; Aschenbrenner 1975). Although the godparent's choice of name usually conforms with standard naming practices, conferring the names of grandparents on the child according to the parents' wishes, I have been told of cases in which the godparent conferred a name not approved by the parents. It was once common in rural areas for parents to be absent from the baptism: they would wait at home for the name to be announced by children attending the service, who would rush home once the godparent and the priest had declared the name.

## NAMING PATTERNS AND NAME DAYS

Despite the huge range of available Christian names, their occurrence in southern European societies is limited, a result of the widespread custom according to which names are repeated in alternate generations. A secondary consequence of name repetition is that certain names predominate within rural communities, resulting in marked regional variation. A clear illustration is provided in a study of electoral rolls of Greek adult male voters (Vernikos 1973).[8] In this countrywide survey, 72 percent of all Greek males were found to share just twenty names; 44 percent had one of six Christian names: Ioannes (John), George, Nicolas, Constantine, Dimitrios, Theodoros. The study showed the geographical variation in the distribution of certain names: for example, Panayiotis is very common in the Peloponnese, Emmanuel/Manolis in Crete, Michalis and Stratis (Efstratios) in the eastern Aegean islands, and Andreas and Spyros in western Greece. A detailed study (Just 1988) of Meganisi, a small Ionian island, records the names of its 205 adult males. Here 50 percent of the men shared seven names: Georgios (28), Nikolaos (17), Gerasimos (16), Stathis (12), Michalis (12), Andreas (11), and Spyros (Spyridon) (10). Gerasimos and Spyridon are especially favored because they are the names of local saints whose relics are revered at local pilgrimage shrines.

The regional and local concentration of personal names allows the celebration of name days to be collectively experienced and generates a sense of commonality and shared endowment among those who have the same name. It is worth noting, too, that Greeks tend to pay attention to names in a way that few Westerners do. The significance of names is reflected in everyday discourse, in the conventional and formulaic phrases people use when introduced: "Your name?" "May you have joy of it!" (*Na charite to onoma sou*, "to take pleasure in your name"). The expression "We have the same name" (*Synonomatoi eimaste*) implies mutual recognition with someone who shares a name day and its celebration.

The name-day celebrations I witnessed in the 1970s in Kokkinia, an urban neighborhood of primarily Asia Minor refugees, represented a pattern common throughout Greece. Name days were public knowledge and their celebration was not optional; all were expected to visit the celebrant. Allowing access to what is normally the private sphere, the name-day celebration opened the house in an auspicious mode and generated a sense of the local community (see Hirschon [1989] 1998: 197, 204–6, 243). The procedure was highly conventional: standard gifts (alcohol, pastries, chocolates) were brought; the *kerasma* (offering of a treat) was of a formalized kind requiring little preparation (a small glass of liqueur, sweets, pastries), while a formal meal for the extended family was offered later in the evening.

Since the 1970s significant changes in these patterns have occurred, most noticeably in the urban centers. The celebration of a name day has now become optional, it often takes place outside the home, and it usually entails major preparation of food. In place of the conventional offerings of liqueur and chocolates, celebrations now reflect the higher levels of affluence in Greek society. Significantly, the celebrations now have a competitive element, so that the number of dishes to be prepared has become daunting. One professional Athenian woman told me that she could not muster the energy to prepare the feast for her husband's name day that year. She would have to offer several new dishes, since repeating the menu from the previous year would not be acceptable! Given the uncertainty, people make telephone calls in advance to inquire: "Are you celebrating (*yiortazeis*)?" "Are you receiving (visitors) (*tha dechtheis*)?" Sometimes the reason for not celebrating is given in practical terms: "No, it's a weekday." As many women are employed and work long hours, the celebration may be postponed to the weekend.

Undoubtedly, changes in employment and gender roles, as well as rising affluence, are factors that influence personal celebrations. The conventional symbolic offering is less acceptable, and more expensive gifts (books, clothes, jewelry, potted plants) are brought. And alternative practices exist. Unmarried men and women might take a group of friends to a cafeteria or a *taverna* and pay for the meal (*tous kernaei*), and would do the same if celebrating a birthday. In Athenian offices, it has become standard practice on a name day for the celebrant to bring a large box of sweetmeats or savory pastries to treat other employees and visitors at work. The standard wish remains "Many years!" (*Chronia Polla!*).

When I phoned to greet Thanos (a professor at the University of Athens who is in his fifties) on his name day, he was not even aware of the day. "Name days aren't celebrated the same way anymore," he responded. "Before, the house was open to anyone on the day. Now you wait till the weekend, you go out with friends or invite them. It's not the same. Birthdays are also celebrated now, but mainly for children. After you're twenty-five, you don't celebrate a birthday."

Leftheris, an eighty year old, celebrates his name day now as an annual family occasion on the nearest weekend after Saint Eleftherios Day, 15 December. His wife complained that the style of celebration has changed so much that it has to be restricted to family and close friends. She spends two days preparing the food, helped by their unmarried fifty-year-old daughter who lives in the same flat. Besides the families of the two married children, including five grandchildren, the other guests are related through spiritual kinship (godparents and marriage sponsors). A variety of foods were offered on the occasion when I was present. Typically, the platters on the large table included roast meat and potatoes, a chicken casserole dish (sometimes a fish dish), several kinds of traditional Greek pies (*pittes*), various stuffed vegetables (*gemista*), salads, and three different kinds of puddings.

Even with the evident changes that have occurred in the style of name-day celebrations, their continued importance is clear. On major feast and saints' days in smaller towns and villages, an air of festivity spreads throughout the locality, as some celebrants take the day off work (civil service employees are allowed a day's holiday on their name day). In Athenian offices, boxes of pastries or savory snacks are passed around, and though home visits are less common for reasons explained above, the minimal expectation is a telephone call to the celebrant. People tell me that they feel affronted if friends fail to express greetings on their name day.

## CELEBRATION OF BIRTHDAYS

Greeks' reasons for not celebrating birthdays in the past are usually pragmatic. People refer to widespread illiteracy in rural communities and say that the recording of births was inaccurate (dates were often written on the back of an icon), and that birthdays were often falsified (e.g., to reduce the marriage age for girls or delay army service for boys). The actual date was of little significance. People say that sometimes birthdays were celebrated only because they fell on significant days (e.g., 25 March, the national Independence Day), or when the person did not have a Christian name (in certain periods, classical names such as Perikles, Priam, Danae, Leda, Daphne, and Kleopatra have been favored, often to the disapproval of clergy).

The state-imposed requirement for civil registration, powerful economic forces, and the pressures of social prestige are all playing a part in establishing new patterns. With the legal reforms of the PASOK government a different awareness of individual identity has been introduced, providing a new rationale for the birthday celebration. I suggest that this new formulation of identity is a key element in the growing practice of having birthday parties. Parents consider birthdays more "European." Classmates and other selected friends are invited, usually to the child's home. The table is decorated with a printed tablecloth and napkins, and a cake is ordered from a pastry shop. In some circles where it is an innovation, parents may express anxiety about "getting it right" and comment that "this is what they do in Europe." Popular magazines run articles with advice about how to hold birthday parties, and the appropriate presents and food. After about age eighteen, it seems that only special birthdays (e.g., a fortieth or fiftieth birthday) are celebrated. I have been told that many older adults ignore birthdays because they draw attention to the aging process.

By contrast with the older pattern of name-day celebrations, birthdays celebrate an individual's birth as a unique event. Birthdays are not public knowledge; they

INDIGENOUS PERSONS AND IMPORTED INDIVIDUALS     303

are selective and require an invitation. Notably, they are neither communal nor inclusive. Therefore, birthdays are not shared, and the house is not open. Birthdays mark one's age, and thus the finite passage of life. In essence, birthdays are the recognition of one's physical being, since they mark the mortality of humans. I suggest that, phenomenologically, the increasing attention paid to children's birthdays generates an awareness of one's unique individual existence.

Although in contemporary Greece recognition of birthdays is undoubtedly increasing, name-day and birthday celebrations are happening concurrently, at the present time. However, with the changes in style, and the introduction of choice, the force of change in all aspects of name-day celebrations is clear.

## DEEPER MEANINGS

Name-day and birthday celebrations represent contrasting symbolic modes of expressing personal identity. The name day has a twofold significance: the social existence of the named person is honored, and the spiritual identity of the person is recognized socially. The name day refers to the sacred realm of eternity, where the fallen condition of humanity has been redeemed and where rebirth and salvation are the reality. In sharp contrast on a symbolic level, a birthday celebration acknowledges a person's physical nature and biological birth and mortality; it marks a person's material existence in the social world. In a Durkheimian dichotomy, a birthday is an expression of the profane or mundane, while a name day is an association with the sacred realm.[9]

A name day is public knowledge, and the style of its celebration promotes a collective and communal awareness of personal identity. In the old pattern, the imperative to participate in name-day celebrations helped people transcend the tensions of daily life and the conflicting family and work interests that inevitably divide a community. The name-day celebration was a force for wider social cohesion. It also crossed temporal boundaries as a result of family naming customs (on which, see above), uniting living and deceased family members across generations. Naming was an act of commemoration; and it is said that the child who bears a grandparent's name "resurrected him/her" (*ton/tin anastithike*) (Kenna 1976; Danforth 1982: 38, 204; Sutton 1998: 182). Name days are also repeated each year, but without a sense of progression. The years that have elapsed since the saint's martyrdom are disregarded, and even when the year of martyrdom is known, the anniversary is rarely acknowledged. In essence, name days transcend linear time and human mortality. The name day exists in (sacred) ritual time, in a liturgical timelessness, where the notion of coincident synchronic dimensions prevails over the progressive linear model of the secular world. A community of same-name persons and a sense of common identity with the saint are expressed and experienced. In summary, the celebration of name days promotes a collective sense of identity, of living and dead, of relatives and nonrelated, and creates an open, inclusive sense of community among all who share a holy patron's name. Name days are essentially sacred, and their celebration should also be seen as the social manifestation of a religious worldview.

The most obvious explanation for the changes discussed above is that they are simply a mimicry of Western practices, a leap into modernity, a new type of consumerism, an imported fashion, all of which are part of the picture. My interest in this analysis, however, is to uncover the cosmological implications of the new pattern, in terms of Dumont's suggestion that societies might be seen to shift from "holistic" or "collective" to "individualistic." The changes discussed can be summed up in terms of the contrast between a locally defined notion of a "person" and an imported idea of an "individual." We can use the writings of theologians as a guide in following this line of thought, as the tradition of the Eastern Orthodox Church contains rich sources for an indigenous anthropology.

In accordance with the supposition that Orthodox precepts have been assimilated into the Greek worldview and have widespread ramifications in social practice (Hirschon [1981] 1993; [1989] 1998: chaps. 9, 10), some elements relevant to the current topic need to be presented. According to this way of thinking, the nature of the human being (*o anthropos*) is conceptionalized in relation to the nature of the Divine Being. The first key element in this indigenous anthropology is the understanding of the nature of the human person. In this worldview the human person has been given a divine archetypal referent. Man and woman are created in "the image and likeness of God" (Gen. 1:26). The human person is seen to be an icon of God.[10] In this theocentric view, "human beings cannot be understood apart from divine being for the divine is the determining element in our humanity" (Ware 1986: 4). This conceptualization provides, as it were, a blueprint for the traditional Greek understanding of human nature (Paparizos 2000: 147–50; see also Hann and Goltz and Hanganu, this volume).

The second key element is the understanding of the nature of God, in whose image humans are created. The Eastern Orthodox Church places great emphasis on the Trinitarian nature of God: God consists of three distinct but united persons or hypostases (a term Orthodox writers prefer, because it avoids the many connotations of the Latin "persona"). These three divine hypostases—Father, Son, and Holy Spirit—are undivided but distinct; they exist in reciprocal relationship, in an interchange of mutual love. Kallistos Ware (1986) develops the idea of the human person and the Trinitarian character of God and goes on to point out that it is only in relationship with others and with God that our full human nature can be realized (1996: 12–16). The essential point is that "the being of God is a relational being: without the concept of communion it would not be possible to speak of the being of God" (Zizioulas 1985: 17). The emphasis in Orthodox writings on the relational and social aspect of the human subject underscores the distinction between the notion of the "individual" and that of the "person." The importance of these precepts is also noted by Gabriel Hanganu (this volume) as it affects social relations in an Eastern Christian social context. The Greek word for each is suggestive of the contrast between them: *atomo* (individual) as opposed to *prosopo* (person). This polarity can be represented schematically as follows:

HUMAN SUBJECT

| as Individual | as Person |
|---|---|
| *to atomo* | *to prosopo* |
| unit, indivisible | face to face |
| self-contained | involved, in relationship |
| separation | communion |
| competitor | co-worker |
| possessing, keeping | sharing |
| I, me, mine | We, us, our, thou |

Although I have represented these as binary oppositional categories in an ideal-type analysis, most Orthodox writings on the subject of the human person do not present the individual and the person as mutually exclusive categories (Yannaras 1984:. 21). Rather, the individual is held to be the core of the person, so that the connection between these two states is situational and dynamic. Full personhood cannot be achieved without the achievement of true individuality. In short, the central notion in the Greek conceptualization of the human subject is that of the socially engaged "person," *to prosopo.* This can be depicted as antithetical to the individual, *to atomo;* in a wider interpretative framework, however, the two categories are not opposed but hierarchically structured. The one subsumes the other: the individual is the core of the person, is a state of primary self-awareness, but it is subsumed within the more embracing notion of the person, the full expression of the construction of the human. The fully developed person exists in relationship with others as a fully integrated individual. The charter or archetypal model for this conceptual approach is that of the human being created in the "image and likeness" of the Trinitarian God.

## CONCLUSION

We are now in a position to return to some of our earlier observations. Greek society is firmly grounded in kinship and family relationships. Every Greek is primarily a member of a family, and consequently the Greek individual is always embedded in networks of given (ascribed) relationships, and is essentially a relational being. I contend that the Greek notion of the human subject has not always corresponded with that of the individual in the modern Western sense. The celebration of personal identity through the name day, essentially a communal festivity, is a critical index of this. The emphasis on the birthday is, I argue, a shift toward a different sense of the human subject, in the direction of a more Western construct of the individual.

Dumont's query regarding the change from a "holistic" or "collective" mode of thinking to a more individualistic one is therefore aptly illustrated in terms of the changes in personal celebrations. Similarly, the outcry over the issue of new ID cards that omit religious affiliation can be seen as reflecting the "collective" or "holistic" character of Greek society. Religion is conceptualized as a communal endowment, a crucial element of national identity. This perception has a theological basis, too, for, in the Orthodox view, the church is coterminous with society. In terms of Christian belief, the rite of baptism confers full membership in both everyday society and the eternal religious community. However, with the modernizing reforms of the PASOK government, the separation of religion from nationality and citizenship, and the development of more individualized, secularized forms of personal identity, I suggest that a shift is under way, eroding the collective and holistic and promoting the individualistic and atomized, and that this can be charted in social transformations.

The changes in personal celebrations have multiple causes, and I have indicated that their effects are not superficial. Certainly they are a response to wider politico-economic forces, for the imported construction of the individualistic human subject is better suited to the needs of the market economy of late capitalism. I have tried to show that the changes are also an expression of a deeper ontological transformation. In the frivolity of detail regarding name-day and birthday celebrations, we can observe a shift of cosmological import, corresponding to Dumont's contrast between "holistic" and "individualistic" societies. As Greece moves from its status as a "holistic" society to full integration in Europe, I conclude that a fundamental aspect of the Greek worldview is changing. The paradigm of the human subject is shifting from the Eastern Orthodox anthropology of the person to a Western anthropology of the individual.

NOTES

1. This survey, conducted by Tnsicap and Gallup International Association, was publicized on 16 November 2005 during a period when church-state relations were under scrutiny. It does not state the sample size or composition but does indicate significant regional differences, the highest proportion of those who call themselves "religious" being in African countries (overall average 91 percent). The lowest was in Hong Kong (14 percent) and Japan (17 percent), while the overall average for Western European countries was 60 percent. www.tns-global.com. During a three-month stay in Athens (Oct.–Dec, 2005; also April 2006), I had the opportunity to observe some aspects of religious practice on a daily basis in various parts of the metropolis and the country. Overall my observations have been made over four decades in various parts of the country in a number of different roles, both personal and professional.

2. Vlachos 2000; the detailed examination of the ID issue in Vlachos's book provided much of the information presented here. I am deeply indebted to Nikos Alivizatos, a constitutional lawyer, for up-to-date information (2006) on legal debates and proposed reforms, to Ioannes Ktistakis for further clarification, and especially to Aigli Brouskou, who alerted me to the existence of long-standing legislation regarding civil registration.

3. In an official poll on 16 September 2000, reported in newspapers, 77.4 percent wanted religious affiliation to be recorded on the ID card, "because they believe that this feature is an 'inextricable part of their self-awareness' [*anapospasto tmyma tis aftosyneidesias tous*]" (Iera Synodou tis Ellados 2000: 29).

4. Awareness of minority groups of Muslims, Jews, and other Christian denominations in the country has not been part of public consciousness in the past (see Pollis 1992). Increasing immigration, illegal and permitted, has effected marked demographic changes. Huge controversy has arisen when Albanian children who excel at school are not allowed to carry the national flag at parades, the accepted recognition of achievement. For characteristic aspects of nationalism in Greece and an exhaustive analysis of notions of the European self, see Herzfeld 2002, 2004; Molokotos-Liederman 2003. For various criteria applying to Greek national identity at different periods and two minority examples, see Hirschon 1999.

5. Many anthropological accounts reveal the value placed on personal autonomy, expressed in different ways, for example, as honor (Campbell 1964) or *egoïsmos* in Herzfeld's copious writings. See Herzfeld's (2002) analysis of the notion of individual and self in the European context. For an analysis of different expressions of the values of freedom and personal autonomy, see Hirschon 2008, and Hirschon 2001 for how such values affect codes of linguistic politeness.

6. For some societies, anthropologists use the idea of "person," for others that of "individual" or that of "self" (see, e.g., contributors to Carrithers 1985). These are, however, ethnographically specific categories, constituting empirical data. Mauss's original essay on the person was the point of departure, but a more rigorous attention to definitional categories is now required.

7. I am mindful of the dangers of essentialism, of sweeping categorizations, and of oversimplification in dealing summarily with so vast a topic. For the sake of argument, I have not avoided the crudeness of using blanket terms such as "individual" and "Western" to designate what constitutes highly differentiated sets of notions. For more sophisticated analyses, see Morris 1991; Herzfeld 2002; 2004: 204–10.

8. I know of no systematic analysis of female names. The male bias in my analysis reflects the ethnographic data, in which there is a clear emphasis on men's name-day celebrations.

9. In the Orthodox Christian worldview, material and mundane dimensions are not seen as opposed to the sacred but are imbued with them, interpenetrated and transfigured in a process of continual communication with the divine world (with regard to material objects, see Hanganu, this volume). Though this significance may not be conscious for the actors in any way, there is ample scope for interpretation in the ethnographic record; see, for example, Campbell 1964; du Boulay 1974; Hart 1992; Hirschon [1981] 1993.

10. This notion, central to Orthodox thinking, has been developed with regard to personhood by a number of theologians; see, for example, Lossky 1957: 121ff.; Yannaras 1984: 19–22; Zizioulas 1985: 33–42; 1991; Vlachos 1999 and 2000; Sakharov 2002: 117ff.; and Ware 1986, 1996.

# REFERENCES

Aschenbrenner, S. 1975. Folk model vs actual practice: The distribution of spiritual kin in a Greek village. *Anthropological Quarterly* 48: 65–86.

Bellah, R., N.R. Madsen, W.M. Sullivan, A. Swidler, and S.M. Tipton. 1985. *Habits of the heart: Individualism and commitment in American life.* Berkeley: University of California Press.

Bialor, P.A. 1967. "What's in a name?" Aspects of the social organization of a Greek farming community related to naming customs. In *Essays in Balkan ethnology,* ed. W.G. Lockwood, 95–108. Kroeber Anthropological Publications 1. Berkeley: Kroeber Anthropological Society.

Campbell, J.K. 1964. *Honour, family, and patronage.* Oxford: Clarendon Press.

Carrithers, M., S. Collins, and S. Lukes, eds. 1985. *The category of the person: Anthropology, philosophy, history.* Cambridge: Cambridge University Press.

Danforth, L.M. 1982. *Death rituals of rural Greece.* Princeton: Princeton University Press.

Du Boulay, J. 1974. *Portrait of a Greek mountain village.* Oxford: Clarendon Press.

Dumont, L. 1986. *Essays on individualism: Modern ideology in anthropological perspective.* Chicago: University of Chicago Press.

Frazee, C. 2002. Catholics. In *Minorities in Greece: Aspects of a plural society,* ed. R. Clogg, 24–47. London: Hurst & Co.

Friedl, E. 1962. *Vasilika: A village in modern Greece.* New York: Holt, Rinehart and Winston.

Hart, L.K. 1992. *Time, religion, and social experience in rural Greece.* Lanham, Md.: Rowman and Littlefield.

Herzfeld, M. 1982. When exceptions define the rules: Greek baptismal names and the negotiation of identity. *Journal of Anthropological Research* 38, no. 3: 288–302.

———. 1985. *The poetics of manhood: Contest and identity in a Cretan mountain village.* Princeton: Princeton University Press.

———. 2002. The European self: Rethinking an attitude. In *The idea of Europe: From antiquity to the European Union,* ed. A. Pagden, 139–70. Cambridge: Cambridge University Press.

———. 2004. *The body impolitic: Artisans and artifice in the global hierarchy of value.* Chicago: University of Chicago Press.

Hirschon, R. [1981] 1993. Essential objects and the sacred. In *Women and space: Ground rules and social maps,* ed. S. Ardener, 72–88. Oxford: Berg.

———. [1989] 1998. *Heirs of the Greek catastrophe: The social life of Asia Minor refugees in Piraeus.* New York: Berghahn.

———. 1999. Identity and the Greek state: Some conceptual issues and paradoxes. In *The Greek diaspora in the twentieth century,* ed. R. Clogg, 158–80. London: Macmillan.

———. 2001. Freedom, solidarity, and obligation: The socio-cultural context of Greek politeness. In *Linguistic politeness across boundaries: The case of Greek and Turkish,* ed. A. Bayraktaroglu and M. Sifianou, 17–42. Amsterdam: John Benjamins.

———. 2008. Presents, promises, and punctuality: Accountability and obligation in Greek social life. In *Networks of power in modern Greece,* ed. M. Mazower, 189–207. London: Hurst & Co.

———. 2009. Religion and nationality: The tangled Greek case. In *When God comes to town: Religious traditions in urban contexts,* ed. R. Pinxten and L. Dikomitis. Oxford: Berghahn.

Iera Synodou tis Ellados. 2000. *Ekklisia kai taftotites* [Church and identity cards]. Athens: Ekdosis Kladou Ekdoseon Epikoinoniakis kai Morphotikis Ypiresias tis Ekklisias Ellados.

Just, R. 1988. A shortage of names: Greek proper names and their use. *Journal of the Anthropological Society of Oxford* 19, no. 2: 140–50.

Kenna, M. 1976. Houses, fields, and graves: Property and ritual obligations on a Greek island. *Ethnology* 15: 21–34.

———. 2008. Onomatodosia, klironomia kai i moira tis psychis: Skepseis yia ti synechisi kai tin allagi ton symvolikon praktikon s' ena Kykladitiko nisi [Naming, inheritance, and the fate of the soul: Some thoughts on continuity and change in symbolic practices on a Cycladic island]. In *Anthropologia kai symvolismos stin Ellada* [Anthropology and symbolism in Greece], ed. E. Alexakis, M. Vrachionidou, and A. Oikonomou, 205–30. Athens: Elliniki Etaireia Ethnologias.

Kitromilides, P. M. 2006. Orthodoxy and the West: Reformation to Enlightenment. In *The Cambridge history of Christianity*, vol. 5, Eastern Christianity, 187–209. Cambridge: Cambridge University Press.

Lixouriotis, I. 1986. Koinonikes kai nomikes antilipseis gia to paidi ton proton aiono tou nioellinikou kratous [Social and legal perceptions of the child during the first century of the modern Greek state], 329–30. Athens: Dodoni.

Lossky, V. 1957. *The mystical theology of the Eastern Church*. London: James Clarke.

Molokotos-Liederman, L. 2003. Identity crisis: Greece, Orthodoxy, and the European Union. *Journal of Contemporary Religion* 18, no. 3: 291–315.

Morris, B. 1991. *Western conceptions of the individual*. New York: Berg.

Paparizos, A. 2000. H taftotita ton Ellinon: Tropoi aftoprodiorismou kai i epidrasi tis ellinikis orthodoxias [The identity of Greeks: Ways of self-identification and the influence of Greek Orthodoxy]. In *"Emeis" kai oi "alloi": Anafora stis taseis kai ta symvola* ["Us" and "Others": Reference to trends and symbols], ed. X. Konstantopoulou, L. Maratou-Alibranti, D. Germanos, and T. Oikonomou, 135–51. Athens: EKKE.

Pollis, A. 1992. Greek national identity: Religious minorities: Rights and European norms. *Journal of Modern Greek Studies* 10, no. 1: 171–95.

Prodromou, E. 1998. Democracy and religious transformation in Greece: An underappreciated theoretical and empirical primer. In *The Orthodox Church in a changing world*, ed. P. Kitromilides and T. Veremis, 99–153. Athens: ELIAMEP, Centre for Asia Minor Studies.

Sakharov, N. V. 2002. *I love, therefore I am: The theological legacy of Archimandrite Sophrony*. New York: SVS.

Schmemann, A. 1976. *Of water and the spirit*. London: SPCK.

Stathopoulos, M. 2005. Prosopiki katastasi kai thriskeftikes epiloges [Personal situation and religious choices]. Paper presented to the Hellenic League for Human Rights, Athens.

Stewart, C. 1992. *Demons and the devil: Moral imagination in modern Greek culture*. Princeton: Princeton University Press.

Sutton, D. 1997. Local names, foreign claims: Family inheritance and national heritage on a Greek island. *American Ethnologist* 24: 415–37.

———. 1998. *Memories cast in stone: The relevance of the past in everyday life*. Oxford: Berg.

Tavuchis, N. 1971. Naming patterns and kinship among Greeks. *Ethnos* 36: 152–62.

Vernikos, N. 1973. La structure des prenoms masculins dans la société grecque en tant qu'instrument pour l'étude des certains phénomènes sociaux. In *Actes du 1er Congrés International d'Ethnologie Européenne,* 187–89. Maisonneuve and Paris: UNESCO.

Vlachos, I. 1999. *The person in the Orthodox tradition..* Livadia: Birth of the Theotokos Monastery.

———. 2000. *Taftotita kai taftotites* [Identity and identities]. Livadia: Birth of the Theotokos Monastery.

Ware, K. 1983. The church: A time of transition. In *Greece in the 1980s,* ed. R. Clogg, 208–30. London: Macmillan.

———. 1986. The human person as an icon of the Trinity. *Sobornost* 8, no. 2: 6–23.

———. 1996. In the image and likeness: The uniqueness of the human person. In *Personhood: Orthodox Christianity and the connections between body, mind, and soul,* ed. J. T. Chirban, 1–13. Westport, Conn.: Bergin & Garvey.

———. 2002. Old calendarists. In *Minorities in Greece: Aspects of a plural society,* ed. R. Clogg, 1–23. London: Hurst & Co.

Yannaras, C. 1984. *The freedom of morality.* New York: SVS.

Zizioulas, J. 1985. *Being as communion.* New York: SVS.

———. 1991. On being a person: Towards an ontology of personhood. In *Persons, divine and human,* ed. C. Gunton and C. Schwobel, 33–46. Edinburgh: Edinburgh University Press.

# 13

# Individual and Collective
# Identities in Russian Orthodoxy

Alexander Agadjanian and Kathy Rousselet

In this chapter we address trends within Russian Orthodoxy from the point of view of the formation of collective and individual identities and their interaction within and around the church. We deal with both discursive and practical domains, and in addition to an analysis of theological debates we draw also upon fieldwork, particularly with regard to worship of the newly canonized Russian royal family.[1]

## RUSSIAN RELIGIOSITY AND IDENTITY FORMATION

Our first key assumption is that social reality cannot be reduced to forms that are either purely "collective" or purely "individual." Religion is practiced and perceived in both collective and individual ways, and these interact and transform each other constantly. It is more appropriate to speak of a hierarchy of identities, from the most personalized and private to the most general and public. In the Soviet Union strong trends of individualism coexisted with the official collectivism (see Kharkhordin 1999). Secondly, the idea of a linear evolutionary process from predominantly collective to predominantly individual forms, a sort of *grand récit* of inescapable individuation, is untenable. Both have always been necessary in the formation and maintenance of the social fabric, and there can be no zero level of individualism (Elias 1987). Thirdly, rhetorical uses of "individualism" and "collectivism" are contingent and must be explained within a particular context. Michael Herzfeld has shown that a dogmatic concept of individualism lies at the core of the modern "western ethos," though in fact the notion of the individual is understood in various ways, even within Europe (Herzfeld 2002). In Russian Orthodoxy we find a spectrum of individual identities shaped both by Eastern

Christian traditions and by the impact of postsocialist disintegration and of the privatization and globalization of religiosity typical of the Western, late modern religious landscape (Beckford 2003; Hervieu-Léger 1999). These diverse factors give "individualism" and "religious community" diverse meanings.

Since the collapse of socialism the Russian Orthodox Church (ROC) has accomplished an impressive renewal of its hierarchy, which is no longer account-able to the state apparatus. The church has regained a huge amount of real estate, old and renovated buildings, monastic and educational institutions, and is again a prominent and quasi-official (in spite of the constitutional principle of secular-ity) component of the symbology of the state. The reconstruction of an imagined community of Russian Orthodoxy has been supported by a mass-media narrative of "revival," which evokes a uniform collective body with a strong group identity tightly linked to national ideals and goals. However, behind the state-run, tele-vised ceremonies and meticulously restored buildings is a church that has under-gone a real deregulation, which is characterized by thriving localism, small-group loyalties, and individually focused beliefs and practices. The discrepancy between the official "monolithic" image and anthropological reality, which is by no means new, is reproducing stereotypes and controversies over the very definition of the *true* Eastern Christian, or Russian Orthodox, tradition. What is *the church?* What are the criteria of "churchliness" (*votserkovlennost'* in Russian)?[2] Elsewhere we have characterized these controversies as "the competition for authenticity" within the tradition (Agadjanian and Rousselet 2006). With respect to the subject of this chapter, multiple questions have risen among the believers over the authentic forms of individual, family, or small group ritual and social involvement, and indeed over the proper form of the church as a collectivity. In the spontaneous creativity of everyday life, individuals adapt social norms, and one observes a behavioral bricolage (de Certeau 1994: 360 passim), "an endless series of negotia-tions among actors about the assignment of meaning to the acts which they jointly participate in" (Turner 1985: 154). But behind the negotiation of meaning by individuals lie conflicts of authority: how much authority is vested in the church "as a whole," in its hierarchy, in a particular priest, a spiritual father, a *starets* (elder), a nonpriestly popular "tradition-keeper," a group of pilgrims, a family, or a particular individual?

To approach this diversity we need to keep in mind three cultural layers of the Russian religious landscape, each with its own discourse about religion. The first, the postsocialist period, gave birth to a reinvented and essentialized "Orthodox Russia," which was perceived as "closing the parentheses of atheism." At the same time we can witness some new trends toward a more selective, more individualized religiosity that have been shaped at least in part by Russia's transition to a market economy and its opening up to more pluralist, global influences.

The second layer is the Soviet period, which began with a severe disruption of institutional continuity. Religious traditions could mostly be transmitted informally, and, though conditions eased in later decades, the ROC remained under governmental control, and in a sense real religious authority stayed outside the formal structures. The institutional atrophy of the ROC was partly compensated by a strongly anti-Soviet and otherworldly "catacomb" Orthodoxy, opposed to both the atheistic state and the "succumbed hierarchy." At the same time informal rural and urban networks of popular religiosity emerged around old women or elders, as well as around priests and intellectuals, extra-ecclesial sacred objects, and so forth (see Kononenko 2006; Bezrogov 2006; Chepurnaya 2005; Panchenko 2005), and these have left their mark on postsocialist religious identities.

Finally, many forms of group and individual religiosity can be explained only with reference to a third layer, the *longue durée* of (Russian) Eastern Orthodox tradition. Since the early 1990s, historians of Russia have criticized the scholarly perpetuation of a fixed image of what religion meant in pre-Soviet Russia: "rigid, hierarchical structure; superficial conception of doctrine; and static, repetitive ritualism" (Kivelson and Greene 2003: 4; see also Shevzov 2003, 2004). Instead, they have shown a diversity of collective and individual forms of worship and socialization both within and outside parish structure. This diversity of "lived religion" is taking similar forms at the beginning of the twenty-first century. Among these, we can refer to a relative looseness of ecclesiastic authority, the vibrancy of small devotional groups, the significance of informal networks across and beyond the formal lines of the church hierarchy, the vague boundaries of the notion of "churchliness" and of the status of being "churched" (*votserkovlennyi*), and a large latitude in the criteria for determining the orthodoxy of norms and rules. In spite of the ruptures of the twentieth century there has been considerable continuity in patterns of institutional structure and forms of identity formation across all three of these cultural layers. To understand this complexity is a methodological challenge, but no analysis of trends can afford to overlook the legacy of the past.

## PERSON AND GROUP IN RUSSIAN
## ORTHODOX DISCOURSE

The tension between collective and individual religiosity in Russian Orthodoxy, first prominently raised in the middle of the nineteenth century by the Slavophiles, has reappeared in totally new forms. One striking example is the debate around the concept and practice of human rights. This new debate was initiated by the hierarchy of the ROC with the aim of finding an alternative to the "Western human rights" ideology. Over many years this debate acquired a wider scope and depth, touching upon the most profound discourses and meanings of religious and cultural tradition.[3] Much of the discussion has focused on the notion of the person and personhood, in opposition to the modern liberal concept of the individual.

The Orthodox critique of the ideology of human rights alleges that to concentrate on the individual is to ignore the community, which is the bearer of common values and traditions. Therefore, if we are to talk about rights at all, group rights must be superior to individual rights. Secondly, for the Orthodox, when the individual's rights, freedom, and self-realization are considered the highest value, there is a danger of total anomie, a *bellum omnium contra omnes*. This is typically illustrated with a caricature of "wild (rugged) individualism" as the dominant ethos of Western societies. Thirdly, as Western individuals are autonomous entities, they tend to be free from foundational meanings and norms, moral and divine; they are simply "mechanical atoms" whose freedom is only limited by the freedom of others. Fourthly and finally, it follows that although the human being is indeed central to the entire Christian tradition, he/she is not an individual (*individuum*), who is "the measure of all things," but a person (*lichnost'*), possessing personhood (same Russian word), whose dignity is not given as "natural and inalienable," but bestowed by God through creation after His image and His likeness, as an ontological possibility, a potential, that may be fully realized only through communion with God. The polysemic English word *communion* has a whole cluster of meanings here. The Eucharistic communion with God (*prichastie*) implies, in the Orthodox discourse, communion in both the ecclesiastical and a wider social sense: "being a part of" (*prichastnost'*) a group or a larger collectivity; the feeling of universal togetherness and catholicity (the word *sobornost'* covers both). Such are the ways through which the individual, as a person, is included in a larger whole, and which define, ultimately, the prescribed forms of religious identities that interest us.

This recent Russian debate confirms individualism as one of the main sins (or blessings) associated with Western modernity. The themes are strikingly reminiscent of earlier anti-Western reactions in other cultures (Muslim, Hindu, Chinese, etc.), but also of critical streams within Western discourse ranging from Marxism to postmodernism and highlighted in the sociological dichotomy between individualist and holistic societies. The issue of individual versus corporate religiosity and the task of how to provide a religious legitimation for liberal modernity have been widely addressed in modern Christian theology. We find a very profound rethinking of the individual in the works of such Catholic thinkers as Jacques Maritain (1882–1973) and John Courtney Murray (1904–1967). As a result, the notion of the individual person, bestowed with human dignity, has become a key notion since the Second Vatican Council.

The Eastern Orthodox tradition, for many reasons that are beyond the scope of this chapter (see Buss 1995; Kharkhordin 1999), either remained aloof from these debates or straightforwardly opposed them. Nikolai Berdyaev (1874–1948) (who influenced Maritain and Emmanuel Mounier) was one of the few exceptions in the emphasis he placed on individual freedom, as a direct link with the promised Kingdom of God, and in rejecting the eschatological significance of any collectivity (Berdyaev [1949] 1990: passim). Other Orthodox theologians sensitive to this personalistic shift included George Florovsky (1893–1979), who tried to formulate "catholicity" (*sobornost'*) as "concrete oneness," Olivier Clement (1921–2009), Vladimir Lossky (1903–1959), and Florovsky's leading disciple, John Zizioulas (b. 1931).

These men are exceptions. The mainstream Orthodox tradition followed a different line. Both Orthodox and Catholic theologians considered the person to be a realization of the divine potential. Yet the Catholic personalists emphasized the person as a concrete individual human being, placing this being above social, communal forms and expressions of humanness. This emphasis was much weaker in Orthodoxy. Alexei Khomiakov (1804–1860) had a strong impact through advancing the idea of collective salvation: "We know that if any of us falls, he falls alone; but no one is saved alone. He is saved in the church, as a member of it, in union with all other members" (Khomiakov 1994: 19). It would be an exaggeration to claim that this radical soteriology of mystical collectivism was shared by the mainstream in the twentieth century. However, in clerical and lay perceptions, communion in a broad sense is indeed the main soteriological strategy; "people-organism" ideas are common, and individual differentiation and competition are undesirable (Chaplin 2005, 2007; Anastasios [Yannoulatos] 2003: 25ff.).

This can be seen very clearly in the official document "The Bases of the Social Concept of the Russian Orthodox Church," which was adopted by the ROC in 2000. This document addressed all kinds of social, moral, political, and publicly relevant issues for the first time in church history (Osnovy 2001). Reference was made for the first time to the "uniqueness of the person" (*unikal'nost' lichnosti*) and the "dignity of the person" (*dostoinstvo lichnosti*), but the document was nonetheless quite clear in criticizing secular individualism and emphasizing the social, communitarian dimension of the church's mission (Agadjanian 2003; Agadjanian and Rousselet 2005). As in the debate over human rights that we mentioned earlier, the individual is hardly articulated as a locus of morality or soteriology, and at times emphatically refuted.[4]

## WORSHIPPING THE ROYAL FAMILY

In this section we set aside the theological debates and explore a striking example of contemporary religiosity—ceremonies commemorating the martyr death of the last Russian tsar, Nicholas II, and his family. The tsar, his wife, their five children, three servants, and a family doctor were murdered by the Bolsheviks in

Ekaterinburg on the night of 16–17 July 1918. Twenty-four hours later in a suburb of Alapaevsk, the grand duchess Elizaveta Fedorovna, her servant Varvara, and the grand duke Sergei Mikhailovich and his personal secretary, as well as four princes of the Romanov dynasty, were also executed.[5] Whereas Elizaveta Fedorovna and Varvara were in 1992 among the first "new martyrs" (*novomuchenniki*) to be canonized by the Russian Orthodox Church, Nicholas II and the members of his family were canonized as passion-bearers (*strastoterpsy*) only at the Jubilee Bishops' Council on 19 August 2000, on the feast of Transfiguration, after very long debates. Since that time, commemorative services have been held annually in Ekaterinburg, attracting thousands of local believers and pilgrims. The majority come from the region of the Urals, but many make their way from Moscow and St. Petersburg, from Ukraine and Kazakhstan. They attend the main night liturgy in the Church on Spilled Blood (Khram na Krovi) in Ekaterinburg, which was built in 2003 on the site of the actual murder (the original building, the Ipatiev house, was destroyed in 1977 when Boris Yeltsin, the future president of Russia, was first secretary of the regional party unit).

Many pilgrims then participate early in the morning in the twenty-kilometer procession from the church to the Ganina Iama (pit), where the corpses, according to the church's official interpretation (contested by other sources), were thrown and then burnt.[6] On the following day some of these pilgrims head to Alapaevsk. The list of religious practices asserting the sense of the "we," the collectivity, is overwhelming in these celebrations, in the surrounding discourses as well as in the forms of worship. However, all these discourses and forms are expressed through interpersonal relations, through groups of friends, and through strong ties between a believer and his/her spiritual father (cf. Mitrokhin 2006). Many participants are skeptical and even suspicious toward the ROC or particular priests. Is it not unusual to hear statements such as "There is nobody to confess to." "We love God, not the priests." "They build churches with dirty money." Other believers, whom we might call religious virtuosi, gather in small groups that are real nodes of social life, centered around priests whom they trust and whom they blindly obey. These people need to get a benediction (*blagoslovenie*) before doing anything (see also Sergazina 2006), and in their narratives they attribute their problems and grief to their failure to obey the *starets* (an elder, spiritual father).

The narratives and practices recognized and approved by the church are constantly combined with the individual stories and acts of particular believers. Initially, the worship of the imperial family as it is now observed in Ekaterinburg was very much a creation of the ecclesiastical institutions. Belief in the holiness of the imperial family came to permeate Russian Orthodox narratives, both written and oral, by the end of the 1990s. However, we should not forget the rather chaotic and fragmentary presence of stories about the saint-tsar and various forms of his popular sacralization that circulated in Soviet times. Many pilgrims in

2006–2007 related how their grandmothers, mothers, or aunts had discovered the real significance of Nicholas II long before he was officially canonized. One informant, whose conversion in the 1980s was prompted by the illness of her son, discovered the tsar in the 1990s thanks to the songs of Janna Bichevskaia, a singer of Russian folk songs and ballads, and to conversations with a priest and a member of her parish. This parishioner had been introduced to this knowledge about the tsar by his history professor in Soviet times, who had shown his students the place where the murder was committed.

The tsar is represented in multiple ways: for example, some laypeople and even some priests present him as the redeemer of sins (Tsar-iskupitel'), although this is considered heretical by the church hierarchy (cf. Knorre 2006). Dogmatically there can be only one Redeemer, but when knowledge of national history is unsteady the church canons, too, may be easily ignored. As a result, various memory transmitters contribute to a multiplication of narratives and interpretations of the imperial family, which intertwine with and occasionally contradict the official discourses of both the state and the ROC. The same diversity can be found in the forms of worship and the liturgical practices around the new imperial saints: while some are set up as canonical by the ROC, others appear in an informal way. Thus one of our informants, a priest from Ekaterinburg region, who is a former dissident, a longtime admirer of Nicholas II, and a convinced monarchist, gathers around himself followers from the entire region, who observe the imperial family according to a set of rituals that the priest himself partly invented.[7] This group also worships Grigori Rasputin, who has never been canonized by the church. Some pilgrims introduce symbolic gestures common to veneration of the saints, such as placing candles and flowers by the hole where the body of Saint Elizaveta Fedorovna was thrown or taking a handful of soil from this holy place.

Many of those who come to the liturgy on 16 July can be considered "tourists" rather than virtuosi believers, for their main motivation is to see (see Kormina, this volume). We need, however, to take a careful look at the criteria used to distinguish "tourists" from "believers." A woman who worked at the monastery described the visitors to the Ganina Iama as follows: "People discover the tsar for themselves for the first time here. Sometimes they cry. The Lord gives everybody a measure of grace to bear, especially when one comes for the first time. . . . Some see the churches . . . some see nature . . . some would stand before the cross and find something there . . . some would go to a service and pray. . . . There are some who don't even speak Russian, [yet] they attend the service and pray . . . everybody in his own way."[8] Another woman who described herself as "not very observant," explained that she did not go to the Church on Spilled Blood, as she believed this church to be a place for officials and the nonreligious (svetskie), but she went eagerly to Alapaevsk, where her mother lived. The place where Grand Duchess Elizaveta Fedorovna was assassinated was for her a namolennoe mesto, "a place imbued with prayers," where thousands of people had prayed before her and where prayer had proved itself efficient thanks to this very intensity (see Kormina, this volume).

Of course we need to be careful not to exaggerate this individual freedom of practice. Prayer itself is never solely an individual gesture related to purely personal needs; it is inscribed into a collective ritual process (Mauss 1909). All acts performed and words uttered draw on various traditions, more or less revived or invented, and more or less recognized by the church as authentic. The range of practices that can be blessed or suggested by a priest, a spiritual father, or some other person is very great. These now include practices dictated by the new economic context of a market economy, to which the ROC has been obliged to adapt itself. In July 2007, at the entrance to the monastery at Ganina Iama the visitor had many opportunities not only to buy a bottle of water or a cake but also to order prayers. One could choose between various forms of prayer, according to what one needed and could afford. Discounts were granted for multiple prayers. Many ordered prayers for relatives and friends unable to attend. Pilgrims crowded around priests who held icons brought from their remote parishes and who offered holy myrrh, which is thought to work miracles. The poor are well served by this market, for they can reach the holy places without having to spend too much money thanks to various facilities and transportation offered by the ROC. While medical care has become expensive and almost out of reach of the very poor, pilgrimage provides an alternative means of healing and ultimately salvation.[9]

### From Defending the Fatherland to Personal Salvation

The worship of Tsar Nicholas II as a saint could be seen by a superficial observer as an entirely political action, evidence of a believer's monarchical agenda. However, political discourse is not emphasized by the believers themselves. Even monarchists tend to argue that Russia is not yet ready for this "true" political system, and that people need first to prepare themselves spiritually.[10] Certainly, the tsar and the whole royal family attract all kinds of "patriots" (patrioty) who eagerly engage in a discourse of nationalist revival and hold that Russia has been corrupted since the early 1990s by the United States and the ideology of liberalism. For example, the Cossacks are very prominent at the Tsar's Days in Ekaterinburg, and they are keenly involved in a reinvigoration of Russian ethnic traditions, folklore in particular.

Tsar Nicholas was canonized as strastoterpets (passion-bearer) not because of his skill in managing the affairs of the state, but rather for his fidelity to his religion and country until his exemplary death. The narratives present him as a sovereign who was close to his subjects, but misunderstood by the elites. The last Russian tsar is cast as the protector of a nation in danger; the message is that, as a sovereign anointed by God, he can again intercede for a country that has been thrown into moral and spiritual crisis. In July 2007, in a small museum in Ganina Iama bearing the tsar's name, there was a section called "A Chain of Time" (Sviaz vremen) that featured pictures symbolizing the greatest patriots and patriotic milestones of Russian history: Alexander Nevsky, the Battle of Kulikovo, Borodino, Marshal Zhukov, and the parade in Red Square on 7 November 1941. This exhibition, portraying threats to the "Fatherland" and how they were overcome, derived from the collection of a local military enterprise that was closed after the collapse of the Soviet Union. Some of its objects were transferred to Ganina Iama by the curator in charge of the museum there. The exhibition was considered by many visitors to be the central element of the museum, but its future was uncertain. The local ecclesiastic authorities were concerned that although the spirit of patriotism could be a vehicle of religious feeling, there was a danger that too much of this spirit suppressed true religion.

The image of the tsar is seen as uniting all Russians. The resulting community exists beyond the borders of the state, especially after the reunion of the Russian Orthodox Church with the Russian Orthodox Church Outside Russia in spring 2007. The latter was in fact the first to canonize the tsar, in 1981. According to Nina Schmit, "This transnational religious community has been formed as a result of exchanges of goods, ideas, and religious attitudes and practices. These reflect a particular social reality in a milieu that hopes ultimately to return not so much to the geographical territory occupied by the nation-state of Russia, but to a mode of religious consciousness known as 'Holy Russia'" (2005: 222). The veneration of the royal family means, above all, the restoration of a way of life permeated with religious values. Nicholas II and his family also became local saints in the region of Ekaterinburg, like Saint Ksenia in St. Petersburg and Saint Matrona in Moscow. The Tsar's Days foster a form of local patriotism throughout the region of the Urals.

To this "patriotic religion," referring both to Russia as a whole and to the region of the Urals ("great and small Fatherlands") we can add another form of collective identity, based on Christian ethical standards and a moral ethos. Again the individual defines him- or herself through a relationship to a collectivity. The royal family becomes a paragon, the exemplar of a perfect family: in the words of one informant, "The tsar's family is love" (*tsarskaia sem'ia eto liubov'*). In the words of a priest, it is "an image of family, love, humility, and gentleness." Children of this family were remarkably well educated, and, most importantly, they were brought up in great humility regardless of their circumstances. The family is the primary link in patriotic discourse, and the education and upbringing of children figure as a priority in pilgrims' narratives.[11] This clearly reflects the legacy of the Soviet ethical code, and it is no accident that many old Soviet films can be found at the Orthodox fair of Ekaterinburg, available for purchase from booths set up by devout Christians and admirers of the tsar. Behind the patriotic exaltation, thoughts about personal salvation in an unstable context where believers are in search of themselves, and of certainty, can also be discerned. The worship of the saint tsar can provide a vehicle for both collective and individual aspirations to salvation. The following narrative of a young religious virtuoso is especially revealing in this sense:

> This man, sorry for putting it like this, the sovereign emperor Nicholas II, he was indeed not an ordinary man. He is alive, he helps you as a man and as a sovereign, as an intercessor. . . it is just this prayer of the tsar that enlightens human souls, so that they can notice him, his help, and, overall, his presence in our life. He is real, a tsar over Russia. He is invisible. And the one who prays has him above oneself, on oneself.[12]

In spite of the impact of Soviet propaganda, the royal family is venerated regardless of its actual historical role. It is common to assert a personal, individual relationship with the tsar and his family. A young woman, thirty-three years old, told of how distant she had felt toward the royal family in the past, and how difficult it had been for her to accept the worship of its members after they were canonized. Eventually an icon of the new saints had been, as she put it, imposed on her; and then she continued: "And always when the saints are repulsed, then [you are attracted] so strongly to them and [you feel] such love, simply understanding your mistake, your error." For this woman, the tsar was somebody who knew how to forgive:

> The tsar, he forgave everybody, so this is not unimportant. . . . For me, this is so simply human. And now, as we have just followed the procession of the cross, I understood many things, that the tsar and his entire family are the passion-bearers [*strastoterptsy*]. . . . They bore passions, and our task is to make peace with each other, and also to bear each other's passions.[13]

This narrative resonates with the official, clerical narrative, but in 2006 this woman walked from St. Petersburg to Ganina Iama for very personal reasons: "I had two daughters who died during delivery. I prayed to the new royal martyrs. This was connected. While praying, only they had an answer to relieve my pain. They are my protectors. They hear my prayer."

### From Collective Responsibility to Personal Repentance

Whether official declarations or personal revelations, forms of repentance give exceptional insight into religious identities. One of the most important collective religious practices during the Tsar's Days is penance (*pokaianie*) for all the sins of the Bolsheviks, the cause of Russia's great crisis. Starting in 1993, and then more intensively after 1998, Patriarch Alexii II called upon the entire Russian people to repent.[14] In Ekaterinburg the all-night vigil (*vsenoshchnoe bdenie*) and the Way of the Cross on 16–17 July are believed to be helpful in purifying the nation. In summer 2007, Cossack leaders were very active in promoting this movement of repentance:

> Godlessness led Russia to Revolution, to the murder of the Tsar as the One Anointed by God, and all his family, to the fratricidal Civil War, to Big Terror [*repressiam*], to the foundation of the Soviet State. . . . There is no future without God! Only with God will Russia revive!
>
> Realization of this axiom leads us inevitably to understanding the tragedy of the twentieth century as our personal tragedy, and this means, in turn, that each of us understands a personal responsibility for Russia's today and tomorrow. . . . Realization of a personal participation in the history of your nation and of your kind [*tvoego naroda i tvoego roda*] can lead to understanding the unity of your nation, your kind, your fatherland [*tvoego naroda, roda, rodiny*], and the responsibility for them. Descendants in the third and fourth generations are responsible for sins of the ancestors. . . . It is your personal repentance before God and before your kind [*tvoim rodom*], before God for your kind, before God for the Tsar, before God and the Royal Passion-Bearer, that is the only way to revive Russia.[15]

This declaration insists on a collective responsibility of the Russian people for the "tragedy of the twentieth century," but at the same time it stresses the importance of personal acts in the pursuit of collective salvation. Russia would not revive without everybody's personal repentance. This idea is not accepted by everybody and annoys some. "Why should we repent for acts that we never committed?" exclaimed one believer participating in a debate on this precise subject organized during the Tsar's Days in 2006.

The call for national repentance is expressed in a significantly different way in the documents of openly monarchical religious groups such as *Za sobornoe pokaianie* (For Universal Repentance). They define the nation's tragedy with reference to the oath of 1613.[16] They prioritize a repentance on the part of the nation [*narod*] as a whole, which needs to perform what they call the "ritual of a universal repentance" (*chin vsenarodnogo sobornogo pokaiania*). The term *sobornyi*, "universal," used here, resonates with the theological concepts we referred to earlier:

> No matter how much we repent personally, we have no power to free ourselves from the oath taken by the Russian people in 1613. There is a curse lying on every Russian because of the violation of this universal oath [*sobornoi kliatvy*], and this curse can only be removed through a universal repentance.[17]

Aside from these acts of repentance for the salvation of Russia, many other forms of contrition can be found among the pilgrims, generally determined by some aspects of social identity. In some cases, for example, repentance assumes a local flavor: the assassination of the royal family is considered by some residents of

Ekaterinburg as their sin, a stigma of disgrace (*kleimo*) that they felt in Soviet times and continue to bear. One woman in her forties said:

> We felt a real shame. First, in a purely atheistic way. . . . "Ah, you are from Sverdlovsk [Soviet name for Ekaterinburg]! From out there where the tsar was murdered!" . . . Then you start to understand that he was not only the tsar but an anointed, and so your pain becomes even stronger. . . . When the construction of the church started, this was a great purity process.[18]

Another woman, baptized in childhood, had been practicing her faith without being specifically devout in worshipping the royal family. However, she said that the family of the tsar was "what brings us together in Ekaterinburg; it is our sad local point of interest." The act of contrition can also help to expiate an ancestral guilt. A young girl told a story about her father, who had been a member of the team that had demolished the Ipatiev house, where the tsar was murdered. This guilt had provoked the disease of her father and her grandmother; her mother had therefore called all surviving members of the family to repent and purify themselves.

## CONCLUSION

The example of the canonized monarchical family shows how religious feelings and behavior combine in a variety of patterns, both collective and individual. These practices generate a sense of community and use a community as a reference point, whether it is an "imagined community" of the Russian nation, a politically bound religious movement (monarchist, patriotic, etc.), a group surrounding a spiritual father, or a family.

Yet individual bricolage is also omnipresent. Processes of individuation have been documented in numerous other studies. The veneration of icons has always had individual healing as a major objective, and new patterns of devotion are being developed to utilize the power of icons for individual success in private and professional affairs of various kinds: student exams, careers, and conflicts at the workplace (Chistiakov 2006). Worship of the relics of Saint Ksenia, who lived in eighteenth-century St. Petersburg, is organized collectively by pilgrims, yet their participation is highly individualized, and they seek grace to support particular personal needs (Filicheva 2006). The same trend is manifested at the "Orthodox fairs" that have become a common feature of the religious landscape in post-Soviet Russia. Inna Naletova (2006) views these fairs as places where the sacred is "thrown" from the church into the world; at the same time the fairs foster the commercialization of church activities. Products such as honey and decorations are sold alongside prayers for the dead and prayers for health. Each fair is a venue for free experiments with "lived religion": parishes, monasteries, and brother-hoods use them to promote new local saints and new kinds of prayers. They attract visitors with extremely diverse individual motivations and demands: most are believers, but some are simply curious and keen to acquire goods that have been touched with "blessing."[19]

Although, as we have seen, no strong notion of the individual entered the mainstream of Russian Orthodoxy discourse, nonetheless the individuation of faith was well rooted in tsarist times and continued throughout the Soviet period along with growing localism and because of the destruction of institutions. The individuation characteristic of the postsocialist setting, despite the institutional revival of the ROC, is a legacy of these earlier cultural layers. It applies to both "religious specialists" and ordinary believers, and it differs from the patterns of religious "privatization" found in the secularized societies of Western Europe. The worship of the Russian royal family shows a more traditional type of interaction between collective and individual religiosity, and the introduction of new com-mercial elements has not led to dramatic changes. Individuation in the Russian case can be construed as a common "vector," ever present *within* the tradition, rather than something radically new.

It might be argued that a new type of individuation is developing in the guise of pilgrim-tourists. Boris Dubin (2006) speaks of the "weakness of imagined com-munities" in Russia, and of the multiplicity of individual religious motivations, which he equates with eclecticism and frivolity in faith, a "light burden," as he calls it (see also Kormina, this volume). The same data can be interpreted as proof of an ongoing individuation, especially characteristic of people who possess what we might call a thin religiosity. Eclecticism and hybridity exemplify this new pattern. Indeed, values and role models have been in flux since the end of the 1980s. The former Soviet lands have experienced a mass-media revolution, and these media (rather than memory, books, sermons, or experience) have become the main source of religious knowledge. Dubin suggests that for young people who are not very religious, Orthodoxy may be merely a part of a new trendy lifestyle. The impact of mass media is also strong among the enthusiasts discussed above, including those who link religiosity with patriotism. However, this community-oriented group is very different from those for whom Orthodoxy is a "light burden." In the worship of the royal family we witness quite the opposite: a clear desire for a strong community. Therefore, when speaking of individualism in today's Russian Orthodoxy we need to distinguish between at least two different types. The first pertains to virtuosi religiosity, or what we can also call a *thick* religious tradition, in which individual expression is tightly linked to collective identities centered around smaller or larger groups, and eventually, the "nation." The second refers to the *thin* religiosity of people who seem to be much less bound to collectivities. Our data suggest that within contemporary Russian Orthodoxy, as a thick religious tradition, individuality, while always present, does not exceed the limits set by the tradition itself.

## NOTES

Fieldwork conducted by Kathy Rousselet in Ekaterinburg in 2006 and 2007 was financed by the Fondation Nationale des Sciences Politiques, Paris.

1. The authors organized three conferences in Moscow in 2003, 2005, and 2006 on the subject of "religious practices in Russia." Some papers originating from these conferences have been published in French, in a special issue of the *Revue d'Études Comparatives Est-Ouest* 36, no. 4 (2005), and then in Russian, as Agadjanian and Rousselet 2006. The anthropology of post-Soviet religiosity remains weakly developed, but see Rogers 2005 and the collection of papers he introduces; see also Kormina, Panchenko, and Shtyrkov 2006.

2. See the discussion of wider and narrower notions of "churchliness" in Chesnokova 2005.

3. A short *Declaration on Human Rights and Dignity* was approved by the World Russian Congress in April 2006, and a much larger official document on human rights was approved by the Bishops Council in August 2008; see Osnovy 2008.

4. See an analysis of the content and significance of the official document on human rights in Agadjanian 2008.

5. Sergei Mikhailovich, Prince Ioann Konstantinovich, Prince Konstantin Konstantinovich, Prince Igor Konstantinovich, and Prince Vladimir Pavlovich Palei.

6. According to the church's own data, in 2007 about 15,000 people attended the main night liturgy, and about 6,000 participated in the procession.

7. See the liturgy on 18–19 July, the Day of Commemoration of the Holocaust Offering of the remains of the martyred St. Royal Family (Den' pamiati vsesozhzheniia ostankov muchenicheski ubieniia Sv. Tsarskoi Sem'i). In 2006 about thirty persons attended, a high proportion of them young.

8. "Liudi zdes' otkryvaiut dlia sebia Tsaria vpervye. Plachut inogda. Gospod' daet blagodat' kazh-domu v tu meru, kotoruiu on mozhet nesti, osobenno kogda v pervyi raz priezzhaet. . . . Kto-to vidit khramy . . . Kto-to vidit prirodu . . . Kto-to postoit u Kresta i chto-to naidet u nego . . . kto-to na sluzhbe pobyvaet, pomolitsia. . . . Byvaiut liudi, kotorye dazhe russkii iazyk ne znaiut, na sluzhbe stoiat, moliatsia . . . Kazhdyi po-svoemu."

9. Though in an informal way, Orthodox prayers were already largely used for healing in the Soviet period. See their use by the "healers" (Lindquist 2006).

10. Most of the responses to a question probing political views can be summarized in three affir-mations: "All powers come from God"; "We have a power that we deserve"; and "Vladimir Putin is not the worse solution." The following reflections can be also heard: "For Russia to have a tsar over it, it is first necessary that people would want to have him, would seek it, that people would feel how bad they are without the tsar. . . . For the power of the tsar is like a symbolic power of God when people understand that there is no power higher than God."

11. Anna, headmistress of a local Orthodox school, said that in her classes she invited her students to look for solutions to problems of family life in the personal diaries of the tsarina Alexandra Fedorovna. She entrusted her own children to the intercession of the royal family during the proces-sion of the cross to Ganina Iama. Another informant said: "We pray to the royal family and especially to the *tsarevich* [prince] Alexei to help our children to enter well into life."

12. "Eto chelovek. Prostite, chto ia tak govoriu. Gosudar' Imperator Nikolai Vtoroi. On byl deistvitel'no ne prosto chelovek, on zhiv, on kak chelovek tebe pomogaet, i kak gosudar', kak zastupnik

. . . Imenno molitva Tsaria, kotoraia prosveshchaet dushi chelovecheskie dlia togo, chtoby oni ego zametili, ego pomoshch' i voobshche ego prisutstvie v nashei zhizni, chto on est' na samom dele. Nad Rossiei est' Tsar'. On nezrimyi. I tot, kto molitsia, tot ego imeet nad soboi, na sebia imeet."

13. "Tsar' on vsekh prostil, to est' eto tozhe nemalovazhno. . . . Dlia menia chisto chelovecheski. I seichas, kogda proshli krestnym khodom, ia poniala mnogo chto. Tsar' i vsia Tsarskaia sem'ia oni strastoterpsy. . . . Oni priterpeli strasti i nasha zadacha byla mirit'sia drug s drugom, tozhe proterpet' strasti drug druga."

14. "The murder of the Royal Family is a heavy burden upon popular conscience that reminds us that many of our ancestors are guilty of this sin, either through direct complicity, approval, or toleration. Repentance for this sin must become a sign of people's unity, which is to be reached not through limitless compromises but through a thoughtful understanding of what has happened with the country and the nation. Only then will it be a unity by spirit, not by form. . . . We call for repentance by the entire nation, all its sons and daughters. Let our memory of the crime committed push us to performing today a universal repentance for this sin of apostasy and regicide [*tsareubiistvo*], followed by fasting and abstinence so that the Lord hears our prayers and blesses our fatherland with peace and prosperity." Message by Patriarch Alexii II, 9 July 1998.

15. *O pokaíanii* (On repentance), an official declaration of the Cossacks (Orenburgskoe kazach'e voisko) on 15 July 2007.

16. The oath of the Zemsky Sobor (Land Council) for "fidelity to the Romanov dynasty until the end of times" was taken at the coronation of the first Romanov.

17. From the leaflet "Za sobornoe pokaianie," which was distributed during the procession to Ganina Iama in 2006.

18. "Styd byl. Snachala chisto ateisticheskii styd . . . 'Oi, Sverdlovsk . . . Da znaiu. Tam Tsaria ubili.' . . . A potom ponimaesh', chto eto ne tol'ko Tsar', a Pomazannik Bozhii. I bol' eshche tiazhelee. . . . Kogda stal stroit'sia khram, eto bylo bol'shim ochistitel'nym protsessom."

19. A trend toward individuation has also been noted for Greece; see Kokosalakis 1996: 146; Hirschon, this volume.

## REFERENCES

Agadjanian, A. 2003. Breakthrough to modernity, apologia for traditionalism: The Russian Orthodox view of society and culture in comparative perspective. *Religion, State and Society* 4: 327–46.

———. 2006. The search for privacy and the return of a grand narrative: Religion in a post-Communist society. *Social Compass* 53: 169–84.

———. 2008. Russian Orthodox vision of human rights: Recent documents and their significance. *Erfurter Vorträge zur Kulturgeschichte des Orthodoxen Christentums* 7. Erfurt.

Agadjanian, A., and K. Rousselet. 2005. Globalization and identity discourse In Russian Orthodoxy. In *Eastern Orthodoxy in a global age: Tradition faces the twenty-first century,* ed. V. Roudometof, A. Agadjanian, and J. Pankhurst, 29–57. Walnut Creek, Calif.: AltaMira Press.

———, eds. 2006. *Religioznye praktiki v sovremennoi Rossii* [Religious practices in today's Russia]. Moscow: Novoe Izdatel'stvo.

Anastasios (Yannoulatos), Archbishop. 2003. *Facing the world: Orthodox Christian essays on global concerns.* Crestwood, N.Y.: SVS.

Beckford, J. 2003. *Social theory and religion.* Cambridge: Cambridge University Press.

Berdyaev, N. [1949] 1990. *Samopoznanie* [Self-knowledge]. Moscow: Mezhdunarodnye otnosheniia. Published in English as *Dream and reality: An essay in autobiography.*

Bezrogov, V. 2006. Vlast' diskursa i religiia v vospominaniiakh o detstve [The power of discourse and religion in the memoirs of childhood]. In *Religioznye praktiki v sovremennoi Rossii* [Religious practices in today's Russia], ed. A. Agadjanian and K. Rousselet, 89–105. Moscow: Novoe Izdatel'stvo.

Buss, A. 1995. The individual in the Eastern Orthodox tradition. *Archives de sciences sociales des religions* 91: 41–65.

Chaplin, V. 2005. Pravoslavie i obshchestvennyi ideal segodnia [Orthodoxy and the ideal society today]. In *Predely svetskosti* [The limits of secularity], ed. A. Verkhovsky, 162–69. Moscow: Informatsionno-analiticheskii tsentr "Sova."

———. 2007. Russkaia pravoslavnaia tserkov', prava cheloveka i diskussii ob obshchestvennom ustroistve [The Russian Orthodox Church, human rights, and the discussions about social system]. *Interfax,* http://www.interfax-religion.ru (accessed 16 October 2007).

Chepurnaya, O. 2005. Nezavisimye religioznye ob"edineniia v Leningrade v 1960–1980-kh gg: Sotsial'no-kul'turnyi analiz [Independent religious associations in Leningrad in 1960s-1980s: A sociocultural analysis]. PhD diss., St. Petersburg.

Chesnokova, V. 2005. *Tesnym putem: Protsess votserkovlenia rossiiskogo naseleniia v kontse dvadtsatogo veka* [A narrow gate: The process of inchurchment of the Russian population in late twentieth century]. Moscow: Akademicheskii proekt.

Chistiakov, P. 2006. Pochitanie chudotvornykh ikon v sovremennom pravoslavii: Bronnitskii spisok ierusalimskoi ikony Bogomateri [Veneration of miracle-working icons in today's Orthodoxy: Bronnitsky copy of the icon of Mother of God of Jerusalem]. In *Religious practices in today's Russia,* ed. A. Agadjanian and K. Rousselet, 273–89. Moscow: Novoe Izdatel'stvo.

De Certeau, M. 1990. *L'invention du quotidien.* Vol. 1, *Arts de faire.* Paris: Gallimard.

———. 1994. *L'invention du quotidien.* Vol. 2, *Habiter, cuisiner.* Paris: Gallimard.

Dubin, B. 2006. Legkoe bremia: Massovoe pravoslavie v Rossii 1990–2000 godov [The light burden: Russian Orthodoxy as a mass religion in the 1990s]. In *Religious practices in today's Russia,* ed. A. Agadjanian and K. Rousselet, 69–86. Moscow: Novoe Izdatel'stvo.

Elias, N. 1987. *Die Gesellschaft der Individuen.* Frankfurt am Main: Suhrkamp Verlag.

Filicheva, O. 2006. Narodnoe pravoslavie v gorode i derevne: sviashchennik i ozhidaniia pastby: Religioznye prazdniki v 2001–2004 godakh [Popular Orthodoxy in cities and in villages: The priest and the expectations of the flock: Religious holidays in 2001–2004]. In *Religious practices in today's Russia,* ed. A. Agadjanian and K. Rousselet, 254–72. Moscow: Novoe Izdatel'stvo.

Hervieu-Léger, D. 1999. *Le pélerin et le converti : La religion en mouvement.* Paris: Flammarion.

Herzfeld, M. 2002. The European self: Rethinking an attitude. In *The idea of Europe from antiquity to the European Union,* ed. A. Pagden, 139–70. Cambridge: Cambridge University Press.

Kharkhordin, O. 1999. *The collective and the individual in Russia: A study of practices.* Berkeley: University of California Press.

Khomiakov, A. 1994. Tserkov' odna [The church is one]. In *Sochineniia v dvukh tomakh* [Selected works in two volumes]. Vol. 1. Moscow: Moskovskii filosofskii fond et al.

Kivelson, V., and R. Greene, eds. 2003. *Orthodox Russia: Belief and practice under the tsars.* University Park: Pennsylvania State University Press.

Knorre, B. 2006. Oprichnyi mistitsizm v religioznykh praktikakh tsarebozhnichestva [The mysticism and religious practices of worshippers of divine tsardom]. In *Religious practices in today's Russia,* ed. A. Agadjanian and K. Rousselet, 384–97. Moscow: Novoe Izdatel'stvo.

Kokosalakis, N. 1996. Orthodoxie grecque, modernité et politique. In *Identités religieuses en Europe,* ed. G. Davie and D. Hervieu-Léger, 131–51. Paris: Editions La Découverte.

Kononenko, N. 2006. Folk orthodoxy: Popular religion in contemporary Ukraine. In *Letters from Heaven: Popular religion in Russia and Ukraine,* ed. J. P. Himka and A. Zayarnik, 46–75. Toronto: University of Toronto Press.

Kormina, J., A. Panchenko, and S. Shtyrkov, eds. 2006. *Sny Bogoroditsy: Issledovaniia po antropologii religii* [Dreams of the Mother of God: Research in anthropology of religion]. St. Petersburg: Evropeiskii universitet.

Lindquist, G. 2006. *Conjuring hope: Healing and magic in contemporary Russia.* New York and Oxford: Berghahn Books.

Mauss, M. 1909. *La prière.* Paris: Félix Alcan, Éditeur.

Mitrokhin, N. 2006. Arkhimandrit Naum i "naumovtsy" kak kvintessentsiia sovremennogo starchestva [The Archimandrite Naum and his followers as a quintessential example of the startsy tradition today]. In *Religious practices in today's Russia,* ed. A. Agadjanian and K. Rousselet, 126–48. Moscow: Novoe Izdatel'stvo.

Naletova, I. 2006. Sovremennye pravoslavnye iarmarki kak vyrazhenie pravoslavnoi very vne khrama [New orthodox fairs: An expression of faith outside the church's fence]. In *Religious practices in today's Russia,* ed. A. Agadjanian and K. Rousselet, 178–98. Moscow: Novoe Izdatel'stvo.

Osnovy. 2001. Osnovy sotsial'noi kontseptsii Russkoi pravoslavnoi Tserkvi [Bases of the social concept of the Russian Orthodox Church]. In *Iubileinyi Arkhiereiskii sobor Russkoi Pravoslavnoi Tserkvi, 13–16 avgusta 2000. Materialy* [Proceedings of the Jubilee Bishops Council of the Russian Orthodox Church, 13–16 August 2000], 329–410. Moscow: Izdatel'skii Sovet Moskovskogo Patriarkhata.

————. 2008. Osnovy ucheniia Russkoi pravoslavnoi Tserkvi o dostoinstve, svobode i pravakh cheloveka [The bases of the Russian Orthodox teaching on dignity, freedom, and human rights]. Published at the official site of the Moscow Patriarchate, http://www .mospat.ru/index.php?page=41597 (accessed 14 December 2008).

Panchenko, A. 2005. Ivan et Iakov: Deux saints étranges de la région des marais (Novgorod). *Archives de sciences sociales des religions* 114: 55–79.

Rogers, D. 2005. Introductory essay: The anthropology of religion after socialism. *Religion, State and Society* 33, no. 1: 5–18.

Schmit, N. 2005. A transnational religious community gathers around an icon: The return of the tsar. In *Eastern Orthodoxy in a global age: Tradition faces the twenty-first century,* ed. V. Roudometof, A. Agadjanian, and J. Pankhurst, 210–23. Walnut Creek, Calif.: AltaMira Press.

Sergazina, K. 2006. Dinamika vozrozhdenia russkoi religioznoi kul'tury [The dynamics of the revival of Russian religious culture]. In *Religious practices in today's Russia,* ed. A. Agadjanian and K. Rousselet, 106–25. Moscow: Novoe Izdatel'stvo.

Shevzov, V. 2003. Letting the people into the church: Reflections on Orthodoxy and community in late imperial Russia. In *Orthodox Russia: Belief and practice under the tsars,* ed. V. Kivelson and R. Greene, 59–77. University Park: Pennsylvania State University Press.

———. 2004. *Russian Orthodoxy on the eve of revolution.* Oxford: Oxford University Press.

Turner, V. 1985. *On the edge of the bush: Anthropology as experience.* Tucson: University of Arizona Press.

# 14

# The Russian Orthodox Church, the Provision of Social Welfare, and Changing Ethics of Benevolence

Melissa L. Caldwell

In winter 1998, during my fieldwork with an international Protestant church in Moscow, I accompanied members of the congregation to a prayer meeting held at a local Russian Orthodox church.[1] The visit was part of a religious exchange set up by pastoral staff from the two churches to foster both interfaith and international understanding and dialogue between the two congregations. Whereas the congregation of the Orthodox church was primarily Russian, the composition of the Protestant congregation was primarily foreign. Approximately one-half of the Protestant congregants were North American and Western European expatriates working in Moscow, and one-half were African students and refugees. The pairing of these two churches was not coincidental: both were actively involved in Moscow's social welfare sector through sponsorship of soup kitchens for elderly and disabled pensioners. Their soup kitchens shared the same space in a local restaurant, and, even though the clients of the two programs were different, most knew each other and socialized both inside and outside the soup kitchens. As a result, the partnership that existed between the two churches extended beyond an interfaith connection to encompass charitable and social aspects as well.

Religious charity has become a vibrant field as the post-Soviet Russian state redefines the welfare sector and its role as a welfare provider. One of the consequences of neoliberal economic reforms has been that Russia has actively shed its identity as a welfare state and instead focused its attentions on developing the country's commercial sectors. In practical terms, as the state has redirected its resources to the private, corporate sector, it has retooled its categories of "need" and reduced support for public-assistance projects, effectively abandoning thousands—perhaps millions—of people who had formerly received state-sponsored social assistance to the generosity of private charities. This shift has coincided with a large-scale religious revivalism among Orthodox and other "traditional" Russian religious denominations, as well as among "new," primarily non-Orthodox Christian denominations. Consequently, both Orthodox and non-Orthodox religious groups, such as the two congregations mentioned above, have been visible and indispensable actors in Russia's religious and charitable welfare spheres during the post-Soviet period. Working individually and together across denominational divisions, religious communities and people of faith have sponsored and operated food programs, drug and alcohol rehabilitation centers, clothing drives, homeless shelters, orphanages and other children's programs, educational programs, and more general vocational training classes. Some religious charities work closely with local and state agencies, especially with local welfare offices, to procure lists of recipients and negotiate spaces to provide services, while others exist independently of official structures, often operating their programs informally and in more personalized and small-scale ways.

Yet despite the similarities in the types of projects that religious groups support, and in the clientele they serve, their reception in Russia, and among Russian citizens, has been mixed. In a curious contrast to the Orthodox Church's historical role as a charitable institution and the significant work that Orthodox churches and their followers are currently doing in Russia, the church has generated criticism from Russian citizens. In particular, even as growing numbers of Russians participate in church services and other ritual activities (see Agadjanian and Rousselet, Kormina, and Naletova, this volume) Russians fault the church not only for not doing enough to help the Russian population, but also for being a corrupt institution that focuses on its own needs and interests rather than those of the general population. By contrast, non-Orthodox religious communities, especially foreign groups, are praised for their activities, their commitment to providing support, and their trustworthiness. In the course of my fieldwork in Russia since 1997, the frequency with which casual conversations and formal interviews on more general topics such as welfare and charity turned into criticisms of the church was striking. For instance, when one woman heard that I was researching religious charities, her first response was that the church does nothing to help Russians. Upon clarification that my current work focused primarily on Protestant religious groups, she amended her response and conceded that Protestant churches did provide help, unlike Orthodox churches.[2] The fact that my interlocutors repeatedly complained that Orthodox churches and church officials ignored the needs of the community revealed that this was an especially sensitive topic for many individuals in Russia.

In this chapter I take up the question of why the increasingly public role of the Orthodox Church has been accompanied by public dissatisfaction, and in particular why the church's efforts to serve its followers and other constituents through charitable projects have generated such resounding public criticism. Through a study that compares the types of services provided by Orthodox communities with the perspectives of ordinary Russians, I suggest that the central issue is not one of theological or liturgical differences, but rather a conflict over the nature of religious communities as social institutions and the ethics of compassion and benevolence associated with these communities. Ultimately, the church is an institution that must address multiple, and often conflicting, needs: the needs of its organization, its staff, its parishioners, its welfare recipients, and the larger Russian nation, as well as its spiritual obligations. Not surprisingly, the church is occasionally unable to satisfy all of the needs and interests of its various constituents, and that reality, when situated within a Russian cultural tradition of entitlement, can encourage the perception among Russian citizens that they are competing with each other and with the church for ever-diminishing resources. Nevertheless, these conflicts are not simply about Russian citizens misrecognizing the church's activities. Rather, individual Orthodox clergy and church staff have at times made choices and promoted ethnonational interests that undermine the church's moral authority as a benevolent and universal provider. Within a context in which Orthodoxy is understood as a quintessential cultural element of a shared Russian identity and heritage, and "Russianness" operates simultaneously (and uneasily) as both an inclusive civic-nationalist identity and an exclusive ethnonationalist identity, public dissatisfaction with the church also arises from the unintended consequences of individual church actions that create hierarchies of deservingness and presumed Russianness among citizens.

I shall focus the discussion in this chapter on three points that offer insight into competing visions of Orthodox benevolence in Russia today. The first point concerns who is responsible for providing charity and whether this charity should be automatic or conditional. The second addresses tensions between civic nationalism and religious nationalism as they play out through the politics of Orthodox charity. Finally, I explore the extent to which charitable activities and business enterprises can be mixed. Collectively, these three aspects reflect ongoing preoccupations with the redefinition of individualist and collectivist responsibility in Russia more generally. This chapter derives from a larger project on faith-based charities in Russia.[3] The material discussed in this chapter comes from research that I have been conducting in Moscow since 1997. During summer 2005, I also spent two months in Tver, a city of approximately 250,000 residents located about 150 kilometers from Moscow. The ethnographic evidence includes personal observations from visits to churches and welfare programs; interviews and informal conversations with charity and church staff, welfare recipients, and other Russians; church publications (brochures, Web sites, magazines, and newspapers); local newspapers; and other publications, including political and commercial advertising materials.

When discussing Russian Orthodoxy, it is crucial to avoid generalizing practices that treat all Russian Orthodox churches as identical. There are in fact significant theological and political differences among individual churches and church leaders (see Knox 2003). Nevertheless, my Russian informants have typically not made these distinctions in their comments. Instead, they have consistently talked about "the church" as a single body. Moreover, despite efforts by clergy to educate Russians about Orthodox theology, my informants were neither knowledgeable about nor particularly interested in doctrinal matters. These individuals treated the church as a social institution analogous to a state agency rather than as an entity concerned with spiritual affairs. An intriguing complication emerged over the issue of morality: although most informants viewed Orthodoxy as a moral system for ensuring personal and social justice (see also Zigon 2008), few described individual churches or clergy or the church as moral entities. When it is appropriate in this chapter I will acknowledge distinctions among churches or church programs; at other times, I will present the generalizing perspectives of my informants, who do not always make these distinctions. As the analysis will illustrate, it is precisely these generalizing practices that complicate efforts by individual Orthodox churches to overcome the criticisms raised against the church as a monolithic entity.

## THE ROLE OF RUSSIAN ORTHODOXY IN SOCIAL WELFARE AND BENEVOLENCE WORK

Religious charity work in Russia coevolved with the Orthodox Church's participation in the state's nation-building projects. As Michael Khodarkovsky has documented for the early modern period, the state's efforts to consolidate its power and create "a single political and religious identity under one tsar and one God" included the use of material benefits by Orthodox missionaries to encourage conversions (2001: 117). As early as the fifteenth century, this use of development programs to entice—or in some cases coerce—non-Christians to convert to Orthodoxy was well established in Russia. Working in coordination with Russian government officials, the Orthodox Church offered converts material goods such as woolen clothing, boots, and cash, as well as assurances that personal property would not be confiscated by the government. Non-Christian nobles who converted were given new titles in the Russian nobility system, as well as cash and land (Khodarkovsky 1996, 2001).

By the nineteenth century, the church's welfare projects had shifted direct support for the church and the state to support for the larger community at both local and national levels. Consequently, the status of welfare recipients as officially recognized adherents to the Orthodox faith and members of any particular church became less important than their personal degree of need. Individual churches and church leaders offered practical support through social welfare programs such as poorhouses, work-relief programs, and soup kitchens (Kaiser 1998; Lindenmeyr 1996). These programs coincided with a move within the Russian Orthodox Church to adopt an explicit theological orientation on charity as a form of moral action that could bring about personal salvation (Kenworthy 2008). By reframing benevolence as a simultaneously personal and social necessity, the church cultivated among its followers permissive attitudes toward begging and a "culture of giving" that came to be seen in the popular imagination as a distinctively Russian trait (Lindenmeyr 1996). According to Adele Lindenmeyr, "Orthodox theology lauded personal, face-to-face charitable giving by men and women alike. Unlike Protestant creeds, Orthodoxy considered individual almsgiving to beggars on the street a worthy outlet for one's piety and a valid way to help others" (1993: 563).[4] Nevertheless, despite this campaign to cast charity as a uniquely Orthodox practice, other religious groups, including Baptist, Lutheran, and Jewish congregations, also provided significant forms of charitable assistance (Coleman 2005; Lindenmeyr 1986).

During the Soviet period, the church lost its position in the social welfare sphere when the state issued a decree in 1929 forbidding religious groups from operating charitable programs (White 1993: 788). When the Soviet state assumed control of the provision of social welfare it turned these programs into entitlements for all citizens and channels for ideological indoctrination. It was not until the 1980s that nonstate charities began reemerging in the Soviet Union in response to concerns about an impending "moral crisis" (790). This shift was accompanied by President Gorbachev's program of *glasnost'*, which encouraged the public revival of religious practices in the Soviet Union and the loosening of restrictions on the importation and production of religious materials. Subsequently, the 1990 Law on Freedom of Conscience eliminated the prohibitions against religious groups participating in charity work (Knox 2003; White 1993: 797). The Russian Orthodox Church and many other domestic and foreign religious congregations and NGOs took advantage of these changes and began establishing both congregations and charities. Often working closely with state welfare agencies and private social programs (both religious and secular), Orthodox churches have provided a wide range of public services for poor citizens and noncitizens: food aid, social activities for disadvantaged youths and the elderly, rehabilitation programs for drug addicts, health care and hospice support, sponsorship of children's shelters, prison chapels, and even public meetings that operate like support groups, where people can gather and talk about their problems (see also Mitrokhin 2004: 294–310).

For the Orthodox Church benevolence activities satisfied two needs. First, charitable projects offered a channel for bringing Russians into the church. In a period of economic instability, membership in a congregation with strong social support was a survival strategy for needy Russians (see also Caldwell 2005). Although parlaying charity into an opportunity for church building was not always the explicit aim of Orthodox and other religious denominations, it was a reality for many congregations. Second, charitable activities affirmed Orthodoxy's return to its theological and moral imperative to help others. This call to benevolence was evident not only in the projects sponsored by the patriarchate and individual churches, but also in the church's public role as a concerned critic of Russia's social problems throughout the post-Soviet period. In 2004, according to church spokesman Vsevolod Chaplin (2006), the church was instrumental in getting the World Russian People's Sobor to adopt The Code of Moral Principles and Rules of Economy, a document based on the Ten Commandments that promotes ethical economic behavior. On the local level, individual believers who have taken up social welfare as a necessary element of their personal religious obligations have organized grassroots charities. Miloserdie.ru, an organization that emerged through discussions about volunteer activities among Orthodox youth in an Internet chat group (the group's name is the same name as the Internet site), is one such charitable group.

Yet despite the considerable work being done by Orthodox churches and followers, and despite the fact that the type and scope of their activities are similar to those sponsored by non-Orthodox religious communities, Orthodox programs can be distinguished in three critical respects. First, non-Orthodox congregations typically receive greater amounts of financial and administrative support from their donors and congregants than do their Orthodox counterparts. This has especially been the case for non-Orthodox Christian groups, both Russian and foreign, that enjoy strong ties with religious communities in Western Europe, North America, and Asia. Second, because many foreign Christian churches are operating quasi-legally or even illegally in Russia, they do not typically maintain formal membership rosters. As a result, there is greater flexibility for Russians who want to receive aid but who do not want to make a commitment to attend services or join a specific religious community. Third, non-Orthodox Christian congregations generally tend to approach their charitable activities through a broader ecumenical lens that does not discriminate according to religious belief or identity, ethnic background, or citizenship status, unlike some Orthodox congregations that make faith and membership a requirement for services.[5]

Nevertheless, these factors are insufficient to explain why so many Russian citizens fail to recognize the work of Orthodox congregations and instead criticize the Orthodox Church for being uninterested in social work, and why many individuals who claim Orthodox heritage choose to participate in welfare programs run by Protestant or other non-Christian religious groups. Rather, public criticism of the Orthodox Church's role as a charitable provider is embedded within the paradox of charity itself. I shall argue that the social codes governing the conditions under which charitable aid occurs cannot be met in reality, and hence the Russian Orthodox Church confuses the very ideal of charity in the Russian context.

## COMPETING ETHICS OF CHARITY, BENEVOLENCE, AND ALTRUISM

In post-Soviet Russia, the terms "charity" (*miloserdie, blagotvoritel'nost'*), "social welfare" (*sotsial'naia zashchita,* literally "social defense"), and "social support" (*sotsial'naia podderzhka*) all designate forms of material and social assistance provided through public, private, secular, and religious social services programs.[6] Charity is typically distinguished as a nonstate activity supported by private groups, both religious and secular. Members of foreign religious congregations and foreign nongovernmental organizations working in Russia often talk about their activities not as "charity" but as "social work," "humanitarianism," or "development," thus linking them to larger processes of salvation economics and millennial capitalism (see Bornstein 2003; Comaroff and Comaroff 2001; Gifford 1990).[7]

Ideologically, charity should be disinterested and anonymous. As Marcel Mauss and others have argued, however, gifts are, by their very nature, socializing forces that draw both giver and receiver into intimate and extended relationships of obligation (Mauss 1990; see also Carrier 1990). Echoing Mauss, Mary Douglas cautions that acts of charity do not necessarily foster positive bonds of social intimacy but can be socially destructive: "Charity is meant to be a free gift, a voluntary, unrequited surrender of resources. Though we laud charity as a Christian virtue we know that it wounds. . . . The recipient does not like the giver, however cheerful he be" (1990: vii). There is no such thing as a free gift, and charitable exchanges are always fraught with expectations on the part of both givers and receivers. Charity is also a social exchange that occurs at multiple levels simultaneously: the exchange of material goods and the exchange of beliefs, values, and even sense of self.

Christian doctrine also shapes how giving is conceptualized and enacted. The very idea of the free or pure gift presupposes a particular type of religious worldview, which envisions "the unreciprocated gift" as a means to personal salvation (Parry 1986: 468; see also Cannell 2004: 338 and Coleman 2006: 181). In the models of religious gifting presented by Mauss, Jonathan Parry, Fenella Cannell, and Simon Coleman, the givers themselves have priority, and the identity and role of the recipient are secondary. For instance, among the Swedish Faith Christians whom Coleman (2006) studied, gifting seems clearly to bring greater benefit to the givers.[8] This understanding of charitable giving as an act of personal religious growth presents a problem for the Russian Orthodox Church as both a religious entity and a charitable institution in Russia today. In the case of the Russian Orthodox Church the nature and directionality of the relationship between givers and receivers becomes confused because the church is both a recipient and a provider of charitable support. Individual churches must balance the needs of their parishioners against the need to renovate church buildings and restore icons and other religious artifacts (Dal Pont 2005). Most churches are dependent on gifts from donors, including parishioners, while other parishioners may be "clients," dependent on the gifts that the church distributes. Because Russians tend to see Orthodox churches as the source of gifts, rather than as shifting nodes within longer chains of dependencies, the act of receiving assumes primacy over the act of giving.

Charities that must solicit resources and then manage the equitable distribution of these resources can hardly avoid modes of operation that sometimes appear commercial and impersonal, and hence less sensitive or responsive to personal need. This is the basic challenge facing the charitable programs of the Russian Orthodox Church today. Because the conflictual nature of the charitable process is disguised by ideologies of altruism and gifting, Russian recipients and other observers often misrecognize the factors that shape the work of Orthodox charities. Instead of seeing how the Orthodox Church is struggling to work within these structural constraints, Russians perceive violations of the social codes about charity and hence of the responsibility of the church to its community. In the rest of this chapter I consider three specific sites of conflict over the nature and purpose of charity and benevolence that shape interactions between the Russian Orthodox Church and Russian citizens.

## VIOLATIONS OF CHARITABLE TRUST

In an essay comparing philosophical perspectives on charity, Jeremy Waldron asked: "Can charity be inactive? Is it possible to be charitable by doing . . . absolutely nothing?" His response was that even though charity requires giving, this giving "need not involve any active or onerous expenditure of effort" (1986: 470). Waldron implicitly confirms one of the central points of Mauss's analysis of the gift: the coercive force of obligation. This issue of obligation is significant for directionality in the charitable encounter in Russia, where there have been misunderstandings over who is responsible for providing assistance—society or the individual—and whether that assistance should be automatic or conditional. This tension is clearly visible in debates between the Russian Orthodox Church and Russian citizens over whether the church is morally required to provide assistance, and it is the direct product of the social and economic transformations currently under way in Russia.

During the Soviet period, the socialist state implemented social welfare programs as an important element in the achievement of modernity, progress, and equality. Food programs were implemented not so much to help poor people as to promote gender equality, by freeing women from their kitchens (Goldstein 1996). During the Soviet period Russian citizens came to see welfare as a benefit and entitlement for all citizens. However, many foreign observers and reformers have suggested that the paternalistic orientation of the Soviet state fostered among citizens an unhealthy dependence on the state. Consequently, one crucial aspect of postsocialist economic transformations has consisted in replacing socialist practices of social support with market capitalist ideals of individualism, autonomy, and personal responsibility (Kornai 2001). Economic reformers have tried to replace personal networks and informal economic practices by expanding the realm of formal, commercial transactions.

The values of personal autonomy and responsibility are also being promoted in the charitable welfare realm. To complement the material services they provide, both religious and secular charities offer medical, financial, and social self-help programs designed to inculcate these values in welfare recipients. The emphasis on personal responsibility and self-help has not been completely embraced by Russian citizens, however. An official at a secular charity told me that staff members were surprised at the level of resistance to the philosophy of personal responsibility that they were encountering among Russians. Their clients were willing to accept the aid provided by the organization but not necessarily the goal of autonomy that accompanied that aid. Clergy in other denominations have noted that one of their biggest challenges in dealing with new Russian members is retraining these new parishioners not to demand assistance but instead to focus on personal spiritual growth and to contribute socially and materially to the life of the religious community. Even Russians who have adapted to these new philosophies of personal responsibility continue to view charitable institutions as having a responsibility to help them resolve their problems. In other words, these individuals may see themselves as displaying personal responsibility by identifying their needs and seeking out the proper channels for meeting those needs, while acknowledging a continuing emphasis on the responsibility of institutions to provide the resources necessary to satisfy those needs.

This conflict between personal responsibility and institutional responsibility plays out in the realm of Orthodox charity. Russian citizens view the Russian Orthodox Church as an essential and indispensable element of the Russian nation (see Davis 2003: 248). At the same time, they see the church, with its long-standing history as a quasi-state entity (Geraci and Khodarkovsky 2001: 3–4), as a civic or social institution that has a moral duty to provide assistance (Caldwell 2004: 84–85). Consequently, in many respects, there is a prevailing interpretation that the Russian Orthodox Church, with all its supporting services, is, like the Orthodox Church in Greece, the birthright of all Russian citizens.[9]

A vivid example of this conflict occurred during the Orthodox prayer meeting described at the beginning of this chapter. Toward the end of the meeting, it was possible for participants to present their prayer requests to the rest of the community. Several individuals outlined spiritual or medical problems and requested that the other participants pray on their behalf. Yet the longer this section of the service continued, the more specific the petitions became.[10] Petitioners began to elaborate personal stories of hardship: one mother described her severely constrained financial situation and asked for material help, while another related stories about disabled family members. The petitioners typically introduced themselves before beginning their personal narratives, and it gradually became apparent that many of these individuals were not members of this church or even affiliated with any other Orthodox church. Rather, they were operating from a cultural perspective that viewed the Orthodox Church as an institution that was required to provide help when asked.[11]

Despite the prevailing view that the Orthodox Church is obligated to provide assistance, the church is undergoing changes that mirror the general trends of Russia's economic transition. In particular, the Orthodox Church is also modifying its long-standing theological emphasis on charity and benevolence to encourage self-help and personal responsibility. As in the experiences of other charitable providers, however, these changes have not been fully embraced or understood by the church's constituents or the wider Russian public. For instance, priests at one Orthodox church in downtown Moscow began offering self-improvement educational programs for parishioners and other local residents, with a focus on strategies for improving personal finances, health, and relationships. The attitudes of the priests bothered some participants. One elderly informant, while praising the topics addressed in the program, drew attention to what she saw as evidence of the church's lack of responsiveness to real needs. As a pensioner with a small monthly income, this woman was unable to afford the high cost of the program materials, which consisted of a thick binder filled with photocopied articles and lecture notes. When she asked the priest who was leading the program if she could obtain the materials at a reduced cost or for free, he informed her that she should save her money and come back to the program when she could pay in full. The woman was upset by the priest's dismissive attitude toward her personal circumstances and what she saw as his deliberate refusal to help ordinary people.

An equally revealing example comes from a comparison of the actions of the two churches described at the beginning of this chapter, when the restaurant that served their respective feeding programs closed unexpectedly for renovation. The two churches had offered the same meals to their (respective) clients, in the same space, and at the same time. When the restaurant closed, the Protestant church quickly relocated its clients to another cafeteria on the other side of Moscow. The Orthodox church, however, did not make alternative arrangements and simply halted operations temporarily without informing its clients. Subsequently, many recipients of the Orthodox program traveled across the city to the program run by the Protestant church, only to be told that they would not be served because it was not their program. Until that event, many clients in both programs did not realize that the programs were separate. Clients in both programs were angered and voiced their displeasure with what they perceived as the Orthodox Church's abandonment of its clients. Few clients criticized the Protestant church for refusing to extend its services to include recipients from the Orthodox program; rather, clients tended to fault the Orthodox program.

Although in the early post-Soviet years many Orthodox and non-Orthodox churches were supported by foreign congregations and private donors, most congregations have since come to rely on the financial support of their own members. In a culture where tithing has not been customary for many years, churches have hired consultants to educate their parishioners and encourage them to support their congregations. Conversations with clergy and charity staff suggest that Orthodox churches have not been as successful as their non-Orthodox counterparts in recultivating this ethic of giving.

These examples show how debates about personal versus institutional responsibility are reframed into debates about the obligation and directionality of aid. For Russians who are accustomed to thinking of charity as an entitlement, and the church as a statelike civic institution with a moral imperative to provide for the needy, actions by Orthodox churches or staff that limit the assistance they receive are perceived to be wrong. The church's failure to uphold its presumed moral imperative to assist the needy is interpreted as an abandonment of Russians and a violation of the proper directionality of the charitable encounter from giver to recipient.

## SELF-INTEREST AND THE ORTHODOX NATION

In addition to challenging the expected directionality of charity, the Orthodox Church has—either explicitly or implicitly—endorsed an exclusive religious nationalism. The types of programs that churches support and the ways in which some individuals frame their requests for assistance communicate the perception that the Russian Orthodox Church has shifted from being an institution that provides help to all Russians, regardless of religious affiliation, to being an exclusionary religious institution that provides assistance only to practicing members of the Orthodox Church. Although petitioners in the prayer service described at the beginning of the chapter did not necessarily feel obligated to belong to the church before asking for assistance, some churches have begun requiring formal religious affiliation before providing assistance.

More significantly, some segments of the church are using religious identity to separate citizenship from ethnonationalist identity. In other words, the correlation of Orthodoxy with Russianness emerges as a means to set up ethnonational hierarchies and discriminate against individuals who are citizens of Russia but do not claim Russian ethnonationality. From the perspective of the church, since Russian and Orthodox identities have historically been coupled in Russian cultural traditions, Orthodox believers are "true" Russians. An often-quoted statement from Dostoevsky illustrates this well: "He who is not Orthodox is not Russian" (cited in Dinello 1994: 87).[12] Nevertheless, in Russian social practice the designation "believer" carries a more general sense of personal spirituality that does not require church attendance or even knowledge about church doctrine or rituals. Although many Russians consider themselves "believers," few of the Russians I have encountered are churchgoers or identify themselves as members of the Orthodox Church—or even as Christians (see Caldwell 2005; cf. Kormina, this volume).[13] From this perspective, then, charitable activities that favor churchgoers and members of Orthodox churches are interpreted as erecting hierarchies of inequality among needy Russians.

This exclusivity is part of the church's larger efforts to respond to the influence of Protestantism, particularly evangelizing Protestantism, in Russia. Despite the religious revival taking place across Russia, which includes an increase in the number of Orthodox churches, monasteries, and seminaries, the church has not enjoyed a similar resurgence in membership. Many observers and church officials have blamed the non-Orthodox denominations that have entered Russia since the early 1990s for attracting potential members away from the Orthodox Church. At the same time, the church has also been concerned with Russia's sharp demographic decline. In response to both sets of pressures, the church has promoted measures to rebuild the Russian nation, such as anti-abortion programs and the encouragement of large families. In the city of Tver there is an Orthodox social welfare organization in the local hospital, but rather than provide material assistance to the hospital and its patients the members of this group focus their activities on anti-abortion activities. The local newspaper *Tverskoi Sobor* regularly printed articles and petitions geared toward helping Orthodox families with many children. One representative article detailed the efforts of one family with eight children to obtain an increase in their monthly welfare payments. The article focused on the contributions this family was making to the country's Orthodox Russian population (Anon. 2005).

Some church leaders have directed their charitable support to programs with explicit patriotic and even xenophobic agendas. The church has approached the state with a view to providing Orthodox chaplains in the military and was also a key supporter and organizer of World War II commemorations in 2005 (the six-tieth anniversary of the end of the war), soliciting donations through slogans such as "Russian, Help Russian" (Podushkov 2004). *Tverskoi Sobor* has published arti-cles and letters from community members about the need to target charitable programs for the elimination of foreigners from Russia, especially people from Central Asia and the Caucasus (see, for example, Mikhailov 2004). At the national level, the Orthodox Church has actively participated in the activities of the pro-Kremlin, nationalist youth political party Nashi. What we see in all these examples is the idea that the church should help only its own—that is, Orthodox Russians. Consequently, ordinary Russians interpret this exclusionary orientation as an effort by the church to require religious identity and/or affiliation as a necessary prerequisite to receiving assistance, a move that disturbs the spirit of selfless altru-ism that many ascribe to religious charity.

Perhaps more significant is that practices that cultivate religious-national dis-tinctions prevent the church from publicly collaborating with non-Orthodox con-gregations to support charitable programs. Staff at a Moscow-based development organization that provides funding and other resources to faith-based medical charities reported that several regional governments barred them from working with non-Orthodox congregations. Regional officials insisted that the organiza-tion support only local Orthodox churches, despite the fact that these churches were unable to provide the appropriate services, unlike the non-Orthodox con-gregations. In Moscow, two Protestant-based charities that had formerly enjoyed strong relationships with local Orthodox churches, and in one case the support of the patriarchate, were informed by church officials that because of the political sensitivity regarding non-Orthodox Christian denominations, the church could no longer continue to support these congregations publicly. The church did not withdraw its support entirely, however, but rather redirected it through informal and unofficial channels, such as making the church's coordinator of social pro-grams available to assist her counterparts in the Protestant churches in generating rosters of eligible clients and negotiating with local businesses. Yet by disguising these ecumenical charitable partnerships, the church risks incurring public criti-cism from Russians who see not the extent of the church's charitable activities but rather the extent of the church's efforts to curtail charitable work more broadly.

## THE CHURCH AS CAPITALIST ENTREPRENEUR

Yet another reality of post-Soviet life that poses challenges for the church's public image is the need to define the church's position in Russia's new economy. Echoing sentiments reported in the popular media, my acquaintances and informants were critical of the church's participation in the market economy and what they saw as its self-interested economic behavior and preoccupation with competition, efficiency, and investment. They were troubled by the increased attention to fund-raising, what Paul Pribbenow describes as "professionalization" (2005: 49), and the blurring of distinctions between the spiritual and the economic. Informants typically focused on the moneymaking activities of the church. In spring 1998 an elderly acquaintance invited me to accompany her on a visit to the newly reopened Cathedral of Christ the Savior in downtown Moscow. This church was destroyed during the Soviet period and had just been rebuilt. My companion specifically wanted to show me the opulent interiors and the names of the donors listed prominently over one of the entrances. As we read through the names of those who had given significant sums of money to fund the reconstruction of the church, she called my attention to a group of wealthy businessmen and venture capitalists who were known to be of Jewish descent. For this Russian woman, the support of these individuals provided evidence of the church's power to command (or coerce) the resources of both Orthodox and non-Orthodox believers. Although she did not use specifically capitalist economic terminology, she formulated a compelling critique by commenting that these Jewish businessmen had most likely recognized that it was in their best economic interest to cooperate with the Russian Orthodox Church.

A similar perspective emerged in a conversation with several women in Tver. As the subject turned to a discussion of local church officials who were supporting themselves lavishly at the expense of local residents, one woman reminded me of a previous conversation in which we had discussed priests who owned expensive luxury automobiles. A second woman then compared the types of cathedrals that were currently being built in Russia, and concluded that only the Russian Orthodox Church possessed the financial resources necessary to build grand cathedrals such as those. In many ways the views of these women were accurate: the church has become an extremely prosperous business. Among its corporate interests, it bottles water under its own label, the St. Springs brand; runs food and religious souvenir shops; has founded banks, factories, and hotels; and is engaged in oil exporting (Davis 2003; Knox 2003; Mitrokhin 2004). In summer 2005 it indirectly launched a new cable television station—Spas (Savior) TV. Billed as "the country's first Orthodox channel," the station presented a combination of "analytical programs, call-in talkshows and historical programs hosted by priests and historians" (Yablokova 2005: 3). Although the Spas channel is not officially administered by the Russian Orthodox Church, the patriarch reportedly gave his blessing to the venture, and priests participated in the programs. In a comment released to a religious news Web site, the chief editor of the Spas channel stated: "This should be a modern business project" (3).

At one level, entrepreneurial activities (as when individual churches rent out space in their church buildings and compounds to commercial enterprises) are a means of raising funds for essential rebuilding efforts (Knox 2003).[14] According to Nathaniel Davis, the church had difficulties overcoming the economic crises of the early 1990s and was on the verge of bankruptcy (2003: 212–13). However, activities that might in the case of secular organizations be considered fiscally responsible and necessary for infrastructure maintenance have met with growing displeasure among Russian citizens, who criticize the church for focusing on its own interests and ignoring or even aggravating the plight of local people. Rumors have circulated that certain church activities may in fact provide a cover for profiteering and money-laundering (215). Nikolai Mitrokhin has observed that the lack of discussion about how the Orthodox Church is using funds received from Western charities does not necessarily mean that these monies are going into private pockets, but the lack of information about these funds remains problematic (2004: 474).

Similar criticisms have emerged over the church's efforts to recover property seized by the state during the Soviet period. A young woman who works as an instructor at a local *detskii sad* (nursery school) in Tver blamed the church for the closure of a local youth center and for "[throwing] children out on the street." She said that local church officials had claimed the building as church property that had been confiscated by the state during the Soviet period. More generally, Tver residents were critical of local churches' efforts to use their power as property owners to curtail local social activism programs. For example, the church had evicted NGOs, including a prominent environmental organization, from church-owned office buildings. In Moscow in the late 1990s a secular charity that operated a feeding program found itself in a heated battle with a local Orthodox church. The charity operated in an empty lot owned by the church and adjacent to the church building. According to aid workers, church officials became concerned that the charity's homeless clients presented an unpleasant image to parishioners and passersby. The church locked the empty lot and forced the charity to move its food distribution activities to another, more discreet location.

The types of assistance programs provided for elderly believers also contribute to the image of the church as a self-interested actor. It is a long-standing tradition in Russia to offer senior citizens of limited financial means work as cleaners of churches, vendors in church kiosks, and cooks for church programs. People in need of food or shelter can also go to the monasteries or convents, where they cannot be turned away. Special "elders' homes" (*bogadel'ni*) provide senior citizens with shelter while they perform housework and other support jobs for a nearby church (Mitrokhin 2004: 293–94). Although these forms of assistance are ostensibly intended to help the needy, they also subsidize the overall functioning of the church.

Market competition also emerges as an important theme in Orthodox activities and perspectives. In Tver, local press coverage of Orthodox and non-Orthodox charities alluded to competition among organizations and their supporters over both access to resources and moral authority in the community (e.g., Anon. 2005; Mikhailov 2004; Podushkov 2004). Such competition is another cause of the discomfort many Russians feel about the church's role as a commercial body. The church's new emphasis on turning a financial profit and using charity as a means to appropriate the labor of its recipients is considered antithetical to the goals of both religious morality and charitable morality. As Susan Harding notes in her work on American fundamentalist Christian ministries, "The whole point of giving to a God-led ministry is to vacate the commercial economy and to enter another realm, a Christ-centered gospel, or sacrificial economy in which material expectations are transformed" (2000: 109). Similarly, for Russians, visibly capitalist activities violate a sense of sacredness, a point that acquires additional significance in Russian social practice, where there is a strong taboo against calling attention to money in requests for help. Money-based interactions are perceived to transform personal relationships of friendship and mutual support into relationships of impersonal commercial exchange (Frisby 1998; Lemon 1998; Pesmen 2000).[15]

Ironically, at the same time that Russians are quick to criticize the church for its commercial greed, many citizens themselves display a remarkable entrepreneurial spirit in their own religious practices. Some churchgoers approach their own religious practices (including material manifestations in terms of religious texts, clothing, and other paraphernalia) as a form of consumption (see also Kormina and Agadjanian and Rousselet, this volume; and Naletova 2006). Religious affiliations become commodities that offer practitioners a range of material, social, and spiritual resources, and selective participation becomes a matter of strategic choice. Thus Orthodox churches that do not make these resources available for free to petitioners invite public criticism and prompt many Russians to turn their attentions to other denominations (Caldwell 2005).[16] Underlying this rejection is the pervasive notion that the church has sacrificed its unique role as a religious institution to become just one more economic enterprise in Russia. Critics see the church as a moneymaking business. One woman in her sixties commented with disgust that all the church did was take money and never gave it out. Her eighty-seven-year-old mother agreed: "Yes, they just take and take."

## CHRISTIAN GIVING AND THE PARADOX OF RUSSIAN ORTHODOX CHARITY

Both Orthodox and non-Orthodox Russian citizens see the church as a corrupt and immoral institution, undermining society rather than supporting it. At the heart of these criticisms are debates over the nature and place of self-interest and responsibility in contemporary religious life. Even as Russia's political officials and business leaders actively promote neoliberal market ideologies based on ideals of self-interest, personal responsibility, and individual autonomy, these models are seen by ordinary Russian citizens as antithetical to the purposes of the Orthodox Church. Russians who see the Orthodox Church as their national birthright also see its material resources as their legitimate legacy. This perspective is encouraged by church officials who present Orthodoxy as an essential feature of national identity. Yet this image can backfire when churches must direct funds toward their own projects, even when those projects ultimately benefit church members, because ordinary people see this as a violation of the trust between church and citizen.

At another level, such criticisms of the Russian Orthodox Church's activities raise the universal tensions of charitable benevolence. As the Russian state withdraws from the welfare sphere and emphasizes personal autonomy and responsibility, individual citizens are forced to reorient their own survival strategies and expectations. Because non-Orthodox religious groups are perceived as adhering more closely to Russian traditions of social support and mutual responsibility, these groups garner greater respect and have a better reputation for reliability than Russia's own, indigenous religion. These new dilemmas provide a useful lens for viewing the ways in which Russian identities themselves are being defined and contested. The selective distribution of charitable aid to particular groups of Russians—individual churches, church officials, and specific groups of church followers—establishes new boundaries within the Russian population and excludes non-Russians and noncitizens altogether. This development is greatly at odds with the church's long history of using charitable projects as a means to bring people into the church and into the Russian nation. Conflicts over the nature of benevolence are at one level about who is allowed into a welfare program, but at another level they raise larger issues of national identity and the changing value of collectivism within postsocialist Russian society.

For anthropological studies of religion, the recent experience of the Orthodox Church in Russia offers insight into a set of perennial definitional questions. From the perspective of most ordinary Russians, it is appropriate to consider religion an institution of entitlement. They expect the church, like the state, to provide resources to its constituents. Yet there is also a persistent notion that the church, as an enduring part of the Russian nation itself, will outlast any particular state formation. Even as citizens recognize, albeit unwillingly, that the changing political and economic philosophies on which the Russian state is based mean that the government can no longer provide support to its citizens, they seem less willing to concede that the same changes also affect the church. Rather, public opinion holds that the church is failing in its essential responsibility to Russia.

The realities of Orthodox charity in postsocialist Russia also illuminate the extent to which religiously inspired moral imperatives to help others are ideologies that are not always met, and cannot possibly be met, in daily practice. The ability of the church to generate funds and distribute them is always constrained by the necessity of balancing multiple interests among multiple actors. Russians who criticize the church for focusing on its own needs rather than on the needs of ordinary people call attention to an aspect of gifting that has been largely overlooked in anthropological analyses of gifting, and particularly in analyses of Christian gifting: the ethics of receiving. Orthodox charity provides a reminder that systems of morality also determine the proprieties of receiving. In Russia, the Orthodox Church is caught in a double bind as it negotiates its multiple roles of giving and receiving.

Although Orthodoxy's theological and practical emphasis on social justice and well-being is not unique among religious denominations both in Russia and elsewhere, Russians nonetheless treat the Russian Orthodox Church differently by holding Orthodox churches accountable in ways that they do not for non-Orthodox congregations. Underlying these tensions is a larger debate over whether Orthodoxy is in fact a spiritual or a social movement. Whereas my interlocutors typically included spirituality as an aspect of their experiences in other religious venues (Catholic, Protestant, and non-Christian), spirituality was rarely mentioned when they discussed their experiences with Orthodoxy. Rather, they focused almost exclusively on Orthodoxy as a cultural and material resource. This insistence on materiality complicates contemporary understandings of Orthodoxy as a religious movement or an essential quality of an ethnonational identity. From a theological standpoint, Orthodoxy may well be oriented toward otherworldly experience, but from the perspective of ordinary people, Orthodoxy is an institution embedded within a this-world domain of real-life needs and circumstances.

Ultimately, the experiences of Russia's Orthodox Church are instructive for considering the precarious nature of religious institutions more generally as they attempt to balance their needs and responsibilities as spiritual communities against their roles as social institutions, particularly in settings where these religious communities enjoy status as part of the national heritage. In the specific case of Russia, the Orthodox Church finds itself caught in an untenable position in which its efforts to regain its status as the national church are at the same time undermining its popularity. By emphasizing its legitimate claim to Russia's historical and national legacy, the Orthodox Church has itself disentangled the spiritual and theological from the practical.

## NOTES

Funding for this project was provided by the U.S. Department of Education (Title VI); the Mellon Foundation; and the Kathryn W. and Shelby Cullom Davis Center for Russian and Eurasian Studies, the Department of Anthropology, and the Committee on Degrees in Social Studies at Harvard University. The University of California, Santa Cruz, provided support for later stages of this project. I thank Chris Hann, Hermann Goltz, my colleagues at the conference on Eastern Christianities, and the anonymous reviewers for their suggestions on how to improve this chapter.

1. I discuss this Protestant community and its charitable welfare programs elsewhere (Caldwell 2004, 2008).

2. Colleagues who described my research to their Russian friends and acquaintances reported similar responses.

3. I talk more specifically about the ethics of salvation and benevolence among Protestant aid workers elsewhere (Caldwell 2008).

4. In this article Lindenmeyr also describes how charitable activities provided deeply pious women with "a special model of female poverty" (1993: 563).

5. For instance, several of the Christian communities with which I have worked serve clients who come from Orthodox, Protestant, Catholic, Jewish, Muslim, Hare Krishna, and atheist backgrounds, among others. Although some Orthodox programs are similarly ecumenical in their outreach, other congregations prefer or even require religious affiliation for their programs. Jewish and Muslim congregations typically provide services only to fellow members of their faith or to local congregations.

6. Because discourses of charity and assistance are rendered in both Russian and English, and Russian and foreign aid workers often move back and forth between the two languages, it is often difficult to specify which term is regularly used in which context.

7. In their discussion of "millennial capitalism," Comaroff and Comaroff point to post-Soviet societies as striking examples of salvation economics (2001: 2).

8. Elsewhere, I have described similar perspectives among volunteers in a Protestant charity in Moscow (Caldwell 2008).

9. I thank Roger Just for pointing out this comparison.

10. Conversations with visitors from the Protestant church revealed that they found this practice the primary and most striking difference between their two congregations. Protestants were surprised that individuals who were not members of this Orthodox church, and in some cases did not know anyone who was a member of the church, felt comfortable attending the service specifically in order to share intimate details about their lives and ask for the help of strangers.

11. More generally, churchyards are spaces where beggars congregate in the hope of presenting their stories and gaining assistance. Although some churches permit this type of activity, others actively discourage it by chasing individuals out.

12. For a more detailed discussion of the complexities of civic, ethnic, and religious national identities in Russia, see Agadjanian 2001.

13. Khodarkovsky points out that in early modern Russia "conversion was spiritual least of all; it generally involved only a nominal transfer of religious identity" (1996: 269).

14. Non-Orthodox religious communities also rent out empty offices in their buildings, although I did not hear as many criticisms of non-Orthodox churches that did this as I did of Orthodox churches.

15. For more extended treatments of these practices, see also Ledeneva 1998 and Lindquist 2006.

16. On a visit to an Orthodox monastery in Moscow with an elderly Protestant friend, my companion repeatedly called my attention to the prayer request sheets that were made available outside the church for visitors. What my friend found most astounding was that the papers were available for free. She commented that this was highly unusual and evidence that this church was far more progressive and welcoming than the other Orthodox churches in the neighborhood.

# REFERENCES

Agadjanian, A. 2001. Revising Pandora's gifts: Religious and national identity in the post-Soviet societal fabric. *Europe-Asia Studies* 53, no. 3: 473–88.

Anon. 2005. Pomogite razobrat' Treugol'nik! Otkrytoe obrashchenie k gubernatoru Tverskoi oblasti D. V. Zeleninu [Help fix the triangle! Open appeal to the governor of Tver Oblast D. V. Zelenin]. *Tverskoi Sobor* 4, no. 54: 3.

Bornstein, E. 2003. *The spirit of development: Protestant NGOs, morality, and economics in Zimbabwe*. New York: Routledge.

Caldwell, M. L. 2004. *Not by bread alone: Social support in the new Russia*. Berkeley: University of California Press.

———. 2005. A new role for religion in Russia's new consumer age: The case of Moscow. *Religion, State & Society* 33, no. 1: 19–34.

———. 2008. Social welfare and Christian welfare: Who gets saved in post-Soviet Russian charity work? In *Religion, morality, and community in post-Soviet societies,* ed. M. D. Steinberg and C. Wanner, 179–214. Washington, D.C.: Woodrow Wilson Center Press.

Cannell, F. 2004. The Christianity of anthropology. *Journal of the Royal Anthropological Institute* n.s. 11: 335–56.

Carrier, J. G. 1990. Gifts in a world of commodities: The ideology of the perfect gift in American society. *Social Analysis: Journal of Cultural and Social Practice* 29: 19–37.

Chaplin, V. 2006. Post-Soviet countries: The need for new morals in economy. *The Ecumenical Review* 58, no. 1: 99–101.

Coleman, H. J. 2005. *Russian Baptists and spiritual revolution, 1905–1929*. Bloomington: Indiana University Press.

Coleman, S. 2006. Materializing the self: Words and gifts in the construction of Charismatic Protestant identity. In *The anthropology of Christianity,* ed. F. Cannell, 163–84. Durham, N.C.: Duke University Press.

Comaroff, J., and J. L. Comaroff. 2001. Millennial capitalism: First thoughts on a Second Coming. In *Millennial capitalism and the culture of neoliberalism,* ed. J. Comaroff and J. L. Comaroff, 1–56. Durham, N.C.: Duke University Press.

Dal Pont, G. E. 2005. Charity law and religion. In *Law and religion: God, the state, and the common law,* ed. P. Radan, D. Meyerson, and R. F. Croucher. London: Routledge.

Davis, N. 2003. *A long walk to church: A contemporary history of Russian Orthodoxy.* 2nd ed. Boulder, Colo.: Westview Press.

Dinello, N. P. 1994. Religious and national identity of Russians. In *Politics and religion in Central and Eastern Europe: Traditions and transitions,* ed. W. H. Swatos, Jr., 83–99. Westport, Conn.: Praeger Publishers.

Douglas, M. 1984. *Purity and danger: An analysis of concepts of pollution and taboo.* London: Ark Paperbacks.

———. 1990. Foreword (No free gifts) to *The gift: The form and reason for exchange in archaic societies,* by M. Mauss. Trans. W. D. Halls. New York: W. W. Norton.

Frisby, T. 1998. The rise of organised crime in Russia: Its roots and social significance. *Europe-Asia Studies* 50, no. 1: 27–49.

Geraci, R. P., and M. Khodarkovsky. 2001. Introduction to *Of religion and empire: Missions, conversions, and tolerance in tsarist Russia,* ed. R. P. Geraci and M. Khodarkovsky, 1–15. Ithaca, N.Y.: Cornell University Press.

Gifford, P. 1990. Prosperity: A new and foreign element in African Christianity. *Religion* 20: 373–88.

Goldstein, D. 1996. Domestic porkbarreling in nineteenth-century Russia, or who holds the keys to the larder? In *Russia, women, culture,* ed. H. Goscilo and B. Holmgren, 125–51. Bloomington: Indiana University Press.

Hammack, D.C. 2005. Donors, intermediaries, and beneficiaries: The changing moral dynamics of American nonprofit organizations. In *Good intentions: Moral obstacles and opportunities,* ed. D.H. Smith, 183–203. Bloomington: Indiana University Press.

Harding, S.F. 2000. *The book of Jerry Falwell: Fundamentalist language and politics.* Princeton: Princeton University Press.

Honey, L. N.d. The myth of a moral vacuum: Competing voices in Moscow's new spiritual landscape. Unpublished manuscript.

Kaiser, D.H. 1998. The poor and disabled in early eighteenth-century Russian towns. *Journal of Social History* 32, no. 1: 125–55.

Kenworthy, S.M. 2008. To save the world or to renounce it: Modes of moral action in Russian Orthodoxy. In *Religion, morality, and community in post-Soviet societies,* ed. M.D. Steinberg and C. Wanner, 21–54. Washington, D.C.: Woodrow Wilson Center Press.

Khodarkovsky, M. 1996. "Not by word alone": Missionary policies and religious conversion in early modern Russia. *Comparative Studies in Society and History* 38, no. 2: 267–93.

———. 2001. The conversion of non-Christians in early modern Russia. In *Of religion and empire: Missions, conversions, and tolerance in tsarist Russia,* ed. R.P. Geraci and M. Khodarkovsky, 115–43. Ithaca, N.Y.: Cornell University Press.

Knox, Z. 2003. *Russian Orthodoxy and religious pluralism: Post-Soviet challenges.* CERC Working Papers Series, The University of Melbourne, no. 1/2003.

———. N.d. Religious freedom in the Putin era. Unpublished manuscript.

Kornai, J. 2001. The borderline between the spheres of authority of the citizen and the state: Recommendations for the Hungarian health reform. In *Reforming the state: Fiscal and welfare reform in postsocialist countries,* ed. J. Kornai, S. Haggard, and R.R. Kaufman, 181–209. Cambridge: Cambridge University Press.

Langan, J. 2005. Philanthropy, charity, subsidiarity, and solidarity: A basis for understanding philanthropy in catholic social teaching. In *Good intentions: Moral obstacles and opportunities,* ed. D.H. Smith, 166–80. Bloomington: Indiana University Press.

Ledeneva, A.V. 1998. *Russia's economy of favours: Blat, networking and informal exchange.* Cambridge: Cambridge University Press.

Lemon, A. 1998. "Your eyes are green like dollars": Counterfeit cash, national substance, and currency apartheid in 1990s Russia. *Cultural Anthropology* 13, no. 1: 22–55.

Lindenmeyr, A. 1986. Charity and the problem of unemployment: Industrial homes in late imperial Russia. *Russian Review* 45, no. 1: 1–22.

———. 1993. Public life, private virtues: Women in Russian charity, 1762–1914. *Signs* 1, no. 3: 562–91.

———. 1996. *Poverty is not a vice: Charity, society, and the state in imperial Russia.* Princeton: Princeton University Press.

Lindquist, G. 2006. *Conjuring hope: Magic and healing in contemporary Russia.* New York: Berghahn.

Mauss, M. 1990. *The gift: The form and reason for exchange in archaic societies.* Trans. W. D. Halls. London: Routledge.

Mikhailov, A. V. 2004. Nuzhna nasha pomoshch' [Our help is needed]. *Tverskoi Sobor* 23–24, nos. 49–50: 11.

Mitrokhin, N. 2004. *Russkaia Pravoslavnaia Tserkov': Sovremennoe sostoianie i aktual'nye problemy* [The Russian Orthodox Church: Contemporary conditions and actual problems]. Moscow: Novoe Literaturnoe Obozrenie.

Naletova, I. 2006. Sovremennyi pravoslavnye iarmarki kak vyrazhenie pravoslavnoi very vne khrama [New Orthodox fairs: An expression of faith outside the church's fence]. In *Religious practices in today's Russia,* ed. A. Agadjanian and K. Rousselet, 178–98. Moscow: Novoe Izdatel'stvo.

Parry, J. 1986. The gift, the Indian gift, and the "Indian gift." *Man* n.s. 21, no. 3: 453–73.

Pesmen, D. 2000. *Russia and soul: An exploration.* Ithaca, N.Y.: Cornell University Press.

Podushkov, D. L. 2004. Kul'turnye i sotsial'nye Proekty Udomel'skogo Russkogo Sobraniia I Udomel'skogo Fonda Predprinimatelei [Cultural and social projects of the Udomelskii Russian Board and the Udomelskii Business Fund]. *Tverskoi Sobor* 12, no. 38: 4.

Pribbenow, P. 2005. Common work: Jane Addams on citizenship and philanthropy. In *Good intentions: Moral obstacles and opportunities,* ed. D. H. Smith, 38–53. Bloomington: Indiana University Press.

Turner, P. 2005. Philanthropy's inconstant friend, religion. In *Good intentions: Moral obstacles and opportunities,* ed. D. H. Smith, 127–45. Bloomington: Indiana University Press.

Waldron, J. 1986. Welfare and the images of charity. *The Philosophical Quarterly* 36, no. 145: 463–82.

White, A. 1993. Charity, self-help, and politics in Russia, 1985–1991. *Europe-Asia Studies* 45, no. 5: 787–810.

Yablokova, O. 2005. Orthodox believers get own channel. *The Moscow Times,* 27 July.

Zigon, J. 2008. Aleksandra Vladimirovna: Moral narratives of a Russian Orthodox woman. In *Religion, morality, and community in post-Soviet societies,* ed. M. D. Steinberg and C. Wanner, 85–113. Washington, D.C.: Woodrow Wilson Center Press.

# Epilogue

## Ex Oriente Lux, *Once Again*

### Douglas Rogers

*Ex Oriente lux* ("From the East comes light") is the title of an oft-cited poem by the late nineteenth-century Russian Slavophile philosopher V. S. Solovyov. The poem, written in 1890, envisioned a special role for Holy Russia in the reunification of a Christendom that had been divided for close to a millennium:

> And a light shone from the East
> And heralded and promised
> What had been impossible.
>
> . . . . . . . . . . . . . . . . . . .
>
> That light from the East
> Reconciled East and West.

Nearly a century later, Jaroslav Pelikan introduced *The Spirit of Eastern Christendom (600–1700)*, the second volume in his magisterial series on the history of Christian doctrine, with reflections on the phrase *ex Oriente lux* (1974: 1–7). Pelikan's series remains one of the few studies of Christianity written in the West to incorporate the churches of the Orthodox East effectively and comprehensively into its understanding of Christian history and theology. The old phrase *ex Oriente lux* deserves mention in the pages of the present volume as well, for the collective project its authors are engaged in is, in an important sense, heir to the intellectual labors of both Solovyov and Pelikan. To be sure, this book is neither a call for Russia-led ecumenism nor a study of the development of doctrine. It does insist, however—along with too few others like it—that anthropological conversations about Christianity as a social, historical, and cultural formation are impoverished when they neglect the diverse experiences and manifestations of Eastern Christianity.

What we require is a unified analytic field, a set of ongoing conversations that move across and actively reflect upon the East-West divide in their efforts to understand the significance of Christianity in human social and cultural life, past and present. In this brief epilogue, I point to three particularly fruitful ways in which light from the East might illuminate new terrains for the anthropological study of Christianities and of religion more broadly.

## CHRISTIAN SELVES AND PERSONS

One important strand of anthropological scholarship, dating almost to the discipline's origins, associates Christianity with the creation of more "modern" human beings—often glossed as bounded, inward-looking individuals. Marcel Mauss (1985) and Louis Dumont (1986), for instance, each had something to say about the emergence of these modern Christian selves; each, like Max Weber before him, accorded special attention to variants of Protestant Christianity in his analysis. More contemporary anthropologists have taken up this line of inquiry by following Christian missionaries as they sought to foster the growth of Christian notions of selfhood in European colonies and postcolonies. In this large and still-expanding body of literature, Christian missions have often been understood to be the leading edge of incorporation into the modern capitalist world system (esp. Comaroff and Comaroff 1991). Peter van der Veer, summing up an impressive collection dedicated to this phenomenon, writes that "it is under capitalism that the entrepreneurial bourgeois self with his urge for self-improvement becomes the bearer of modernity. . . . I would argue that both Catholic and Protestant missions carry this new conception of the self . . . to the rest of the world" (1996: 9). In one of the most innovative contributions to this strand of anthropological inquiry, Webb Keane (2007) has suggested that secular Western social scientists and Protestant missionaries often navigate a common set of dilemmas that spring from shared semiotic ideologies and assumptions about the nature of the material world.

Where should we place Eastern Christians in this conversation, aside from correcting the common slippage whereby Western Christianity has so often come to stand for Christianity as a whole? We might ask, along with Sergei Kan (1999) or Paul Werth (2001), what was different about Orthodox missions and their links to non-Western views of modernity and selfhood. We might also ask, along with Catherine Wanner (2007) or Mathijs Pelkmans and his collaborators (2009), what emerged from the intersection of postsocialist transformations and Western missionaries in the 1990s and 2000s.[1] We might also consider whether the inclusion of Eastern Christians in our field of vision requires more substantial expansion of anthropological conversations about Christianity as they concern personhood and subjectivity; this is what some of the chapters of this volume suggest we might profitably do.

The chapters by Renée Hirschon and Alexander Agadjanian and Kathy Rousselet join long-running conversations about the differences between—and interactions of—a putatively Western (and Western Christian) "individualism" and an Eastern Orthodox emphasis on holistic and collectivist forms of personhood. Hirschon, specifically aligning herself with the mode of analysis employed by Dumont in his *Essays on Individualism,* suggests that the trend toward celebrating individual birthdays (and, concomitantly, away from spiritually and socially significant name days) is diagnostic of broader, deeper, more pervasively individualizing transformations in Greek society. Agadjanian and Rousselet make a somewhat different point for Russia, ranging widely over several religious domains to suggest that multiple varieties of individualism and collectivism combine at any given time; individuation is not, then, entirely new in Russian Orthodoxy, although it seems now to be emphasized to a greater extent than in the past.

Given the fact that one important thrust in the recent anthropological study of Christianity—especially that emerging from European colonial contexts—theorizes conversion from non-Christian religions to Christianity as the crucible par excellence for the creation of modern individuals, it is of considerable comparative interest that both of these chapters understand these processes to be unfolding without corresponding switches in religious affiliation or identification. On this score, the line of analysis pursued by both Hirschon and Agadjanian and Rousselet more closely resembles historical studies of the emergence of individualism in Reformation Europe than, for instance, the explorations of Christian conversion in the colonial encounter that, under the influence of Peter van der Veer (1996), Joel Robbins (2004), and others, have become so central in the anthropology of Christianity. In new studies of Eastern Christianity, that is, there may be room for productive reengagement with the early works of Mauss and Dumont.

A second group of chapters takes up broadly similar issues of Christian personhood and subjectivity but largely avoids the already heavily burdened and often ideological labels of "individual" and "collective." These chapters approach issues of personhood and subjectivity through careful ethnographies of the Orthodox sensorium: the world of icons, elaborate rituals, and liturgies that Christians—Western and Eastern—so often identify as distinctively Orthodox. Gabriel Hanganu's analysis of a rural Romanian Orthodox icon procession unites detailed ethnographic description with the theology and visual anthropology of the icon to suggest that icons have "cross-realm" biographies, biographies that are not fully appreciated in existing approaches to either icons or the "social life of things." Applying this approach to the icon of Saint Ana in a Romanian village yields the provocative suggestion that the varieties of human personhood envisioned and practiced in Eastern Orthodoxy occupy a midpoint between the individualism of Western Christianity and the "distributed" or "dividual" personhood often asserted to prevail in non- or pre-Christian areas of the world. In Sonja Luehrmann's chapter, this brand of comparison between Orthodoxy and other religious traditions does not take place through her analysis alone. In present-day Marii El, she shows, the specificity of Orthodox icon veneration is a pressing concern for clergy and laypeople themselves: it must be constantly compared to and distinguished from both Protestant and pagan practices. Luehrmann shows that the diocese of Marii El positions itself in these debates by being much more lenient toward manifestations of pagan "idolatry" than toward Protestant "iconoclasm"—or, in other words, toward the deification of, rather than the rejection of, the material world.

Luehrmann carefully phrases the intervention she wishes to make in broader conversations in and beyond anthropology. Her claims about Marii El do not necessarily apply to Eastern Orthodoxy writ large, she suggests (although they are usefully seen as one chapter in the centuries-long struggles over images, icons, and the nature of the material world in Christianity). Her point is, rather, that the particular configuration of debates about the materialities and immaterialities of being a proper—that is, nonheretical—Christian person in Marii El raises important analytic questions about Christian practice that might be productively explored in other times and places as well. This strikes me as just the right tone for studies of Eastern Christianity to adopt as they seek to engage and transform the Western tilt in existing scholarship on the anthropology of Christianities. As the wide variety of explorations of Christian subjectivity and personhood in this volume amply attests, we are unlikely to arrive at an "essential" Eastern Christian notion of personhood that is not so diluted and abstracted as to account for the actual practice of precisely no one. Far better, as many of these chapters persuasively suggest and Luehrmann articulates most clearly, to point to particular configurations of Eastern Orthodox Christianity that reformulate broader debates and discussions at an analytic level, and, in this way, influence the shape of future scholarship. One desirable outcome of anthropological attention to Orthodox Christian persons and subjects might be, then, additional impetus to shift from our long-running emphasis on individualism in Western Christian contexts themselves.

## THE POLITICS OF CHRISTIANITY

The chapters in this volume are also instructive for thinking about the intersection of Christianity and politics, whether we conceptualize politics in its classic manner as a domain of interactions and struggles among interest groups—"the state" among them—or, following Foucault's writings on power, as a diffuse array of disciplinary and discursive formations through which subjects are formed. Again, potentially significant shades of difference with Western Christianity emerge through careful ethnography based in the Christian East.

Alice Forbess's ethnography of an Orthodox convent most fully engages Foucault and his followers on the topics of Christianity, power, and subject-formation; her brand of analysis overlaps considerably with the chapters on Eastern Christian selfhood and personhood I have already highlighted. Forbess suggests that the monastic life she encountered in Romania was based less on following a specific monastic rule or submitting oneself to certain disciplines than on a broad range of loosely defined efforts to reunite oneself with God, to achieve the divinization written of by church fathers. These Orthodox nuns are guided on the path to Christian salvation less by adherence to doctrinal texts than by the pursuit of what Forbess, following Harvey Whitehouse, calls an "analogic" mode of religious knowledge transmission based on mystery and ultimate unknowability. Broadly similar instances of mysticism and analogic religious knowledge appear in other chapters of this book, from Naletova's "kenotic communities" in pilgrimage to Naumescu's study of monastic exorcisms in Ukraine. Taken together, these chapters suggest that some reorientation of the ways in which Christianity is implicated in fields of power and subject-formation is in order. As Michael Herzfeld (2004: 48) has also pointed out in his ethnography of Greek artisans and their apprentices, the techniques of Christian discipline that are so central to Talal Asad's masterful and influential *Genealogies of Religion* (1993) are often distinctively Western Christian in origin. They need to be expanded, and perhaps substantially rethought, if we are to apprehend correctly the relationships between Eastern Christianity and modes of power and domination, state-formation and subjectivity.

Christian churches have long been acknowledged to be important political actors in the more traditional sense of politics: church leaders speak and direct their followers to act on the national and international stage; they lend their moral authority to the legitimation of political and state agendas; and their members are often deeply engaged in very local struggles where there is no discernible dividing line between "religion" and "politics." On this score, too, the particularities of Eastern Orthodoxy are interesting and potentially instructive for anthropologists of Christianity. Again and again in these chapters, we find politically fraught encounters between and among Christian churches that are only understandable if we take into account Eastern Orthodoxy's particular brand of Christian unity: a family of autocephalous, largely self-governing, and nation-state-based churches, all of them "in communion" with each other but not overseen by a centralized authority on the model of the Roman Catholic Vatican. This flexible organizational structure persisted even in the former Soviet bloc, in a landscape with a bewildering variety of overlapping—and often contentious—boundaries among nations, states, ethnic groups, and Christian denominations. This complexity is, of course, nothing new to historical or social scientific studies of the region, but it has not yet been appreciated in the wider anthropology of Christianity and of religion.

Several chapters illustrate these dynamics. The fallout of the Estonian Church crisis of the early and mid-1990s—in which the Patriarchate of Moscow and the Patriarchate of Constantinople quarreled over which body had administrative authority over parishes in newly post-Soviet Estonia, eventually bringing the entire Eastern Orthodox Church to the brink of schism—forms the crucial backdrop for Jeffers Engelhardt's study of liturgical hymns in Estonia. Through careful attention to the singing style of *akathist* hymns, Engelhardt is able to show that the particular styles of singing at the Church of St. George in Setomaa, Estonia, continue to show the influence of the Petseri (Pechory) monastery, located across the border in the Russian Federation. In the local Orthodox liturgy, in other words, the Estonian-Russian border—still fraught, defended, and heavily ideologized in so many ways—is reimagined and subordinated to a broader Orthodox ethics of liturgical singing.

Melissa Caldwell explores a different dimension of the particularities of Eastern Orthodox political organization in her ethnography of social welfare and charitable organizations in Moscow. Russian Orthodox charity, Caldwell shows, is often caught between civic nationalism and religious nationalism. The close identification of the Russian Orthodox Church with the Russian state would appear to mandate the provision of social welfare resources to all citizens; yet, in practice, Russian Orthodox benevolent associations have been shifting to restrict assistance exclusively to Russian Orthodox believers. But the church is not safe from critique even on this territory: the common postsocialist indictment of the Russian state for failing to provide social services has rubbed off on the Russian Orthodox Church as well, and their representatives analogously criticized for failing to take care of their flocks. As Caldwell notes, this situation has much to do with the ongoing political and economic transformations of post-Soviet Russia. Read in the context of the anthropology of Christianity, it shows some of the entailments and consequences of the close association between state and church in Eastern Christian political/religious organization.

In Maria Couroucli's ethnography of popular Saint George's festivals on an island near Istanbul, we see with particular clarity that the political formations in which Eastern Christians participate extend beyond the nation-state to empire and its aftermath. Like Glenn Bowman's ethnography of Macedonian "mixed shrines," Couroucli's study reveals a range of symbolic and ritual ways in which contemporary Orthodox and Muslim communities interact and intertwine outside of—and sometimes in spite of—the official positions staked out by their respective religious authorities.[2] Moreover, Couroucli places the present-day configurations of Orthodox-Muslim syncretism in the context of more than a century of large-scale political reconfigurations, for archival research demonstrates that such syncretisms are not new in Turkey. They extend back at least to the Ottoman period, when they also quietly challenged the official separation of religious communities

envisioned by the *millet* system. As Couroucli astutely notes, however, these practices should not be understood as simple continuities with an Ottoman past;
rather, the high attendance at recent Saint George's festivals can be attributed in
part to a new nostalgia for the imagined tolerance of the Ottoman empire, a nostalgia that is intimately connected to struggles over Turkey's efforts to establish a
minority rights record that will speed entry into the European Union.

In sum, the chapters that focus their attention on the politics of the Eastern
Churches reveal a Christian world aspiring to unity and cooperation among a
family of coequal churches, but always caught up in shifting borders of state,
nation, ethnic group, religion, and territory. (Complicating this matter further, of
course, is the fact that careful ethnography shows that matters "on the ground"
are often considerably more complicated than they are in the official church statements and pronouncements that guide many analyses.) This history of schisms
and near schisms, and of moments of tolerance and intolerance, at the layered and
constantly shifting boundaries of faith, nation-state, empire, and European supra-
state might be productively mined for insights that Eastern Orthodoxy can contribute to the anthropological study of religion and politics more broadly. If
studies based in the Western Christian world have been particularly useful for
their treatments of individual conversion to Christianity—of people moving
across religious boundaries—then perhaps the study of Eastern Christianity might
be analogously instructive about a closely related but analytically distinct issue:
the dilemmas and reconceptualizations that result from the movement of state,
national, or imperial boundaries across communities of Christians (well illustrated here by the breakup of the former Yugoslavia and Estonia's declared independence from the Soviet Union). Once again, my aim is not to argue for the
absolute distinctiveness of the Christian East, but for an appreciation of the ways
in which its particularities—of political organization in this case—might reformulate research agendas and questions across the anthropology of Christianity.

## CHRISTIAN HISTORIES

As the editors note in their introduction, a concern with historical continuity and
unchanging tradition has long been a distinguishing feature of much Eastern
Orthodox theology and even everyday discourse. This emphasis, they and several
contributors note, stands in contrast to the emphasis on rupture and discontinuity
that Joel Robbins (2007) rightly identifies in many Western Christian—largely
Protestant—contexts. This mode of historical consciousness does seem to be very
widespread in the Orthodox world: as Anna Poujeau's chapter on the revival of
monasticism in the Greek Orthodox Church of Antioch in Syria reminds us,
Eastern Christian models of historical authenticity and roots in a remote past are
to be found well outside Eastern Europe and the former Soviet Union. Nevertheless,

we find particularly interesting and challenging analytical problems when these frequent assertions of long-term continuity rub up against the pervasive discontinuities of the postsocialist transformations that form the backdrop for most of these chapters. How, then, do Eastern Christians understand and fashion their own histories of continuity, even as the vast majority of them have found themselves in new, specifically postsocialist circumstances?

Jeanne Kormina provides one ethnographically nuanced answer: by casting new interest in old rites—such as pilgrimage—as a quest for a particular kind of authenticity. By searching for simplicity, purity, and antiquity, the Russian pilgrims Kormina interviewed are also creating a particular kind of Eastern Christian historical consciousness. This historical consciousness is born in key part, she shows, of the specifically post-Soviet moment. Even as they participate in long-running Russian practices whereby authenticity is sought through sensuous experience and by investing objects with sacred meanings, post-Soviet pilgrims counterpoise these practices to the perceived problems and disorders of the present day, including those ascribed to the official Orthodox hierarchy itself. Pilgrimage practices participate, as Kormina nicely puts it, in efforts to "avoid history, or at least the traumas of recent history."

There is, to be sure, no reason to associate the fashioning of this kind of "antihistorical" historical consciousness with Eastern Christianity exclusively. Indeed, something like this has often characterized Christian practice under conditions of "modernity" elsewhere in the world. However, we might still ask how specifically socialist and postsocialist modernities color quests for authenticity. In the case of Russian pilgrimage, Kormina points to one important clue: post-Soviet pilgrimage derives a significant part of its form from the Soviet heritage and tourism industry, with its distinctively socialist ideologies and practices. Other authors make similar suggestions, such as Luehrmann's claim that the styles of argument in post-Soviet religious debates in Marii El echo those of Soviet antireligious campaigns.

Reckoning with Christian histories can be a different kind of task from the perspective of those with positions within or closer to official church hierarchies, as Stéphanie Mahieu shows in her study of the tension between Latinization and Byzantinization trends among Greek Catholics in both Romania and Hungary. At stake in the debates she traces is the establishment of continuity with authentic Eastern Catholic traditions as envisioned and led by the Vatican's Congregation for the Oriental Churches beginning in 1990. The official Vatican program of Byzantinization, Mahieu demonstrates, unfolded in shades of dispute and disagreement with local practitioners, many of whom had become accustomed to the incorporation of certain Latin prayers and rites. These attempts to shape and reshape Christian historical consciousness progressed differently in Romania and Hungary for reasons that are to be found, once again, in the proximate history of the socialist period. In Romania, where political campaigns had a pervasive impact on the organization of the church, "revival" entails a radical rupture with the socialist past, and there has been more room for newly trained priests to promote the recovery of authentic Byzantine rites. In Hungary, where Greek Catholics were not repressed in the socialist period, there has been more local affection for Latin rites despite the efforts of the official hierarchy. Here, as in many of the chapters, the precise shapes of socialist efforts to secularize and modernize societies appear as crucial determinants of postsocialist efforts to establish new kinds of continuity with the Christian past.

Taken together, these chapters challenge anthropologists to incorporate the Orthodox and Catholic East into their discussions and analyses of Christianity as a social, cultural, and historical formation. "Eastern," that is, should no longer serve as the marked counterpart to the unmarked "Western" in descriptions of Christianity. This volume thus participates in one of the still larger projects that anthropologists working in and on postsocialist societies often set themselves: the reformulation of social and cultural theories based on ethnography carried out in a part of the world that has just begun to get the full depth and breadth of worldwide anthropological attention it has long warranted. As was the case with earlier, similar moves in Anglophone anthropology, such as the emergence of the "anthropology of Europe" as a field of research, this kind of strategy can produce novel theoretical insights not because it reveals essential differences but because it permits us to ask new questions of established assumptions and paths of analysis.

## NOTES

I am grateful to Melissa Caldwell and Sonja Luehrmann for their instructive comments on an earlier version of this epilogue. Some of the issues on which I touch here are also treated at greater length in Rogers 2009.

1. Although Wanner and Pelkmans focus largely on Protestant communities, their studies deserve mention here because the encounters they trace have unfolded—not without controversy—on territory that Eastern Christians have often considered to be their privileged domain.

2. Although Bowman does not choose the frame of imperialism for his study, one way to explore the comparative insights afforded by his analysis would be to cast the former Yugoslav dynamics as following from the waning of Soviet imperial ambitions in Eastern and Southeastern Europe.

## REFERENCES

Asad, T. 1993. *Genealogies of religion: Discipline and reasons of power in Christianity and Islam.* Baltimore: Johns Hopkins University Press.

Comaroff, J., and J. L. Comaroff. 1991. *Of revelation and revolution: Christianity, colonialism, and consciousness in South Africa.* Chicago: University of Chicago Press.

Dumont, L. 1986. *Essays on individualism: Modern ideology in anthropological perspective.* Chicago: University of Chicago Press.

Herzfeld, M. 2004. *The body impolitic: Artisans and artifice in the global hierarchy of value.* Chicago: University of Chicago Press.

Kan, S. 1999. *Memory eternal: Tlingit culture and Russian Orthodox Christianity through two centuries.* Seattle: University of Washington Press.

Keane, W. 2007. *Christian moderns: Freedom and fetish in the mission encounter.* Berkeley: University of California Press.

Mauss, M. 1985. A category of the human mind: The notion of person, the notion of self. Trans. W. D. Halls. In *The category of the person: Anthropology, philosophy, history,* ed. M. Carrithers, S. Collins, and S. Lukes, 1–26. Cambridge: Cambridge University Press.

Pelikan, J. 1974. *The spirit of Eastern Christendom (600–1700).* Vol. 2, *The Christian tradition: A history of the development of doctrine.* Chicago: University of Chicago Press.

Pelkmans, M. 2009. *Conversion after socialism: Disruptions, modernisms, and the technologies of faith.* Oxford: Berghahn Books.

Robbins, J. 2004. *Becoming sinners: Christianity and moral torment in a Papua New Guinea society.* Berkeley: University of California Press.

———. 2007. Continuity thinking and the problem of Christian culture. *Current Anthropology* 48, no. 1: 5–38.

Rogers, D. 2009. *The old faith and the Russian land: A historical ethnography of ethics in the Urals.* Ithaca, N.Y.: Cornell University Press.

van der Veer, P., ed. 1996. *Conversion to modernities: The globalization of Christianity.* New York: Routledge.

Wanner, C. 2007. *Communities of the converted: Ukrainians and global evangelism.* Ithaca, N.Y.: Cornell University Press.

Werth, P. 2001. *At the margins of Orthodoxy: Mission, governance, and confessional politics in Russia's Volga-Kama region, 1827–1905.* Ithaca, N.Y.: Cornell University Press.

# CONTRIBUTORS

ALEXANDER AGADJANIAN is Professor at the Center for the Study of Religion, Russian State University for the Humanities, Moscow.

GLENN BOWMAN is Senior Lecturer in the Department of Anthropology, University of Kent, Canterbury.

MELISSA L. CALDWELL is Associate Professor of Anthropology at the University of California, Santa Cruz.

MARIA COUROUCLI is Senior Researcher at the CNRS, Laboratoiere d'ethnologie et sociologie comparative, Université Paris Ouest Nanterre-la Défense.

JEFFERS ENGELHARDT is Assistant Professor in the Department of Music at Amherst College.

ALICE FORBESS is British Academy Postdoctoral Fellow at Goldsmiths College, University of London.

HERMANN GOLTZ is Professor for the History and Theology of the Orthodox Churches at the Martin Luther University, Halle-Wittenberg.

GABRIEL HANGANU is a Community Manager, Research Technologies Service, University of Oxford.

CHRIS HANN is a Director of the Max Planck Institute for Social Anthropology, Halle.

RENÉE HIRSCHON is Senior Research Fellow and Lecturer in Anthropology at St. Peter's College, Oxford University.

JEANNE KORMINA is Assistant Professor in the Department of Sociology, Higher School of Economics, St Petersburg.

SONJA LUEHRMANN is a Killam Postdoctoral Fellow in the Department of Anthropology at the University of British Columbia.

STÉPHANIE MAHIEU is García-Pelayo Fellow at the Centro de Estudios Políticos y Constitucionales, Madrid.

INNA NALETOVA is a Research Fellow at the Institute for Practical Theology, University of Vienna.

VLAD NAUMESCU is Assistant Professor of Anthropology at the Central European University, Budapest.

ANNA POUJEAU is a Postdoctoral Fellow at the Laboratoire d'anthropologie sociale et culturelle, Université de Liège. Senior Researcher at Sciences Po, Centre d'études et de recherches internationales, CNRS, Paris.

DOUGLAS ROGERS is Assistant Professor of Anthropology at Yale University.

KATHY ROUSSELET is a Directeur de Recherches at the Fondation Nationale des Sciences Politiques, Centre d'Études et de Recherches Internationales, Paris.

# INDEX

icon veneration, 5, 12, 15, 23n16; Council of
Nicaea and, 45, 57–58; pilgrimage, 240, 244,
245, 249–51, 251*fig*, 256*fig*, 259–60, 260*fig*;
proper attitude, 60–61; Romanian
rain-seeking ritual, 33–42, 34*fig*, 35*fig*, 38*fig*,
47, 52–53, 353; Russian Orthodox, 56–76,
240, 244, 245, 249–51, 251*fig*, 256*fig*, 259–60,
260*fig*, 322; Soviet science and, 64–68
identity: ID card, 289, 292–94, 307n3;
individual/collective, 12, 297, 304, 306,
311–25, 331; religious vs. ethnonationalist,
104, 340; religious nationalistic, 339–41;
syncretic, 197–98. *See also* national identity;
personal identity
idolatry, Russian Orthodoxy and, 57–58, 63–64,
66, 74–75, 354
Ignace IV Hazim, Patriarch, 185, 186
images, 12, 42–48, 50; "corpothetics," 45;
East-West differences, 42–46, 58–59, 88,
134; of God, 42–44, 47–48, 71, 304–5;
idolatry, 57–58, 63–64, 66, 74–75, 354; as
presence, 59, 74; prohibition against
making, 57–58; as representation, 59, 74;
Volga region, 56–76. *See also* art; icons;
imagistic mode; statues
"imagined community," 10, 228, 231, 234, 322,
323
imagistic mode, of religiosity, 5, 16, 147,
155–57, 160–74
India: cultural politics, 49; Oriental Orthodox
churches, 1, 9
individualism, 12–13, 18–19, 307n5; Greece and,
13, 289–307, 353; and holism/collectivism,
12, 297, 304, 306, 311–25, 331, 353;
origins, 296–97; and person, 18–19, 289–90,
296–98, 304–5, 315, 353; pilgrim, 282;
Russian postsocialist, 311–25, 337; Western
Christian, 12, 18–19, 353; wild (rugged), 314
Indonesia, Dutch Calvinist missionaries, 62
interiority, Christianity, 3, 10, 146
Internet, charitable projects through, 334
Ioann, Archbishop of Marii El, 61*fig*, 62, 76n10
Ionescu, Nae, 133
Ioshkar-Ola: Ascension Cathedral, 61, 61*fig*;
Charismatic Christian Center, 66–67, 68*fig*;
Protestants, 66–69
Islam: anthropology of, 5–6; Christianity's roots,
4; as heresy or deviancy in Christianity, 211,
213, 217n13; Oriental Orthodox churches
close to, 16; Ottoman, 9; pan-Arabism and,
179. *See also* Muslims

Istanbul: Christian numbers, 9; Constantinople/
Byzantium becoming, 4, 222; "cosmopolitanism," 222–23, 234; Rum Orthodox Greek
community, 221, 223, 232, 235n6; Saint
George's festival, 220–36, 356–57

Jääts, Indrek, 111
John Chrysostom, Saint, 14, 80, 86
John of Damascus, Saint, 43, 57–58
*al-Joumhouriya*, 186
József, Father, 84–85, 93
Judaism, 4, 291

Kan, Sergei, 352
Kapferer, Bruce, 167
Kaspirovski, A., 276–77
Keane, Webb, 59, 352
Kemalists, 225, 232
*kenosis*, 13, 240–41; pilgrim community,
240–65, 355
Khodarkovsky, Michael, 332, 347n13
Khodr, Metropolitan Georges, 179–80
Khomiakov, Alexei, 315
kinship: Greek relations, 297, 305; naming
practices associated with, 298, 303; spiritual,
299. *See also* family
Kligman, Gail, 7
Kohl, Karl-Heinz, 59
Kõllamägi, Anna, 107, 108–9
Kolodiivka monastic community, Ukraine,
156–74; exorcisms, 160–74; last Tuesday
service, 163–68
Kopytoff, 49
Kormina, Jeanne, 13, 21, 267–86, 358
Krupin, Vladimir, 258
Kuraev, Andrey, 282

Ladinskaya, Melitina, 268
language: Aramaic, 183–84; church singing,
108; Greek Catholic churches, 84, 86–87;
Russian charity, 347n6; Seto, 110, 112, 113
Larkin, Brian, 48
Last Day, Orthodox theology, 44
Latinization, 97n4; Greek Catholic, 80–94, 96,
97n2, 358–59
Latour, Bruno, 82–83, 85, 96
Leach, Edmund, 6
Lebanon: civil war, 180; Greek Orthodox
churches, 179–80, 189n1; independence
(1941), 179; Maronite Church, 189n4,
190n12; Syrian army in, 178

TEXT
10/12.5 Minion Pro

DISPLAY
Minion Pro

COMPOSITOR
Toppan Best-set Premedia Limited

INDEXER
Barbara Roos

PRINTER AND BINDER
Thomson-Shore, Inc.